Medieval Women on Film

Medieval Women on Film

Essays on Gender, Cinema and History

Edited by KEVIN J. HARTY

McFarland & Company, Inc., Publishers
Jefferson, North Carolina

ALSO AUTHORED OR EDITED BY KEVIN J. HARTY

The Holy Grail on Film: Essays on the Cinematic Quest (2015)

The Vikings on Film: Essays on Depictions of the Nordic Middle Ages (2011)

Cinema Arthuriana: Twenty Essays, rev. ed. (2002)

King Arthur on Film: New Essays on Arthurian Cinema (1999)

The Reel Middle Ages: American, Western and Eastern European, Middle Eastern and Asian Films About Medieval Europe (1999)

Frontispiece: **Cate Blanchett as Marian in Ridley Scott's 2010 film** *Robin Hood*

Names: Harty, Kevin J., editor.
Title: Medieval women on film : essays on gender, cinema and history / edited by Kevin J. Harty.
Description: Jefferson : McFarland & Company, Inc., Publishers, 2020. | Includes bibliographical references and index.
Identifiers: LCCN 2020005809 | ISBN 9781476668444 (paperback : acid free paper ∞) ISBN 9781476639000 (ebook)
Subjects: LCSH: Women in motion pictures. | Middle Ages in motion pictures. | Historical films—History and criticism. | Feminism and motion pictures.
Classification: LCC PN1995.9.W6 M387 2020 | DDC 791.43/6522—dc23
LC record available at https://lccn.loc.gov/2020005809

BRITISH LIBRARY CATALOGUING DATA ARE AVAILABLE

ISBN (print) 978-1-4766-6844-4
ISBN (ebook) 978-1-4766-3900-0

Front cover: Katharine Hepburn as Eleanor of Aquitaine in the 1968 film *The Lion in Winter* (AVCO Embassy Pictures)

Printed in the United States of America

McFarland & Company, Inc., Publishers
Box 611, Jefferson, North Carolina 28640
www.mcfarlandpub.com

For Kathleen and for Rick

Table of Contents

Preface

The essays in *Medieval Women on Film* continue a conversation about the many ways in which film has portrayed medieval women that began in 1999 in Kalamazoo, Michigan, at the annual International Congress on Medieval Studies. The always kind, supportive, and generous Dr. Paul Szarmach, then director of the Medieval Institute at Western Michigan University, asked Alan Lupack, Virginia Blanton, and me to organize a film festival for the Congress. The festival would screen three films: any film set in the Middle Ages on Wednesday night, a film tied to the Arthurian Legend on Thursday night, and a film reflecting the complicated and intriguing lives of women in the Middle Ages on Friday night. The Thursday night film was sponsored by the International Arthurian Society, North American Branch (IAS/NAB), which agreed to offer a panel of papers on the film that it sponsored, and the Friday night film was sponsored by the Society for Medieval Feminist Scholarship (SMFS), which agreed to offer a panel with papers on the film that it sponsored. Paul provided free popcorn for all three nights, and I supplied handouts with production details and a brief bibliography for each film that was screened.

The film festival continued for a decade, screening 30 films introduced by scholars from a variety of disciplines who were attending the Congress, and offering 20 panels of three and four papers by presenters new and familiar, again drawn from a variety of disciplines. Many of those papers would go on to be published as journal articles and book chapters, and the *Medieval Feminist Newsletter* would in 2000 publish as its first volume in its Subsidia Series an entire issue devoted to the topic of medieval women on film. Discussion of cinema medievalia has continued at the Kalamazoo Congress, and at other academic and professional meetings worldwide, and "medieval film" has now been long established as a field of scholarly inquiry that is taught at the secondary and college and university levels and that is increasingly examined in master's theses, doctoral dissertations, journal articles, monographs, and online platforms. My hope is that the essays in *Medieval Women on Film* will inspire others to continue this line of serious scholarly inquiry into "medieval film" in general, and into how such film portrays women in particular, since such inquiry has, to paraphrase *Piers Plowman*, already proven for more than two decades to be a fair field full of folk .

In editing *Medieval Women on Film*, I have incurred a great many debts, first and foremost to those colleagues who were willing to contribute their essays to this collection. My own work on this collection has been generously supported at La Salle University by two provosts—Dr. Joseph Marbach (now president of Georgian Court University) and Dr. Brian Goldstein—and by the now dean emeritus of the College of Arts and Sciences,

Dr. Thomas Keagy. My colleagues Gerard Regan, Megan Bennis, and Eithne Bearden in the Interlibrary Loan and Reference Departments of La Salle's Connelly Library have happily (I hope) put up with my numerous requests for materials, and I have been further cheered by the support of John Baky, Director Emeritus of the Library, and of my generous colleagues: Br. Emery Mollenhauer FSC, Dr. James Butler, Bob Heybach, and Eileen Barrett. In London, Olwen and Gordon Terris, Sheena Napier, Rick Fisher and Marcus Tozini, David Barrable and Simon Cunniffe, and Gary Yershon and Matthew Saxton offered assistance, meals, and even lodging when I needed it. I also acknowledge the generosity and kind support of Paddy and Dr. Roger Simpson in Norwich, Professor Jeffrey Richards in Lancaster, Professor John Marshall in Bideford, and Dr. Jamie Wood in Lincoln. Anastasia Kerameos and her colleagues at the British Film Institute's Reuben Library in London and Nancy Goldman and her colleagues at the Pacific Film Institute in Berkeley also answered any number of research queries that I had, as did Arlene Zimmerle at Bryn Mawr College's Canady Library. I owe thanks as well to Michael Klossner, retired from the Arkansas State Library, who has continued to alert me to "medieval film" sightings. My longtime friends Matthew McCabe and Charles Wilson, Peter Rudy and Richard Meiss, Ron Haynes, Nannette Lee Miller and Olga Barrera, the late Jeff Petraco, Kenneth W. Kaukola, Helena White, Dr. Linda Merians, Dr. Jonathan Good, Dr. Barbara Tepa Lupack, and Dr. Alan Lupack supported this project in more ways than they know. As always, the editorial and support staffs at McFarland have been unfailingly helpful throughout the publication process that brought this collection into print. Finally, I owe my greatest debt in this endeavor to Kathleen Harty and to Rick Tempone, to whom this volume is dedicated with gratitude and love.

Medieval Women on Film

An Introduction

KEVIN J. HARTY

On and off the screen, medieval women have lived more complicated lives than have generally been allowed them both within the academy and in popular culture, and, thanks to the work of any number of scholars who have continued to show us how to reread and reexamine those lives, we are coming to a better understanding of the variety and fullness of the lives led by medieval women, fictional and historical.

Just how multi-faceted medieval women's screen lives can be is suggested by the still that serves as the frontispiece for this collection of essays. At first glance, a medieval woman appearing on the screen in head-to-toe armor can be no one else but Joan of Arc. But Cate Blanchett is not playing Joan; she is the Greenwood's Marian, in a still from Ridley Scott's 2010 film *Robin Hood*. While the film does at least initially allow its Marian a status beyond that of damsel in distress, it eventually situates her safely enclosed in Robin's arm—her attempt at self-definition finally thwarted by the agenda of a film tradition that focuses exclusively on Robin's establishing his bona fides, often at Marian's expense. But the still is further complicated by Blanchett's earlier screen appearance as a decidedly different armed woman, the title character in the 1998 film *Elizabeth*, where the armor-clad monarch delivers her August 9, 1588, speech to troops assembled at Tilsbury in Essex to repel an anticipated Spanish invasion: "I know that I have the body but of a weak and feeble woman, but I have the heart and stomach of a king, and of a king of England too."[1] In this collection's frontispiece, Blanchett's fictional Marian is then first channeling the historical Joan of Arc and then in turn herself as the historical Elizabeth I. In cinema medievalia, the fictional and historical lives of women often overlap.

Film has embraced medieval women for more than a century, and that embrace has been anything but monolithic—indeed, it has at times been downright contradictory. Women, both historical and fictional, have appeared in film as role models, as saviors, as seducers, as villains, as saints, as sinners, as she-devils, as viragos, as victims, and as victimizers. Perhaps nowhere is this multiplicity of contradictory roles more apparent than in one of the most ubiquitous and long-lasting myths of western European history and culture, the Arthuriad. As early as the 12th century, a commentator, long thought to be the poet and theologian Alanis de Insulis (c. 1128–c. 1203), could ask rhetorically:

Whither has not flying fame spread and familiarized the name of Arthur the Briton, even as far as the empire of Christendom extends? Who, I say, does not speak of Arthur the Briton, since he is also better

3

known to the peoples of Asia than to the *Britanni*, as our palmers returning from the East inform us? The Eastern peoples speak of him, as do the Western, though separated by the width of the whole earth…. Rome, queen of cities, sings his deeds, nor are Arthur's wars unknown to her former rival Carthage, Antioch, Armenia; Palestine celebrates his acts.[2]

The Arthur whose "flying fame" was so widespread and familiar would soon enough be the Arthur of the Knights of the Round Table, but that homosocial world would see its ranks expanded to include women in their multiple and contradictory roles. So fittingly, this volume begins with two essays examining the conflicting portraits of two of the principal women within the world of Arthur, his wife, Guinevere, and his half-sister, Morgan.[3]

Amy S. Kaufman offers a reading of four very different film Guineveres who struggle to negotiate their sexuality in light of the feminist movement. Gone is Guinevere as passive victim or shameless seductress, readily found both on and off the screen in earlier retellings of the Arthuriad. One thinks of Tennyson's abject queen, whose characterization borders on the misogynistic. As Alan Lupack points out, in the last meeting between Arthur and his disgraced queen, Guinevere "adds to the drama if not by her words then by her body language—she grovels and, when he [Arthur] pauses in his speech to her, she creeps" closer laying her hands around his feet.[4] Kaufman argues that, in these four films, the burden which Guinevere's sexuality presents is not inherently her problem; rather, in light of the women's movement, filmmakers must negotiate a tricky character whose newfound strength and agency counter the stereotypes that have previously been attached to her portrayals, themselves deeply rooted in deeply ingrained anxieties about women and the ways in which they express their sexuality.

Thus Vanessa Redgrave's Guenevere in Joshua Logan's 1967 filmed version of the Broadway musical *Camelot* finds herself cast in a conservative film made in an increasingly radical decade, for which Redgrave herself would continue to be a spokesperson off-screen. Logan's solution is at times half-hearted, as his film simultaneously attempts to embrace female sexual liberation while also displaying an uneasiness with, if not fear of, unbridled female desire. Early in the film, a clearly baffled Arthur will wonder in song "How to Handle a Woman." *Camelot* will never really figure out how to solve the riddle implicit in the song's lyrics. At the end of the film, Arthur fails, but Guenevere is repressed, banished to a penitential life as a fitting end to her failed attempt to embrace the erotic. That she appears shorn of her locks, of the hair which throughout the film symbolizes her internal state, only further serves to signal her final loss of agency, freedom, and identity.

In his 1981 film *Excalibur*, John Boorman empowers Guenevere by embracing the mythopoetic, both as generally articulated in Jungian archetypes and as refashioned by a number of feminist writers. Boorman offers a feminism that does not so much challenge the masculine as complement it. Unbalanced sexuality, masculine or feminine, is seen in the film as a threat. And Boorman's Guenevere can flourish because she is divested of all the darker, destructive elements of femininity—the film invests these in Morgana, the queen's cinematic foil. Camelot is still in ruins; Arthur is still defeated; Guenevere still does her penance within the walled enclosure of the convent; but in a noteworthy rejection of a tradition that Tennyson's groveling Guinevere only exaggerated, Boorman's Arthur does not condemn his queen, but begs for her forgiveness. As progressive as such a reversal is, it is nonetheless not without its downside. The conflicting portrayals of Guenevere and Morgana give expression to what is at best a polarized embrace of a view of feminine desire that Logan could not bring himself to follow through with, and that Boorman seems not to be wholly comfortable with either.

The 1990s ushered in the postfeminist theory that any opposition between agency and oppression in feminism might simply be found in the eye of the beholder. Postfeminism would then offer a challenge to any filmmaker attempting to bring so complicated a character as Guinevere to the screen. And, unfortunately—or not surprisingly—Jerry Zucker's 1995 film *First Knight* consistently failed to meet that challenge. As I have elsewhere argued, nothing about the film "quite works,"[5] not least its portrayal of Guinevere, who in *First Knight* is at first quite happily a queen in her own right and then too soon the willing child bride of a much older Arthur, the sacrifice of her autonomy not proving too high a price to pay for the safety of her people. Such contradictory views on female agency are the result of Zucker's decision to make a film not about Arthur and Guinevere, but about Lancelot, whom he sees in the mold of the stereotypical American hero who succeeds by merit and skill rather than by lineage. By nature, the film's Lancelot is a huckster and a shameless roué, and Guinevere suffers as a result of his characterization in this way. Ultimately, Guinevere is reduced to little more than a prize to be won and traded by men, first by Arthur and then by Lancelot, who here, unlike in other versions of the Arthuriad, cinematic or otherwise, actually gets the girl. For Zucker, feminism is at best a nice dream with decided limits; it cannot prevail in a world dominated by male violence. In such a world, Zucker argues, male violence can only be countered by more male violence.

In contrast to Zucker's defeated queen, Anton Fuqua's 2004 *King Arthur* presents Guinevere as a battle-hardened warrior princess whose links to the land she defends counter those associated with Arthur in, say, *Excalibur*, where the secret of the Holy Grail is that the land and the king are one. Indeed, Arthur here is a Roman soldier—an outsider, at least at first, to the land that he will eventually defend and rule though marriage to Guinevere. And Guinevere's female agency can be successfully portrayed in part because there is no love triangle involving Lancelot and Arthur—Lancelot, here a debased cad, is killed off long before Guinevere's wedding to Arthur. And with him dies any cultural anxiety in the film about female sexuality. But perhaps Fuqua's Guinevere is too good to be true—or to imitate. As Kaufman points out in a final note, the next major Arthurian film, Guy Ritchie's 2017 *King Arthur: Legend of the Sword* felt that the easiest way to handle a woman such as Guinevere was to eliminate her character completely from the film's screenplay.

If Guinevere is allowed multiple cinematic characterizations, her foil, Morgan, is more singular in her film embodiments. As Usha Vishnuvajjala points out, Morgan often makes possible Arthur's queen's redemption or quasi-redemption by default, whether in big budget or in independent films that include her as a force with which to be reckoned. Within the complicated Arthuriad, Morgan has an even more complicated role. She is initially Arthur's benevolent sister, more fairy spirit than mortal. But her character soon undergoes a marked shift from benevolence to malevolence in different national medieval traditions and in more modern post-medieval retellings of the tale of a woman blessed with immortality who becomes an evil enchantress bent on undermining successive generations of heroes in a vain attempt to claim Camelot or Excalibur, and, through them, world domination for herself.[6]

Vishnuvajjala discusses three categories of Arthurian film in which Morgan appears: those in which she is an adversarial character with whom other characters, especially

Arthur, most reckon; those in which she is potentially sympathetic; and those in which she is a figure of pure evil and malice. In the first category, Morgan appears as an adversary, though an ineffectual one. In the 1953 film *Knights of the Round Table*, Anne Crawford's Morgan is Uther Pendragon's sole legitimate heir—her half-brother Arthur is a bastard. Her claim to the throne, disallowing gender bias and the practice of primogeniture, is thus more legitimate than Arthur's, but it is Arthur who sits on the throne, not she. Her ally in the film is Modred, with whom she plots unsuccessfully to undermine Arthur's Round Table by exposing Guinevere and Lancelot's relationship. Modred here is not her son, as he is in other traditions, but her paramour, and his death at the hands of Lancelot twice defeats Morgan. It deprives her of a potential spouse and of the throne which she considers rightly hers, by eliminating the one person who might champion her cause and claim. Legal claims aside, she is ultimately ineffectual and powerless in a film that repeatedly grants agency to men and not to women.

A very different kind of Morgan, but one who is also defeated by male agency, is Virginia Field's Morgan in the 1949 film version of *A Connecticut Yankee in King Arthur's Court*, where she appears as Arthur's niece, and is opposed not by her uncle but by the modern-day interloper, Hank Martin.[7] As with other film versions of Twain's novel, the 1949 film deflates the misanthropy and pessimism of its source, substituting instead plots that play romantic and familial conflicts off against each other. Here Morgan's ally is Merlin—in later films her nemesis—and both prove no match as villains to the enterprising Yankee who has time travelled back to their midst in Camelot. Morgan's foil is Alisande, another of Arthur's nieces, who initially is engaged to be married to Lancelot, but who quickly turns her affections to Hank. And the rivalry with Morgan here is once again familial; each claims the right to inherit Arthur's throne. Morgan's depiction makes repeated use of time honored, but nonetheless offensive, sexist tropes, and she is little more than Merlin's handmaid and sidekick in his plots to undermine Camelot. Here once again, any attempt to add nuance to her character is useless, since she soon becomes largely insignificant in a Camelot where all real power is vested in men.

Later Morgans would be more complicated—beautiful, morally ambiguous, but ultimately punished by those closest to her. Emma Sutton's Morgan le Fay in the 1984 *Sword of the Valiant*, Stephen Weeks' second attempt to bring the 14th-century Middle English romance *Sir Gawain and the Green Knight* to the screen,[8] is punished for her sorcery by being turned into a toad. In the original English source, Morgan is the *magistra ludi* directing the Green Knight in an elaborate plot to undermine Arthur and the world of Camelot; in Weeks' film, she interferes in a game that the Green Knight has set into motion himself, and is punished by her onetime ally for doing so. That punishment is further reinforced when, as a toad, she is cleaved in half by Gawain and disappears from the film. Women like Morgan in Weeks' film hold what power they can at a price—as Morgan herself admits earlier in the film, "Nothing is free."

Helen Mirren's Morgana in John Boorman's 1981 film *Excalibur* is a woman with decided agency. Arthur's half-sister—she even watches as he is conceived—she eventually becomes mother to his son Mordred, with whom she plots, having first defeated Merlin, to destroy the Round Table and all that it stands for. Her character moves along a continuum that allows her both vulnerability and power. But she ultimately proves too clever by half, overestimating her abilities to hold in check the male-centered and male-empowering world in which she lives. The much vaunted "charm of making" is not her salvation but her final undoing. The power it holds is only briefly hers to wield, and that power is finally used against her by a magician with powers greater than hers, Merlin. Morgana seems at one point to direct the quest for the Holy Grail, but here too her agency is an illusion—a charm easily broken. The secret of the Grail is that the land and the king are one—women have no role, no real power in the world of the supernatural, whether that world be pagan or Christian. Excalibur is protected by women—Guinevere and the Lady of the Lake—but it is only for a man to possess and to use in battle. Morgana, literally deprived of her youth and beauty, is killed in disgust by her son Mordred who will himself die at the hands of Arthur. Arthur, it seems, however, does not die. The last scene of the film sees him adrift on a barge at sea accompanied by three queens who will cure him and ensure his immortality. Arthur will come again. The same cannot be said for Morgana.[9]

More recent cinematic Morgans are presented with little nuance. They are almost cartoonish as they exist solely to cause trouble which will lead to the central conflict in the films in which they appear. In *The Sorcerer's Apprentice*, Morgan and Merlin are the only Arthurian characters in a film set in present-day New York. *Dragons of Camelot* hues more closely to a traditional cast of Arthurian characters, but the futuristic Camelot which it presents also provides Morgan with little in the way of backstory to flesh out what is essentially her one-dimensional character. Both films tie into what Vishnuvajjala rightly sees as a backwards view of the medieval aimed at displacing modern misogyny into a pseudo-historical setting. Such displacement allows us to cope with real modern social problems at a safe distance. Quoting Finke and Shichtman, Vishnuvajjala notes that "the flip side of ... nostalgia is to associate the medieval with barbarity, superstition, and violence from which civilization ... is supposed to have rescued us."[10] Film Morgans, Vishnuvajjala sadly concludes, must be contained, controlled, and defeated, all in the name of human progress.

To modern and postmodern audiences, the great love affair of the Middle Ages is not that of Lancelot and Guinevere but of Tristan and Isolde. While the story of their love would in the late Middle Ages be linked to the Arthuriad, it is a story long told throughout medieval Europe, and a story that would rise and fall in its popularity in the post-medieval world.[11] That filmmakers from a number of countries working within different cinematic traditions would turn to it for inspiration more than a dozen times only testifies to the enduring appeal that the story of two originally medieval, ill-fated lovers continues to have.

In the legend, Joan Tasker Grimbert argues, Isolde is the stronger character—more passionate, more cunning, more alluring, and more determined than her lover. Wagner may be the source for such a gendered reversal of hero and heroine—his Isolde is intent on establishing her own agency. And his 19th-century opera revived interest in the legend into which early film makers eagerly tapped. But the first great film version of the legend would not be made until the middle of the Second World War in France, the 1943 Delannoy/Cocteau film *The Eternal Return*.[12]

The film is not set in the Middle Ages, however, and changes the names of the protagonists to Patrice and Nathalie, whose blonde hair sets them apart from everyone else in the film. And the action takes place in nondescript locations without any link to history or geography—better to emphasize the timelessness of the story that the film tells. As the film's Nietzchean title and opening quotation suggest, mythic stories like that of Tristan and Isolde are destined to be recycled through history—they know no temporal or geographical boundaries.

Unfortunately, such a successful translation of the legend to the screen did not find a totally successful sequel in the next attempt to film the story of Tristan and Isolde, Tom Donovan's 1979 film *Lovespell*. Donovan eagerly embraces the legend's medieval origins stressing its Celtic roots, the tension it exposed between pagan and Christian traditions, and the possibility it afforded for a woman to successfully establish her own agency without the aid of a male companion. Indeed, in the film, it is Isolt who is more comfortable with the adulterous relationship that she enters into than Tristan. And Donovan rearranges characters and their motivation from a number of medieval sources to highlight the on-screen presence of his marquee star, Richard Burton. But Burton's Mark is not one of his most stellar performances, and the film ends with a bit of a muddle. The strong willed Isolt seems equally in love with both her husband and her lover, and, while Isolt loses Tristan, Mark also loses Isolt in an ending that is not nearly as tidy as it may seem.

Veith von Fürstenberg's 1981 *Fire and Sword* offers an even more headstrong Isolde and attempts to layer onto the legend a message about the senselessness of war. The result is a mixed success, but one that attests to the malleability of the legend and its ability to withstand whatever a filmmaker attempts to do with it. That these two films were made in Ireland and in Germany provided filmmakers with a rich legacy into which to tap. How successfully they did so, however, is a matter of some critical debate, as Grimbert makes clear.

The Eternal Return offers a nontraditional, and, interestingly, more successful translation of the legend; so too does the 1988 Icelandic film *In the Shadow of the Raven*, which grafts the legend onto the rich traditions of Old Norse mythology and the family saga.[13] Grimbert argues that the result may be the most unorthodox film in the cinematic Tristan canon. But the love story finds a ready home in an 11th-century Iceland already facing a conflict between an old pagan and a new Christian religion. And the film successfully integrates the couple's passion for each other into a more universal message of Christian love. Ísold represents the violence of the pagan past; Trausti, a Christian alternative to revenge and blood feud, assured of success by his survival and that of their daughter Sól. But Ísold too finds redemption—her image becomes the model for that of Mary Magdalene in an altarpiece created near the end of the film to celebrate the triumph of Christianity.

The most recent Tristan and Isolde film, Kevin Reynolds' 2006 *Tristan & Isolde*, introduces a Marke who is Arthur-like in his desire to unite all of Britain against a common enemy, the King of Ireland. The war with the Irish provides the backdrop for the love story that the film tells. And the love affair threatens the outcome of that war, since an enraged Marke will presumably be a less effective opponent. Marke does eventually defeat the Irish and reign in peace for the rest of his life, but Tristan is a casualty of the war with the Irish, even though a more than magnanimous Marke is willing to allow Tristan and Isolde to secure their love by escaping from Cornwall before the promised apocalyptic final battle. Reynolds' film then adds a depth to Marke not previously seen in other film versions of the legend. But the most interesting character to watch is Isolde, who can defy our gender expectations in her on-screen characterizations, characterizations that owe much to a long tradition that sees her as the strongest of the three members of the ill-fated love triangle in which she is involved.

Perhaps second only to the Arthuriad in popularity is the legend of yet another English medieval fictional character, Robin Hood. The Hoodian legend would develop later than the Arthuriad, and would showcase a decidedly different hero, an anti-establishment foil to the establishment Arthur, a hero more comfortable in the Green-wood than in the castle.[14] And while Arthur has his Knights of the Round Table, Robin has his band of merry men, whose number varies depending upon which narrative thread someone is interested in following. The world of Robin Hood is markedly homosocial. Only one woman is a constant in the Hoodian legend, the Lady or Maid Marian, who, as Valerie B. Johnson shows, despite the best efforts of some film directors, finds herself repeatedly consigned to the secondary, and ultimately passive, role of damsel in distress—no Isolde is she.

Non-cinematic Marians fare better than their on-screen counterparts. But whether on the large or the small screen, Marian is victimized by the fiscal conservatism of the film industry, and by the unexpectedly dismissive attitude toward her often propagated by neomedievalism. The first major Robin film, Douglas Fairbanks' 1922 blockbuster, set a pattern for the cinematic Marian, from which her character has been at best only fleet-ingly able to escape. Subsequent film Marians are defined by the love of a good man, Robin, or by an unsuccessful attempt to rewrite the past in a way that allows them just brief moments of self-definition and agency. In both cases, her focus is never on herself, but rather on Robin, whose motives she can help to explain to film audiences.

Marian plays second fiddle regardless of how Robin Hood is characterized. In the 1922 Fairbanks film, Robin is famously afraid of women, and he must almost be dragged kicking and screaming to the nuptial altar by King Richard. In the 1938 Errol Flynn film, Robin is more self-assured—almost cocky in his dealings with men and women. Marian at first finds him repulsive in part because he is a Saxon, but eventually she comes to see him in an entirely different light, when she finally realizes that her fellow Normans are such incredibly cruel cads and villains. However, her change in attitude provides her with no real agency; it victimizes her and makes her even more dependent upon Robin, who must now rescue her from her fellow Normans who plan to execute her for, among other things, being a traitor to her race.

Both Enid Bennett's 1922 and Olivia de Havilland's 1938 Marians seem closer to courtly heroines—to the women of the Arthuriad who at times seem to serve one sole purpose: to inspire men to deeds of derring-do, including their own rescue when they are in moments of distress. Both Marians suffer from the gaze of both the camera and the audience—they are passive objects of beauty on display to delight the active men who surround them. And these two film Marians set the pattern for every film and television series that followed, thereby preventing Marian from achieving a cinematic narrative uniquely her own. The hope that post–Second War Marians would fare any better because of the multiple social revolutions afoot in society would prove false. As Johnson argues, conservatism would again win out, and unruly Marians would be tamed by their Robins.

The animated 1973 feature length film represents, not surprisingly, the Disneyfication of the Robin Hood legend and all that such a transformation implies.[15] A child-friendly version of the legend must needs downplay anything that might prove inappropriate for a young audience. And Marian is offered as a counter to any social movement that would offer women self-empowerment and agency. The animated Marian is simply an object of love. Any feminine agency that the film allows is vested in her companion and servant, a portly hen, who initially does appear to have genuine agency, but, we eventually learn, her agency is really in the service of her mistress and then easily replaced by Robin who is, in the final analysis, her true rescuer.

The 1976 *Robin and Marian*, which can be read as an anti-establishment—especially anti–Vietnam War—film,[16] would seem to present the perfect opportunity for a filmmaker to present a different kind of Marian, one who is able to embrace the anti-establishment sentiments of the decade in which the film was produced and released. But Audrey Hepburn's Marian is a woman in conflict with both her past and present selves, and the film's (mis)treatment of Marian—if not its misogyny—denies her any real chance of self-determination. Robin has abandoned her in the past, and his return forces her to abandon the new life that, in his absence, she has created for herself as a nun. The reunion of Robin and Marian strikes a Wagnerian note light. She does act in the film's final scenes, but the result of her actions is that she poisons both Robin and herself. Quoting Sharon Lux, Johnson notes that the best that can be said of the film's ending is that it allows Marian an "agency of desperation."[17]

More recent films may not put Marian into such desperate situations, but they nonetheless offer her initial strength and independence only to deprive her of them in the service of developing an imperfect Robin Hood character. In such films Robin is a work in progress, and what leads him ultimately to success is the love of a good woman who is content to stand behind and support him. Marians of the 1990s may reflect the third wave of feminism, but again Hollywood's attention to the bottom line—to what conservative movie audiences will pay to see—precludes allowing Marian to develop her own narrative or a competing narrative to that offered for Robin Hood. Once again, Marian becomes an object from romance, a woman over whom men battle—in a comic sendup of such Marians, Mel Brooks's 1993 *Robin Hood: Men in Tights* literally secures Marian's safety and virtue with a chastity belt, but the comedy here has an edge. Decidedly neomedieval, initially in a positive way because of its views on so many important cultural issues, the Brooks film nonetheless ends up finally endorsing rather than rejecting a misogyny that is the dark side of neomedievalism.

Ridley Scott's 2010 *Robin Hood* might seem to be an appropriate cinematic vehicle for allowing Marian to step out from behind Robin's shadow, especially since Russell Crowe begins the film as an impostor intent upon ensuring his own safety by pretending to be better than he is. Cate Blanchett's Marian is an impressively skilled woman—she can manage a castle and lead an army. But, by the film's end, she proves no match for the hyper-masculine Robin Hood that Crowe becomes, and into whose arms and embrace she willingly melts.

Johnson argues, convincingly, that filmmakers have never really seemed to know what to do with Marian. She too easily fits into a neomedievalist trope—that of the damsel in distress—a trope that film audiences are decidedly comfortable with and willing to pay to see. Whereas film Guineveres, Morgans, and Isoldes exist along a continuum that allows them differing degrees of agency, film Marians at best have depth and independence secondarily. First and foremost, film Marians stand by their men, whose lives offer endless opportunities for deeds of derring-do, including coming to the aid of their Marians.

If film Marians frustrate us by reinforcing gender-dismissive stereotypes that subject women to the gaze, thereby allowing them to be little more than passive objects in a world full of active men—who are as prone to act badly as they are to act heroically—cinematic medieval women, as portrayed in Fritz Lang's great medieval two-part 1924 cinematic epic, *The Nibelungen*, lead fuller, more complicated, action-filled lives, which nonetheless lead to tragic consequences, but tragic consequences of their own making.

As Donald L. Hoffman points out in his analysis of the film, the dueling queens also reflect dueling agendas for the two parts of the film, one from the director, and one from his wife Thea von Harbou, who wrote the screenplay for her husband's cinematic epic. Lang's film, like his life, is freighted with 20th-century politics. *The Nibelungen* is variously viewed as a reaction to the First World War and an anticipation of the Second—though such prescience seems to stem from a backwards look at German medievalism. Von Harbou was more clearly a Nazi fellow traveler—Lang would find himself hauled before the House Un-American Activities Committee for alleged Communist sympathies, while von Harbou would spend some time after the Second World War in a British denazification camp.

The Nibelungen is not only one of the greatest medievalist films, it is also one of the greatest films ever made, by any barometer. It is truly epic in the sweep of its story, in its monumental sets, and in the depths of the passions with which it imbues its characters, especially the wronged Kriemhild. The two parts of the film are a study in contrasts—each is dominated by a different strong woman character. Part one would appear to be Brunhild's; part two, clearly Kriemhild's. But in a reading which he admits borders on the allegorical, Hoffman shows how the two parts of the film complement each other. While they are two parts of the same film, they essentially tell two very different stories in very different ways.

Siegfried more readily reflects German mythology—it presents a blond, purely Teutonic hero and a wild, mountain heroine who at first rules her kingdom without any male interference. Her freedom—her independence and agency—link her to ideologies with which von Harbou would readily identify, "blood and soil" nationalism, and the modernist ideal of the New Woman. While she and Siegfried meet tragic ends, they are essentially positive figures. Although she turns vindictive when she feels slighted by Kriemhild and betrayed by her husband, Brunhild remains a tragic figure of romance, betrayed yet avenged. The film carries with it an aura of nationalism and myth which reflects the glory of the German people—unfortunately such a view will be invoked later not to unpack the tragic on screen but to drive a national agenda whose consequences would be all too horrific.

In *Kriemhilds Rache*, the cinematic focus shifts from myth to history—cynicism replaces Romanticism. Kriemhild is a decidedly different kind of heroine than Brunhild. The ending of the second film leaves us with neither myth nor history. Kriemhild is indeed powerful, calculatingly and relentlessly so, but for the wrong reasons. What motivates her is an unquenchable thirst for vengeance. So unquenchable and so unfeminine is that thirst that she is characterized as a "she-devil" in the medieval poem that is the film's principal source. She cannot be a man, but she also cannot be a woman. She is totally othered. The clash of myth and history, the clash of the two queens, and the clash of the two parts of the film leave us with nothing but a wasteland. A woman may become all powerful, but to what end. Lang reimagines the image of the medieval woman—she is not like any of the Guineveres, Morgans, Isoldes or Marians that we have seen. She is something else—something unsettling and subversive which shows that moving beyond gender stereotypes can be a fraught cinematic exercise.

Would medieval women fare better on the screen under the direction of women filmmakers?[18] The Lang film shows that women screenwriters can be as uncompromising as their male counterparts in bringing medieval women to the screen in ways that at best allow them limited agency. But at least one film—written and directed by a woman, whose role in Nordic film is iconic—takes a decidedly different approach, and the result is a more positive, nuanced, and complex portrayal of the emotional life of women and response to female erotic desire: Liv Ullmann's 1995 film of *Kristin Lavransdatter*. As Joseph M. Sullivan shows, Ullmann faced an uphill battle with the male-dominated Norwegian film industry in bringing her vision of the first book in Sigrid Undset's trilogy (1920–1922) to the screen.[19] The project also was fraught from the start because the novel upon which the film is based holds such a special place in Norwegian (and Scandinavian) culture in general and literature in particular. Indeed, Sullivan suggests that the novel may well be the most well-known example of medievalism as historical fiction. And it remains so nearly one hundred years after its publication.

The novel is notable—and in some quarters controversial—for both its sensitive portrayal of characters, male and female, and its detailed depiction of early 14th-century Norwegian life. The accuracy of those portrayals and of that depiction has remained the focus of continued scholarly debate. Undset certainly had a solid enough background in the Middle Ages to know of what she wrote; in drafting the novel, she would make use of primary historical and literary medieval texts, as well as late 19th- and early 20th-century scholarly works.[20] But the novel's appeal lies also with the author's conviction that the story she tells of love, loss, and betrayal, from a uniquely feminine perspective, is universally timeless. Ullmann is able to translate what is distinct and important about the novel to the screen, while also adding her own touches to the film's screenplay, as Sullivan points out what in her film Ullmann has kept, intensified, and innovated from the novel.

Ullmann's film intervenes in its source by emphasizing more fully the power of female desire. So powerful is that desire that the film's Kristin rebels against male imposed prescriptions against sex outside of marriage—and that rebellion is ultimately shown to be a rebellion against not only her father, her family and her church, but also against nature itself. While the novel takes an at times ambiguous stance on Kristin's loss of virginity, the film sees the loss as a consensual act on Kristin's part, and allows that a lack of true romantic passion may be as much due to male reluctance as to female hesitancy. Thwarted sexual desire knows no limits; it can plague men as well as women, and younger as well as older lovers. Ullmann further explores female desire in expanding from the novel the relationship between Kristin and her sister Ulvhild. In the film, their difference in age is minimized, and the crippled Ulvhild is able to bond with Kristin in a way that she can at least share in her sister's emotional life vicariously. Indeed, the film's emphasis on the bonds of sisterhood is one with the greater attention that it pays to female friendships in general, thereby providing audiences with a multi-faceted and more in-depth examination and sustained appreciation of the power of female desire. Paralleling the film's discourse on romantic, erotic love and desire is an added focus on maternal love further to explore the complexities of women's interior lives. And despite the best efforts of the male-dominated Norwegian film industry to limit the depth and complexity of Ullmann's reading of Undset's novel, the film presents a decidedly different—and refreshing—cinematic portrayal of medieval women that recognizes the complexities of their desires and emotions in a positive and affirming way.

But Ullmann's film holds a unique place in the canon of films about medieval women. Indeed, as Andrew B.R. Elliott shows in his analysis of Bernard Tavernier's 1987 film *La Passion Béatrice*, film is more than capable of depicting women being subjected to unimaginable depths of cruelty, depravity, and violence.[21] Our reconstructions of the medieval are prone to see the Middle Ages as a well of violence and brutality. Tavernier's film espouses such a view. The film is based on real events, but events which occurred in the Renaissance, not the Middle Ages. The four children of the rich and powerful Count Francesco Cenci murder their father after he has raped his daughter, Beatrice, and abused her siblings. The three eldest are executed; the youngest, a boy only 12 years old, is sold into captivity as a galley slave. Patricide—the ultimate attack upon male supremacy—is, therefore, the ultimate transgression that must be punished no matter what extenuating circumstances surround the crime. And the story of the Cencis would remain so fascinating to post-early modern audiences that it would be retold throughout the 19th and 20th century by any number of writers, and filmmakers.[22]

As he has in a number of earlier publications,[23] Elliott suggests that part of the problem with depictions of medieval women, on film or in other media, lies with the ideology that informs the ways in which we do (and don't) view the Middle Ages. Entrenched views of gender roles reinforce cinematic stereotyping of women. In short, we misperceive medieval women because we want to—again Tavernier takes an historical incident of patricide from Renaissance Italy and resituates it in a medieval world riddled with violence against both men and women. The film is divided into three acts which empower the eponymous heroine with a kind of begrudging agency that allows her to react to the men around her rather than to act on her own. Tavernier's heroine operates in a fragmentally-presented view of a Middle Ages relentlessly descending into chaos and brutality—but the director's approach, as overwhelming as it may seem to audiences, also prevents them from constructing any kind of coherent whole for the medieval world to which they are introduced. Instead, Tavernier gives us an almost Manichean view of a world in which men are the personification of violence and women, by nature devoted and nurturing, are finally undone by a madness that rejects any attempt at being humane or compassionate. The film becomes a study of love and hatred in which hatred will clearly win out. The patriarchal hierarchy in place in the film's medieval world allows brutality and violence to go unchecked. The shift in temporal setting makes the film a study of a specific kind of brutality and violence, that of the Middle Ages, onto which film audiences can displace their own fears and anxieties. Any debates about gender in the film are part and parcel of a neomedievalist fantasy. Such debates are not about the distant ancestors of Tavernier's audiences, but about those audiences themselves. As such, Tavernier echoes Umberto Eco's view that, in looking at the Middle Ages, we are really looking at our own infancy.[24] In hoping to find the medieval, we are really hoping to find our roots, and, in a film like Tavernier's, we find a challenge to our misconceptions about gender, and a reinforcement of them in a way that allows masculinity not only to triumph brutally, but also to do so at the expense of women.

Cinema medievalia has also found inspiration in the lives of historical women from the Middle Ages. The four final essays in this collection discuss the very different ways in which filmmakers have attempted to tell the stories of Lady Godiva, Heloise, Eleanor of Aquitaine, and Joan of Arc. The 11th-century Godiva, Countess of Mercia, who died sometime shortly after the Norman Conquest, has been the subject of a complex legend, mixing history and myth. Remembered most often because of her naked horseback ride through the streets of Coventry to spare the townspeople from oppressive taxation, she has, since the 13th century, become a cultural icon to advance any number of agendas, particularly about women and their roles in society. These agendas, further rooted in a continuing interest both in voyeurism and in medievalism, have found their expression in history, literature, art, and popular culture, and in a cinematic tradition that, as Sandra Gorgievski details, at times offers a mix of the political and the pornographic.[25]

Originally, Godiva's story is one reflective of private piety, but it would eventually develop into a powerful erotic myth, that continues to fascinate us today. From the modern perspective, Godiva's naked ride is an act of transgression, but the idea of a woman on a horse offering assistance to her fellow citizens has deep roots in Eros-laden classical traditions built around images of women deities on horseback. Cinema would first ignore Godiva's link to the erotic in several silent films heavily indebted to an 1840s poem by Tennyson—lines from which would be incorporated into the films as intertitles. But a strong tradition had already developed before Victorian times to replace Godiva's pious historical origins with a rival tradition concentrating on the erotic, though the transgressive behavior in such a tradition is then vested in a man, the Peeping Tom, who is blinded for his attempt to view Godiva's nakedness, when the townspeople otherwise avert their eyes to spare Godiva any shame for her nakedness. The 20th century then inherited two conflicting visual images of Godiva—a contemplative wife safely modest behind the walls of her chamber carefully planning her ride and a totally exposed countless, head bowed, naked except for her long, often red, hair, which covers her breasts. The latter image grew out of civic processions in Coventry, which became a hugely popular commercial attraction for almost 200 years beginning in the late 17th century.

Silent films about Godiva emphasize the sentimental and the melodramatic—the Godiva whom they depict is one with other silent screen heroines who are initially long-suffering but eventually rewarded for their virtue and determination in the face of a variety of dangers. Godiva's next major screen appearance would be in a very different kind of film, a 1955 swashbuckler with a political agenda grounded in the Cold War. That agenda depicts Godiva's ride against a backdrop in which the conflict between Saxon and Norman plays out in a reimagined 11th-century England where loyalty to the crown is a major political concern—questions of politically loyalty would, of course, inform American public discourse and haunt Hollywood in the 1950s. Since the actress who played this very different reimagining of Godiva, Maureen O'Hara, had already become an icon of feminine adventurism, it is not surprising that the film allows her Godiva to move from humiliation to triumph, and to become a role model for those who would put their duty to the commonweal above any personal, selfish gain. Alas, her reward is a little too gender-constricted—as the swashbuckler shifts genres after her ride to become a romantic comedy in which a fainting Godiva falls into her husband's arms as he whisks her away to a life of presumed marital bliss.

Later Godiva films, often only obliquely related to the competing medieval and post-medieval versions of her legend, would offer a decidedly different image of the countess. In such films, Godiva's ride becomes little more than a pretext for soft-core pornographic voyeurism and exhibitionism, or for decidedly inept variations on more successful romantic comedies. While the cinematic tradition of Lady Godiva is not as rich and varied as that say of fictional characters such as Guinevere or of historical figures such as Eleanor of Aquitaine, playing Godiva on film, according to Gorgievski, allows an actress simply to "disguise herself as," rather than to attempt to impersonate, the Countess of Mercia. Film Godivas continue a tradition in which she becomes a figure intended for a kind of mass entertainment where spectators are more active than passive in helping to shape the version of the legend that they see.

If film Godivas objectify the countess's body, a very different interest in a medieval woman's mind and heart emerges in the one major film to assay the life of Heloise (1090–1164), who may be best known today because of her love affair and subsequent correspondence with Peter Abelard (1079–1142). But Heloise was justifiably famous in her own right as a (reluctant) nun, a writer, a scholar, and an abbess. Her letters, most of which do not survive, hold a special place in French literature, offering as much a view into her mind as they do her heart. And their influence would be seen in later literature, especially as a model for epistolary writing. Trained in Latin, Greek and Hebrew, Heloise was already an accomplished scholar by the time that she first met Abelard when she was in her early 20s. Subsequently, under Abelard's tutelage, she was schooled in medicine and other areas of study, and she would outlive him to found a number of religious communities.

Fuller details about Heloise's life are scarce, and her story has perhaps been told most fully in an historical novel, Marion Meade's 1979 novel *Stealing Heaven*, which was in turn the source for Clive Donner's 1988 film of the same title. But, as Kristin L. Burr points out, the novel and the film take decidedly different approaches to the story they tell. Most importantly, the film largely ignores the second half of the novel, which details Heloise's trials and tribulations after Abelard's castration. In doing so, the film erases events in her life which give us a better view of how extraordinary that life really was. In the novel, Heloise is a fully-developed three-dimensional character—she is much less so in the film. And in its selective approach to the novel, the film downplays the complexity of Heloise's character as well as that of Abelard, but with decidedly different results. The novel is decidedly less sympathetic to Abelard than the film, with the result that, in the film, his character benefits from Donner's selectivity in bringing details from his source to the screen. At the same time, the film's compression of Heloise's fuller story and its virtual elimination of Meade's critique of the limited options available to women in the Middle Ages render Heloise less interesting, and less complex. Donner's Heloise is still a remarkable woman, but her life is reduced to a story about frustrated love, and she is more often than not defined simply by her relationship with Abelard. As Burr notes, the film highlights Heloise's life solely in terms of her relationship with Abelard with the result that the real Heloise is ironically hidden on the screen from us in plain sight.

One of the most powerful, wealthy, and influential women of the Middle Ages was Eleanor of Aquitaine (1124–1204). She was first Queen of France, marrying Louis VII, with whom she went on the disastrous Second Crusade and had two daughters. Then, after their marriage was annulled, she quickly married the Duke of Normandy, who would become Henry II of England, and with whom she had five sons and three more daughters. For filmmakers interested in portraying a complex medieval woman whose story was rooted mainly in history, Eleanor has proven a subject hard to resist—though, as Fiona Tolhurst points out, such attraction has led to decidedly different on-screen portrayals of a woman who would be queen of two kingdoms because of the importance and power she first held as the Duchess of Aquitaine, a position that made her the most eligible royal bride of her time.

Cinematic portrayals of Eleanor reflect two conflicting traditions about her that blend history and myth. From the Middle Ages, filmmakers could look back to the Black Legend of Eleanor, which presents her in highly unflattering terms as both a queen and a mother. The legend accuses Eleanor of a laundry list of transgressions including treason, rebellion, cross-dressing, treachery, incest, licentiousness, usurpation, and murder. Countering the legend is the so-called Golden Myth, a 20th-century reevaluation of Eleanor's life in light of Second-wave Feminism that validates Eleanor as genuinely exceptional and heroic and emphasizes her influence and achievements. Further coloring the various screen portrayals of Eleanor were social views about women and their roles during the decades in which the films were produced.

Despite its release during the resurgence of the feminist movement that began in the early 1960s, *Becket* presents a largely powerless and totally disrespected Eleanor because it focuses almost exclusively on the relationship between Henry and Becket, a relationship in which women have a decidedly secondary role. In contrast, *The Lion in Winter* presents a more complicated Eleanor, reflecting both the Black Legend and the Golden Myth, thanks in no small part to Katharine Hepburn's forceful, at times over-the-top, scene-stealing portrayal of the queen in the film. So memorable is Hepburn's portrayal of Eleanor that it haunts the 2003 made-for-television remake of *The Lion in Winter*, in which Glenn Close is at best Hepburn light because of what Tolhurst calls the "Hallmarking" of the entire plot of the stage play that was the source for both films. In keeping with its sendup of the legend of Robin Hood, *The Zany Adventures of Robin Hood* offers a comic Eleanor, who once again blends legend and myth. Janet Suzman's Eleanor is a sex-starved woman whose power is nonetheless something to be reckoned with. The 2010 *Robin Hood* presents an entirely good Eleanor, but Eileen Atkins' queen is disrespected by her sons and ultimately powerless to change the disastrous course of English history that highlights her son John's reign. But, perhaps surprisingly, there is one especially positive cinematic portrayal of a powerful and wise Eleanor, that of Martita Hunt (who would later play *Becket*'s much disempowered Empress Mathilda) in Disney's 1952 film *Robin Hood and His Merrie Men*. Hunt's Eleanor reflects both the Golden Myth and contemporary attitudes about possible roles for American women after the Second World War.

For 125 years, Joan of Arc has been the poster child for cinema medievalia, as I detail in the final essay in this collection. The Maid of Orléans appears, directly or indirectly, in more films than any other medieval woman, historical or fictional. Thanks to the records of her original trial in 1431 and those of the nullification of that trial's verdict in 1456, Joan's life may well be the most documented of any medieval person, so filmmakers have had an abundance of primary sources to which to turn—or which to ignore—as they sought to bring their own vision of Joan to the screen. Jehanne films fall into three broad categories: films that depict her life, or at least an incident from her life; films in which characters play Joan on stage or screen; and films in which characters channel Joan as an avatar. A cinematic depiction of Joan is often freighted in an ongoing debate over whether she is more properly seen as a daughter (and eventual saint) of the Church or as the mother of a nation. Other agendas further color the screen lives of Joan, just as they do the lives of Joan in multiple other media and forums. Just as history gives us no one Joan, film follows suit—though it is quite clear that the corpus of Jehanne films dictates that the lady is indeed for burning. So, unexpectedly, we come full circle at the end of this collection of essays which begins with the fictional Guinevere being threatened with burning at the stake for sexual misconduct and which ends with the historical Joan of Arc being burned at the stake for multiple trumped up transgressions.

NOTES

1. Text in the first volume of *The Norton Anthology of English Literature*, ed. Stephen Greenblatt and others, 8th edition (New York: Norton, 2006), pp. 699–700.

2. Quoted in Roger Sherman Loomis, ed., *Arthurian Literature in the Middle Ages: A Collaborative History* (1959; rpt. Oxford: The Clarendon Press, 1979), p. 62. The bibliography for primary and secondary texts that form the Arthuriad is overwhelming. Some convenient jumping off points are Helen Fulton, ed., *A Companion to Arthurian Literature* (Oxford: Blackwell, 2009); Anne F. Howey and Stephen R. Reimer, *A Bibliog-*

raphy of Modern Arthuriana (1500–2000) (Cambridge: D.S. Brewer, 2006); Alan Lupack, *The Oxford Companion to Arthurian Literature and Legend* (New York: Oxford University Press, 2005); and Daniel P. Nastali and Phillip C. Boardman, *The Arthurian Annals: The Tradition in English from 1250 to 2000*, 2 vols. (New York: Oxford University Press, 2004).

3. Guinevere's name, depending upon the text or film, is spelled either "Guinevere" or "Guenevere." Morgan's name is spelled even more variously. For fuller discussions of the complicated portrayals of Arthurian women, two collections of essays provide convenient starting points: Thelma Fenster, ed., *Arthurian Women* (New York: Routledge, 1996); and Bonnie Wheeler and Fiona Tolhurst, eds., *On Arthurian Women: Essays in Memory of Maureen Fries* (Dallas: Scriptorium Press, 2001). Medieval film has increasingly become the focus of critical scholarly inquiry, and again the bibliography can overwhelming. For starters, see Kevin J. Harty, *The Reel Middle Ages: American, Western and Eastern European, Middle Eastern, and Asian Films About Medieval Europe* (Jefferson, NC: McFarland, 1999).

4. Lupack, p. 151.

5. Kevin J. Harty, "Cinema Arthuriana: An Overview," in *Cinema Arthuriana, Twenty Essays*, ed. Kevin J. Harty (Jefferson, NC: McFarland, 2003), p. 23.

6. See the 2019 film *The Kid Who Would Be King*, where Morgan's long-planned plans for world dominance are abruptly foiled by a group of high school students. For a quick overview of Morgan's shifting roles in multiple retellings of the Arthuriad, see Jill M. Herbert, *Morgan Le Fay, Shapeshifter* (New York: Palgrave Macmillan, 2013); and Kristina Pérez, *The Myth of Morgan La Fey* (New York: Palgrave Macmillan, 2014). For an earlier discussion of Morgan's cinematic portrayals, see Maureen Fries, "How to Handle a Woman: Morgan at the Movies," in *King Arthur on Film: New Essays on Cinema Arthuriana*, ed. Kevin J. Harty (Jefferson, NC: McFarland, 1999), pp. 67–80.

7. While filmmakers may repeatedly have claimed Malory as their source, Twain's novel is the most referenced literary source for Arthurian films, made-for-television films, and television programs. See Elizabeth Sklar, "Twain for Teens, Young Yankees in Camelot," in *King Arthur on Film*, ed. Kevin J. Harty, pp. 97–108; and Alan Lupack and Barbara Tepa Lupack, *King Arthur in America* (Cambridge, Eng: D.S. Brewer, 1999), pp. 308–314.

8. The first was in 1973. Neither film is successful in adapting the Middle English poem to the screen. The later film also uses Chrétien de Troyes' twelfth-century French romance *Yvain* as a source.

9. In Malory, Arthur is accompanied by four queens, one of whom is Morgana.

10. Laurie A. Finke and Martin B. Shichtman, *Cinematic Illuminations: The Middle Ages on Film* (Baltimore: Johns Hopkins University Press, 2010), p. 19.

11. The most comprehensive survey of the legend of Tristan and Isolde remains Joan Tasker Grimbert, ed. *Tristan and Isolde: A Casebook* (1995; rpt. New York: Routledge, 2002).

12. Jean Delannoy directed the film from a screenplay by Jean Cocteau.

13. The film is part of a Viking trilogy which taps into Old Norse mythology and the tradition of the family sagas.

14. Stephen Knight remains the indispensable source for discussions of all things Robin Hood. See his *Robin Hood: A Complete Study of the English Outlaw* (Oxford: Blackwell, 1994), and *Robin Hood: A Mythic Biography* (Ithaca: Cornell University Press, 2003).

15. Disney made several forays into the cinematic Greenwood. See Kevin J. Harty, "Walt in Sherwood, or the Sheriff of Disneyland: Disney and the Film Legends of Robin Hood," in *The Disney Middle Ages: A Fairy-Tale and Fantasy Past*, ed. Tison Pugh and Susan Aronstein (New York: Palgrave Macmillan, 2012), pp. 133–152.

16. See Kevin J. Harty, "Robin Hood on Film: Moving Beyond a Swashbuckling Stereotype," in *Robin Hood in Popular Culture: Violence, Transgression, and Justice*, ed. Thomas Hahn (Cambridge: D.S. Brewer, 2000), pp. 96–99.

17. Sherron Lux, "And the 'Reel' Marian," in *Robin Hood in Popular Culture*, p. 154.

18. Women directors have throughout cinema history been in the distinct minority. And any early pioneers behind the camera who were women have been all but forgotten. The invention of the narrative action film is generally credited to Alice Guy-Blaché (1873–1964), who over a twenty-five year career directed, produced, wrote or oversaw more than 700 films including medievalist films about William Tell (1900), Faust (1903), and Victor Hugo's Esmeralda from *The Hunchback of Notre Dame* (1905). On her life and her career in almost every aspect of the film industry, see Janelle Derrick, *Illuminating Moments: The Films of Alice Guy-Blaché* (Portland, OR: BookBaby, 2017); and Alison McMahan, *Alice Guy-Blaché: The Lost Visionary of the Cinema* (New York: Continuum, 2002).

19. The trilogy consists of *The Wreath* (1920), *The Wife* (1921), and *The Cross* (1922).

20. In 1915, Undset had published a Norwegian adaptation of Malory's *Le Morte Darthur*.

21. While misogyny may regularly inform cinematic depictions of medieval women, as essays in this collection attest, the films that subject women to inhumane treatment and violence—including rape and murder—are few. Joan of Arc films may well, of course, feature her death at the stake, but other films depicting violence against women—for instance, Ingmar Bergman's 1959 *The Virgin Spring* and Paul Verhoeven's 1985 *Flesh & Blood*—are exceptions rather than the rule.

22. See Belinda Elizabeth Jack, *Beatrice's Spell: The Enduring Legacy of Beatrice Cenci* (New York: Other Press, 2005).

23. See the endnotes to his essay below.

24. Umberto Eco, "Dreaming of the Middle Ages," in *Travels in Hyperreality*, trans. William Weaver (London: Picador, 1987), p. 65.

25. For a detailed study of the Godiva legend, see Daniel Donoghue, *Lady Godiva: A Literary History of the Legend* (Malden, MA: Blackwell, 2003).

Liberating Guinevere

Female Desire on Film

Amy S. Kaufman

In the 1967 film *Camelot*, King Arthur laments his inability to control a wayward, perplexing wife in the song "How to Handle a Woman." This short musical number reflects one of the Arthurian legend's most prominent problems: how to handle its female characters—specifically a desiring woman like Guinevere.[1] As Fiona Tolhurst notes, "Guenevere has always been, and continues to be, a means of exploring how sexuality defines women's identity for each author who re-creates her."[2] And Guinevere's troubling sexuality is not just about the desire she receives from her many admirers; instead, what makes Guinevere's character problematic is the desire that she feels.[3]

One would think Guinevere's desire might be the natural focus of feminist revisions to her character in cinema. But, on the contrary, filmmakers have struggled with their newly complicated relationship to Guinevere and her sexuality since the rise of the feminist movement. No longer will audiences tolerate a passive victim or a shameless seductress. A liberated Guinevere has to be strong, have agency, and somehow evade the misogynistic stereotypes that stalk her through literary history. Negotiating such a tricky character means filmmakers have to decide what strength means, how innocence is defined, and what counts as "choice." It also means grappling with evolving anxieties about women and sex in each cinematic generation.

Camelot *(1967): The Babe in the Woods*

Scholars agree that Joshua Logan's 1967 film version of the Lerner and Lowe musical *Camelot* was a conservative movie in an increasingly radical era.[4] And yet, its portrayal of Guenevere also struggles to integrate the feminist discourse of its time. Betty Friedan had published *The Feminine Mystique* in 1963, the same year Gloria Steinem went undercover to investigate the Playboy Club. In 1964, Title VII had banned sex discrimination. In 1967, Valerie Solanas released her *SCUM Manifesto*, and the Pill was on the cover of *Time* magazine. By the film's debut in 1967, women's liberation was definitely in the water.

The focus of women's liberation, at least in popular discourse, was sexual freedom. Alice Grellner sees *Camelot*'s Guenevere as "wanton," but the queen's unabashed sexuality may have been shaped, in part, by the anti-repression philosophies of the 1960s.[5] The Kinsey reports had been out for over ten years, and writers like Friedan and Helen Gurley Brown had been promoting sexual liberation and female desire for most of the decade.[6] *Camelot*'s Jenny—as the film calls her—is vibrantly sexy, and flaunts her desires in a way that speaks to these specific movements. On her way to marry Arthur, she complains, "Was there ever a more inconvenient marriage of convenience? Here I am, at the golden age of seductability, and was my fate sealed with a kiss? No, sealed with a seal." She attempts to escape her wedding caravan as it stops for her hair to be arranged, eschewing feminine frippery here and throughout the film, which often shows her with mussed hair and simple clothes.

Camelot's Jenny also displays compassion and courage. She and Arthur run into one another by accident during her flight from the hairdresser, and Arthur introduces himself as "Wart" (his childhood nickname in *Camelot*, by way of T.H. White). Guenevere asks the lowly "Wart" to run away with her, but they are caught by Arthur's guards, so she tries to protect him, mounting a defense on his behalf by throwing snowballs. She is kind to the doddering, lost King Pellinor, even when the knights mock him. As her affair with Lancelot heats up, she considers Arthur's feelings. For instance, when Lancelot asks her to run away with him, she responds, "And this man we both love, what would you have us do, force him to declare war on you?" She also considers the greater good, warning Lancelot that their actions could get people killed. "I never wanted to love you," she says. "Your God arranged it. Your God must solve it. Arthur is my husband. I must stay with him as long as he wants me." She even leaps at Mordred's sword when he attacks Lancelot, slicing open her bare hand, but knocking her enemy to the ground.

Guenevere is also witty and clever. She does not fall for Lancelot right away; she finds him unbearably pompous. Her verbal repartee reveals both her quick mind and her ability to see through Lancelot's condescending arrogance. When Arthur asks Lancelot to share his "new plan" for training knights, Lancelot asks, "Would not madame find it tedious?"

Vanessa Redgrave as Guenevere in the 1967 film *Camelot*.

She responds, icily, "I have never found chivalry tedious … so far. May I remind you, *cher monsieur*, that the Round Table happens to be my husband's idea." Then she repeats the entire sentence in French and launches into an interrogation that highlights Lancelot's egotism:

> GUENEVERE: "And whose abilities would serve as the standard, *monsieur*?"
> LANCELOT: "Certainly not mine my lady. It would not be fair."
> GUENEVERE: "Not fair in what way?"

LANCELOT: "I would never ask anyone to live by my standards, my lady. To devote your life to the tortured quest for perfection in body and spirit. Oh, no, I would not ask that of anyone."
GUENEVERE: "Tell me a little of your quest for the perfection of the spirit. Have you jousted with humility lately?"
LANCELOT: "Humility."
GUENEVERE: (Pronouncing the French): "*Hu-mil-i-té*. Or isn't it fashionable in France these days?"

Her attack is so merciless that Arthur interrupts her, saying, "Well, we had best discuss the program elsewhere. You look far too beautiful, my dearest, to have anything on your mind but frolic and flowers." At this point, Guenevere's role in the film and in Arthur's life takes a turn, as Laurie A. Finke and Martin B. Shichtman argue: "From this moment, Guenevere will be systematically excluded from the public affairs of the Round Table…. No longer Arthur's business partner, no longer a consort, she is reduced to mere decoration, exiled to the world of love and leisure."[7] This scene, especially in light of Finke and Shichtman's analysis, highlights the fact that the sexual revolution was not all incense and peppermints: its treatment of women was, as Gloria Steinem's exploration of the Playboy Club reveals, highly infantilizing.[8] Likewise, despite Guenevere's conversational cleverness in *Camelot*, she rarely has anything on her mind besides what one might call the "feminine" virtues. Her concerns are simple, earthy, sensual, and decidedly gendered. Even as she interrogates Lancelot, she has to talk around the pie she's busy eating with her bare hands. The first shot of Guenevere presents her bundled up like a little girl, being carried through the forest on a bed of white furs, hooded, with the blankets drawn up to her chin and a tiny greyhound tucked beside her. She behaves like a bored child while people try to explain serious, dangerous situations to her. She's eager to meet the "bandits and brigands" her nurse warns her about in the forest, and, when Arthur lectures her on England's divided kingdoms, she lies on a bed of furs, naked, kicking her feet, her hair sex-tousled. When Arthur tries to explain his plans for the Round Table, which he hopes will bring an end to violence in England, the film flashes from scene to scene in which he pontificates and she reveals her inattention and boredom: she shops for dishware while he blathers, or she cleans a horse. And, disturbingly, Jenny's childishness is part of her sex appeal. In the scene that features the song, "The Lusty Month of May," Jenny leads a full-on flower child free love ode to sex in which she's surrounded by canoodling couples, while also playing on a swing and a seesaw.[9]

Although Arthur, and the filmmakers, seem to embrace Jenny's childlike appeal, the transgressive undercurrents of her character speak to a fear of female sexuality that the film cannot fully reconcile. Her sexuality, unconstrained, is always in danger of leading to violence. Consider the lyrics of Guenevere's first song, "The Simple Joys of Maidenhood," where she longs not only for romance but also for erotically-motivated aggression. Her heartfelt pleas include: "Shall two knights never tilt for me,/And let their blood be spilt for me?" and "Shall a feud not begin for me?/Shall kith not kill their kin for me?" The song is almost a Freudian essay on female narcissism set to catchy music. It captures Jenny's longing to be a desired object who drives men to horrific acts of violence, sometimes even against herself. When Arthur first encounters her in the woods, he promises not to hurt her, but she protests:

GUENEVERE: "You lie! You'll leap on me and throw me to the ground!"
ARTHUR: "I won't do any such thing."
GUENEVERE: "You'll throw me over your shoulder and carry me off!"
ARTHUR: "No, no, no I swear by the sword Excalibur I won't touch you!"
GUENEVERE: "Why not? How dare you insult me in this fashion? Do my looks repel you?"

As appalling as this exchange is in the 21st century, it aligns with some aspects of the sexual revolution's concept of "liberated" desire. So-called "rape fantasies" were thought to lurk in the female psyche, and even liberal thinkers advertised the expression of such fantasies as a remedy for unhealthy female sexual repression.[10]

However, the film's surface embrace of sexual liberation is belied by its fear of unconstrained female desire. Guenevere isn't merely interested in airing her secret fantasies of being corrupted: she is also corrupting all the men around her. As Guenevere gets closer to engaging in extramarital sex, the film's imagery, and the knights in her company, grow more violent. Before she becomes Lancelot's lover, she provokes three of Arthur's best knights to joust with him by promising them favors and playing up their clear attraction to her in the song "Then You May Take Me to the Fair."[11] Her promises are juxtaposed with the knights' pledges to commit graphic acts of violence. Sir Lionel says he will "smash and mash" Lancelot if he can take her to the fair; when Guenevere asks, "A mighty whack?" Lionel responds, "His skull will crack." She tempts Sir Sagramore with an invitation to the ball, and he vows to serve Lancelot "*en brochette*":

> GUENEVERE: "You'll pierce right through him?"
> SAGRAMORE: "I'll barbeque him."
> GUENEVERE: "A wicked thrust?"
> SAGRAMORE: "Twill be dust to dust."

Guenevere enforces the connection between his violence and her sexuality by caressing Sir Sagramore's spear while he promises to impale his fellow knight. From Sir Dinadan, she extracts a promise that Lancelot's "shoulders will be lonesome for his head." "You'll open wide him?" she asks sweetly, and Dinadan responds, "I'll subdivide him." But even as her knights promise to stage violent displays of masculinity, Guenevere simultaneously feminizes them. As she and Sir Lionel sing, he holds her yarn, and, while she sings with Sir Sagramor, she primps by checking her own reflection in his shield. Sir Dinadan makes his bloody vows while lying on the ground beside her as she fans herself in a hammock. By the end of "Take Me to the Fair," Guenevere has gotten them all drunk, and they're dancing on a table alongside her dog.

As the last few verses of "Take Me to the Fair" demonstrate, Guenevere's erotic violence threatens the realm's stability. Her chaotic desires strain against Arthur's philosophical attempts at logic, peace, and order. For instance, the existential crisis that leads Arthur to form the Round Table—the realization that "might doesn't always mean right"— provokes this response from her: "What are you saying? To be right and lose couldn't possibly be right." Arthur tries to explain himself, asking, "Why do we have wars in which people can get killed?" Her conclusion is that ladies love to see knights in armor, and she dismisses the whole idea of the Round Table, dubious that knights would ever want to do "such a ridiculously peaceful thing."

Eventually, Guenevere's cocktail of *Eros* and *Thanatos* poisons Arthur's civil society by driving men away from logic, order, and law.[12] Lancelot's love seems like an illness: when he realizes he has fallen for the queen, he confesses, "Terrible feelings burn within me," and from this point on, he is constantly sweating. When she and Lancelot meet for a tryst and he sings "If Ever I Would Leave You," they have snuck into a garden full of dead trees. Cobwebs surround them, and they sing beside an empty cage. The scene is stark, infertile, and barren, as if nature itself has been corrupted by their passion. Lancelot challenges every knight who accuses him of adultery to trial by combat, and he is always on the verge of murdering knights who are merely telling the truth. Arthur himself is aware of the affair, but he does not want to punish them, so he loses his grip on the Round Table, even threatening Pellinor with a choice between exile or execution. When Arthur stops "thinking too much" and reacts based on emotion, snipping and snarling like an animal, the viewer knows that he has also been "infected."

Arthur struggles to stave off violence for a time by establishing a system of trial by jury instead of by combat. But law and order are no match for chaotic femininity, which will ultimately destroy Arthur's pursuit of peace. Though Mordred is the one who intentionally breaks up the Round Table, he is in some ways riding the tide that Guenevere created. And Mordred is the same kind of feminine, id-ruled creature as the queen. When Arthur first offers to knight him, Mordred—slim, lithe, and mischievous—protests that he loves decadence and leisure too much. He uses "feminine" wiles similar to Guenevere's to provoke discord among the knights: gossip and whispers in the dark eventually lead Arthur's knights to ride drunk and on horseback into the Round Table room in a scene that reminds the viewer of the table-dancing celebration of violence at the end of "Take Me to the Fair." As Arthur and Lancelot rush in to stop Mordred and the knights, a horse breaks the Round Table, the symbol of civilized order crushed under the weight of an animal. The literal collapse of the Round Table and the fall of Camelot represent the death of *logos*, which, in the 1960s, was still considered the property of the rational male. Indeed, when the queen is about to be executed, Mordred channels Lacan to taunt his father: "Kill the queen," Mordred says, "or kill the law."

Ultimately, it is unclear whether the film endorses the queen's or the law's survival. Camelot's fall and Arthur's crushed dreams of equality are tragedies, but the filmmakers also weave imagistic tragedy into scenes of Guenevere's repression. For instance, Guenevere's hair often symbolizes her internal state. When she is "herself," her hair is wild, sexy, and free. But society's constraints bind her locks. Her hair is tied back when she tries to hide her love from Lancelot, enclosed beneath gold mail at Lancelot's awkward knighting ceremony, and bound in a braid when she is led to the stake. In the end, when Jenny joins a nunnery, Arthur pulls back her hood and gasps: her beautiful hair has been chopped short. Then again, what appears to be repression may merely be the imposition of order. Jenny's wild hair is bound when she submits to marriage, knighthood, religion, and the law, which are all forces that keep violence at bay.

At the end of the film, Guenevere and Lancelot return to Arthur and offer to pay for their sins, but Arthur refuses. His knights, he says, only want revenge, "the most worthless of causes," not justice. Arthur laments the impending war: "It's those old, uncivilized days, come back again. Those days, those dreadful days we tried to put to sleep forever." But who woke those dreadful, dark ages up again? Surely it was Guenevere, shivering and crying in her shorn hair, begging for forgiveness that she never receives (at least, not in the film[13]), and doomed to a lifetime of penance for her erotic nature, which filmmakers never really could figure out how to "handle."

Excalibur *(1981): Neopagan Pixie Dream Girl*

Excalibur, written at the height of the neopagan movement, uses the same gender binary as *Camelot*, only it flips the hierarchy, finding power in the feminine.[14] Long recognized by scholars like Martin B. Shichtman, Kevin J. Harty, Norris J. Lacy, Susan

Aronstein—and even director John Boorman himself—as a mythopoetic film, *Excalibur* draws on a reverence for nature and Jungian archetypes for its vision of an ideal king and ideal masculinity.[15] However, feminism had its own mythopoetic moment in the late 20th century. Mary Daly's 1978 *Gyn/Ecology* deftly deconstructed patriarchal myth to usher women to the "Gates of the Goddess"; Merlin Stone's *When God Was a Woman* hit the shelves in 1976; Carol P. Christ's "Why Women Need the Goddess" emerged in 1978; and Sallie Gearhart and Susan Rennie even developed a feminist tarot deck in 1976.[16] By the time *Excalibur* was released, mythopoetic feminism had saturated popular culture. Of course, mainstream entertainment often ignored the "Destroyer" aspect of the Goddess invoked by scholars like Daly and Stone. Instead, pop culture merged mythopoetic feminism with a comfortable biological essentialism in order to redeem "the feminine" without challenging male supremacy. The Goddess was all things nurturing and protective, the yin to man's yang, the moon to his sun, the soft, loving mother to his harsh, unyielding father.

And from the moment we see Boorman's Guenevere, Cherie Lunghi, we know that she will be the scabbard to Arthur's sword. She appears while her father's castle is under siege, and she defends herself bravely, but only with a shield, reinforcing the protective nature of her gendered power. Guenevere is also a healer: she bandages injured knights, including Arthur, ably sewing his wounds and tearing off the thread with her teeth. Guenevere embraces her sensuality and chases Arthur, bringing him little cakes that she's prepared, which are imbued with mysterious herbs. "I've made these only for you," she says, "I've mixed into them things that will heal you, but not too quickly, and they'll make you a little sleepy so you can't escape."

In *Excalibur*, gender is both essentialized and complementary: Boorman seems to believe that masculine and feminine forces must remain balanced, and that danger lies in an excess of one or the other. For instance, as Aronstein and Finke and Shichtman point out, Uther is the film's model of toxic masculinity, and he is constantly wearing armor, which represents his separation from nature.[17] Uther even leaves his armor on when he rapes Arthur's mother, Igrayne; the rape scene, as Finke and Shichtman argue, "seems all the more brutal because his armor makes him seem inhuman."[18] And, throughout the film, armor is a sign of alienation from nature. At one point, Lancelot has a nightmare in which he is fighting an empty suit of armor. He awakens to find himself naked, wriggling, and impaled near his groin by a sword. "Guenevere!" he cries. "I fight against myself. Oh, God!" Although some scholars read this scene as Guenevere's lust "wounding" Lancelot sexually,[19] in *Excalibur*'s erotic lexicon, armor is an obstacle to man's all-important union with nature, which Boorman describes as "the source of things"; being cut off from nature, he explains, is "incredibly dangerous…. It's a process of profound alienation and leads to neurosis."[20] The "self" Lancelot battles may be the civilized self, a man with no heart and no passion—an empty metal suit. In sharp contrast, when Lancelot and Guenevere finally unite, their naked bodies twist together in the forest, surrounded by lush greenery and a baby deer.[21] Their natural, easy lovemaking is juxtaposed with scenes of Morgana using cold, intellectual spells to encase Merlin in an alien-looking crystal. Lancelot and Guenevere's egalitarian embrace also functions as a visual antidote to Igrayne's violent, unbalanced rape in the beginning of the film.

As Aronstein points out, *Excalibur* "explores the potential abuses of patriarchy, particularly a patriarchy that espouses aggression and individualism," especially when Uther's patriarchal legacy constantly threatens to undo Arthur.[22] Boorman even explains that, when Arthur is shown with a beard, the viewer is "supposed to see that he's behaving like Uther."[23] When Arthur battles Lancelot for the first time, he allows pride to overtake him, and Excalibur breaks under the strain of his violent masculinity. Uther's masculine arrogance drives him to rape the wife of an ally and to start a war; when Arthur, fully armed in steel, comes upon Lancelot and Guenevere's pale, perfect, entangled bodies in the forest, he abandons his sword between them, breaking his vow as the land's protector, which blights the land and symbolically severs their perfect union.[24]

Like *Camelot*, *Excalibur* also dramatizes the conflict between the law and the heart, but *Excalibur* favors Mother Nature over the Law of the Father. Laws, after all, are made by men, but love is a product of nature and should not be denied. Arthur's repressive objectivity drives Guenevere into another man's arms. The accusations against her and Lancelot begin before the lovers have any physical contact. But, when she is accused by Gawain, Guenevere finds that her husband will not defend her. Arthur uses the law as a justification for inaction on her behalf: "My laws must bind everyone," he says, "high and low, or they're not laws at all." "You are my husband," Guenevere argues, and Arthur responds, "I must be king first." "Before husband?" she asks. "If need be," he tells her. "Before love?" she demands. When Lancelot fights for Guenevere, he is gravely wounded, and she chastises her husband: "Look at your laws now. Look what they have done."

Like *Camelot*, *Excalibur* also uses Guenevere's hair to indicate her repression: her hair is wild and free when she is happy and loved, and it is covered when she has to suppress her true nature. During the trial by combat, Guenevere's hair hides beneath a golden cowl. After Arthur abandons Excalibur, Guenevere joins a convent, and she is shown with her hair stuffed into a nun's white wimple, living cloistered in a lightless, lifeless space. But despite Arthur's betrayal, Guenevere has kept to her proper role: she has been holding Excalibur, protecting it, serving as its sheath. And in a stunning reversal of legend, Arthur begs *her* for forgiveness.[25] As Lancelot dies on the battlefield, he asks Arthur if Guenevere is queen again, and Arthur answers that she is. The barge that carries Arthur's body away also carries women dressed in white habits, clearly in Guenevere's image. These final scenes imply a return of power to the female archetype, the lover and protector Guenevere represents, and they absolve her of any guilt for her passion, which is, after all, a natural response in a film that prizes nature above all else.[26]

Of course, to elevate Guenevere, the film has to purge her of all the "undesirable" aspects of the goddess, which it summarily invests into Morgana. As Marion MacCurdy points out, women in *Excalibur* are "drastically polarized."[27] Part of the reason Guenevere can flourish is that Morgana exists as her foil, absorbing all the "dark" aspects of femininity and leaving the queen to revel in the light.

First Knight *(1995): The Guinevere Next Door*

The late 20th century saw feminist theory come into its prime, but, by the early 1990s, Susan Faludi could argue in *Backlash: The Undeclared War Against American Women* that the previous decade had experienced "a powerful assault on women's rights, a backlash, an attempt to retract the handful of small and hard-won victories that the feminist movement did win for women."[28] In 1991, Gloria Steinem shed light on this anti-feminist backlash in films such as *Fatal Attraction* and *Working Girl*, which denigrated the independent, career-oriented woman in favor of her softer, male-dependent opposite.[29]

The 1990s also resounded with declarations of "postfeminism," a philosophy that rode the waves of postmodernism and relativism to argue that oppression and agency might just be in the eye of the beholder. In other words, it was a time, if a filmmaker wanted to make a feminist Guinevere, to proceed with extreme caution. How does a film make Guinevere strong, but not threatening? How does it absolve its heroine of adultery but still present a proper love story? And how does a film make her sexy enough to attract audiences but avoid sexual exploitation?

First Knight is Jerry Zucker's incredibly tepid and strange answer to these conundrums.[30] As Harty argues, "nothing in *First Knight* quite works," and its attempt at feminism is no exception.[31] *First Knight*'s Guinevere, Julia Ormond, is bursting with early '90s girl power, whether she's leaping from a carriage or playing a rousing soccer game with her hands tied behind her back.[32] She's in charge of her own kingdom and cares deeply for its people, who run to her for help after being attacked by the villainous Malagant. "He means to frighten us into submission," a villager complains to her, and she responds, "Don't worry. I'm not the yielding kind."

Guinevere is reluctantly persuaded to enter into an arranged marriage with Arthur, even though she wants "to live and die in Leonesse." But the film must negotiate her independent sentiments with audience palatability: one can hardly make King Arthur look as though he's carting off an unwilling child bride. So, incongruously, Guinevere decides that she is in love with Arthur, despite her distaste for marriage. Once she is convinced that sacrificing her autonomy is an acceptable exchange for her people's safety, she muses, "Arthur wears his power so lightly. He has such gentleness in his eyes. I've never known anyone like him. How could I love anyone more?"[33]

This scene presents one of the many inane contradictions that arise as *First Knight* attempts to integrate "girl power" into its own version of the Arthurian legend. Part of the problem is that *First Knight* is really Lancelot's story, as both Jacqueline Jenkins and Susan Aronstein point out: it is a proto–American narrative in which Lancelot "rises by skill and merit" rather than lineage.[34] The need for Lancelot to develop from what Aronstein calls a "huckster" into a faithful knight results in scenes that desperately, and unsuccessfully, try to balance an agential Guinevere with a Guinevere who needs to be the "Holy Grail" that will redeem Lancelot.[35]

The most egregious example of the film's contradictory views of female agency occurs when Guinevere is being delivered to Arthur for marriage. Malagant's men attack her carriage, and girl-power Guinevere rescues her ladies-in-waiting, then jumps from the carriage herself. Enter Lancelot, played awkwardly by Richard Gere, who no sooner rescues her from a crossbow bolt than another man grabs her from behind and demands that Lancelot drop his sword. What ensues may be one of the most cringe-inducing scenes in Arthurian film history: Lancelot *pretends* to be a rapist in order to rescue the damsel in distress. He asks the villain, "Can I have her when you're done?" But Guinevere's captor isn't interested in rape, so Lancelot has to persuade him, crooning: "Have you ever seen anything so beautiful?"; "You don't want her? Her soft skin, sweet lips … young, firm body"; "I'll hold her for you. It won't take long"; "Look at her. She wants it." As this disgusting dialogue plays out, Guinevere manages—coaxed by Lancelot's gazes and words—to get her hands on the crossbow. Together, they "reverse" the rape expectation when Lancelot says to the now-overheated villain, "Turn her around. Look into her eyes. See what she's got for you." When the man eagerly complies, Guinevere shoots him with the crossbow.

Guinevere's "penetration" of her potential rapist doesn't quite have the cathartic effect the filmmakers intended. Instead, we are left with the sick feeling of narrowly-avoided horror and a lingering reminder of Guinevere's persistent vulnerability: despite her bravery, her talent for sports, her longing for independence, and her ability to kill a man in cold blood, she must rely on the protection of a man who violently objectifies her and threatens to rape her as a "joke."

Only it wasn't actually a joke. Lancelot pursues Guinevere relentlessly as he leads her through the forest. After she accuses him of insulting her with his come-ons, he grabs her and kisses her: "Now I've insulted you," he says. Then he hints that he's interested in her body as his reward. "My man will pay you," she answers him, pretending not to know what he means. "I don't want money," he tells her. Then, he plays that ever-so-reliable ladies' night card: "I can tell when a woman wants me. I can see it in her eyes." He forces one more kiss on Guinevere, promising, "I won't kiss you again until you ask me to," which he insists that she will do before she is married. It seems clear that Gere's Lancelot is not based on Sir Thomas Malory's best knight, who once cut off a man's head for being "a theff and a knight" and "a ravyssher of women."

If *First Knight* can't quite figure out how to reconcile its 1990s Guinevere with its "American hero" Lancelot, it is also at a loss for how to handle her marriage to the benevolently paternal King Arthur. For instance, the film uses Guinevere's white horse—a gift from Arthur—as an imagistic sledgehammer to demonstrate her wild, free spirit. As Arthur gives Guinevere a tour of Camelot, he reminisces about her childhood, when he and her father were the best of friends. "Remember when you joined our hunt?" he asks her. "You were fearless." "My father's word was 'reckless,'" she answers. "He was always sparing with praise," Arthur responds. In the very next scene, Guinevere receives the gift of her equine clone, which she rides bareback, her hair flying. The horse is meant to assure us that Arthur, who is Guinevere's father's age, will be an adoring husband because he loves her independence. We are meant to forget that Guinevere and the horse were both taken from their natural habitats and made into possessions to be passed from owner to owner.

Unfortunately, despite its constant attempts to insist on Guinevere's sound mind and free spirit, *First Knight* never *really* lets us forget that Guinevere, like the horse, is a prize to be won and traded. In one early scene, Lancelot enters a contest to win a kiss from the future queen, whose lips are being auctioned off as if she were a prize piglet at the fair. As the crowd chants for Lancelot to kiss Guinevere, Arthur encourages him to claim his "prize." Lancelot then shows us the illusory nature of consent, which is really *his*, not Guinevere's, to give or take: he demands that she ask for his kiss so he can fulfill his sleazy pickup artist prophecy that she'll ask him for a kiss before she's married. When she refuses, he declares, "I dare not kiss so lovely a lady. I only have one heart to lose" and kisses her hand. But we know it's coming, don't we, that debased request for a kiss after a series of so many forced kisses in the forest? After all, Lancelot is our hero.

The film insists that we understand Guinevere's consent in all of her exchanges, that—with the pseudo-logic of postfeminism—her willingness to participate in her own oppression makes the oppression itself disappear. Arthur confirms multiple times that she really wants to marry him. But, when he offers to release her from their engagement, she responds, "I want to marry you. Not your crown or your army or your golden city. Just you." And yet, *First Knight* can't fully commit to this watered-down version of autonomy. For instance, Guinevere never appears to have sex with Arthur—or anyone, for that matter. She's kidnapped by Malagant before her wedding night, and, even after her return, the viewer is never subjected to any form of marital contact between the king and queen beyond a kiss. Thus, Guinevere remains chaste and innocent.[36] When she and Lancelot are finally caught in their long-awaited (or long-dreaded) kiss, they are trying to do the right thing: Lancelot has declared that he will leave Camelot. And yes, Guinevere does ask for his kiss, although it's after her wedding, and she describes it as an obligation: "I owe you a kiss," she says. As they kiss for the first (consensual) time, Arthur walks in on them.

Here is where Arthur loses his paternalistic patience: we're treated to a scene of Sean Connery raging at a church altar with flames reflected in his eyes, screaming, "Why?"— in what is, perhaps, the first believable scene in the whole film. He interrogates both lovers separately, declaring Guinevere innocent, but admitting that he built up an artificial construct of his bride: "I dreamed the dream of you. It was a sweet dream … while it lasted." But he cannot control his ire against Lancelot, whom he charges with treason.

The film may intend to suggest that Arthur's jealousy makes him an unworthy king: Rebecca Umland and Samuel Umland argue that "Arthur's January love for Guinevere 'weakens' and distracts him from his important military and political duties—duties at which he has excelled most of his life."[37] And, as indelicate as it may be to point out, Connery's Arthur appears utterly impotent: he has not, as far as we know, bedded his wife, and he is unable to protect his kingdom from external threats in the form of Malagant, or internal ones in the form of Lancelot, both of whom explicitly jeopardize the virginal body of his queen. He literally pays a fatal price for this impotence during Lancelot's trial for treason: Malagant attacks and one of his soldiers fatally wounds Arthur with a crossbow bolt (one of the film's many phallic symbols) as Malagant declares, "I am the law!" Just in case our Freudo-Lacanian Oedpial detectors are not yet sounding alarms, Arthur drops his sword, but the sword *gleams* at Lancelot in the sunlight. Lancelot picks up the sword and slays Malagant, who dies sprawled across Arthur's throne.

On his deathbed, Arthur grants Lancelot his sword, his kingdom, and, of course, his wife. Guinevere's transfer to a worthier man is meant to be a happy ending.[38] But the film has destroyed our illusion of agency one too many times. Guinevere ably rules a kingdom only to surrender it to a man. She deftly attempts to escape her own abductions but must always be rescued by a man. She speaks at Camelot's war council, but, although she sits in the room with the Round Table, she sits apart, on a throne against the wall; the men who sit at the table with their swords before them, markers of their superior agency, decide whether her words will matter. Ultimately, the film seems to indicate that Guinevere must learn a harsh lesson about the limits of feminism: individuality and independence, autonomy and consent, are sweet dreams, while they last. But they must surrender to a cinematic vision in which male violence is the only force that can regulate male violence.

King Arthur *(2004): Guinevere, Warrior Princess*

First Knight has been criticized for its wimpy portrayal of Guinevere,[39] but these days, it's easy to forget that female action heroes are a relatively recent phenomenon. It wasn't until 1996 that *Ms. Magazine* ran a cover story on the show *Xena: Warrior Princess* and declared, with some degree of shock, "Xena: She's Big, Tall, Strong—and Popular."[40] It took until the 21st century for Hollywood to dream up a Guinevere who could be a physical match for men, and she materialized in Anton Fuqua's 2004 *King Arthur*, a film which, as Virginia Blanton points out, used promotional posters of Guinevere, played by Keira Knightley, armed with a bow and a scowl.[41]

Based on the "Sarmatian theory" of Arthur's origins proposed by C. Scott Littleton and Linda Malcor,[42] the 2004 *King Arthur* proposes that Arthur is actually a Roman soldier stationed in Britain who commands a team of Sarmatian knights contracted into service to Rome. Arthur and his men defend Roman interests against the blue-painted native Britons (called "Woads" in the film), but, when they are sent to rescue a Roman noble from Saxon invaders, they discover Guinevere in the Roman's dungeon. She has been tortured, but she soon recovers and proves to be a fierce warrior who aids Arthur in his battles, recruiting Woads to fight for him and teaching him to love, defend, and ultimately lead the British people.

That Guinevere is a hardened warrior in a film that claims historical authenticity is significant.[43] Her martial skills are meant not to be shocking, but *authentic*—not exceptional, but representative. In this way, she is monumentally important; she is a transgression not so much against medieval tradition and society, but against our understanding of it, and, therefore, our understanding of women's historical potential.[44] Blanton argues that both Guinevere's role and her symbolism intentionally reverse gendered expectations. She focuses her analysis on Guinevere's now-iconic line to Lancelot as they face down Saxon enemies on a lake of ice: "Don't worry. I won't let them rape you." Guinevere delivers this line looking like nothing so much as the Roman goddess (and medieval British favorite) Diana, her hair and ethereal blue dress flowing, her bow nocked.[45] As Blanton explains,

> The bow and arrow is a potent symbol of penetration and sexual congress, in essence an emblem of virility. As an instrument of death, moreover, the bow indicates the emergent masculinity of Guinevere in a film centered on martial prowess, and this scene signals that we as the audience should be prepared for surprising upheavals in the gendered order of the medieval world as it is portrayed here.[46]

King Arthur also rewrites Arthurian symbolism in a striking way: the links between the king and his land, his power and his people, which informed earlier cinematic versions of the story, are invested in Guinevere herself.[47] When she meets Arthur, she calls him "the famous Briton who kills his own people." She shifts Arthur's alliance away from the Roman oppressors and convinces him that Woads "belong to the land." It is, she tells him, "the natural state of any man to want to live free in their own country." "I belong to this land," she insists. "Where do you belong, Arthur?" As Russell Peck points out, Guinevere's wedding to Arthur at the film's finale is steeped in Celtic themes that reinforce the ties between the queen and the land. Held at a rock formation that looks like Stonehenge, the proceedings are led by Merlin, and his presence, the couple's shared cup, and the flaming torches mark the pagan nature of the ceremony. Guinevere is clad in white *and* blue—telling, as two worlds—Roman and Briton, Christian and pagan, unite through her efforts, and Merlin announces, "Arthur and Guinevere, our people are one, as you are."

Admittedly, using Guinevere as a symbol of Britain ushers in a whole new set of problems: namely that Guinevere, and her people, will be colonized by Arthur. Blanton and Harty both suggest that Guinevere surrenders her agency at her wedding,[48] and the film also falls victim to the predictable hegemonic trope in which a colonizer turns out, by strange fortune, to be the chosen leader of the people whom he is originally trying to colonize. However, Peck argues that the wedding suggests an ideology in which "women are agents of power, physical strength, poetry, and imagination, in no way subordinated to patriarchy as they are in Roman Catholicism and Protestantism."[49] The intention certainly seems egalitarian, but the trouble may be that, like Stonehenge itself, there are, as we recently discovered, unexpected layers of meaning buried beneath the surface.

For the most part, though, if female agency is the goal, then the film succeeds. Guinevere makes her choices with deadly aim. But perhaps this new empowerment of Guinevere is only possible because the filmmakers have swept all ethical obstacles from her path: namely, the love story with Lancelot, which has been so utterly excised from this version of the legend that the film kills off Lancelot before her wedding, just to make sure, and even beheads Tristan, that other infamous adulterer, for good measure! Matthews offers the explanation that there is "little time for love in the harsh and uncompromising times in which these people lived,"[50] but there's plenty of time for sex, at least with Arthur. Guinevere comes to his tent and mounts him with the romantic words, "What tomorrow brings, we cannot know." This scene allows her guilt-free sexual agency, since this act of monogamous lovemaking will lead to marriage.

So, while Guinevere has progressed as a warrior and as a leader, cultural anxieties about female sexuality—specifically female desire—are still at play.[51] This time, however, a man bears the burden: poor Lancelot is sacrificed upon the altar of Guinevere's virtue. Not only does he die ingloriously—shot, of course, by a crossbow—but he is also a complete cad. Renowned throughout medieval literature for his purity and fidelity, albeit to a married queen—so much so that if any woman wants him she has to cast a spell and disguise herself as Guinevere—here Lancelot has been transformed into a veritable base recreant, worse than his counterpart in *First Knight*. When Bors indicates that one of his sons is a good fighter, Lancelot quips, "that's because he's mine." He is also self-interested, making sweeping statements like "I don't give a damn about Romans, Britons, or this island!" and campaigning to abandon both Guinevere and a helpless boy when they're being pursued by their enemies. He even considers deserting Arthur during the climactic battle against the Saxons; heaven only knows what drives him back. Perhaps it's some kind of repressed memory of the Lancelot that once was.

Keira Knightley as Guinevere in the 2004 film *King Arthur*.

King Arthur revitalizes, but also revises, Guinevere, cleansing her until she is completely error-free. Her passion has turned into cold calculation and political strategy, her wandering heart laser-focused on her future husband, her physical strength matchless, her virtue impeccable. And one can't help but wonder if this transformation was a sign of things to come. In contemporary feminist philosophy, to put it kindly, the perfect can be the enemy of the good. Thanks to the lightning-fast response time of the Internet, the world is awash with sharp-eyed critics, each primed to notice the slightest media misstep. What kind of Guinevere can navigate such a minefield? The troubling answer may be the one provided by Guy Ritchie's 2017 *King Arthur: Legend of the Sword*, which has no Guinevere at all.

When Vanessa Redgrave sings of May in *Camelot*, she celebrates the freedom that spring brings: "Those dreary vows that ev'ryone takes,/

Ev'ryone breaks./Ev'ryone makes divine mistakes...." Is there room for a divine mistake or two in our modern conception of Guinevere? Is a flawless Guinevere still human enough to tug at our heartstrings? Will she escape the constraints of perfect aim and perfect virtue? Or, from now on, will we all be bound by duty to keep from breaking our dreary vows?

NOTES

1. Depending on the film in question, Guinevere's name is spelled differently. For the sake of consistency, I'll use "Guinevere" unless I am discussing a specific film character or using a direct quotation. Citations for the 1967 *Camelot* are from *Camelot*, directed by Joshua Logan, Warner Brothers, 1967.

2. Fiona Tolhurst, "The Once and Future Queen: The Development of Guenevere from Geoffrey of Monmouth to Malory," *Bibliographical Bulletin of the International Arthurian Society* 50 (1998): 308 [272–308].

3. Amy S. Kaufman, "Guenevere Burning," *Arthuriana* 20.1 (2010): 78 [76–94].

4. Susan Lynn Aronstein, *Hollywood Knights: Arthurian Cinema and the Politics of Nostalgia* (New York: Palgrave Macmillan, 2005), pp. 92–98; Laurie A. Finke and Martin B. Shichtman, *Cinematic Illuminations* (Baltimore: Johns Hopkins University Press, 2009), p. 162; Leah Haught, "Performing Nostalgia: Medievalism in *King Arthur* and *Camelot*," *Arthuriana* 24.4 (2014): 97–126.

5. Alice Grellner, "Two Films That Sparkle," in *Cinema Arthuriana, Twenty Essays*, ed. Kevin J. Harty (Jefferson, NC: McFarland, 2002), pp. 121–122 [118–126].

6. In *The Feminine Mystique* (New York: Norton, 1963), Betty Friedan specifically challenges the idea that women can only be fulfilled "in sexual passivity, male domination, and nurturing maternal love" (p. 66). See also Helen Gurley Brown's *Sex and the Single Girl* (New York: Bernard Geis, 1962), which touts sexual autonomy as the key to women's liberation.

7. Finke and Shichtman, p. 173.

8. Gloria Steinem, "A Bunny's Tale I" and "A Bunny's Tale II," *Show Magazine* (May 1963): 90, 92, 94, 114; (June 1963): 66–68, 110.

9. Grellner, pp. 124–125.

10. In fact, a certain presidential candidate in the 2016 American Democratic primary had written several essays on the topic throughout the 1960s and 1970s. See Tim Murphy, "'You Might Very Well Be the Cause of Cancer': Read Bernie Sanders' 1970s-Era Essays," *Mother Jones* (July 6, 2015), www.motherjones.com.

11. Finke and Shichtman argue that these songs and scenes teach the audience to "long for aristocracy" and that Guenevere's requests for knightly violence on her behalf "reinforce her privilege" (p. 165), but I think the subconscious fear of the destructive nature of female sexuality is also at play. These readings are not mutually exclusive: both anxieties seem alive and well in this version of Guenevere.

12. See Rebecca A. Umland and Samuel J. Umland, who attribute this to the love triangle itself in *The Use of Arthurian Legend in Hollywood Film: From Connecticut Yankees to Fisher Kings* (Westport, CT: Greenwood Press, 1996), p. 94. Finke and Shichtman attribute it to infidelity and its threat to "stable, monogamous families" (pp. 176–177).

13. In Alan Jay Lerner and Frederick Loewe's 1960 Broadway production of *Camelot*, Guenevere says, "So often in the past, Arthur, I would look up in your eyes, and there I would find forgiveness. Perhaps one day in the future it shall be there again." After she embraces Arthur and looks up at him, she says, "Oh, Arthur, Arthur, I see what I wanted to see."

14. *Excalibur*, directed John Boorman, Orion, 1981.

15. Martin B. Shichtman, "Hollywood's New Weston: The Grail Myth in Francis Ford Coppola's *Apocalypse Now* and John Boorman's *Excalibur*," in *The Grail: A Casebook*, ed. Dhira B. Mahoney (New York: Routledge, 1999), p. 566 [561–574]; Kevin J. Harty, "Cinema Arthuriana: An Overview," *Cinema Arthuriana, Twenty Essays*, p. 21; Norris J. Lacy, "Mythopoeia in Excalibur," in *Cinema Arthuriana, Twenty Essays*, p. 35 [34–43]; Umland and Umland, p. 31; Aronstein, pp. 149–160; Finke and Shichtman, p. 86. Boorman insists that *Excalibur* "has to do with *mythical* truth, not historical truth" in Harlan Kennedy, "The World of King Arthur According to John Boorman," *American Film* 6.5 (March 1981): 31 [30–37].

16. Mary Daly, *Gyn/Ecology: The Metaethics of Radical Feminism* (Boston: Beacon Press, 1978), p. xlix; Merlin Stone, *When God Was a Woman* (New York: Harcourt, 1976); Carol P. Christ, "Why Women Need the Goddess," *Heresies 5: The Great Goddess Issue* (1978): 8–13; Sallie Gearhart and Susan Rennie, *A Feminist Tarot* (Watertown, MA: Persephone Press,1976).

17. Aronstein, pp. 155–156; Finke and Shichtman, p. 50.

18. Finke and Shichtman, p. 50.

19. Marion MacCurdy, "Bitch or Goddess: Polarized Images of Women in Arthurian Literature and Films," *Platte Valley Review* 18 (1990): 8 [3–24].

20. Dan Yakir, "The Sorcerer: John Boorman Interviewed by Dan Yakir," *Film Comment* 17.3 (June 1981),

50 [49–53]. Finke and Shichtman argue that women are outside of nature, "objects of exchange between men—like Guenevere—or as incomprehensible threats—like Morgana" (p. 82). I will argue, however, that Morgana and Guenevere function in a binary that aligns Guenevere with nature and exiles Morgana firmly outside it.

21. As Aronstein notes, "the film's imagery undermines [an] easy equation between adultery and evil" (p. 158). See also E. Jane Burns, "Nostalgia Isn't What It Used to Be: The Middle Ages in Literature and Film," in *Shadows of the Magic Lamp: Fantasy and Science Fiction in Film*, eds. George Slusser and Eric S. Rabin (Carbondale: Southern Illinois University Press, 1985), pp. 86–97.

22. Aronstein (p. 155). However, see Finke and Shichtman who argue that Boorman's film "seems far too much in thrall to its myth of masculinity to achieve the distance required for an ironic critique of the very myths it adoringly invokes" (p. 80).

23. Kennedy, p. 34.

24. Aronstein, p. 158. However, see Shichtman, who thinks the land falls apart because of "the king's failure to assert authority" ("New Weston," p. 567). See also Umland and Umland, p. 139.

25. Umland and Umland, pp. 122–123.

26. See MacCurdy who thinks that Lancelot is Guinevere's victim (p. 8).

27. MacCurdy, p. 22.

28. Susan Faludi, *Backlash: The Undeclared War Against American Women* (New York: Three Rivers Press, 1991), pp. 9–10. Part of the backlash was, as Jacqueline Jenkins and Susan Aronstein both note in their analyses of *First Knight*, a "crisis in masculinity." See Jenkins, "First Knights and Common Men: Masculinity in American Arthurian Film," in *King Arthur on Film*, ed. Kevin J. Harty (Jefferson, NC: McFarland, 1999), p. 81 [81–95]; and Aronstein, pp. 197–205.

29. Gloria Steinem, "Women in the Dark: Of Sex Goddesses, Abuse, and Dreams," *Ms.* 37 (February 1991): 36 [36–37].

30. *First Knight*, directed by Jerry Zucker, Columbia Pictures, 1995.

31. Harty, "Overview," p. 23.

32. Aronstein calls this scene "nicely democratic" p. 198. Umland and Umland also note the independence and resourcefulness of *First Knight*'s Guinevere (p. 96).

33. As Aronstein points out, Guinevere really doesn't want to marry Arthur, but "Arthur and Camelot signify protection" (p. 199).

34. Aronstein, pp. 199–200; and Jenkins, pp. 81–91.

35. Aronstein, p. 201.

36. Shira Schwam-Baird argues that *First Knight* avoids the love triangle because Hollywood is "allergic to tragedy," "King Arthur in Hollywood: The Subversion of Tragedy in First Knight," *Medieval Perspectives* 14 (1999): 202–213. See also Aronstein, p. 204.

37. Umland and Umland, p. 98.

38. Aronstein, p. 205.

39. See, for instance, Virginia Blanton, "'Don't Worry: I Won't Let Them Rape You': Guinevere's Agency in Jerry Bruckheimer's *King Arthur*," *Arthuriana* 15.3 (2005): 91–111. Film citations are from *King Arthur*, directed by Anton Fuqua, Touchstone Pictures, 2004.

40. Donna Minkowitz, "Xena: She's Big, Tall, Strong—and Popular," *Ms. Magazine* 7.1 (July/August 1996): 74–77.

41. Blanton argues that this Guinevere exists because of a "contemporary desire for strong female characters, ones that are integral and active agents in the plot line" (p. 92).

42. C. Scott Littleton and Linda Malcor, *From Scythia to Camelot* (London: Routledge, 1994).

43. As Aronstein argues, "*King Arthur* is about the dismantling of myth; from its very beginning frames—and indeed from its first press releases—the film establishes itself as 'the truth behind the myth,' promising to strip away the layers of fantasy and fable to reveal Arthur's 'true identity'" (p. 206).

44. As Kevin J. Harty points out, Knightley's "'kick-ass' Guinevere is a definite improvement over previous screen Guineveres and not totally outside the realm of the possible"; however, see Blanton, who argues that "Guinevere is more about contemporary fantasies of 'girl power' than about historical truth." Kevin J. Harty. "*King Arthur* Directed by Antoine Fuqua (review)," *Arthuriana* 14.3 (2004) 123 [121–123]; Blanton, p. 97.

45. In the previews, Guinevere says "*hurt*," not "rape." Apparently, this role reversal was, in 2004, not quite ready for prime time.

46. Blanton, p. 92.

47. Russell A. Peck, "Antoine Fuqua's *King Arthur* within Imaginary Boundaries of the Celtic World," *Arthuriana* 26.2 (2016): 93 [86–109]. See also Blanton, p. 93; and Aronstein, p. 209.

48. Harty, "*King Arthur* (review)," p. 123, and Blanton, pp. 103–104.

49. Peck, p. 92.

50. John Matthews, "A Knightley Endeavor: The Making of Jerry Bruckheimer's *King Arthur*," *Arthuriana* 14.3 (2004): 114 [112–115].

51. Blanton argues that Guinevere's representation illustrates contemporary anxieties about women's physical capabilities: "women in warfare, women who want to be equal to men on all playing fields" (p. 93).

Adversary, Sister, Scapegoat

Morgan le Fay on Film

Usha Vishnuvajjala

A cursory search for characters named "Morgana" or "Morgan le Fay" on the Internet Movie Database brings up an astonishing 61 results, including film, television, and video games, in which Morgan has been played by such diverse actors as Candace Bergen, Jenny Agutter, Joanna Lumley, Helena Bonham Carter, Julianna Margulies, Alicia Witt, Fran Drescher, Tom Savini, and, if we count the character Turkey Morgan in Michael Curtiz's 1937 Arthurian boxing film *Kid Galahad*, Humphrey Bogart.[1]

Some of these entries are episodes or arcs of well-known TV series, including *The Twilight Zone* and *Doctor Who*, and some are low-budget straight-to-video films such as 1998's *Camelot: The Legend*, which IMDB summarizes as "the legend of Guinevere and Lancelot, retold as a loopy, animated musical." For the purposes of this essay, I will focus on English-language feature films in which Morgan/Morgana plays a substantive role: Tay Garnett's 1949 adaptation of *A Connecticut Yankee in King Arthur's Court*; Richard Thorpe's 1953 *Knights of the Round Table*; John Boorman's 1981 *Excalibur*; Stephen Weeks's 1984 *Sword of the Valiant*; Jon Turteltaub's 2010 *The Sorcerer's Apprentice*; and Mark Lester's 2014 *Dragons of Camelot*.[2]

These six films can be grouped loosely into three categories based on their treatment of Morgan. Although the films vary widely in their production values and popularity, their narratives and sources, and their settings, I group them as follows:

1. Films in which Morgan is depicted as an adversary to Arthur or to other main characters with some hint at motives: *A Connecticut Yankee in King Arthur's Court* (1949), *Knights of the Round Table* (1953).

2. Films that depict Morgan as a nuanced and potentially sympathetic character: *Excalibur* (1981), *Sword of the Valiant* (1984).

3. Films in which an uncomplicatedly evil Morgan is a plot device: *The Sorcerer's Apprentice* (2010), *Dragons of Camelot* (2014).

We can see right away that these categories also fall along chronological lines. Mid–20th century depictions of Morgan were fairly neutral: they depicted her as an adversary, but not an overwhelmingly evil character, and not a terribly powerful one either. The two films from the 1980s (the decade that also produced Marion Zimmer Bradley's feminist Arthurian novel *The Mists of Avalon*) present the most interesting and sympathetic

Morganas, with *Excalibur* going so far as to add new facets to Morgana's childhood experiences that help explain the depth of her desire for vengeance against Arthur and Merlin. The two films from the 21st century swing dramatically to the opposite pole from those of the 1980s: they reduce Morgan to a mere plot device, a simple evil force who sets actions into motion and creates the need for a (young, male) hero to defeat her.[3]

These different ways of portraying Morgan do not overlap easily with other ways of categorizing medievalist or Arthurian films or texts. Just as films about King Arthur "do not easily fit into any one cinematic genre," films depicting Morgan do not fall easily into any one style of medievalism.[4] David Matthews has suggested classifying medievalism (across media) into the "*gothic* or *grotesque* Middle Ages, entailing the assumption that anything medieval will involve threat, violence, and warped sexuality" and the "*romantic* Middle Ages" in which violence against women exists but is found alongside "knights, shining armour, and chivalry."[5] For Matthews, these two categories can coexist in a single work, but still constitute "the chief dualism in contemporary understandings of the Middle Ages, whether scholarly or popular."[6] Both of these modes of depicting the Middle Ages are present in each category of film I have described above: *Knights of the Round Table* and *Excalibur* both contain gruesome scenes full of rotting corpses and desolate wastelands, as well as a great deal of violence; *Connecticut Yankee* falls primarily into the romantic category, but also depicts one of Arthur's subjects dying of the plague; *Dragons of Camelot* and *The Sorcerer's Apprentice* both depict Morgan as part of the grotesque Middle Ages alongside (male) characters who seem to hail from the romantic Middle Ages; *Sword of the Valiant* is more romantic than grotesque, but certainly depicts the Middle Ages as a mysterious and threatening time.

Drawing on other taxonomies of medievalism, we find that some of these films also fall rather neatly into categories described by scholars of medievalism: both *Dragons of Camelot* and *The Sorcerer's Apprentice* fit into what Umberto Eco identified as "the Middle Ages as a *pretext*" which Matthews further describes as texts in which "the historical background of the Middle Ages is used as a setting, but there is no real interest in the history."[7] Some of these films use the Middle Ages, or the clash between the Middle Ages and the present day, as a source of comedy, but those that do so (*Connecticut Yankee*, *The Sorcerer's Apprentice*), do so in different ways.

Louise D'Arcens has differentiated between three types of comic medievalism: laughing at, in, or with the Middle Ages.[8] D'Arcens notes that "comic texts such as Twain's [on which one of the films discussed here is based] that laugh *at* the Middle Ages seem to affirm a progressivist model of history which emphasizes the breach between periods, and arguably validates and advocates for modernity for its implicitly more evolved culture."[9] We see this presentist laughter as much in *The Sorcerer's Apprentice* as we do in Garnett's adaptation of Twain, but in Turtletaub's film, the Middle Ages that must be laughed *at* are represented entirely by Morgan, while the Middle Ages that must be laughed *with* are represented by Nicolas Cage's character, who hails from the same time and place as Morgan. Clare Simmons draws two slightly different categories of medievalist humor: "incongruity dependent on received cultural impressions of what the medieval period should be like" and "ironic hindsight," both of which appear in these films.[10] None of these classifications is meant to privilege one mode of medievalism as more authentic or "real" than others; as Pam Clements has written, the search for so-called authenticity in medieval studies or medievalism "is always the search for a chimera," as definitions of authenticity in medievalism have evolved continuously.[11]

Midcentury Morgan: Friendly Foe

Two midcentury films, Richard Thorpe's 1953 *Knights of the Round Table* and Tay Garnett's 1949 *A Connecticut Yankee in King Arthur's Court*, frame Morgan as a somewhat ineffective adversary—to Arthur and Hank Martin, respectively—with whom Arthur's court also has a friendly or familial relationship. Both films depict her as one of many potential sources of conflict, rather than the primary source of evil in the Arthurian world. Although quite different in their depiction of the Middle Ages, their genre, and their style, the commonality between these two films suggests that the filmmakers and audiences of this era did not find Morgan either threatening or sympathetic, but saw her as somewhat marginal, even though her claim to the throne is supposedly the cause of much of the conflict in *Knights of the Round Table*.

Knights of the Round Table sets up a different relationship and conflict between Arthur and Morgan than that of most medieval and post-medieval Arthurian texts: they are both children of Uther Pendragon, but Arthur is illegitimate while Morgan is legitimate. *Knights* also collapses various time periods and cultural clashes into a single conflict for the throne of "England," but rather than magnifying Morgan's adversarial role, this collapse serves instead to decenter Morgan. The film opens with chaos and anarchy following the withdrawal of Rome from "England," as Arthur, Merlin, and a few knights ride through destruction and carnage to a small seaside fortress, where they meet Morgan le Fay and her champion, Modred. Arthur and Morgan greet each other cordially if a bit formally—"God keep you, stepsister"; "God spare you, stepbrother"—before one of Morgan's knights begins a debate that reveals that Arthur and Morgan are not actually stepsiblings, but half-siblings, with Morgan the legitimate heir to Uther's throne and Arthur a younger and illegitimate son who, according to Merlin, still stands to inherit because he is a man. This reorganization of the familial relationships in the film serves to lend some sympathy to Morgan, who seems to have every reason to view herself as Uther's rightful heir.

This first scene continues with Merlin leading Arthur, Morgan, and Modred to a sword stuck in an anvil and reading its inscription, which names it as Excalibur and declares that whoever pulls it out is the rightful king of England. Morgan asks how they can know that it is "the sword the legend spoke of," suggesting a backstory that is never revealed; again this narrative arc conflates a series of timelines and conflicts, in which the sword famous for making Arthur king is already famous before it does so, and for reasons having to do, perhaps, with the withdrawal of Rome. Modred, acting as Morgan's champion, fails to pull it out, and Arthur, of course, succeeds as ominous string music gives way to triumphant horns playing a fanfare. Modred insists that the sword is not the true sword, and that it is, rather, witchcraft, for which he will ensure that Merlin is hanged. Modred's relationship to Morgan and Arthur is never explained, but it seems, as Kevin J. Harty writes, that he "is either her husband or paramour."[12] His and Morgan's relationship to "witchcraft" or magic seems to be purely oppositional, which is an interesting way to cast Morgan, who has long been associated with magic, witchcraft, sorcery, and even necromancy.

Morgan's role in any Arthurian film or text is bound up in the film's or text's depiction of magic and religion. *Knights of the Round Table*'s setting is overtly Christian, indicated not only by Arthur and Morgan's greetings to each other but also by a scene afterwards in which Modred's knights decide to kill a man instead of bribing him to keep silent, asking, "Was there ever enough gold in all Christendom to silence a traitor?" right before they throw him off a cliff, and by Arthur and Lancelot both crossing themselves when Perceval first mentions the Holy Grail. But Arthur and Merlin also hold a council of local kings and nobles (including Morgan, the King of the Picts, and King Mark of Cornwall) at a stone circle that resembles Stonehenge, and Merlin remarks that the laws of the rule of England are as old as the stones they stand under. But *this* scene is closely followed by a scene in which Lancelot and Arthur celebrate Christmas by exchanging presents and saying the words "Christ is born" when church bells (although they are at an encampment in the woods) announce midnight. Morgan's relationship to Christianity is not clearly explained, but Modred's accusation that Excalibur has been faked using Merlin's "witchcraft" serves to dismantle or at least undermine any association of Morgan and Modred with paganism or magic, and Morgan's greeting to Arthur marks her as at least outwardly Christian. Like the conflation of timelines and conflicts from various Arthurian texts, the rearrangement of the characters' relationship to both Christianity and magic serves to complicate Morgan's role, making it difficult to place her firmly into the category of ally or enemy to Arthur or to the political order.

The collapsed or rearranged timeline is evident in the film's other relationships as well. For example, before the formation of the Arthurian court, we see Lancelot riding through "England" in search of the great hero Arthur of whom he has heard from the harpist Gareth, even though in Malory's *Morte*, Arthur has achieved little fame and Gareth has achieved none (and possibly not been born) before the formation of the round table (the *Morte* is the text in which Gareth appears the most). Lancelot comes across Elaine, the maid of Astolat and Perceval's sister, who has wished at a magic pool on May Eve "for a knight to come riding and carry [her] off" (she seems to take on the naïve or provincial qualities that Perceval usually has). But these events happen to a Lancelot who is already established as a great knight, and during the reign of an adult Arthur who knows his parentage and believes himself the rightful heir of his father's throne. The Saxons are never mentioned, nor is the word "Britain." In short, the film makes significant interventions into the relationships, allegiances, and motives of the main characters it pulls from medieval Arthurian texts, with the result that Morgan is an interesting but not central character.

Rather than Lancelot and Guinevere being banished or driven from court for an affair, a rift between Lancelot and Arthur results from Arthur's refusal to execute Modred after their major battle for the throne of England (which they both survive). Lancelot meets Guinevere after this rift forms and on the eve of her wedding to Arthur, when he comes across a castle where she is being held prisoner and offers to serve as her champion. Morgan resurfaces when Lancelot, reconciled with Arthur, begins spending too much time with Guinevere, and Morgan, together with Modred, sets out to catch Lancelot and Guinevere together. Their ineffectiveness as foes is demonstrated with a shot of Morgan and Modred exchanging disappointed glances when Lancelot and Elaine decide, with Guinevere's blessing, to get married and go north in service of Arthur, and Merlin asks Morgan soon afterwards which of them grieves more for Lancelot's departure, hinting that he knows of her intention to sow discord among Arthur's inner circle. When Lancelot sends the court word of Elaine's death, and sends his infant son, whom he asks Arthur and Guinevere to care for and send to his grandfather in France, Morgan insists that Lancelot must come back to court, but Merlin objects. Morgan and Modred decide in private that they will arrange Merlin's death so no one suspects them of engineering a scandal, and, soon after, Arthur finds Merlin dead in his chamber.

Morgan's role in the film escalates when Lancelot, having returned to court, seems to be romancing a new woman, Vivian; it is primarily Morgan who encourages Guinevere's jealousy until Guinevere goes to talk to Lancelot in the middle of the night, and Morgan and Modred arrange for knights to catch Lancelot and Guinevere together. When Arthur refuses to sentence Guinevere and Lancelot to death, instead banishing them, Modred objects and leads a faction against Arthur, wounding him mortally, and "evil days returned to England." Although Morgan is largely

Anne Crawford as Morgan Le Fay in the 1953 film *Knights of the Round Table.*

absent from the events that take place once Lancelot and Guinevere have been discovered, the events are framed as resulting in part from her interference. The power dynamic between her and Modred, however, means that, unlike a Morgan who is Mordred's mother, she cannot be considered the sole perpetrator of a plan carried out by the two of them together. She reappears briefly after a final battle between Lancelot and Modred to weep over the dying Modred's body, a scene that demonstrates both her grief and the relative powerlessness she is left with at the film's end, despite being Uther's only legitimate heir.

Although it is a vastly different film in almost every way, Tay Garnett's *A Connecticut Yankee in King Arthur's Court* (1949) also depicts Morgan as both an insider to the court and a largely ineffective foe, although her target is the modern interloper Hank Martin rather than Arthur himself. The film softens some of the harsher edges of the novel, in which Tom Shippey reads Hank Martin as "view[ing]the Middle Ages with open horror, compounded by ethnocentric nationalism" because "Twain was clearly counterpunching to an already established vision of the Middle Ages which he disliked" for nationalist reasons.[13] This softening gives the film space to play out the romantic and familial conflicts at length. Garnett's film depicts Morgan as a niece of King Arthur, who is allied with Merlin and frequently in competition with Arthur's other niece, Alisande. Although the portrayal of the two women falls into many visual stereotypes—Morgan has dark red hair and red-painted lips and is frequently seen wearing red or green dresses and hairstyles or headdresses that are sharp or angular, while Alisande has lighter red hair and subtler makeup and is most often dressed in soft pastel or earth-toned dresses that are draped softly and emphasize her curves, with her hair worn down or softly veiled—the film's treatment of Morgan is not as stark as those in the 21st-century films discussed below.

The film begins in 1912, with a flashback of Martin's youth as a mechanic in Hartford, where he is knocked unconcious in a thunderstorm and wakes up in Arthur's Britain to Sir Sagramore challenging him to battle in the year 528. Martin enters the castle as Alisande is performing a song and dance for the court. Sagramore introduces Martin as a marvelous monster he has found, and Merlin urges the king to have him killed. Martin proves that he is not a monster, at a fair-like trial complete with jesters and food vendors, despite Morgan reminding Arthur that the Romans used the "more amusing procedure" of boiling their victims alive. He is knighted "Sir Boss" and allowed to attend a party, at which Sagramour explains to him who everyone is. Morgan is introduced to him as Arthur's niece, whom Merlin would like to see inherit Arthur's throne, and then to Alisande as another niece who is engaged to Lancelot. When Arthur introduces Martin to the crowd, Morgan immediately comments that he is dangerous, and Merlin tells her to dance with him. This scene represents Morgan's first serious attempt to interfere in Martin's participation in the court, but it is prompted by an order, not a suggestion, from Merlin.

Morgan's purpose within the plot of Garnett's film is to serve as a sort of weak villain who provides some plot tension until the central conflict of the film materializes, but her non-narrative purpose as a visual foil to Alisande is much more interesting. The film highlights the seeming distance between Martin and Alisande, represented by their mismatching costumes in the ball scene and the cinematographer's hesitance to frame both of their faces in the same shot very often, and juxtaposes that distance with visual cues that suggest a similarity or affinity between Morgan and Martin. The fact that Martin and Alisande fall in love and are impervious to Morgan's influence helps to underscore the film's idea that seemingly disparate people or time periods can coexist, and, in fact may constitute something more interesting than pairs which seem to match right away, as Morgan and Martin do visually. This idea is demonstrated at the level of plot in the ball scene by the fact that the medieval characters need only a minute to adjust to the modern music Martin has played, and to enjoy it. In the half-sung, half-spoken conversation Martin and Alisande have outside the ball, they emphasize this point in an exchange that is shot partly from the perspective of the eavesdropping Morgan and Merlin, in which Martin and Alisande are once again framed side-by-side in the same shot after a lengthy scene of shot/reverse-shot dialogue, when Martin tells Alisande, "All I'm trying to tell you, honey, is: even if you lived up in my day, around 1905, I'd still feel the same way about you. Time isn't important if it's a real thing." The plot-level argument that superficial temporal divides are meaningless is emphasized by the visual cues that Martin matches more closely with Morgan, but fits better with Alisande.

Morgan's ineffective interference continues when the lovers agree to meet the next day, and Merlin and Morgan decide to try to find Lancelot, Alisande's fiancé, and bring him back to cause trouble for the lovers. There is no real reason for this interference except a desire to harm both Alisande and Martin, although we may guess that Morgan and Alisande are competing for Arthur's favor and his throne. Before Lancelot returns, Alisande confesses to Martin that she is engaged to Lancelot but does not love him and would rather be with Martin. When Lancelot, summoned by Morgan and Merlin, enters Martin's smithy and challenges him, they agree to joust. At the joust, a gleeful Morgan tells Arthur that she expects to see Martin's blood, and Merlin tells Lancelot that he has cast a magic spell on his "evil opponent." Morgan and Merlin are dressed in matching black and gold here in this scene, while a nervous Alisande, sitting at Arthur's side, wears all white, matching Martin's tunic. Martin escapes death by riding away and coming back sans armor so he can fight Lancelot using a lasso instead of a lance and a sword. Again, Morgan's role in the plot is rather minor and is largely overshadowed by the comic anachronism of Martin's fighting style and the tension of the battle to the death of the film's main character. But her role as a foil to Alisande, both in her appearance and her demeanor, is substantial and serves to highlight both the difference between Martin and Alisande and the ways in which those differences are quite easily surmountable.

As *The Sorcerer's Apprentice* would do decades later, the film uses the different historical periods from which the characters come to depict its main character, Martin, as having knowledge and abilities that Morgan and others do not, including the ability to start a fire in his hands (with matches), the knowledge of how to help a young girl whose father has the plague, and the ability to make a working handgun in the smithy he opens.[14] But the humor at the expense of anachronism is most frequently aimed at Arthur himself; it does not serve as a thin veneer over misogyny as it does in *The Sorcerer's Apprentice*. The film's central conflict is not caused by Morgan; instead, the small, humorous conflicts caused by Morgan and Merlin are displaced by Martin's realization that Arthur has no idea most of his subjects are poor, starving, plague-ridden, and hate him, and the second half of the film follows Arthur, Martin, and Sagramore as they travel around the country so Arthur can see how his subjects really live.

Like *Knights of the Round Table*, *Connecticut Yankee* depicts Morgan as very much a member of Arthur's family, competing with her relative—either her sister or cousin in this case—for an inheritance that it seems may be rightfully hers. She is a foe to Arthur at times, but is the source of only one of several conflicts, and not the most serious one. Although at times she is depicted using fairly predictable misogynist tropes—she is redheaded, dark-lipsticked, and angular compared to the fairer and softer-looking Alisande, and she is bloodthirsty and frequently gleeful compared to Alisande's shy modesty—she is also not particularly powerful, instead depicted as doing Merlin's bidding, and failing even at that. Although she does not end the film in circumstances as tragic as those of the Morgan of *Knights of the Round Table*, neither does her story unfold in a way that suggests she will be particularly powerful or significant after the events of film.

The Morgana of the 1980s: Vulnerability and Vengeance

If the Morgan of the midcentury films discussed above is nuanced but largely insignificant to the overall narratives of the films, the Morgana that appears in the films of the 1980s is considerably more complicated. In both John Boorman's *Excalibur* and Stephen Weeks's *Sword of the Valiant*, Morgana is powerful but ultimately punished by those closest to her for that power. In both films, she is depicted as a beautiful woman whose actions are morally ambiguous—she is neither a hero nor a villain.

Stephen Weeks's 1984 *Sword of the Valiant* represents Morgan as someone who suffers as well as causes suffering. In a plot drawn largely from *Sir Gawain and the Green Knight* but incorporating lengthy sequences and tropes from a number of other Arthurian romances, Weeks re-interprets a number of women from medieval Arthurian texts.

Morgan first appears when Gawain is on his journey to find the Green Knight. He stops along the way, remarking that he is starving, and attempts to hunt a unicorn, which disappears when he shoots it. He and his squire, Humphrey, happen upon a lavish tent in the woods, which the lighting and sound effects indicate is magical like the unicorn. Inside, they find beds and cushions, and a large platter of fruit and meat and a jug of wine magically appear. Once they have eaten and are lounging and remarking on how expensive the tent's furnishings look, a group of red lights appears before them and materializes into a smiling woman with long dark hair and heavily made-up eyes, wearing a jeweled red dress. She tells them the furnishings are costly, then encourages them to keep eating as long as they are willing to pay. When Gawain's squire warns Gawain that the woman, Morgan, is the devil's decoy, she responds by asking, "Am I not fair?" She is shot in extreme close-up, with the camera close on her face and then her hand as her red-painted nails trail over her legs and her throat. Gawain draws his dagger and threatens her, but she reveals that she knows the Green Knight's riddle, which he is on a quest to solve. She suggests that he stay with her and ride to Lyonesse the next day.

When Gawain rides to the spot to which she directs him and blows into a horn hanging by the sea, shots of him are intercut with shots of Morgan cackling over a crystal ball built into what looks like a green human skull. The horn calls up a black-clad knight, reminiscent of the Knight of the Spring/Well from the *Yvain/Ywain* story, and Gawain defeats him, is separated from Humphrey, and meets the Lady Linet, who saves him with her magic ring. Linet tells Gawain that he is in the "lost land of Lyonesse," from which they cannot escape, and the two fall in love despite the fact that the much older Lady of Lyonesse, a loathly lady figure, expects Gawain to take the Black Knight's place as her husband. When Gawain and Linet try to escape and guards attempt to execute her, she gives him her magic ring so that he can escape and save himself, and the ring transports him to a barren wasteland, from which we once again see Morgan watching him in the crystal ball. The Green Knight bursts into her tent and reprimands her. Their exchange, Morgan's last human appearance in the film, demonstrates that the power she seems to have comes with its limits:

> GREEN KNIGHT: Morgan! Stop your meddling.
> MORGAN: Meddling? I was only having a little … fun.
> GREEN KNIGHT: You know Gawain and Linet weren't to meet yet. Give him back! You're spoiling
> my game.
> MORGAN: And, *if* I give him back, what will you give me in return?
> GREEN KNIGHT: You've interfered with my game with your black deeds and trickery, and now you
> dare to bargain with me? No one bargains with the Green Knight. No one!
> MORGAN, having turned into a small red toad: Mmm. Quite impressive. But stay with me tonight,
> and show me some better tricks? Please?
> GREEN KNIGHT: Well, we'll see.

Not only is Morgan punished by being turned into a toad, but her "interference," for her own pleasure and entertainment, is also an unacceptable incursion into the Green Knight's game, even though the latter seems to exist only for *his* pleasure and entertainment. Unlike in *Sir Gawain and the Green Knight*, in which the Green Knight is acting on Morgan's commands when he challenges Gawain, or *Yvain*, in which Morgan is a healer whose ointment cures Yvain's madness, this Morgan seems to be merely a lesser sorcerer than the Green Knight, subject to his whims and under his power. When he turns her into a toad, she is reduced to begging him for his company in a sexually suggestive way, perhaps because her sexuality is the only power she can now draw on. Later in the film, Gawain slices her in two with his sword. Her toad form breaks in half and reveals itself to be an empty ceramic frog; later, the Green Knight also dissolves into dust on being struck by Gawain's sword.

If the film's ultimate repudiation of the Green Knight's game can be interpreted as a critique of its cruelty—toward Gawain, Linet, Humphrey, and others—it can also be interpreted as a critique of his cruelty toward Morgan who, whatever her own actions, seems to have met a fate disproportional to her wrongs. Although the violence of Gawain breaking her toad form in half with his sword is mitigated by the fact that the blow turns her into something that is not alive and not sentient, and by the fact that he cannot possibly know that the toad is she, it is still a rather gruesome ending for the character who set Gawain on course to meet Linet, and its cruelty is amplified by the fact that she is never mentioned again in the film. While we can read the film as taking a certain amount of pleasure in the cruel behavior Morgan is subjected to, which can perhaps be understood alongside the pleasure the film takes in showing the loathly Lady of Lyonesse having aged and died alone in her castle, we can also see the film's critique of the Green Knight's cruelty to Morgan alongside that of his cruelty to others. Ultimately, *Sword of the Valiant* shows us that women can hold some power and manipulate some events for their own entertainment and pleasure but, unlike the Morgan of *Sir Gawain and the Green Knight*, they will be punished for it. As Morgan herself says to Gawain in the tent scene, "Nothing is free."

The Morgana of Boorman's *Excalibur* has a much more complex relationship to power structures than Weeks's Morgan, and a much more substantial role than the Morgan in any of the other films discussed in this essay. *Excalibur*'s writers claim that the film is based on Malory's *Morte*, but the film depicts Morgana's early experiences with Uther Pendragon—and those of her mother—in much more detail and much more intimately than Malory's work or any medieval text.[15] Perhaps it is no surprise that the film came out of the same decade as Marion Zimmer Bradley's *Mists of Avalon*, which tells the story of Arthur's life and reign from the perspective of the women closest to him: his mother, his sister, and his wife. *Excalibur* depicts Morgana's rise to power (such as that power is) as a bit of a mirage: she is young and vulnerable at the film's beginning, but Uther finds her threatening, perhaps because of her constant presence at Igrayne's side and her constant witness to his deceitful behavior. By using his belief in her power over or threat to him to punish her, he creates his own enemy.

Excalibur is ostensibly the story of the acquisition and loss of Arthur's sword Excalibur, or more generally the story of the rise and fall of first Uther and then Arthur Pendragon. But just as in Malory where, as Dorsey Armstrong writes, "knightly combat and its language are, in a sense, produced and given meaning by Malory's women," the story of the Pendragons' rise and fall in *Excalibur* is largely produced by their interactions with the film's women; it is even Guinevere who keeps Excalibur safe in a convent during the Grail Quest.[16] The war that begins Malory's text also begins *Excalibur*, and in both cases, it is motivated by Uther's desire for Igrayne, wife of the Duke of Cornwall. But Malory's Igrayne is portrayed as her first husband's intellectual and strategic equal, understanding Uther's intentions and advising her husband to leave Uther's castle. Boorman's Igrayne is powerless in comparison, appearing first when commanded to dance by her husband and again as she waits with her ladies while Uther is attacking the castle she is in. This difference in Igrayne's role necessarily sets the tone for a difference in her daughter Morgana's role. Although she first appears after Uther and Igrayne's wedding in Malory, Morgana's first appearance in Boorman's *Excalibur* is as a young girl on the night her father is killed, and on which Uther Pendragon, bewitched by Merlin to look like her father, comes to her mother's bed. In a striking scene that does not appear in any medieval English text, Gorlois's death and Merlin's trickery are conveyed to the audience by the young Morgana sitting up in bed saying, "my father is dead!"

This introduction follows Igrayne's own sympathetic portrayal, in which she is ordered to leave the table of ladies she is seated with at a feast and dance for the knights by her husband ("My wife will dance for us! Igrayne! Dance!"), who then tells Uther, "you may be king, Uther, but no queen of yours will ever match her." The dance is sexually suggestive, and the camerawork even more so, with close shots of her face and chest and long shots showing her body silhouetted against the light of wall sconces. The shots of her face and body alternate with shots of knights looking both admiringly and threateningly, and of Gorlois looking satisfied. As the dance becomes more frenetic and Igrayne dances closer to the table at which Uther is seated, her twirling is replaced with pelvic thrusts and writhing, and both the music and the editing become faster and faster until the dance ends abruptly with Uther shouting, "I must have her," Gorlois screaming, and Igrayne gasping and falling to the floor. This scene cuts straight to the siege in which Uther's knights kill Gorlois, and only a brief shot of Igrayne and two of her ladies inside the besieged castle indicates that there are stakes in this battle for her as well.

When Morgana sits up in bed and announces that her father is dead (although he is not quite dead yet), a scantily clad Igrayne runs over from her own bed and tries to comfort the weeping Morgana, when she is interrupted by Uther-as-Gorlois and tells Morgana, "Look, here's your father. It was just a dream." Uther summons Igrayne and, leaving Morgana in her own bed just a few feet away, she and Uther have sex. At one point during the sex scene, Uther looks up and makes eye contact with Morgana, who is watching, frightened, through a net. The camera cuts to Gorlois, impaled and dying but still alive, then back to Uther and Igrayne, then back to a now-dead Gorlois, then to Merlin, saying, "The future has taken refuge in the present." The next scene shows Igrayne and Morgana being escorted out of the castle to view Gorlois's body, with the ends of two swords still protruding from his chest. Igrayne's disbelief is juxtaposed with young Morgana's quiet, accepting grief. The scene ends with Morgana, no more than seven or eight years old, reaching over to close her father's eyes.

This opening highlights Morgana's vulnerability and powerlessness, and the following scene, which takes place at Arthur's birth approximately nine months later, highlights the ways in which Uther sees her as a threat. When Uther arrives at Igrayne's bedside, demanding, "What is it, lady?" about the baby, he looks at Morgana and says, "send the girl away." Despite Igrayne's protests that she is only a child, Uther shouts, "Out!" and, as a scared Morgana runs off, he tells Igrayne, "She watches me with her father's eyes." Despite now knowing that the baby, Arthur, is a boy, Uther continues to refer to him as "it," asking, "is it his or mine?" Igrayne then confesses that she does not know who came to her bed that night, but that she knows now it can't have been her first husband, who was already dead. This scene is familiar from Malory's *Morte*, except that in the *Morte*, Igrayne is still pregnant with Arthur, the two are married, and Uther then confesses that it was he and reassures Igrayne. In *Excalibur*, Igrayne only learns that Uther is the father when Merlin appears and reminds Uther that the baby now belongs to him, as payment for transforming Uther to resemble Gorlois on the night Arthur was conceived, and, as a result, Igrayne is angry. She becomes angrier still when Uther tears the newborn Arthur from her breast and hands him to Merlin, saying, "Take the devil child." As Merlin carries Arthur away, we see Morgana within earshot of Igrayne's screams. Looking even smaller and younger than before as she is shot standing in a stone archway below her mother's bedroom, she asks Merlin, "Are you the mother and the father of the baby now, Merlin?" He does not answer, but this series of exchanges that Morgana sees and participates in sets in motion her plans for vengeance, not only towards Uther, but also towards Merlin as well.

When the grown Morgana, now played by Helen Mirren, appears later in the film, at Arthur's wedding to Guinevere, she approaches Merlin, introduces herself, and says, "I remember you. When my brother Arthur was born, you came and took him away," before describing herself as "a creature like you." After quizzing her on the magical properties of various plants and minerals, as the wedding goes on in the background, Merlin agrees to induct her into "the way of the necromancer." When we next see Morgana, she appears with Guinevere in Camelot, as they walk down a set of stairs talking intimately and laughing together. Their easy intimacy is interrupted by Guinevere seeing Lancelot ride up to deliver a combination Perceval/Gareth character to Arthur. As Guinevere's face lights up and she lifts a hand in greeting to Lancelot, then lowers it slowly as she realizes he is going to ignore her, Morgana's expression shifts too, and she turns and walks back up the stairs, looking shrewdly over her shoulder at Guinevere as she does so.

In the dinner scene that follows at court, mimicking the early scene in which Gorlois orders Igrayne to dance, Morgana appears to be flirting with Gawain when we hear her telling him to "watch Guinevere" and "remember what I told you about them." Rather than this exchange being part of a plan devised by Morgana herself, though, it immediately becomes clear that she is seeking Merlin's approval when she sees Merlin in a dark corner and approaches him, remarking, "Your eyes never leave me, Merlin." They argue, with Morgana suggesting that Merlin is in love with her and Merlin telling Morgana she can never have the power that she claims he promised her. Their quarrel is interrupted by Arthur, who half-jokingly demands to know whether Merlin is his counselor or his sister's. The conversation between Arthur and Merlin further reinforces both Morgana's role in the kingdom's downfall and the fact that she acts not on her own behalf, but for Merlin. When Arthur asks, "Where hides evil, then, in my kingdom?" the camera lingers on a long shot of Morgana, framed between Gawain and Lot in the foreground and standing in front of and below Merlin, who is walking up a staircase in the background, before Merlin answers, "Always where you least expect it." This shot suggests that the evil which seems to be orchestrated by Morgana is really Merlin's doing. The consequences of Morgana's machinations become evident immediately, when Gawain claims that Lancelot is the source of any evil in Camelot, accuses the queen of treason, and is challenged by the king.

During the trial, though, Morgana appears as worried as anyone else while waiting for a champion to fight for Guinevere, and as relieved as anyone else when Lancelot appears at the last minute, as Perceval is about to fight Gawain. Standing with the other women of the court, but slightly apart from them and marked by her signature purple veil while they are all in shades of white and gold, she watches the action with what seems like as much uncertainty of the outcome as anyone else at court, but the camera shows her reactions nearly as much as those of Arthur and Guinevere, making it impossible for the viewer to forget her role in bringing about the combat.

Later in the film, Merlin tells Arthur and Morgana, separately, that he is leaving Camelot. Morgana, running after him, asks to be taken with him and to learn the "charm of making," which Merlin promised to pass on to her. The scene of the two of them entering a crystal cave is intercut with Lancelot and Guinevere consummating their relationship in the woods, and Morgana is shown visions of them and of Arthur finding them. As Merlin begins to show her the magic "in the eyes of the dragon," we see Arthur, far away, driving Excalibur back into the stone, right between the sleeping, naked Lancelot and Guinevere. As Morgana screams in horror from what Merlin is showing her, the ground trembles and Merlin collapses, shouting, "Excalibur!"

Helen Mirren as Morgana in the 1981 film *Excalibur.*

The moment Morgana has been waiting and working for has, like everything else in her life, been inadvertently thwarted by Arthur. This time, though, Morgana is able to convince a weakened, delirious Merlin to tell her the "charm of making," binding Merlin in the crystal cave. She tells him that he has now "trapped yourself by the same sorcery you used to deceive my mother. You're nothing. Not a god, not a man. I shall bind a man, and give birth to a god." Making good on her promise to avenge not only herself and her father, but her mother too, she finds the sleeping Arthur, repeating the charm to make him think she is Guinevere until it is too late. The camera shows Guinevere saying to him in Morgana's voice, "I have conceived a son, my king. My brother," and then transforming into Morgana's face. This scene cuts straight to Morgana giving birth in a castle in a lightning storm, wearing only her purple veil and pulling the baby out herself. Arthur is then shown standing behind a priest who is asking God to "save us from Morgana and save us from her unholy child." As he raises a chalice to the sky, a bolt of lightning comes through the window and hits Arthur, knocking him unconscious, hinting at Arthur's complicity—whether through his own actions or those of his father—in the destruction that Morgana and Mordred will bring to Camelot. The following montage of the land withering and people starving suggests that the sins of Uther are to blame for Britain's current state. It is a sick and weak Arthur who orders his knights to find the Grail.

Even the Grail quest here is directed largely by Morgana. When Perceval is searching for the Grail and despairs of ever finding it after ten years of searching, it is a young Mordred who arrives to lead him to it, and instead leads him back to a cave in which Morgana is living. Morgana tells him there is no Grail, and that he should serve her instead like the other knights who have chosen her over Arthur. Perceval refuses, however, and Mordred orders the knights to hang him; he survives only because the dead knight hanging above him is wearing spurs, which sever the rope Perceval is hanging from. As he is hanging there, the window of white light in front of him closes, and he sees himself walking into Camelot, where he can see the Grail floating in mid-air, pouring wine or blood, as he crosses a drawbridge into the castle. He hears a man's voice saying, "What is the secret of the Grail? Whom does it serve?" and is so frightened that he turns around and flees the castle, climbing over the closing drawbridge just in time. As he falls from the drawbridge in his vision, he falls from the tree that he is hanging from and wakes up. This vision, which Morgana inadvertently allows him to have, is what makes it possible for Perceval to find the Grail.

When Perceval returns to Camelot, he is able to achieve the Grail and heal the king because he correctly answers the question posed to him upon seeing the Grail. Although Morgana and the Grail are framed as equal but opposite supernatural forces in this section of the film, it is still, in a sense, Morgana who leads Perceval to the secret of the Grail. Arthur rallies his troops and rides to battle against Mordred, riding first through a barren wasteland that begins to turn green around them, then through a field of wildflowers and blossoming trees as "O Fortuna" from *Carmina Burana* plays over them. The fertility of the land is, of course, the result of Arthur's rejuvenation upon drinking from the Grail, but the images of trees blossoming juxtaposed with the newly powerful maternal Morgana, and with Perceval's realization that it the Grail's power lies not in its Christian holiness but in its link to Arthur and the land, suggests a deeper level of connection between Morgana's magic, the rebirth of the land, and the return of Arthur's health.

When Arthur is approaching Mordred's army, he stops at a stone circle and wishes for Merlin. "If only you were at my side, my friend, to give me courage. There are no war tricks that will fool Mordred and Morgana.... Where are you, Merlin?" Merlin appears and tells Arthur in a dream: "You brought me back with your love." The reawakened Merlin then appears as a vision in Morgana's cave, remarking to a sleeping Morgana that she must be beautiful because she used the magic she stole from him to keep herself so young. He confesses that he used his dragon's magic to trick Igrayne, then persuades her to recite the charm of making, allowing him to take the magic back from her. Smoke pours from her mouth as she recites the charm in her sleep, and, when Mordred is summoned by her guards to investigate the "fog" rising from her tent, he finds an old woman he doesn't recognize, whom he strikes and then strangles. Notably, the ship on which Arthur is borne away has three, not four, queens keeping watch over him; in Malory's *Morte*, one of the four queens is Morgana.

The 21st Century's New Misogyny Towards Morgan

From the nuanced, complicated, and often very human depictions of Morgana in the 1980s, the cinematic world seems to have made an abrupt shift in how it portrays her character by the early 21st century. Despite sympathetic, feminist portrayals of Morgana on television, such as in the miniseries *Mists of Avalon* and in the BBC series *Merlin*, the two 21st-century feature films that feature Morgan in a major role both cast her as a simple villain who exists primarily as the instigator of the film's central narrative conflict. The two feature films of the past two decades to feature Morgan are very different films. One, Jon Turtletaub's *The Sorcerer's Apprentice*, is an action-comedy with reasonable commercial success, set mostly in New York City in the present day, and not an Arthurian film in most respects: Morgan and Merlin are the only Arthurian characters to appear. The other, Mark Lester's nearly-unheard-of, straight-to-DVD sci-fi film *Dragons of Camelot*, is more of a traditionally Arthurian film in the sense that it is set in Camelot after Arthur's death and populated with characters from various Arthurian texts, but the futuristic Camelot and the unusual relationships between characters make it difficult to read alongside other Arthurian texts and films. What these two films have in common, however, is that neither makes any attempt to represent Morgan as a human character with motives and experiences of her own; they both use her simple evil as a plot device to tell a story in which a young man must save the world from evil wreaked by an evil and extremely powerful Morgan le Fay. They both fall into the category of films Eco describes as using the Middle Ages as a pretext, but they go further and use the idea of an evil Morgan as a pretext.[17]

The Sorcerer's Apprentice uses Morgana as the instigator of much of the film's action, in a narrative that begins in "Britain, 740 A.D." where the "great and powerful Merlin," who holds "the fate of mankind" in his hands, has put his trust in three apprentices while Morgana tries to destroy him. The film's opening voiceover describes her as "a sorcerer beyond evil: Morgana le Fay, Merlin's most deadly enemy." By winning over one of Merlin's three trusted apprentices, Horvath, Morgana manages to steal what the voiceover calls "sorcery's most dangerous spell, known as 'the rising,' giving Morgana the power to raise the dead and slay mankind." The two remaining apprentices, Veronica and Balthazar, try to stop her; Veronica does so by "sacrific[ing] herself for Balthazar" and taking Morgana's soul into her own body, where it tries to "kill her from the inside." Balthasar is able to freeze Veronica and Morgana in time with a spell to preserve Veronica's life, but she is unable to act. The mission left to Balthazar by the dying Merlin is to find Merlin's successor, whose purpose is to kill Morgana.

Unlike *Excalibur*'s Morgana, *The Sorcerer's Apprentice*'s Morgana is little more than a plot device; she instigates the film's conflict, creating the conditions for 90 very silly minutes of Nicholas Cage and Alfred Molina playing battling eighth-century sorcerers living in 21st-century New York while socially-awkward college student David (Jay Baruchel) discovers his magical powers, becomes Merlin's successor, and wins the heart of his dream girl by explaining physics to her (being a sorcerer, according to Balthasar, accounts for David's aptitude in physics) and by using magic to save her from a mugger. For a film whose plot is ostensibly set into motion by the actions of a woman, the film's female characters are incredibly one-dimensional and almost always positioned as impediments to the film's main quest, either because they are villains or because they are distractions. For example, Balthazar lets Dave cut his training short to see a girl because Dave says he has been waiting ten years to see her again, which reminds Balthazar of his own love, Veronica, whom he has been waiting 1250 years to see again. This concession to distraction threatens the mission, reinforcing the film's portrayal of women as impediments to the success of "good" sorcerers.

When Morgana is released from Veronica's body and the doll that holds them both trapped in time, she is depicted not as fully embodied, but as a sort of collection of floating molecules that she can move on command, with a deep, distorted voice. Dave is able to defeat her because of his powers of sorcery, but also his knowledge of physics: right before he destroys her by electrocuting her, he tells her he didn't come alone but "brought a little science with me," reinforcing presentist stereotypes of medieval people as ignorant and superstitious.

Lester's *Dragons of Camelot*, though a very different, and even worse, film, uses Morgana's character in a similar way. The film begins with a woman dressed in black using bloodied hands to carve runes into a rock next to a cave overlooking a lake. The woman's words begin as a spell: "Lord of dragons, father of serpents, by the ancient laws of magic, this mark summons you. This mark traps you. This marks binds you to my will." As a dragon roars in the mouth of the cave above her, her words reveal her to be Morgan, saying, "My brother Arthur lies on his deathbed. This day will be his last. When he is dead, I will wear his crown. To take his kingdom, I need a dragon. Give me one of your sons." A smaller dragon emerges from the cave and approaches Morgan after a brief shot of an old man—the dying Arthur—lying in a bed. Shots of Morgan flying on the dragon are intercut with shots of the dying Arthur lying pale in bed as Merlin prays or chants over him.

Dragons of Camelot is a poorly-written low-budget film and its influences are difficult to trace: a dying Arthur in bed, with Guinevere and Galahad (here Guinevere and Lancelot's son, though Arthur treats him as his own) at his side, who says he knows he was "wrong to disband [his] knights" over jealousy of Guinevere and Lancelot's affair. This relationship between characters does not fit into the narrative of Malory's *Morte*, Tennyson's *Idylls*, or any other text that I can identify. But the film still opens with the tired trope of a simply evil Morgana who, with no explanation, is bent on destroying Camelot and killing or imprisoning everyone in it, strange behavior for someone who claims to want to rule now that her brother, the king, is dead. Early scenes after Arthur's funeral feature Morgana breaking a woman's neck with her bare hands after hearing the woman refer to her as a witch, and cracking Excalibur into pieces with a jet of magical green light. While the plot—Galahad and a few remaining knights he rounds up fight Morgana's dragons and eventually defeat her—and the formal elements of the film do not bear much analysis, the fact that the impetus for the entire film's plot is Morgana's wickedness is worth noting. Like *The Sorcerer's Apprentice*, *Dragons of Camelot* takes for granted that audiences know certain things about the Arthurian story, and one of those things is that Morgana is an evil, murderous witch.

The trajectory of cinematic representations of Morgan in the 20th century saw us turning to increasingly interesting and nuanced representations of her by the 1980s. Why might the following three decades have seen her reduced to a misogynist plot device, in which many of the characteristics given to her by medieval writers have disappeared entirely? The simplest explanation would be that the culture that produced these films (both *Dragons* and *Apprentice* are American films) has grown more uncomfortable with the idea of powerful women. But this simple explanation is complicated by two factors: other media—such as television and novels—have continued to portray Morgan as an interesting and sympathetic character, and this same period has also seen an abundance of films about powerful women, both historical and fictional. The 21st century has also seen increased numbers of women in high levels of the U.S. government. What might we make, then, of the misogyny with which these two feature films depict Morgan?

I suggest that the films, like our culture more generally, are falling into a trap of periodization: as we see what looks like a trend towards more and more representation of women as nuanced, sympathetic, funny, and powerful in narratives set in or near the present-day, we are ever more prone to displacing our own misogyny into a pseudo-historical setting. Scholars of medieval literature and of medievalism have noted the tendency to depict a backwards Middle Ages in order to frame our own time as progressive, and of the tendency to displace the more disturbing misogyny, violence, nationalism, and racism of our own time into fantasies of the past in order to cope with them only at a safe distance.[18] "The flip side of … nostalgia," Laurie A. Finke and Martin B. Shichtman write, "is to associate the medieval with the barbarity, superstition, and violence from which civilization (modernity) is supposed to have rescued us."[19] That the idea of such a Middle Ages is represented by Morgan in these two recent films suggests that the displacement of contemporary misogyny onto the past creates a dangerous illusion that male characters from such a barbarous past can evolve, while female characters cannot. If, as Andrew B.R. Elliott has argued, cinematic representations of the Middle Ages are judged as authentic by audiences based on what those audiences expect to see, rather than by what is historically accurate, what does it mean that audiences—even for a children's film like *The Sorcerer's Apprentice*—have come to expect an evil Morgan le Fay to be defeated by men whose knowledge, even if they are from the past like she is, has supposedly evolved beyond the superstition and witchcraft of the "past?"[20] Perhaps the evolution of cinematic depictions of Morgan over the last seven decades serves to reinforce what many of us already suspect to be true: that the nexus of competing medievalisms, pseudo-histories, periodization, and suspicion of what we don't understand as "witchcraft" serves to place blame for society's ills where many other discourses do: on seemingly powerful women, who must therefore be contained, controlled, and defeated for the sake of human progress.

NOTES

1. *Arthur the King*, directed by Clive Donner, Comworld Productions, 1985. "A Day in Beaumont/The Last Defender of Camelot," *The Twilight Zone*, directed by Philip DeGuere, Jr. (as Philip DeGuere), and Jeannot Szwarc, 1986. *Prince Valiant*, directed by Anthony Hickox, Constantin Film, 1997. *Merlin* (two untitled episodes), directed by Steve Barron, 1998. *Mists of Avalon* (two untitled episodes), directed by Eli Udel, 2001. "And the Rule of Three," *The Librarians*, directed by Marc Roskin, 2015. "Camelot," *Live from Lincoln Center*, directed by Lonny Price, 2008. *Knightriders*, Laurel Films, directed by George A. Romero, 1981. *Kid Galahad*, directed by Michael Curtiz, Warner Brothers, 1937. (See The Internet Movie Database, www.imdb.com.)

2. *A Connecticut Yankee in King Arthur's Court*, directed by Tay Garnett, Paramount, 1949. *Knights of the Round Table*, directed by Richard Thorpe, MGM, 1953. *Excalibur*, directed by John Boorman, Orion, 1981. *Sword of the Valiant: The Legend of Sir Gawain and the Green Knight*, directed by Stephen Weeks, Golan-Globus, 1984. *The Sorcerer's Apprentice*, directed by Jon Turtletaub, Disney, 2010. *Dragons of Camelot*, directed by Mark Lester, Titan Global, 2014.

3. Jill M. Hebert, *Morgan le Fay, Shapeshifter* (New York: Palgrave Macmillan, 2013), p. 1, argues that scholars seem to struggle to reconcile what seem like contradictory aspects of Morgan's character, despite having no such difficulties reconciling dueling aspects of male characters like Arthur.

4. Kevin J. Harty, "Introduction," *Cinema Arthuriana: Twenty Essays*, ed. Kevin J. Harty (Jefferson, NC: McFarland, 2002), p. 7.

5. David Matthews, *Medievalism: A Critical History* (Cambridge: D.S. Brewer, 2015), p. 15.

6. Mathews, p. 15.

7. Umberto Eco, *Faith in Fakes*, trans. William Weaver, 1986, quoted in Matthews, p. 17.

8. Louise D'Arcens, *Comic Medievalism: Laughing at the Middle Ages* (Cambridge: D.S. Brewer, 2014), pp. 10–11.

9. D'Arcens, p. 12.

10. Clare Simmons, "Humor," in *Medievalism: Key Critical Terms*, ed. Elizabeth Emery and Richard Utz (Cambridge: D.S. Brewer, 2014), p. 109.

11. Clements, Pam. "Authenticity," in *Medievalism: Key Critical Terms*, p. 26.

12. Harty, p. 15

13. Tom Shippey, "Modernity," in *Medievalism: Key Critical Terms*, pp. 150–151.

14. As Louise D'Arcens writes in "Presentism," in *Medievalism: Key Critical Terms*, Garnett's Martin is a perfect example of "modern protagonists, despite being ordinary people, [being] granted elevated status in their medieval settings, as a result of their contact with quotidian scientific innovations" (p. 185).

15. Norris Lacy, "Mythopoeia in *Excalibur*," *Cinema Arthuriana*, ed. Kevin J. Harty (Jefferson, NC: McFarland 2002), pp. 34–43, notes, "In his closing credits, [Boorman] tells us that he and Rospo Pallenberg adapted the text of Malory, the quintessential Arthurian story for Anglophones."

16. Dorsey Armstrong, *Gender and the Chivalric Community in Malory's Morte d'Arthur* (Gainesville: University Press of Florida, 2003), p. 2.

17. Eco, quoted in Matthews (see note 7).

18. For example, see Geraldine Heng, *Empire of Magic: Medieval Romance and the Politics of Cultural Fantasy* (New York: Columbia University Press, 2003); and Kathleen Davis, *Periodization and Sovereignty: How Ideas of Feudalism and Secularization Govern the Politics of Time* (Philadelphia: University of Pennsylvania Press, 2008). Patricia Clare Ingham argues in *Sovereign Fantasies: Arthurian Romance and the Making of Britain* (Philadelphia: University of Pennsylvania Press, 2001), that the Gawain-poet's "narrative strategies deploy a misogynist gender hierarchy to help us forget moments of exotic difference" (pp. 131–132), which can help us to see how misogynist portrayals of Morgan may be deployed to mask other problems raised by a text or film, or to seemingly collapse them into what looks like a tidy binary when they in fact involve complicated questions of nationalism, race, and periodization alongside misogyny.

19. Laurie A. Finke and Martin B. Shichtman, *Cinematic Illuminations: The Middle Ages on Film* (Baltimore: Johns Hopkins University Press, 2010), p. 18.

20. Andrew B.R. Elliott, *Remaking the Middle Ages* (Jefferson, NC: McFarland, 2011), p. 215.

Isolde on the Silver Screen

Enraptured, Resolute and Shrewd

Joan Tasker Grimbert

More than a dozen films produced between 1909 and 2006 have sought to recreate the legend of Tristan and Isolde.[1] It is a reflection of the enduring transcultural appeal of this story that eight countries have contributed to this archive: France, Italy, Luxembourg, Spain, Ireland, Germany, Denmark, Iceland, and the United States.[2] If Great Britain is not represented, it is doubtless because the love story of Lancelot and Guinevere is dearer to Anglo-Saxon hearts.

Isolde, unlike Guinevere, has no recorded history beyond the romance she shares with Tristan. Starting in the 11th century, the troubadours situated the Irish princess within the passion that bound her to her lover, where she displayed qualities not only of hyperbolic love ardor and wondrous beauty, but also the great cunning she needed to conceal the couple's subversive love from King Mark, who was her husband and Tristan's lord and maternal uncle.[3] In these lyrics and in the 12th- and 13th-century Tristan romances, Isolde appears more alluring than her lover, and her capacity for ruse has captured the attention of feminists and fired the imagination of the many filmmakers who endow her with more initiative than Tristan.

Curiously, Richard Wagner may have unwittingly underscored Isolde's superior strength of character by creating for his opera, *Tristan und Isolde*, a willful heroine intent on forging her own destiny. Wagner sought to reduce Gottfried von Strassburg's 13th-century poem—which he disparagingly called the "medieval saga"—to what he believed was the legend's essence, a tale of love and death. The love potion was central to the medieval legend, and Wagner retained it, but he gave Isolde a prime role in manipulating the drink to achieve her own ends. In all the medieval versions of the legend, Tristan and Isolde ask for wine to staunch their thirst onboard the boat taking them from Ireland to Cornwall where Isolde is to marry King Mark. But they are handed, *by mistake*, the love potion brewed by Isolde's mother for her daughter to share with her husband on their wedding night. In Wagner's opera, however, Isolde, who is determined that she and Tristan will die rather than live to see her marry Marke, asks Brangäne for the flask containing poison. But her nurse, who cannot bear to see her mistress perish, hands her the love potion instead. Isolde consumes the "poison" before passing the goblet to Tristan, who has agreed to the death pact.[4]

Wagner is responsible for having dramatically revived the legend, which, after

50

spreading rapidly throughout Europe during the Middle Ages, had virtually faded from sight in the early modern period. The composer's extraordinary "music drama," which was completed in 1859 and debuted in 1865, exerted a powerful influence on the visual arts.[5] Albert Capellani, who was the first to bring the legend to the screen, actually tried to adapt Wagner's opera in his silent film *Tristan et Yseult* (1909).[6]

In subsequent films, we see borrowings from the earliest Old French and Middle High German versions of the legend. But since these works have come down to us only in fragmented or incomplete form, early filmmakers no doubt relied on the prose romance that Joseph Bédier had composed for his contemporaries in 1900.[7] For his *Roman de Tristan et Iseut* (*Romance of Tristan and Iseut*), the eminent medievalist took episodes from the late 12th-century poems by Beroul, Thomas of Britain, and Eilhart von Oberg, and from Gottfried (ca. 1210), weaving them into a coherent narrative that became an immediate bestseller and was translated into numerous languages.

Bédier's impact on modern adaptations of the Tristan legend soon rivaled Wagner's, in part because it suggested to artists of every stripe that the medieval legend in all its varied forms offered quite promising avenues of inspiration. Maurice Mariaud was the first filmmaker to use Bédier's romance, basing his 1920 film *Tristan et Yseut* so closely on it that the author sued him for plagiarism! (Mariaud's film was silent, but for some of his intertitles, he lifted whole phrases from Bédier's romance.[8]) Bédier deserves praise for having brought the *medieval* legend to the attention of the general public, but the direct influence of his novelistic romance—which owed too much both to the author's creativity and to Wagner's influence[9]—began to wane in the 1960s and 1970s with the publication by Penguin of the first English translations of the actual, freshly edited, medieval poems of Beroul, Thomas, and Gottfried.[10]

Although filmmakers drew increasingly on these poems as source material, Wagner's transformation of the potion scene—which celebrated a memorable conjunction of two compelling themes, love and death—influenced numerous cinematic adaptations. In his 1911 silent film, *Tristano e Isotta*, Ugo Falena introduced a new character, a slave girl Rosen, who accompanies her master Tristano to Ireland to fetch Isotta for his uncle. Sensing that Tristano, of whom Rosen is enamored, has fallen in love with Isotta, she pours poison into the couple's goblets, but the "Fairy Morgan" (Morgan le Fay) intervenes to change the poison into a love potion.[11] The passion that overwhelms Tristano and Isotta convinces them to escape before Isotta's wedding. Horrified, Rosen denounces the lovers to the king. He charges after them, but, surprised to find them asleep on the ground fully clothed, he spares them, leaving his sword and crown as a sign. When the lovers awaken, they misinterpret his gesture, and, despairing of ever being able to surmount their passion, they stand ready in the final scene to plunge into the sea. Although the episode in the forest is a variation on the one found in Beroul's poem (and recorded in Bédier's romance), the lovers' conscious decision to seek refuge in death seems inspired by Wagner, as does the poison/potion scene.

It is noteworthy that Falena's variation of Wagner's potion scene makes his own heroine seem more innocent. Less calculating than Wagner's Isolde, Isotta does not consider poisoning herself or Tristano, and, by fleeing the palace with her lover before her wedding, she avoids committing adultery. We shall see that, in most of the subsequent film adaptations of the legend, the heroine blithely follows the lead of Wagner's Isolde to heed the dictates of her heart, seemingly unafraid to sin. Since the present volume highlights the role of medieval women in the history of cinema, I will focus in the following pages on five films in which female agency is underscored in the unfolding of the lovers' destiny.

L'Éternel retour/The Eternal Return *(French, 1943)*

Although *The Eternal Return* was directed by Jean Delannoy, Jean Cocteau wrote the screenplay, infusing it with his own sensibility.[12] As the title and the initial quotation by Nietzsche suggest, the film's creators sought to underscore the universality of the Cornish lovers' passion: certain stories, especially those that have attained a mythic status, are recycled continuously through time. Cocteau felt that film was "the sole vehicle possible for achieving the equilibrium between the real and the unreal, for elevating the story to the level of the legend."[13] Thus, whereas the screenplay follows closely the plot found in Bédier's romance,[14] Cocteau dispenses with the medieval setting and even updates the protagonists' names to Patrice and Nathalie. Like Cocteau's *Orphée*, *The Eternal Return* is set in modern times. Moreover, the action takes place in sites shorn of any recognizable links to history or geography—the sea, the island, the bar, the castle, the mountains, the garage, then back to the same island and sea.[15]

Cocteau was, by nature, very receptive to Wagner's love and death complex, but he clearly delighted in adapting episodes from the medieval poems that he found in Bédier. Patrice (Jean Marais), an orphan, lives in the castle of his widowed uncle Marc (Jean Murat) with the Froissin family, consisting of Marc's sister, her husband, and their son Achille, a malevolent dwarf who is jealous of his cousin.[16] Having convinced his uncle to remarry, Patrice motors over to the island to find him a bride. In a biker bar, he finds Morholt, a towering bully taunting a beautiful woman named Nathalie (Madeleine Sologne), who (in a nod to Wagner) happens to be Morholt's fiancée.[17] A fight ensues, and when Morholt stabs Patrice, Nathalie takes her champion home to restore him to health. Soon enamored of her winsome patient, Nathalie is sorely aggrieved when he proposes to take her back to the castle to become his uncle's bride. But she agrees, if only to escape a worse fate—marrying Morholt. Nathalie's guardian, Anne, entrusts her with a love potion (which she labels "poison"), asserting that whoever drinks of it will love all their life and after. Since Nathalie does not believe in the potion's power, instead of using it on her wedding night as instructed, she stores the bottle in her medicine cabinet.

Patrice and Nathalie—both dazzling blonds, who stand out from the dour Marc and the zany Froissin family—share an attraction that is obvious to all. One afternoon, believing they are alone in the castle, they settle down in front of a blazing fire with drinks that Patrice has mixed—into which Achille has surreptitiously slipped Nathalie's "poison." The young people marvel at the effects of the "cocktail," and, although they do not of course die at this point, from that moment on they seem destined to do so, since they can no longer control their desire when they are together and languish when apart. Marc is eventually forced to banish them, but, after a spell in their mountain cabin, where Nathalie contracts a mysterious disease, her husband comes to take her back.

Meanwhile, Patrice finds another home and another Nathalie. We recall that, in the medieval legend, Tristan is taken in by the Duke of Brittany and, believing that Isolt the blonde has forgotten him, agrees to marry Isolt of the White Hands. Wagner ignored this part of the legend, which is preserved not in Gottfried, but in the poet's original source, Thomas. Although it is duly recorded by Bédier, many filmmakers have followed Wagner's

Madeleine Solonge as Nathalie la blonde and Jean Marais as Patrice in Jean Delannoy and Jean Cocteau's 1943 film *L'Éternel retour*.

lead, preferring the "condensed" version of the legend. But, happily, Cocteau chose to follow Patrice into exile, and the last part of the film introduces characters that are as entertaining as the Froissin family.[18]

Patrice's friend Lionel, who owns a garage in town, takes him in, and his sister, a brunette named Nathalie (June Astor), promptly falls in love with him. When Lionel proposes that they marry, Patrice insists on returning first to the castle to make sure his beloved truly has forgotten him, as he suspects. While he attempts in vain to attract Nathalie's attention under the window he erroneously thinks is her bedroom, Achille spies him and shoots him in the leg. Lionel manages to get his wounded friend to safety—where his sister, Patrice's prospective bride, awaits them.

Nathalie la brune is in many ways a more attractive figure than her blonde counterpart. Lively and engaging, she is certainly the stronger of the two, and, like Isolt of the White Hands, her jealousy leads her to precipitate the hero's death. The wedding is to take place on the same island where Nathalie la blonde had lived with Anne. Patrice is taken there to recover from his wound, but, because it has become badly infected, he convinces Lionel to return to Marc's castle to fetch his beloved. Lionel is to replace the red pennant on the boat's mast with a white scarf if she is aboard. Overhearing the plan and learning of Patrice's enduring passion for his first love, the distraught fiancée realizes he will never marry her, for she herself is just the shadow of the shadow of his first love. So, whereas the returning boat (which carries both Nathalie la blonde and Marc) gaily sports a white scarf, Nathalie la brune lies to Patrice. Although she feels immediate remorse and reverses herself, her deception has already dealt the fatal blow. Patrice expires, as does his beloved upon arriving—too late. In the final scene, we see the lovers lying side by side on overturned boats in the boathouse, which has been transformed into a chapel.

Lovespell or Tristan and Isolt *(Irish, 1979)*

Unlike *The Eternal Return*, which was greeted with great enthusiasm by the general public under the German Occupation,[19] *Lovespell*, directed by Tom Donovan, was a critical failure. Norris J. Lacy has called it "a tepid and tedious film with very little to commend it," and notes that it went straight to video without having a theatrical release.[20] Nevertheless, the film is intriguing and is included here for several reasons: the director's insistence on underscoring the legend's Celtic roots, the blending of Christian and pre–Christian traditions, the depiction of a headstrong heroine, and the rather bizarre ending which seems like an incoherent use of source material.

Not only did Donovan shoot his film in Ireland, he assembled an impressive cast of Irish and British actors. The Irish actors include Kate Mulgrew (Isolt), Geraldine Fitzgerald (Bronwyn), and Cyril Cusak (King Gormond of Ireland); Richard Burton (Mark) is Welsh, and Nicholas Clay (Tristan) is English. Donovan also used film titles based on the *Book of Kells* and Irish folk music composed by Paddy Moloney and performed by The Chieftains.[21] Moreover, he chose to evoke the Druidic religious practices of a country depicted as a recent convert to Christianity. Finally, he named Isolt's tercel Cuchulain (after the hero of the Irish saga *The Wooing of Emer*) and gave it symbolic importance.

Donovan's intractable heroine may owe something to an Irish saga that has been identified as an analogue of the Tristan legend, *The Pursuit of Diarmaid and Grainne*.[22]

The dead lovers in Jean Delannoy and Jean Cocteau's 1943 film *L'Éternel retour*.

As we shall see in another variation on the potion scene, Isolt asserts her right to choose her own lover even though she has agreed to wed King Mark in accordance with her father's wishes. Her relationship with Mark is fraught with ambiguity from the moment she meets him riding through her father's countryside. She reacts aggressively when Mark tries to take possession of her sparrow-hawk, but she inexplicably changes her tune when she meets him in her father's hall: she apologizes for her behavior and even offers him Cuculain. The king is touched by this gesture.

Therefore, when Tristan is wounded by Morholt, he is sent to Isolt not only to be healed but also to convey Mark's marriage proposal. During the time it takes Isolt to cure Tristan, the two young people become increasingly fonder of each other. Appalled by this turn of events, Bronwyn, who learned about herbs from Isolt's deceased mother (a priestess of the old religion), decides to brew a love potion for Isolt to share with Mark on their wedding night. Bronwyn tells her, "The two who use the contents of this flask in love are bound forever together through life past death and into the hands of God."

Like Patrice and Nathalie, their counterparts in *Lovespell* need no love potion to fall in love. But unlike them, they confess their love and proceed to consummate it on board the ship en route to Cornwall before even drinking the potion! Although Isolt intends to marry Mark, she thinks Tristan can remain a friend and even her lover, a prospect Tristan finds intolerable. Given his recalcitrance, Isolt decides to bind him to her by pouring the potion into a glass of wine that she offers her unwitting lover. While promising always to care for and comfort Mark, she swears that Tristan is her heart and her life. As the two consume the potion, she intones, "Through life past death and into the hands of God."

We are told that, when Ireland became Christian, people were forbidden to brew potions. By breaking this interdiction, Bronwyn signals her desperation. Is her mention of God with regard to what she intends as a loving cup for the married couple an attempt to transform this pagan brew into something resembling the wine of the Eucharist? If so, when Isolt reprises Bronwyn's formula as she offers the potion to her lover, her action borders on the sacrilegious, since she is using it to aid and abet a passion that undermines the marriage sacrament. But it may be that Donovan meant simply to show Isolt emphasizing the supreme right of lovers to live out their passion in the eyes of an accepting God.[23]

If so, Tristan is never wholly convinced of that right. When Isolt suggests that they can carry on as lovers even after she weds, he seems horrified at the thought of committing adultery, which to him is clearly a much greater betrayal than what he has just done. Once Isolt is married, she apparently avoids having sexual relations with her husband (unlike her medieval counterpart), so when Mark catches his wife and nephew meeting secretly, he is doubly outraged: as in Beroul, he hands Isolt over to the leper colony and imprisons Tristan. When Tristan manages to escape and to rescue Isolt, the two flee to the woods. It is only then that Tristan is told about the potion, and, although he accepts that they will always love each other, he seems determined never to bed Isolt again for as long as she is his uncle's wife. When he places his sword between them that night, it is a symbol of his steadfast loyalty to Mark, and his uncle reads the sign correctly. He takes back Isolt but feels he must banish Tristan.

Like Cocteau, Donovan opts to include the part of the legend where Tristan meets Isolt of the White Hands in Brittany, but he gives the episode a rather bizarre twist. Tristan meets the second Isolt after a band of ruffians mortally wounds him. The maiden does what she can to heal him, but when she fails, Tristan sends for Isolt of Cornwall. Although Breton Isolt is clearly attracted to her patient, Tristan never contemplates marrying her. Therefore, she has no reason for resentment, unlike Isolt of the White Hands—and even Nathalie la brune. Indeed, this maiden actually hopes that Queen Isolt will be able to come heal Tristan and live with him forever after! Clearly, then, it will fall to someone else to draw the story to its tragic end, and that will be Mark.

When Isolt learns of Tristan's plight, she begs her husband to take her to him, but, since Mark believes she is too ill to make the trip, he promises to bring Tristan to her and to raise a white sail if he is onboard and a black sail if he is not. Upon arriving in Brittany, Mark tells Tristan he has come to take him "home" because Isolt is dying. On board the ship, with the white sail flying high, Mark explains to Tristan that, despite his betrayal, he still thinks of him as a son. Tristan responds by cruelly informing his uncle that he and Isolt have loved each other since they first met in Ireland and had slept together before arriving in Cornwall. He also tells him about the potion, adding that given the drink's force, there is no appeal except to God: he and Isolt will love each other "through life past death and into the hands of God."

This bold revelation is too much for Mark to bear. Although there is no evidence that Tristan has changed his resolve not to bed Isolt as long as she is married to Mark, his arrogant confession infuriates his uncle. While Isolt stands on the cliff reveling at the sight of the white sail, Mark abruptly unfurls the black sail, and his wife falls onto the rocks below. Tristan plunges into the water, followed by his uncle, who, apparently repentant, helps him swim ashore. Collapsed on the beach, the youth reaches out and just barely touches the fingers of his lover's outstretched hand. The final shot shows Mark, hapless and helpless, standing alone in the water. No doubt he regrets having precipitated the death of the two people he loved most in the world.

Critics such as Lacy have wondered why Donovan changed Thomas's ending so radically. Why does he transform Isolt of Brittany from a vengeful spouse into a compassionate bystander? Why does Mark decide not to take his ailing wife to Tristan in Brittany, choosing instead to fetch his nephew and bring him back to her in Cornwall? After all, Tristan appears to be in worse shape than Isolt, although dying of love is a real phenomenon. Mark's erratic behavior has also been the object of critical scrutiny. He swings abruptly from outrage to compassion when he finds the lovers in the forest and then from compassion back to outrage when, at the end, Tristan confirms his uncle's suspicions that he had betrayed him. But Mark has the same extreme mood swings in Beroul's poem, especially since the lovers evade several traps set for them by the dwarf Frocin and the jealous barons before Tristan is banished from Cornwall.

No doubt Donovan's decision to transfer to King Mark the role that Isolt of Brittany usually plays in the lovers' demise was motivated by Richard Burton's star caliber. We have seen that Mark makes an early appearance in the film and is on screen for the entire second half. Indeed, except for the time that Tristan and Isolt spend falling in love in Ireland and making love on the boat to Cornwall, Mark dominates the film. Donovan's decision to increase Burton's screen time means that Isolt's relationship with her husband receives as much emphasis (or more) as the one she has with her lover.

If Burton's performance has also been found wanting, he does shine in a tender scene that underscores the symbolic importance of Cuchulain, Isolt's tercel. The bird refuses to bond with the king, a recalcitrance that clearly parallels Isolt's. As his wife lies close to death, Mark wistfully recounts the difficulty he once had taming a willful goshawk. At one point, he believed he had triumphed, but, when the bird suddenly struck him and drew blood, he reacted by dealing his beloved pet a blow from which it never recovered. Mark tells Isolt that it was a lesson he thought he would not have to learn twice. The film's ending confirms that he never did learn that lesson.

Feuer und Schwert: Die Legende von Tristan und Isolde (Fire and Sword) *(German, 1981)*

This film, directed by Veith von Fürstenberg, was made shortly after *Lovespell* and features an even more willful heroine (the ravishing Antonia Preser). Isolde's desire and initiative drive the plot from beginning to end, as she strives to overcome both Tristan's desire to respect his oath of allegiance to Marke and the strange apathy he displays at certain moments.[24] Much is made of her knowledge of sorcery. Like *Lovespell*, *Fire and Sword* includes several memorable episodes from the medieval poems, leading Meradith McMunn to assert that both films are quite "faithful" to the legend, even though that fidelity—in each case—is rather superficial, since some episodes are stripped of their original symbolism[25] or seem extraneous. It is especially true of the inclusion of a second Isolde, whose role in *Fire and Sword* is every bit as inexplicable as in *Lovespell*.

Also puzzling are some of the changes that von Fürstenberg made in the first part of the film. Throughout *Fire and Sword*, the director underscores the bloody conflict between Ireland and Cornwall; totally senseless, it will culminate in the apocalyptic death not only of the lovers but also of nearly all the principals. Thus, it seems fitting that the film begins with the single combat between Morolt and Tristan (Christoph Waltz). Tristan triumphs, but, grievously wounded, he sets himself adrift in a boat that arrives in Ireland where he is rescued and brought to a convent to be healed. As in the legend, Tristan conceals his true identity, claiming to be the minstrel Tantris. But so does Isolde, strangely enough: she tells Tristan her name but says she works in the convent as a maid. This mutual deception allows the two to fall in love gradually in an idyllic setting—beautifully filmed—that instills in them a taste for the pastoral life. When Tristan decides he must return to Cornwall, he promises to come back for her.

In Cornwall, meanwhile, Marke's barons have persuaded the king to accept Ireland's offer of Princess Isolde's hand, even though Dinas (Peter Firth) has counseled him against the alliance, and Marke does not want to disinherit his nephew. When Tristan arrives, though, he urges his uncle to proceed with the plan, saying that he himself would not make a good king. The youth claims to have but two yearnings, one to serve Marke and the other to go fetch his "common girl": she is also named Isolde, he adds—"a good omen."

But Tristan's return to Ireland, which reveals the young people's true identity, is a painful shock for both. Isolde boldly proposes that they flee, unlike in the legend where it would be unthinkable to choose social alienation, but Tristan refuses to betray his uncle. Seeing no alternative to losing her lover, Isolde brews a potion and warns Brangane, "Those who drink this potion will fall in love forever and ever in life and death," a formula that recalls *Lovespell*. On board the ship bound for Cornwall, Isolde summons Tristan. After he has recounted the story of his parents, Rivalen and Blanchefleur,[26] and underscored his gratitude and undying devotion to Marke, Isolde hands him the potent "wine" and tells him there's no point in resisting its effects. As they lie naked caressing each other, Brangane spots the empty goblet and shrieks, "She poisoned you, lord. She made the wind stand still. Now it will take revenge."

The lovers' arrival in Cornwall and their attempts to pursue their affair resemble the corresponding scenes in *Lovespell*, except that von Fürstenberg includes piquant details that have no real consequences. For example, both Donovan and von Fürstenberg present a wedding celebration featuring musicians and jugglers. In a lovely touch that recalls Achille's role in *The Eternal Return*, von Fürstenberg introduces a juggling dwarf, who mischievously lifts up the tablecloth to reveal (to us) that the lovers are holding hands. He does not denounce them, however, for that role is left to Andret, who is intent on destroying Marke's marriage to the "Irish witch." Isolde's reputation for sorcery is well known and frequently underscored in this film.[27] On her wedding night, she hands Marke a goblet with a sleep potion in the hope that he will fail to notice that she is not a virgin. Although he refuses, saying that he has had enough wine, Marke does not perceive that anything is amiss. When he does eventually realize that Isolde's obvious lack of affection for him must mean she is having an affair, he believes it is with Dinas. Both Brangane and Governal warn the lovers to be more cautious, and, although Andret fails to offer Marke clear proof of their betrayal, the king reluctantly banishes Tristan.

From this point until the film's end, the plot becomes impressionistic and even disjointed, in part because the director incorporates elements from the medieval poems in a somewhat willy-nilly fashion. For example, when Governal returns to the castle to tell Isolde that Tristan is ill and needs her, he is disguised as a beggar, recalling one of Tristan's own disguises on his furtive visits to Cornwall from his exile in Brittany in the *Folies Tristan*. And von Fürstenberg situates the episode from Beroul in which Marke discovers Tristan and Isolde in the woods *after* Isolde has followed Governal back to the forest. Marke finds the couple awake and, concluding that they are indeed guilty of Andret's charges, takes them both back to Cornwall to be punished. As in Beroul, Marke intends to burn Isolde at the stake, but members of the leper colony persuade him to hand her over to them, not to be used as a common woman—as in Beroul (and *Lovespell*), where the punishment fits the crime (a *contrappasso*)—but rather to heal their disease! Tristan is imprisoned in the chapel, but escapes when he crashes through a stained-glass window depicting a knight conquering a dragon. One could argue that this image (which recalls how Tristan won Isolt in the medieval legend by killing the dragon that was ravishing Ireland) anticipates symbolically how the youth will rescue Isolde from the lepers, after which they will go back into hiding.

A title announces that three years have passed.[28] The Irish are again waging war on Cornwall—with Andret's help—while the Cornish offer fierce resistance. Tristan retreats into the forest with Dinas, who urges him to make peace with Marke and then perishes in the conflict. Isolde wants to return to Cornwall, because she feels responsible for the war, but Tristan is surprisingly apathetic. Marke decides that the only way to end the conflict would be for Isolde to submit to a judgment of God. In a scene drawn from Gottfried's poem, Isolde pronounces the oath that she has never had relations with anyone but her lord Marke and gamely grasps the red-hot iron, which chars her hands and causes her to faint. But the king believes her.

Meanwhile, Tristan, who has presumably retreated to Brittany, rescues a maiden from raiders who have set fire to her hut. On an incomprehensible impulse, he derisively "baptizes" her Isolde and says she's the Queen. In the very next scene, we see him, grievously wounded, waiting for his beloved to come to him. We only learn why in the scene that follows: back in Cornwall, Governal tells Isolde that Tristan was struck by a lance while trying to settle a quarrel between two foraging soldiers. Isolde wants to set out immediately, but the Irish (led by Andret) have surrounded the castle. In order to protect Isolde, Marke attacks the Irish, and Andret is slain.

In recounting the lovers' final moments, von Fürstenberg fuses Thomas's traditional ending with the film's pervasive theme of senseless war. Back in Brittany, "Isolde" the maid anxiously stands watch. Having learned the crucial signal, she tells Tristan that the sail on the returning boat carrying Governal and the Queen is black. Tristan cries out, "Isolde!" and promptly dies. When Isolde arrives to find him dead, she lies down beside him and expires. In the final scene, we see Governal lighting the funeral pyre, an apocalyptic image that recalls the film's original title, *Fire and Ashes*. As Brangane had told Governal earlier, their departure from Ireland had come to no good.

I Skugga Hrafnsina/In the Shadow of the Raven (Icelandic, 1988)

Until now, we have been examining films whose plots contain elements that can be traced back either to Wagner or to the earliest medieval poems (as conveyed by Bédier or by subsequent translators), and we have seen how various directors adapted this source material to suit their purposes. No doubt the most unorthodox contribution to the Tristan film archive is *In the Shadow of the Raven*, a film directed by Hrafn Gunnlaugsson as part of his Viking trilogy. The director strays so far from the legend that we might not even recognize it as an adaptation if he had not chosen to call his main characters Trausti (Reine Brynolfsson) and Ísold (Tinna Gunnlaugsdóttir) and included a love potion brewed by the heroine's mother. When asked which version of the legend he had in mind, Gunnlaugsson claims to have followed no particular one, inspired mostly by a dimly remembered bedtime story that his grandmother had told him as a boy and that he thought of adapting to the plot of a film that was also shaped by indigenous Icelandic mythology and its tradition of family sagas.[29] *In the Shadow of the Raven* shares with *Lovespell* the fact that it is set in a newly Christianized country, Iceland in 1077, and thus features a fusion of pre–Christian and Christian rites that could have been disconcerting if the director had not crafted a coherent picture of the conflict between the old and the new ways. Gunnslaugsson also presents a heroine who is determined to control her own destiny in matters of the heart and uses the potion to that end. Although there is no King Mark figure to whom Trausti owes allegiance, there is a triangle of sorts: Ísold's father has betrothed his daughter, an unwed mother (and thus "damaged goods"?), to the bishop's son, Hjörleifur. Hjörleifur and his domineering mother, Sigrídur, are intent on the marriage because they seek to consolidate their power in the country. Thus, the bishop's family turns out to be the main adversary of Trausti and Ísold.

The potion dominates the first part of the film. Ísold's mother brewed it and gave it to her daughter to share a love that would last a thousand years with the man of her choice. As such, it is Ísold's most prized possession, and three separate scenes illustrate her determination to control her fate. When a quarrel between Ísold's clan and Trausti's over a beached whale results in the death of Ísold's father, Eríkir, and the torching of their abode, she runs from her home, carrying her daughter and the potion. Then, firmly—and erroneously—convinced that Trausti was the one who slew her father, she returns to the burning house in search of a weapon and faints, only to be rescued by the man she considers her mortal enemy. Trausti, in an attempt to revive her, calls for a flask of water but is handed the one containing the potion. He puts it to her mouth before taking a healthy swig of it himself, at which point Ísold, on opening her eyes, recognizes it and spits it out, screaming, "Murderer, murderer!" She will tell him subsequently that she did not want to be bound forever to the man she believed had murdered her father.

The second and third potion scenes occur in the chapel of Trausti's mother Edda, where Leonardo, an artist whom Trausti had brought back to Iceland, is painting an altarpiece. In the first of these scenes, Trausti hopes to make peace with Ísold. When she, intent on revenge, tries to stab him, he wrestles her to the ground, then covers her with kisses (no doubt an effect of the potion), but he eventually comes to his senses, only to be cruelly mocked by her. By the time the third potion scene takes place, Ísold has had a total change of heart. Trausti has just been forced into single combat with the bishop's son, and, though triumphant, he has demonstrated his desire to avoid violence by refusing to kill his opponent.

At the beginning of the film, Trausti had just returned from Norway as an ordained priest, and he resists the temptation to continue using the sword to combat his enemies as the old ways dictated. After his combat with Hjörleifer, Ísold draws Trausti into the chapel and brazenly offers him the potion. Wielding the same knife with which she had once threatened to kill him, she cuts their palms and joins them, thus sealing their mutual love with a blood pact inspired by the pre–Christian Odinic religion. Unwitnessed, this pagan act will be followed by a Christian wedding celebrated in the presence of all. It is only on their wedding night that Ísold will allow Trausti to make love to her, an act that is cruelly interrupted when the bishop's family treacherously sets their house on fire, and Hjörleifur mistakenly kills Ísold.

The protracted process by which the potion is consumed is very different from what we have seen in other versions of the legend. Ísold maintains control over the precious liquid, and, even after finally offering it to Trausti, she insists on waiting until they are properly married to consummate their love. At that point she tells him, "Every great deed a man does is merely a dream of love ... and now you have me and I have you. Can we wish more than that love seals peace upon the whole land?"

Ísold's dream of love is not the exclusive passion we associate with the Tristan legend: it chimes with Trausti's desire for a universal, forgiving love. When his mother warned him to beware of Ísold, whose mother was a witch, he showed her a sketch of the altarpiece destined for her chapel. It depicts the Crucifixion, but, in the spot to the lower right of the Cross, which is usually reserved for the Virgin Mary, Leonardo has depicted a woman in red whom Trausti identifies as "Mary Magdalene, the woman who loved Christ." "The sacred work of Christ was a single dream of love," he explains: "the love of all mankind, but also the love of a woman." Thus, Trausti makes a clear connection between a woman popularly—though erroneously—cast as a former prostitute[30] and the witch's daughter; indeed, Leonardo uses Ísold as his model for the Mary Magdalene figure, as can be seen in the final version of the altarpiece.

It is the explicit integration of the couple's love passion into the Christian message of universal love that makes this film unique in the Tristan film archive. But that process of integration in newly Christianized Iceland is not an easy one. As Claudia Bornholdt notes, "the Christian values and ways of dealing with conflict and confrontation quite literally clash with an indigenous Icelandic culture that is grounded in pagan German concepts of kinship and honor. In this pre–Christian society, revenge and thus blood feud were considered the means to uphold the family's and the individual's honor and position in society."[31] As we have seen, Ísold tries to avenge the death of her father by threatening Trausti with a knife, whereas Trausti eschews the sword as a way of dealing with his enemies. Only as a last resort does he stoop to killing when he must avenge the murder of his wife by the bishop's deceitful family. Ísold and Trausti are worthy representatives of the old and the new religions, respectively. Since Trausti has become a Christ figure by the end of the film, his brand of Christianity promises to win out, as his survival and that of Ísold's aptly named daughter Sól[32] seem to indicate. Nevertheless, the Odinic tradition, symbolized by the raven, continues to cast its shadow. As Edda tells her son on her deathbed, "The God who created the sun has always been my God. And he has listened to my prayers. Whether he is called Christ or Ódinn is of no importance."

Tristan & Isolde *(American, 2006)*

In most of the films discussed above, we have been able to recognize the sources either as Wagner's opera or the medieval poems as conveyed by Bédier's popular romance. If *In the Shadow of the Raven* stands out as an exception, it is because Gunnlaugsson was intent on setting what little he knew of the legend in the context of medieval Icelandic culture and history, in part as recounted through the family sagas. In the case of the latest entry in the Tristan film archive, directed by Kevin Reynolds and co-produced by Ridley Scott of *The Duellists* fame, the historicizing impulse was so dominant that it seemed to override all other concerns.

In a manner reminiscent of Antoine Fuqua's *King Arthur* (2004), Reynolds sought to recreate the period associated with the "historical" Arthur, and thus the "historical" Tristan, although if Arthur's links to history are tenuous, Tristan's are virtually nonexistent. Politics are not absent from the medieval legend, but the only war featured pits Ireland against Cornwall and is settled once and for all when Tristan slays the Morholt. As we have seen, in *Fire and Sword*, which also focuses on politics, Ireland continues its raids on Cornwall, and the war between the two lands does not end until nearly everyone is dead. Reynolds, for his part, expands the legend's power struggle in a different way. He presents a sixth-century conflict in which Lord Marke of Cornwall strives first and foremost to unite Britons, Angles, Saxons and Picts, so that they can present a united front against King Donnchadh of Ireland. Here, although Tristan's fight with Morholt results in the elimination of Ireland's star warrior, it does not take place in a single combat but rather during a skirmish between the Brits and the Irish in a dark wood. The war between Britain and Ireland stretches over the entire length of the film and becomes more complicated when Donnchadh finds allies in the Lord of Wessex (Wictred), and eventually even Marke's nephew Melot. Tristan's defeat of Morholt serves mostly to send the youth, wounded by his adversary's poisonous sword, out to sea on a funeral barge that will deliver him into Isolde's arms, thus initiating the love idyll. The political situation is complex and confusing,[33] but it is, frankly, the most engaging element of what is essentially an action film. Next to it, the love story often appears humdrum and even lackluster.

Nevertheless, one of the film's purposes was clearly to introduce the legend to young audiences. Posters and other promotional materials included the tag line: "Before Romeo

& Juliet, there was Tristan & Isolde." But it is hard to imagine what people unfamiliar with the legend could have gleaned from the film, for it owes little to the usual medieval and modern sources of inspiration. The names (especially the spelling of Isolde and of Marke) recall Wagner, as does the fact that Isolde is betrothed to Morholt, although she is unaware that Tristan slew him, and, had she known, she would have been grateful because she had no desire to wed him. The main debt the film owes to the medieval poems is the conflict in Tristan's mind between his love for Isolde and the allegiance he owes Marke, who, however, is not his maternal uncle but rather the kindly lord who rescued him in the enemy raid in which the boy's parents perished. Marke himself loses his right hand, significantly, for Tristan becomes his right-hand man, a favoritism that, in another nod to Wagner, makes the king's nephew Melot jealous.

Sophia Myles as Isolde in Kevin Reynolds' 2006 film *Tristan & Isolde*.

Surely it was to attract and engage a young audience that Reynolds offered the role of Tristan to James Franco. But the actor, who, five years previously, had played the lead role in a James Dean biopic to great acclaim, clearly did not know what to do with a character that he could not "research" in the same detailed way. He practiced brandishing a sword and riding a horse, but, when it came to expressing emotions, he settled for channeling a modern American adolescent. Given Rufus Sewell's fine portrayal of an energetic and endearing Marke, it is hard to see why Isolde (Sophia Myles) prefers Franco's Tristan.

We can't blame it on the potion, because there is none. Reynolds must have thought that teenagers would scoff at the idea that an herbal brew could induce love. Certainly, the situation is romantic enough as it is: the two young people fall in love in Isolde's seaside retreat while Tristan is convalescing from the poisonous wound inflicted by Morholt.[34] The cinematography—gorgeous views of Ireland and the sea—and Anne Dudley's haunting score make the budding romance more believable. In one key scene that is strangely anachronistic, Isolde reads aloud from a little printed book the final stanza of John Donne's poem "The Good Morrow":

> My face in thine eye, thine in mine appeares,
> And true plaine hearts doe in the faces rest,
> Where can we finde two better hemipheares
> Without sharpe North, without declining West?
> Whatever dyes, was not mixed equally,
> If our two loves be one, or, thou and I
> Love so alike, that none doe slacken, none can die.

Although Tristan scoffs at what initially seems like so much romantic nonsense, it is shortly thereafter that they finally make love, and both lovers recall this exact stanza at key moments in the film.

Tristan soon returns to Britain, leaving behind a woman he believes is a lady-in-waiting at the Irish court. (Isolde's deception here is similar to that of her counterpart in *Fire and Sword*.) Tristan comes back to Ireland on learning that Donnchadt is holding a "tournament" with his daughter as the prize. By defeating Wictred, Tristan wins the tournament—actually a slugfest involving swords, daggers, and maces—and promptly announces that he has won the Irish princess for Marke, only to discover that the veiled woman seated next to Donnchadt is his very own beloved. On the boat bound for Cornwall, the lovers rue their misunderstanding, but Tristan insists on fulfilling his promise to Marke, adding that the alliance will avoid a hundred years of bloodshed. Isolde has different priorities, however, and, like her counterparts in *Lovespell* and *Fire and Sword*, feels little loyalty to her husband. She has always chafed at having to bow to her father's plans to marry her off—first to Morholt, then to Lord Wictred, and finally to King Marke. Isolde tells Tristan that there is more to life than duty and death, which explains why, even after marrying Marke, she remains undaunted in her desire to pursue her romance. Meanwhile, Tristan seems horribly conflicted and makes no effort to hide his disarray. He spends the second half of the film plunged into a gloomy daze, and Franco plays the tortured soul to the hilt.

Reynolds fashions a dénouement that underscores his priorities. Marke's enemies band together to reveal the lovers' betrayal to their newly coronated king, who is naturally enraged. Upon learning the whole story, though, he is willing to allow the two to escape the apocalypse that threatens to engulf Britain. But Tristan refuses to abandon Marke in his hour of need. He tells Isolde that he will not have it said that their love brought down a kingdom! In the ensuing scenes he slays Wictred but receives a mortal wound and asks Marke to take him to the river, where Isolde is awaiting him. Tristan dies as Isolde kisses him and repeats the poem. In two epigraphs, we learn that Marke defeated the Irish, rebuilt Castel d'Or, and reigned in peace until the end of his days. Isolde laid Tristan under the ashes of the Roman ruin where they used to meet and planted two willows "that grew forever intertwined ... then disappeared."

Conclusion

In most of the films discussed above, the Isolde figure generally appears stronger or more resolute than her lover, although, if Tristan often seems less independent-minded, it is because he is bound to Mark by strong blood and feudal obligations. We might be tempted to see in Isolde's cinematic characterization the influence of modern feminism. Yet, as far back as the 11th and 12th centuries, medieval poets and romancers presented Isolde as a very compelling figure. A few centuries later, Wagner recognized Isolde's capacity for ruse and her strength of character when he had her manipulate the love potion to serve her own ends. Most filmmakers have simply picked up on these cues and developed them cinematically.

There are three fascinating entries in the Tristan film archive that I have not discussed here because each is so idiosyncratic that it constitutes a category all its own. Yvan Lagrange's *Tristan et Yseult* (1972), a "visual opera," demystifies the legend by situating it at the intersection of the four main elements and exploring the two primordial instincts of the human race: individual survival and reproduction.[35] Jytte Rex's *Isolde* (1989) presents the heroine as a librarian whose ex-husband, a manipulative politician, tries to blackmail her lover, a mercenary, into killing her. Luis Buñuel's *Tristana* (1970), based on the novel by Benito Pérez Galdós also stands out, for the eponymous heroine actually displays characteristics that we associate with *both* Tristan and Isolde![36]

Appendix: Film Versions of the Legend of Tristan and Isolde

1909	France	*Tristan et Yseult* (Albert Capellani)
1911	Italy	*Tristano e Isotta* (Ugo Falena)
1920	France	*Tristan et Yseut* (Maurice Mariaud)
1943	France	*L'Éternel retour/The Eternal Return* (Jean Delannoy; sc. Jean Cocteau)
1970	Spain	*Tristana* (Luis Buñuel; based on the novel by Galdós)
1972	France	*Tristan et Yseult* (Yvan Lagrange)
1979	Ireland	*Lovespell* or *Tristan and Isolt* (Tom Donovan)
1981	Germany	*Feuer und Schwert* (Veith von Fürstenberg)
1981	France	*La Femme d'à côté* (François Truffaut)*
1988	Iceland	*I Skugga Hrafnsina/In the Shadow of the Raven* (Hrafn Gunnlaugsson)
1989	Denmark	*Isolde* (Jytte Rex)
1989	France	*Connemara* (Louis Grospierre)
1998	Italy	*Il Cuore e la spada* (Fabrizio Costa)
2002	Luxembourg	*Tristan et* Iseut (Thierry Schiel)
2006	U.S.	*Tristan & Isolde* (Kevin Reynolds)

Unlike many scholars, I do not believe that Truffaut had the Tristan legend in mind, specifically, when he conceived of this modern tragic love story. See Joan Tasker Grimbert, "Truffaut's La Femme d'à côté *(1981): Attenuating a Romantic Archetype—Tristan and Iseult?" in* King Arthur on Film, *ed. Harty, pp. 183–201.*

Notes

1. The spelling of the heroine's name varies. Here, I use "Isolde," except when discussing works where an alternate spelling predominates. The spelling of other characters' names, such as Mark and Brangane, also varies. For an extensive overview of the legend, see *Tristan and Isolde: A Casebook*, ed. Joan Tasker Grimbert, Arthurian Characters and Themes 2 (New York: Garland, 1995; rpt. Routledge, 2002), pp. xiii–ci.

2. See the Appendix above for a full listing of these films.

3. In three strophes of his song *Non chant per auzel*, Raimbaut d'Aurenga praises Iseut for gifting her virginity to Tristan and concealing her deceit from Mark. For the original text and English translation, see Bernard O'Donoghue, *The Courtly Love Tradition* (Manchester: Manchester University Press, 1982), pp. 120–123.

4. In previous articles cited below, I have analyzed the potion scene in various films, most recently in "Variations on a Transcultural Phenomenon: The Potion Scene in Four Film Versions of the Legend of *Tristan and Iseult*," in *The Legacy of Courtly Literature: From Medieval to Contemporary Culture*, ed. Deborah Nelson-Campbell and Rouben Cholakian (New York: Palgrave MacMillan, 2017), pp. 133–149.

5. See Christine Poulson, "'That Most Beautiful of Dreams': Tristan and Isoud in British Art of the Nineteenth and Early Twentieth Centuries," in *Casebook*, ed. Grimbert, pp. 325–356.

6. Capellini adapted numerous classical works. For this film, he may have followed the lead of Edwin S. Porter, who in 1904 filmed *Parsifal*, a silent film that involved actors in the cinema hall performing Wagner arias. See Paolo Cherchi Usai, *Silent Cinema—An Introduction* (London: BFI Publishing, 2000), p. 9.

7. Joseph Bédier, *Le Roman de Tristan et Iseut* (Paris: L'Édition d'Art H. Piazza, 1900). For an excellent translation and introduction, see Joseph Bédier, *The Romance of Tristan and Iseut*, trans. Edward J. Gallagher (Indianapolis: Hackett, 2013). Bédier, a well-known medievalist, was working on a scholarly edition of the medieval Tristan poems at the time he penned his modern adaptation.

8. See "Dire de M. Joseph Bédier à MM. Les Experts (1921–1923):'Mon Roman de Tristan au Cinéma,'" in Alain Corbellari, *Joseph Bédier, Écrivain et philologue* (Geneva: Droz, 1997), pp. 619–627.

9. "Bédier contre Wagner," in Corbellari, pp. 157–164; Joan Tasker Grimbert, "Bédier et la légende tristanienne," *Romanische Studien* 7 (2017): 68–78.

10. Gottfried von Strassburg, *Tristan, with the surviving fragments of the 'Tristran' of Thomas*, trans. A.T. Hatto, Penguin Classics (London: Penguin, 1960); *The Romance of Tristan by Beroul and The Tale of Tristan's Madness*, trans. Alan S. Fedrick, Penguin Classics (London: Penguin, 1970).

11. See Kevin J. Harty, "A Note on Maureen Fries, Morgan le Fay, and Ugo Falena's 1911 Film *Tristano e Isotta*," in *On Arthurian Women, Essays in Memory of Maureen Fries*, ed. Bonnie Wheeler and Fiona Tolhurst (Dallas: Scriptorium Press, 2001), pp. 313–318. As Harty points out, Falena's introduction of the love-smitten

slave girl Rosen adds a second love triangle to the story (p. 315). In the thirteenth-century prose *Tristan*, Tristan and Iseut both inspire passionate love in various other characters, who either commit suicide or attempt to do so.

12. For an analysis of this film and its relation to Cocteau's work, see Joan Tasker Grimbert and Robert Smarz, "*Fable* and *Poésie* in Cocteau's *L'Éternel Retour*," in *Cinema Arthuriana—Twenty Essays*, rev. ed., ed. Kevin J. Harty (Jefferson, NC: McFarland, 2002), pp. 220–234.

13. Jean Cocteau, *Du Cinématographe*, ed. André Bernard and Claude Gauteur (Paris: Belfond, 1973), p. 163.

14. Stephen Maddux, "Cocteau's Tristan and Iseut: A Case of Overmuch Respect," in *Casebook*, ed. Grimbert, pp. 473–504.

15. Meradith T. McMunn, "Filming the Tristan Myth: From Text to Icon," in *Cinema Arthuriana*, ed. Harty, pp. 211–219 [214].

16. Inspired by the dwarf Frocin in Beroul's poem, Achille is played to perfection by the inimitable Piéral. He is a stand-in as well for the jealous barons in Beroul.

17. Wagner was the first to make Morholt the heroine's betrothed rather than her maternal uncle, reasoning no doubt that his audience would not know that, in the Middle Ages, the maternal uncle was second only in importance to the father. In the opera, Isolde is angry with Tristan in part because she has fallen in love with him and in part because he slew her betrothed. Most filmmakers will follow Wagner's lead, although they will change Morholt into a thoroughly despicable character.

18. Maddux, "Cocteau's Tristan and Iseut," correctly notes that the parts of the film where the secondary characters play a prominent role are among the best (501–504).

19. Jean Marais, *Mes Quatre Vérités* (Paris: Éditions de Paris, 1957), pp. 134–136.

20. Norris J. Lacy, "*Lovespell* and the Disinterpretation of a Legend," *Arthuriana* 10.4 (Winter 2000): 5–14 [5].

21. McMunn, "Filming the Tristan Myth," p. 212.

22. On this work, see W.J. McCann, "The Celtic and Oriental Material Re-examined," in *Casebook*, ed. Grimbert, pp. 3–35, esp. 25–27.

23. Beroul and Gottfried allow the heroine to survive the Judgment of God, by which she dubiously proves that she has never betrayed her husband. In Beroul, she cleverly fashions an ambiguous oath, but, in Gottfried, she does not.

24. For a detailed plot summary and perceptive analysis, see Alain Kerdelhue, "*Feuer und Schwert*, Lecture matérielle du myth," in *Tristan et Iseut, mythe européen et mondial. Actes du Colloque des 10, 11 et 12 janvier 1986*, ed. Danielle Buschinger (Göppingen: Kümmerle, 1987), pp. 182–198.

25. See Lacy, "*Lovespell*," 5–6.

26. This is the only film that alludes to the love story of Tristan's parents, which anticipates his own. It was recounted by Gottfried (following Thomas)—and reprised by Bédier.

27. Kerdelhue, "*Feuer und Schwert*," p. 188.

28. This notation reminds us that the potion's effects wear off after three years in Beroul and after four in Eilhart, at which time both lovers desire to return to court. Here, though, there is no mention of a mutual change of heart.

29. Jane Chance and Jessica Weinstein, "National Identity and Conversion Through Medieval Romance: The Case of Hrafn Gunnlaugsson's Film *Í Skugga Hrafnsins*," *Scandinavian Studies* 75 (2003): 417–438 [429]. The Tristan legend was well known throughout Scandinavia in the Middle Ages, thanks to a Norwegian adaptation of Thomas's poem (1226) and an Icelandic version (ca. 1400). On what the film owes to those poems and to the indigenous family sagas, see Joan Tasker Grimbert and Claudia Bornholdt, "'The Love of All Mankind but Also the Love of One Woman Alone': Hrafn Gunnlaugsson's *Shadow of the Raven*," in *The Vikings on Film: Essays on Depictions of the Nordic Middle Ages*, ed. Kevin J. Harty (Jefferson, NC: McFarland, 2011), pp. 83–95.

30. Contrary to widespread belief, nothing in the Bible supports the popular conception of Mary Magdalene as either a prostitute or Jesus's lover. A faithful follower of Jesus, she was present at his Crucifixion and his Resurrection. In the sixth century, Pope Gregory the Great arbitrarily conflated the unnamed sinner in Luke 7 with Mary Magdalene, an error that the Church corrected in 1969.

31. Grimbert and Bornholdt, "Love of all Mankind," p. 89. Gunlausson places recurrent motifs (the raven, the white veil) in key scenes to guide our reading of the film. Odin is known as the Raven-god because two messenger ravens sit on his shoulders (p. 88).

32. "Sól—the Icelandic and classical name for the sun, source of light and truth—is at once a diminutive of her mother and the continuation of the lovers' vision (Chance and Weinstein, "National Identity," p. 436.)

33. Internecine strife leads to shifting alliances that reach across the Irish Sea, as the pact between Lord Wictred and King Donnchadh illustrates.

34. Morholt had boasted to Isolde that he too "dabbled in elixirs," showing her the poison he could apply to his sword to paralyze his adversary in battle—which explains why Tristan appears to be dead following his combat with the Irish champion.

35. See Jean Marcel, "La Dernière Métamorphose de Tristan: Yvain Lagrange" (1972), in Jean Marcel, *Pensées, passions et prose* (Montréal: L'Hexagone, 1992), pp. 244–251.

36. See Donald L. Hoffman, "Tristan la Blonde: Transformations of Tristan in Buñuel's *Tristana*," in *King Arthur on Film: New Essays on Arthurian Cinema*, ed. Kevin J. Harty (Jefferson, NC: McFarland, 1991), pp. 167–182. After this current essay went to press, I published the following article on film treatments of the legend of Tristan and Isolde: "Tristan in Film," *Arthuriana—Special Issue in Honor of Kevin J. Harty*, guest editors Alan Lupack and Barbara Tepa Lupack, 29.2 (Summer 2019): 47–63.

Maid Marian

Neomedievalism and the Misogyny in the Reel

VALERIE B. JOHNSON

> "Oh, Robin, you're so brave and impetuous!"
> —Maid Marian, *Robin Hood* (1973)

Introduction

The "reel" Maid Marian is an object of masculine attention, the subject of the Gaze[1]: a damsel in distress who must be rescued by the gallant Robin Hood; a lady of quality for whom Robin strives to be worthy; an heiress whose marriage is controlled by the Crown. As Sherron Lux so aptly observes of the reel Marian, whether cinematic or televised, "even when Marian is little more than a beautiful plot device, she is not only brave and loyal but also attempts to claim agency for herself."[2] But the Marian of the reel is not the only Marian: audiences of film encounter Marian in ballads, in novels, in comics, art, and more. Those Marians are rarely as marginalized as the Marian of cinema; those Marians retain the agency that cinematic Marians battle to obtain but are never permitted to retain. This begs the question: what are viewers to make of the Marian of neomedieval cinema, a "beautiful plot device" and a character whose narrative development is to continually seek agency that must be surrendered to complete the arc of Robin Hood's desires, character development, and benefit?

I argue in this essay that Marian's characterization and treatment in neomedieval cinema is inexorably linked to the fiscal conservatism of filmmaking. These characterizations are complex: independence, for audiences to mentally classify Marian as a "strong independent woman"; dependence, so Robin Hood's rescue and claiming of "his" woman becomes a major plot point; marginalization, both physical and emotional, to ensure Marian never overshadows Robin. This marginalization after independence punishes the character for her actions: if Marian fights against an undesired marriage at the start of the film, the resolution of the movie is a marriage to Robin Hood (*Robin Hood*, 1991); if Marian banters wittily upon her introduction, her final words will be cloying statements of love after helpless screams (*Robin Hood: Prince of Thieves*, 1991); if Marian is physically active and dynamic by her own choice, the film will end as she is embraced and lifted by Robin Hood (*Robin Hood*, 2010).

Stephen Knight proposed in *Reading Robin Hood* that "Marian studies" has as much merit as "Robin Hood studies," arguing that Marian's history in the "Robin Hood tradition is both the history of form, seen through generic change, and also the history of content embodied in a range of ideological meanings."[3] I argue that a major block to developing a tradition of Marian studies is posed by conservative cinematic anti-feminist feminism: Maid Marian has changed only slightly since 1922, largely due to neomedieval desires for women (and specifically white women) to be historically situated within the reductive yet hyper-real binary of medievalism and neomedievalism.[4] A woman character like Marian has two opportunities for representation in these films. The first is to be a "historical" through-line for conservative modern (white, heterosexual, American) feminism, showing viewers how a socially-elevated woman can navigate her place in a man's world, yet still thrive by securing the love of a good man. The second is to de-historicize her, presenting an apparently modern Marian as an aspirational or representative modern fantasy to rewrite the past. Both of these options encourage tokenization, no matter how good or ill their intentions; indeed, the gender balance of a Robin Hood film (or ballad) is never equal. Marian's ability to act for her own interests and motives is always exceptionally circumspect, and never the focus of the narrative. Her narrative actions largely serve to bring her close to meeting Robin, supporting Robin, and allowing Robin to explain his motives to the audience.

Neomedievalism pulls the past into the present without concern for accuracy, and consequently neomedieval perspectives are problematic for women viewers and women characters. Neomedieval films embrace images of women that are products of modern misogyny. When attempts are made to interrogate women's historical circumstances in these stories, the critique draws near-exclusively on clichés arising from Victorian-inspired medievalism, *or* an urgent need for the modern post-feminist world to be radically better than the medieval world. Lorraine K. Stock and Candace Gregory-Abbott note that cinematic treatments of Marian and the women of Sherwood are "depictions of … marginalized female archetypes … [that] reflect the shifting roles experienced by women in the past century," and these archetypes are enshrined in neomedival depictions of Marian.[5] Neomedieval archetypes dictate Marian's behavior, her story potential, her narrative role, and ultimately her value; the ease with which the ephemeral nature of neomedievalism interlaces with cultural minimization of women is chilling. This ease of erasure is what prompts my argument that neomedievalism dictating Marian's behavior is a simultaneous push forward and pull back that ultimately does more harm than good.

Men do not escape this damage, for misogynistic cultural practices harmfully shape masculine imagery and notions of manhood. Robin Hood himself is often subjected to topical and politically charged medievalism that explores contemporary matters of justice and moral rigor in the face of immoral laws. The difference between Robin Hood and Maid Marian, however, is that Robin is both the narrative center of the story and a beneficiary of neomedievalism's gendered binaries. Though it is theoretically possible to create a major Robin Hood film without Marian (an unsatisfying prospect that no studio has achieved), Robin's journey and character are the focus of a Robin Hood film. Robin's name serves as the title, the narrative flows from his perspective, and he is centered in story and frame by filmmakers. Marian is always already a secondary character; her narrative function is to be the love interest within the "Robin-Hood-and-Maid-Marian" story unit. Marian will never be the focus of a film or television series without a thorough reworking of the Robin Hood figure: this concept has only been attempted once in the comedic television series *Maid Marian and Her Merry Men* (1989–1994). In the "real" world, women lead without devaluing men; the fact that in the reel world this is unthinkable outside of comedy demonstrates the potential toxicity of such representation.

I assert that patterns in Marian's characterization in major Robin Hood films are indicative of fiscal conservatism in cinematic storytelling, a conservatism that links insidiously to the dark underside of medievalism, heritage, and fictionalized notions of the past. The medieval is profitable: well-known medieval stories have long been considered stable investments for filmmakers. The Robin Hood tradition has consistently produced blockbuster films since the 1920s: though Allan Dwan's 1922 collaboration with Douglas Fairbanks is the best known, Robin Hood films were made continually beginning in 1908.[6] The success of larger films mandates that productions with more modest budgets must reference the blockbusters to remain relevant. Blockbuster Robin Hood films consistently resist references to more obscure productions; fiscal conservatism and profit demand that filmmakers stick with what works when huge budgets are involved. Lower-budget productions have more freedom, but consequently don't provide audiences with the comforting repetitions of the past that maximize blockbuster profits. An effect of this overreliance on the blockbuster—usually summer deliveries, which generally maximize profit by avoiding nearly every form of controversy, including diversity, feminism, and complex political messages—is that the "typical" Robin Hood film is exceptionally risk averse, focused on action and adventure, and consequently minimizes efforts to advance or revolutionize women's roles or depictions.[7]

I propose considering neomedievalistic depictions of Maid Marian as actant fictions: stories and narratives used by audiences to understand the present within the context of a constructed fictional past, privileging exciting storytelling and comfortable affirmations over factual accuracy or challenges to the status quo. Audiences whose access to the Middle Ages is through popular culture often receive narrative stereotypes: these impressions are delivered as plot and transform into immutable historical fact. Neomedieval film productions, drawing as they do upon historical imagery while maintaining the iconography that allows audiences to relate to the characters and settings, consistently transform fictions into perceived realities through psychological shortcuts that characterize film reception.[8] Thus, the prejudices of the present are imported to the past: the lack of women or persons of color in Robin Hood films subliminally convinces viewers that the Middle Ages were masculine and white.[9] Popular understanding of the Middle Ages is rooted in over exaggerations of stereotypes (for example, that women were denied all agency; that rape and sexual assault were commonplace and condoned); often these stereotypes are prioritized over demonstrable evidence contradicting the presumption.

The consequences of such distorted thinking are manifold. I argue that neomedievalism's attempts to "historicize" gender in Robin Hood cinema does not result in the "strong independent woman" role model. Instead, such efforts reproduce extremely modern American social norms of gendered and sexual behavior. Productions draw upon narrative stereotypes and produce reciprocal cycles of misunderstanding, inherently demonstrating to audiences that such norms are universal across time and space. Audiences cannot know what is narrative convenience and what is historical fact, and the narratives they consume have historicized (and thus normalized) horrific treatment of women. Because those productions were fiscally successful (and often prevalent in childhood), nostalgia has already begun to look back at these fictions and long for a "return" to an utterly fictional golden era—and the profit-driven mindset of cinematic production cycles takes up the narrative anew in an attempt to cater to audience desire.

The cinematic Marian is a paradox: she is a model for modern feminism and simultaneously an example of dutiful feminine submission to her man, and contradictions allow vast narrative flexibility and utility. The modicum of independence she has achieved in other media (novels, television, and more) is decidedly less advanced in cinema. The intent of this essay is to focus on the subtle changes made in Marian's representation in major cinematic works. I identify and explicitly address a pattern in Marian's characterization that is familiar to feminist viewers: audiences are introduced to a Marian who is spunky and spirited, independent with a touch of the wild … until she meets Robin Hood. In short order Marian falls into Robin's orbit as a prospective romance partner. Once she has been classified as Robin's "love interest," Marian is overshadowed, and her potential independence is brutally negated by the narrative: she is forcibly parted from Robin and threatened with rape or unwilling marriage to Robin's chief (masculine) foe. The independent, even feminist, Marian of the film's beginning is invariably menaced with gendered violence that negates her status as a person to reconfigure her as Robin's weakness.

"Darling, you could help": Enid Bennett (1922) and Olivia de Havilland (1938)

The two landmark Robin Hood films of the first half of the 20th century are *Douglas Fairbanks in Robin Hood* (1922) and *The Adventures of Robin Hood* (1938), starring Fairbanks and Errol Flynn. The Fairbanks and Flynn Robin Hoods owe great debts to the 19th-century stage, while exploring the valences of the new medium. The long running television series *The Adventures of Robin Hood* (1955–60), which has recently experienced a critical renaissance due to scholarly nostalgia and interest in political activism within the production company, drew heavily on the popularity of both films for its looks, characterizations, and treatment of Marian. Though the three Robin Hoods are all different with some quite marked differences, the Marians are all variations on a theme: youthful, slightly naïve, and exceptionally spirited, girls on the cusp of womanhood who are often possessed of a sharp tongue but rarely the social power that would allow her to evade the consequences of her words. The means of her oppression vary; the results, however, are static.

Bennett's Marian must match a Robin (first the Earl of Huntingdon) who is, generously, a man-child; Bennett does so by presenting Marian as capable of both playful enthusiasm and cool detachment. The film establishes Bennett's Marian as an object of courtly and chivalric love, and the scope of the impressive sets, lingering wide shots of gaily blowing banners, and intertitles grandly proclaiming that here the "lofty battlements of the castle look down upon the chivalry of England in all its glory," prompt viewers towards a feeling of nationalistic fervor commonly found in the matter of Britain. Into this Arthurian setting Marian is introduced, even before we meet the Earl of Huntingdon: the intertitles proclaim that "high above the clash of lance and shield in joust and tourney, the fairest maiden was chosen to reign for a day as the Queen of Love and Beauty." Despite this positioning as distant and remote, the lady on a pedestal—or in this case a decorative throne for a May queen—Marian emerges from a tent with a group of gaily clad women, their long sleeves, hair, and skirts fluttering in the wind. Marian smiles and gestures happily, explaining her girlish enthusiasm for her role and conveying brightly cheerful humility to the audience, who is quickly told that she is "Lady Marian Fitzwalter, from whose slim white hands would fall the chaplet of valor on the victorious knight." The audience, of course, knows that this knight will be the Earl of Huntingdon, despite the rapid introduction of Sir Guy of Gisbourne as a sexually menacing threat.

Marian, meanwhile, is situated within a community of women: one lady hands her the crown, and she crowns herself while another brings out a mirror for her to adjust the crown's fit on her hair, smilingly checking with the other ladies that all is in place. She is part of a supportive and loving community, despite the efforts of men to turn them against each other, first in courtship of Huntingdon and later, after Marian has secured Huntingdon's devotion, by demanding that the ladies betray Marian when interrogated by Prince John. Marian's continual placement within positive and healthy feminine communities provides her with emotional support—she does not have to bear the weight of representation as the sole woman that so many other Marians must endure—as well as furthering the hints that Marian is both lover and mother to the childish Huntingdon. The tourney scene establishes these threads of community: the ladies are enthusiastic and pleased for Marian's good fortune—there is no hint of jealousy, and they touch hands gently as they collect their veils (draped casually over arms or held, the easier to give to a favored knight) and depart for the viewing stands, and Marian for the dais upon which the Queen, as iconic figure of untouchable beauty, will watch. This community is dissolved when Sir Guy approaches her, roughly gathering up a loose end of the veil draped over her left arm and declaring in an expository intertitle, "Your veil for a favor, fair lady, that you may see it worn in victory." Marian coolly and silently rebuffs him, turning to signal to a lady in waiting—raising right her hand, finger extended, to appear very much a statue of grace and judgment—and handing over the veil to an attendant, who quickly departs as Marian turns her back to ascend her flower-strewn dais, her long train flaring beautifully behind her as she climbs. Bennett's switch from girlish and slightly naïve camaraderie with fellow ladies to cool and remote statue in the face of Sir Guy's overly hasty request is impressive, and reminds the viewer that Marian is more icon than woman in this moment. Here, she is the Queen of Love and Beauty, the embodiment of chivalric courtly love and representative of all such ladies: untouchable but expected to grant her favor once to the exemplary knight.

Marian's introduction as an object of chivalric adoration thrusts her into the game of courtly love, where a lady is expected to select a knight and he to adore her, perform feats of arms to impress her, and engage in a softly romantic courtship. Though this brings the man into the larger community, it isolates the woman in service of masculine obsession. The adored lady is less woman or person than museum object: despite the apparent power women hold in courtly love, Marian is trapped within the social script that means a good lady is only suited to the good knight—her rejection of Sir Guy signals this fact, while also displaying the only means of dissent she has available to her. She can only say no once before a knight's persistence would begin to menace her reputation and honor. Likewise, she can only say yes once, since the value of her love is in its rarity and singularity, and her willingness to say yes to Huntingdon is signaled through her anxiety for his safety. Tension and expectation are crafted through Marian's uncertainty—the audience is cued to concern by her facial expressions as she watches, clutching her hands and twisting a ring in concern—and then validated by her enthusiastic body language, arms up and out in sympathetic victory.

The work Marian does is emotional and is typical of the cinematic Marians who will follow: she directs the audience as effectively as the intertitles, using her expressive face and body language to direct our interpretation of Huntingdon's martial experience. Her enthusiasm for his victory seems nearly at odds with her position as the Queen of Love and Beauty, though it is familiar to us after her introduction in the midst of equally expressive ladies, all of whom touched hands and arms in delicate feminine solidarity. The language of touch is exceptionally expressive in silent film, and Bennett's enthusiasm ensures audiences will not see Fairbank's showboating as vainglorious, but rather a spontaneous overflow of boyish energy. This is typical "women's work"—emotional, and unrecognized, but absolutely vital in ensuring the correct masculine message is conveyed. That message, of course, is that the Earl is a Lancelot: strong, favored by the king, and envied by the potential usurper who also covets his woman, largely via his surrogate Sir Guy. Marian's role as supporting object to the Earl's personhood is demonstrated when he fails to recognize or validate the interpretive work of her reactions: when King Richard orders him to accept the victor's crown from Marian, who the camera captures sitting on her throne demurely and sweetly looking off to one side, he shudders and in an intertitle begs, "Exempt me, sire. I am afeared of women."[10]

Marian's work thus shifts from support to contrast: she is woman to his boy, adult to his child, and calm to his fear. Richard has to shove the Earl forward as Marian sweeps to the front of her dais, and Marian's attempts to crown Huntingdon are thwarted by his nervous fidgeting, She purses her lips, clearly taken aback by behavior that she cannot sort into the social script that she is following and which the Earl's immaturity ensures he does not even recognize. When she does get the crown on his head, she raises a hand and proclaims his victory. The Earl skitters backwards at her gestures—feminine and statuesque, Bennett's resemblance to an Edmund Leighton painting like "The Accolade" is unmistakable—and slides down the dais, backing away from Marian only to be surrounded by a bevy of women offering their veils to him. With the community of women dividing into individuals in competition, Marian disappears from the narrative.

The narrative does not return to Marian until Richard asks the Earl, "Why hast thou not a maid?," Rather than allowing Huntingdon to put off the matter, Richard pulls him forward and renews the individual competition among women, offering, "A castle and lands to the maid who wins him." This has the effect of centering relentlessly heteronormative expectations for romance in terms of conquest and contest, pitting the women against each other. It also monetizes love and courtship, which follows from a love-economy in which romantic partners are won along with substantial fiscal security. Marian is too shy to approach the Earl, and this reluctance—indeed, "properly" modest behavior—means that she is alone when the drunk Prince John seizes her and throws her at Sir Guy. Her struggle to escape catches the Earl's eye and he rushes to rescue her (his crowd of suitors following behind), confronting Prince John on the castle battlements as Marian crouches fearfully against a crenellation. Nollen, describing this moment, observes that "material borrowed from the 19th-century tales is merged with typical 1920s romantic twaddle,"[11] but this does a disservice to Marian's story: from the growing hope for the Earl's romantic interest, signaled by Bennett when her back is to Fairbanks and her face to the camera, to the gently ecstatic expressions as the Earl kisses the tips of her sleeves and the hem of her veil, Marian's reactions to the Earl's attention are conveying the restraints she must operate under. She cannot express interest herself; she can only respond to his overtures, and even then her behavior must be restrained—Bennett-as-Marian several times visibly reins herself back, twining her fingers together in various configurations and jerking her arms down to 'properly' clasp her hands in front of her body. This restraint could be read as gently luring the skittish Earl toward suitably heterosexual romantic behaviors, but the beaming smile Marian gives him as the scene ends indicates instead that Marian is blocked by expectations for feminine behavior (be quiet, be modest, don't pursue him) that go beyond managing the Earl.

These behavior expectations do, however, allow Marian to challenge Prince John's reign of terror: she implores him to "have mercy on the people of England," thereby placing herself on Prince John's list of potential dissidents by acting as mediatrix. Her next step is to send a secret message to Huntingdon, conveying the peril to England's people but also the sexual threat to the women in the castle.[12] Huntingdon is the exceptional hero, the character whose story is central to the film's plot, but his exceptionality continually reinforces Marian's position as passive damsel in distress and unable to take independent action beyond her own survival. She can flee the castle, but only after the other ladies urge her towards escape as Prince John advances. This community of women enables them to take collective action: the ladies deliberately delay Prince John, for when he demands to know where she has gone the women disdainfully turn their backs and scornfully maintain their silence. However, the community of women fades from sight after the lady-in-waiting helps Marian fake her own death, and the story shifts from crusade-themed chivalric romance to a typical Robin Hood tale where Marian is functionally a non-presence except to be a damsel in distress for Robin to gallantly save and later marry, cementing his growth from boy to man.

In contrast to the Marian of the 1922 silent film, the Marian (Olivia de Havilland) of the Technicolor classic *The Adventures of Robin Hood* (1938) is sharp-tongued and unafraid to speak her mind. However, like her predecessor, this Marian is equally constrained by a social script that binds women's behaviors severely, though her Robin (Errol Flynn) does not treat her with the distant adoration of a courtly lover. Instead, our first introduction to Marian is in an elaborate feast scene, where she is the only woman present at the high table—other women alternate with men at the low table but none speak or rise to salute Prince John when he is introduced as the "only true defender of the Norman spirit." John further distances Marian (and any woman) from the company of men when he says, "Well, this is what we Normans like. Good food, good company, and a beautiful woman to flatter me. Ey, Lady Marian?" She cannot answer and can only smile winsomely. John's comment is not presented as "evil": he says it cheerfully, and all the characters present agree, representing an instance of casual misogyny that audiences barely register. Whether or not it is noticed, however, it still exists—and defines a woman's purpose as decoration (for male eyes) and to perform verbal (male) ego-stroking. Marian's first words, therefore, must fit this behavioral model—she must be witty but ultra feminine, and therefore cannot actually respond in the affirmative or negative without drawing attention to the fact that he has established that she is an art-object. It is no coincidence that Prince John consequently asks her a series of light questions and refuses to give her a conversational opportunity to answer. She can only smile and tilt her head in response to his first question and smile again when he asks if the trip from London was worthwhile to "see what stout fellows" are in the crown's service in Nottingham. Not until he begins to point to the virtues of a particular man (Sir Guy) does Marian have an opportunity to speak. But given the context, she must speak as a woman, which neomedievalism continually interprets as relentlessly inferior, valuable only for her marriage-potential or as the love interest (and thus inevitably weakness) of the hero.

Neomedievalism also demands that the lady be a visual spectacle: her body is constantly on display, and de Havilland's costumes reveal only her face and hands, though they do show off her figure. Despite this concealing costume, Marian is still the subject of masculine gazes. I would argue that she is well aware of this attention and deeply uncomfortable with it. When Robin bursts into the feast, she tenses and sits stiffly, keeping her eyes on him at all times until Prince John, halfway through a short speech, says Robin's name. Only then does Marian break her gaze and look to John; her shoulders stay slightly tensed the entire time, a contrast to her posture when speaking to John of her potential marriage to the unsuitable Sir Guy. The uncomfortable body language begins when Robin enters the scene, and after Guy and Robin begin to threaten each other verbally she interrupts and stands in an attempt to leave the situation: a classic flight response in the face of danger, with the added factor that as a woman she must seek permission—which is denied—to leave.

Olivia de Havilland as Maid Marian in the 1938 film *The Adventures of Robin Hood.*

The escape attempt redirects Robin's attention to her. Marian is still standing when she is formally introduced to Robin; as she sits, he doffs his cap and sweeps a bow, and offers a pleasant comment. Her disdainful response might be rude, but also offered from an unsafe position she does not wish to occupy. Robin, however, fixates on rudeness and ignores context when he punishes her: he speaks directly to John while staring at Marian, tsking at her, sweeping his eyes down and up her body—a casual act of possession and demonstration of the male gaze that every woman is familiar with in real life but is startling to see in cinema, where every action is chosen for deliberate effect—and says, "What a pity her manners don't match her looks, your highness." Robin is saying that Marian has failed her primary duty: though she is beautiful to his sight, she is not flattering to his ego. Even though John articulated these standards as part of Norman identity, Robin is claiming them for all men by his actions. Robin is reinforcing that a woman's role is universal, regardless of whether she is Norman or Saxon. It is no wonder then that Marian's look hardens rapidly into one of scorn and dislike, and she looks to disagree with him: moments later, Robin articulates his objections to Norman occupation, taxation, and abuses toward Saxons, so Marian says sharply, "you speak treason!" Once again, he sweeps his eyes from breasts to face, before calmly replying, "Fluently." This exchange is one of the most quoted of the film, yet the dialog is accompanied by a standard masculine power assessment and dismissal of a woman's body alongside her verbal objection.

The focus on Marian as woman, and thus object to be possessed or controlled, creates an ideal opportunity for the film to root two narrative arcs in sexual tensions. The first is the rivalry between Guy and Robin over a woman, which will only intensify as Marian is arrested—the most serious charge, of course, is a veiled accusation of miscegenation. The second is a dynamic and changing relationship between Marian and Robin, where they begin as enemies and move to lovers, a common narrative trope.[13] However, this trope is also fundamentally misogynistic: when men and women are initially enemies, the woman is inevitably mistreated, belittled, and dismissed by the man before she becomes worthy of his love by changing her perspective. The trope demonstrates that mistreating women, objectifying them, and speaking over their heads to other men is the beginning of an epic love story. In real life, this sort of behavior is part of an abusive pattern; the narrative, however, glosses such acts as the beginning of a true love story.

Marian's own gaze is never permitted to generate action, except to indicate feminine submission (in context, consent) to romance. This is in line with Laura Mulvey's description of the unidirectional and appropriative nature of the cinematic male gaze (which includes, of course, the camera). Marian is often pictured staring helplessly upward: for example at the outlaws who do not wish to believe she is splitting from her Norman kin to help rescue Robin before he is hanged; at the window of her dungeon cell as the grand action set piece of the film rages above her; at Robin before she drops her gaze to his lips in the forest, apparently inviting a kiss. Moreover, Marian is aware of this gaze: her smile first appears as a means of keeping powerful men happy, for example Prince John in the initial minutes of the feast, or Gisbourne as they ride through the forest. Her smile is a method of retaining her primary social function as decorative exemplar of femininity and desirable marriage object, and is simultaneously a signal to the audience that her feelings are genuine while remaining a narrative method to keep the tone of the film light.[14]

Indeed, her entire body is continually interpreted through masculine eyes in the service of equally masculine goals. The Sheriff hatches the plot to have her present the golden arrow at the tournament in the first place after he observes that Marian seemed less antagonistic to Robin at the end of the forest feast scene. The feast begins with Marian visibly uncomfortable, continually leaning away from Robin though he has seated her at his side. She refuses the foods he repeatedly offers—enormous slabs of meat that the film consistently portrays offering and accepting as peculiarly masculine forms of hospitality—and he will not take no for an answer, which the film excuses because he is the hero and she is his love interest. Furthermore, her bodily integrity and control are continually mocked; when she refuses food or says she is not hungry, Robin mocks her, and when she finally does begin to eat, he laughs loudly at the reversal of the position he forced her to take. He manipulates her into softening her stance through careful use of compliments designed to elicit positive responses: when she demands to know why Robin lives "like an animal," Robin takes her to see the suffering and displaced Saxon refugees and observes that they are "hardly an inspiring sight for such pretty eyes as yours," while claiming that her dawning understanding of his cause is reward enough for his heroic actions. The Sheriff's decision to interpret Marian's body language entirely in the context of predicting Robin's actions—she seemed friendly (or friendlier), so Robin will obviously place himself in danger—fundamentally robs Marian of any form of agency: she is a conduit to Robin because, despite the absurdity of the tournament idea (an observation Guy obligingly voices for the audience), the narrative shows the Sheriff's assessment is ultimately correct. Marian's trembling hands at the archery tournament nearly give away the fact that Robin has arrived because, a scene after the feast, the audience has all the knowledge to be certain that Guy's observation means he has made the connection between Marian's anxiety and Robin's presence.

The films of 1922 and 1938 laid the groundwork for every television series and movie that followed. Marian's presentation in these films of the early 20th century have remained touchstones. These films, despite touches of genuine medievalism in costuming, sets, even the contextual framework for the stories, read as neomedievalism when Marian's character is isolated and analyzed. The neomedieval is typically itself a paradox: as KellyAnn Fitzpatrick so aptly observes, "neomedievalism manages all at once to create a 'hyperreality' more real than reality itself and to carve out its living in the furtive and ravenous consumption of mass-produced commodities, yet also floats disembodied above a seas of already constituted academic disciplines waiting to be formed into something solid and punishable/ten(ur)able."[15] Neomedievalism presents Marian's suffering as so real that it must be relegated to the past for audiences to enjoy the story, a pattern that carries into two major films produced in the wake of civil rights and women's rights.

"It's not a woman's place to interfere": Monica Evans (1973) and Audrey Hepburn (1976)

The Marians of the post–World War II period represent a fascinating negotiation between the representation of Marian (drawing on the films of 1922 and 1938) and significant post-war social revolutions. By the 1970s, women in Robin Hood film and television were represented by Marian, and usually Marian alone; if secondary characters exist, they are foils to Marian. Neomedievalism offers filmmakers an opportunity to address tensions regarding women and womanly behavior, and the Evans and Hepburn Marians exemplify masculine attempts to control unruly women's bodies.

The Walt Disney Company animated film *Robin Hood* (1973) contains two significant female characters who shows feminine duality in action. The slim and highborn vixen Marian is a true lady: sweet, beautiful, well-mannered, slightly politically naïve, and sexually innocent. Her servant, the portly hen Lady Kluck, is designed to contrast Marian's positive qualities: Kluck is caustic, homely, crude and mannish, politically astute, sexually experienced, and strongly implied to desire a cross-species romance with Little John (a bear). This bifurcation overtly embraces the virgin-whore dichotomy. Since virginity is the status most male characters desire to eliminate, Marian is acted upon and coveted for her value as a bride, further cementing Marian's status as a damsel in distress. The secondary woman (if one is included) is usually a servant and will have considerable agency and initiative ... to hold the line until Robin arrives to save the day.

The Disney film is the definitive Robin Hood for at least two generations of now-adult viewers and scores of youth. Once, *The Adventures of Robin Hood* (the 1938 film or the 1950s television series) dominated the childhood memories of Robin Hood scholars and casual enthusiasts alike; the 1973 Disney film has rapidly become the nostalgic anchor for viewers born in the 1970s or later. Its popularity will linger: Disney's marketing strategies and brand-recognition as child-friendly and appropriate ensures this success. Anyone who has taught Robin Hood materials in a 21st-century classroom knows that students continually default to the little fox and his lovely vixen as their internal portraits of Robin and Marian. This means that Marian's passivity, helplessness, and complete configuration as love object—the film introduces her as she sits in her rooms, sighing over a poster of

Robin, wistfully asking Kluck if he might recall her fondly—are fully internalized archetypes.

On the surface, *Robin and Marian* (1976) appears to break this pattern of virginal
passivity: uniquely, this film deals with the titular characters in middle age rather than
vigorous greenwood youth. As Sherron Lux aptly observes, the film's break with tradition
allows a fascinating and nuanced examination of "the contradictions surrounding love,
aging, and outlawry."[16] Audrey Hepburn's Marian has worked through the pain of being
abandoned by Sean Connery's Robin, for she tells him that she'd contemplated suicide:
"When you left, I thought I'd die. I even tried. I went out into the woods not far from
camp, and lay down by a stream and cut myself," and when suicide failed, she discarded
her past life by taking on a new name as a nun. Marian's former obsession with Robin is
not a healthy basis for a renewed relationship with a man who, when told that Marian
lives in the abbey, tells his (male) friends, "Lovely girl. Haven't thought of her in years."
Marian is happy with her new life, and she does genuine good in her role as the leader
of Kirklees Abbey. The viewer must wonder if a portion of that good work is to poison
Robin (and herself) at the end of the film. Her actions stop Robin's foolhardy and destructive rivalry with the Sheriff; Marian is further spared the pain of a life without Robin.

Audrey Hepburn as Marian in the 1976 film *Robin and Marian*.

However, despite the equal billing and closer-to-equal screen time Hepburn received, *Robin and Marian* is characterized by misogyny and mistreatment of women—mostly Marian herself. The film sets the stage for such treatment by its opening sequence: King Richard burns a castle filled with women and children. Though Robin objects to Richard's order, Robin's own treatment of Marian is little more advanced: Robin's behavior utterly and directly destroys Marian's life and works. Lux and Nollen both observe that the film's title was originally meant to be *The Death of Robin Hood*, but the change implies that Marian has equal (if secondary) importance. She does not: the film's tag line is "Love is the greatest adventure of all," but the adventure is only for men. For Marian, love is destruction of all she has built after her attempted suicide. She is a woman whose principles demand that she consciously and deliberately defy King John's order that all clergy of rank depart England.[17] She accepts, even embraces, imprisonment for her civil disobedience; such principles would hardly compromise for past (and painful) love. Yet that is precisely what happens, despite Marian literally being dragged screaming into a second association with Robin. Marian's characterization (in any film) has never been internally consistent within the film or developed for her character's own interests because she is *always* prefigured as Robin's love interest.

Neomedievalism in *Robin and Marian* attempts to elide the fact that Marian's capitulation is painful. Robin behavior is deeply misogynistic, and arguably the only reason audiences do not immediately perceive them as such is due to neomedievalism and presentism applied to Connery's performance. Film is historically (and presently) profoundly misogynistic, as Mulvey demonstrates, and *Robin and Marian* is no exception. Robin's actions toward Marian are classical examples of physical abuse and emotional manipulation. When Robin and his friends first ride into the courtyard of Kirklees Abbey, Marian is treating a sick woman in the tower keep, an image that establishes her as compassionate and skilled. At Robin's hail, Marian bellows from the window, "You there. What in hell do you want?" Robin cannot seem to accept Marian has changed: he engages in a behavior termed "negging," commonly practiced by modern-day anti-woman "pickup artists." Negging is practiced through continual insults from a position of (masculine) power: it presupposes masculine power and punches down by deliberately lowering a victim's social status and internal self-value, until she is pliable and agrees to sex because she believes she will never find better than her abuser. Robin begins negging Marian before she has even fully left the tower: when he sees her nun's habit, he exclaims, "Marian, what are you doing in that costume?" devaluing and insulting her vocation. Her response, "Living in it," does not refute his point; rather, it confirms his assessment. Moreover, Robin does not limit his objections to the spoken word: when Marian attempts to leave with the Sheriff in a peaceful and principled surrender as part of her systematic resistance to King John's unjust order, Robin physically yanks her away from the Sheriff, holding her back and restricting her movement. When reasoning fails to sway him, she shouts shrilly, "It's my life, Robin!" His reply, "You're a fool," accompanies mutual (though uneven) physical assault: she first ineffectively strikes his arm as he restrains her; he then physically assaults her, knocking her unconscious with a single punch to the jaw and slinging her body over the back of his horse.

Marian is a devoted nun and dedicated pacifist. However, her abduction by Robin destroys both these core elements of her identity. After Marian decides to remain with Robin—were the characters anyone but a predestined and traditional love-pairing, I assert that viewers would be trying Robin for assault, kidnaping, and emotional abuse—

she explains her efforts to split her personality from the Marian Robin had known. Her explanation culminates in a nearly manic decision to break her vow of chastity, for it represents a final destruction of her new self and return to the old. She begs Robin to "love me. Make me cry," which is an exceptionally disturbing thing for a woman to say to a man whose desertion had led her to attempted suicide in the past. After taking up with Robin again, Marian is also willing to break her resolve against violence, and is willing to kill: when Robin is severely wounded in his foolish confrontation with the Sheriff and has been brought back to Kirklees Abbey, she pours out a lethal dose of painkillers and overdoses first herself and then Robin.

The film ends as Robin, assisted by the loyal Little John, shoots an arrow out the window to mark their burial spot. The camera is forced to engage in a series of rapid cuts between Robin's struggle and close-up of Marian's face because Little John's position is difficult to acknowledge: he is seated between them, with his back to Marian. The cinematic effort to make the final moments of the film "romantic" by focusing on the two lovers while ignoring the intruding body of John parallels the efforts an overwhelmingly masculine culture makes to include women. A film about death and abuse is rebranded as a story about love, and the destruction of a woman's life work for a man's childish desire to relive his wild outlaw youth is justified as an examination of aging desire and reconciliation of the body's limits. In both film and culture, men do not have to change; women are forced to accept the new designations. Lux observes that Marian's actions are a final grasp at "agency in desperation … but agency nonetheless" that, I contend, she *only* possesses at the end of her life: though this film is a break in the traditional focus on youth, it does, I believe, show that the only control Marian has in cinema is over the end of her own biological life.[18]

"For a thousand, I would turn you in myself": Mary Elizabeth Mastrantonio (1991), Uma Thurman (1991), Amy Yasbeck (1993) and Cate Blanchett (2010)

The bulk of Marian's cinematic history follows a deeply disappointing pattern: though she is usually established as strong and independent, her strength is always deliberately broken or negated by the narrative, usually as a sacrifice for Robin's character development. Robin Hood productions of the 1980s to the present do not change the pattern. What does change, however, is the manner in which Marian's early strength is presented, a development which I assert could permit audiences to recognize the long-standing pattern the character endures.

The Marians of the 1990s represent different aspects of third wave feminism, filtered through neomedieval Robin Hood cinema. One film was a typical summer blockbuster: the neomedieval Kevin Costner vehicle *Robin Hood: Prince of Thieves* was designed, marketed, and performed as a Hollywood blockbuster and remains immensely popular decades later. Feminism in *Prince of Thieves* is conservative, and, I will argue, actively undermined. *Prince of Thieves* also inspired rapid cinematic pushback in the form of Mel Brooks's satiric *Robin Hood: Men in Tights* (1993). Nineteen ninety-one's competing film, titled simply *Robin Hood* and staring Patrick Bergin and Uma Thurman, was smaller in scope, budget, and ambition: the historically weighted film was pulled from consideration and theatrical release by 20th Century–Fox pictures in the face of the Costner juggernaut. As Lux observes, Thurman's Marian is unusually successful in asserting her own agency: she avoids forced marriage to a much older man by disguising herself as "Martin," cross-dressing and cropping her hair to join the unpredictable and deeply violent outlaw band. The film ends as Marian declares "she is a person—her own person" in her wedding vows to Robin to trigger the film's end as "the sun comes out, at last."[19] Despite this success for Marian and a persistent afterlife as a staple of public broadcasting, the Thurman film is a notable dead-end because it was not released theatrically.

The 1990s Marian most likely to be remembered by the general public is *Prince of Thieves*' Mary Elizabeth Mastrantonio. Her introduction appears to be exceptionally feminist: she asserts her own agency, fights Robin Hood to a stand-still, and then defuses a confrontation with the evil Sir Guy while retaining her lands and dignity. However, analysis of her introduction demonstrates that the film is deploying a harmful neomedieval interpretation of feminism that will encourage Marian to be put in her place later in the film. When Robin returns from crusade to find his home burned, he seeks out Marian for an explanation and to fulfill his vow to her brother that he will keep her safe. Marian's servant Sarah assumes her identity in the initial meeting, forcing Robin to visibly swallow back his shock at her broad girth and homely features. His undeniably sexist reaction is played for comedic effect, as well as allowing audiences access to the secret knowledge that this woman is not Marian. After all, any audience familiar with Hollywood sexism knows immediately that overweight or ugly women are never the love interest— and Sarah is presented as both. Robin's determination and heroic potential are problematically tested through the crucible of confronting Sarah's body: when she demands that he leave, Robin refuses and says, "I'm sworn to protect you, my lady." Costner's delivery of the line, moments after the revelation of "Marian's" large body, is rueful; the implicit disgust in his voice links Robin's heroism to his reluctant yet repulsed acceptance of her body and coupling it with his disregard for her agency. The film frames Robin's reaction as context for heroism: Robin is willing to protect a fat, ugly woman against her will, because her brother established a deathbed masculine contract with Robin. Marian further tests Robin's resolve by prodding him with a sword to enforce Sarah's command that he leave the keep, provoking a fight. Their battle is interesting: despite losing her sword early, Marian proves adept with a dagger and Robin must

Mary Elizabeth Mastrantonio as Maid Marian in the 1991 film *Prince of Thieves*.

snatch a hunting trophy of antlers from the wall to defend himself. Once Marian shatters his shield, Robin slams her into a wall; he is unable to force her to release her dagger until he holds her hand over a burning taper. Her feminine yelp of pain startles him, and he fumbles off her mask to stare at her in stunned disbelief until she knees him in the groin—just in time for his companions to arrive, finding Robin rolling in uniquely masculine pain and Marian visibly realizing that Robin is, in fact, himself.

In the following scene, Mastrantonio's Marian is firm with her boundaries and eloquently critiques Robin's abrogation of his responsibilities. She refuses to be baited by Robin's insinuation that despite the plundering of the shire she has held her lands through some unspoken betrayal of right behavior—as she says, "I give [the Sheriff and Gisborne] no reason to take them," reminding Robin that as a cousin to the king it is her duty to care for the people, and as a woman she occupies an infinitely more delicate position than he can even imagine. The sequence establishes Marian as reasonable and logical, far more so than Robin, whose impulses are emotional and centered on masculine pride; as proof, the narrative allows her to soften her position when Robin argues that his time in prison has matured his outlook. Despite this compassion, she does not abide foolishness or false pride: as Gisborne's men close in, Robin still insists that he must protect her. Marian demonstrates wit, nerve, and dedication to her people why loudly accusing Robin of horse theft; the volume of her accusation forces Robin to flee in time to escape.

However, the film does not sustain this version of Marian. Instead she is reconfigured as a romance object and thus a pawn in a sexual-political competition between Robin and the Sheriff. When Marian and Sarah visit Robin's refugee village in Sherwood, the sight of Robin bathing in a waterfall demonstrates to Marian that he is no longer the boy she knew in childhood. They bond over their mutual patristic responsibilities and establish an implicit romantic relationship. Immediately upon her return, the Sheriff (Alan Rickman) captures her as a bargaining chip to use against Robin. The Sheriff also sees the value in marriage to the king's cousin, and expresses sexual desire for Marian specifically, a threat that becomes an active on-screen rape attempt averted only by the PG-13 rating. The Marian who begins the film in armor and fighting the hero to a standstill ends the film screaming in abject terror, rescued from horrific gendered violence in a battle between men that she watches from the sidelines. She is a literal damsel in distress; unlike her cinematic sisters, this Marian cannot escape the unwanted marriage and is assaulted in the progress. The film takes clear and careful measures to absolve Marian of guilt over her own rape, through an elaborate process that is arguably relishing the gendered violence: from screams and struggle, to physical restraints, to Mortianna's declaration that if the Sheriff rapes Marian now a son will result. Every component of the scene renders Marian an abject victim: it works to punish her for her independence at the start of the movie. The Marian of *Prince of Thieves* is thus a strong, canny woman whose strength is violently used against her through highly gendered assaults and threats, and the camera glories in its voyeuristic privilege to watch her assault. *Prince of Thieves* fits the established pattern of establishing intriguing and strong cinematic Marians with the goal of breaking them in service of Robin's motivation, and the film distinguishes itself by adding an unpleasant twist of graphic near-rape.

Prince of Thieves represents, I contend, a moment in which systematic sexual violence against Marian became an acceptable topic to explore openly in visual formats, particularly cinema and television. The discreet and systematic violence—normalized violence—against women introduced in early films was intensified by the domestic abuse threading through *Robin and Marian*. The two 1991 films both tease out the threat of forced marriage by examining implications through masculine and feminine responses, establishing women's reactions to the threats as narratively affective.[20] The Mel Brooks satire film *Robin Hood: Men in Tights* (1993) responds to many of the innovations and changes *Prince of Thieves* introduced in an effort to erase *Prince of Thieves* from the cinematic tradition, while simultaneously privileging an idealized reading of *The Adventures of Robin Hood* (1938). *Men in Tights* features a Marian (Amy Yasbeck) whose sexual future is overtly controlled by a chastity belt that both Robin and the Sheriff battle to open. Notably, her sexuality is intensively heterosexual and centered upon the potential for penetrative vaginal intercourse: this is played for comedic effect to de-intensify the social conditions that enable this centering. The visuals of the Brooks film advocate for a return to the tights-and-tunics costuming of Fairbanks and Flynn and Disney, costuming and ideology that *Robin and Marian* and *Prince of Thieves* both eschewed. The film is intensely neomedieval, in the sense that it deals with modern issues of race, religion, the history of women's rights within the context of a patently ahistorical "medieval" setting. *Men in Tights* has many valuable contributions to the cinematic Robin Hood tradition, but also centers and endorses an insidiously attractive neomedieval misogyny.

The 2010 Russell Crowe vehicle *Robin Hood*, directed by Ridley Scott and co-staring Cate Blanchett as Lady Marion Loxley, offers a partial correction to *Men in Tights* and the 1991 films. Marian is central: Blanchett's Marion teaches Crowe's Robin Longstride (a peasant impersonating her dead husband) the skills, empathy, and motivation he needs to become Robin Hood. Crowe's Longstride is initially unlikable and though his narrative arc is to learn to become Robin Hood instead of Longstride, his primary motivation at the start of the film is for his own safety. He permanently assumes Sir Robert Loxley's identify—along with Loxley's wife—because Sir Walter, Robert's father, determines that Marion (as a woman) will never be able to peacefully hold the estate without a man to serve as the public face. This is an example of neomedievalism: modern stereotypes hold that medieval women could not hold property nor inherit, so neomedieval films take this presumption as fact to glory in the marginalization of women over the duration of the movie.

Blanchett's Marion is a deeply accomplished woman: her archery skills, determination, and caring manage to fill the gap in the narrative where Robin's heroics would routinely fit. However, despite Marion's successes, the typical cinematic pattern reappears: the strong woman is punished and put in her (gendered) place as subservient to the hero. In the film's final act, Robin leads a united English army against a French invasion force landing at Dover; clad in armor that evokes Joan of Arc, Marion brings the small Loxley force to the battlefield. She is struck down, providing Robin the opportunity for hypermasculine heroics against his enemy—and a striking visual portrait as Robin carries the armored Marion out of the surf in his arms, bridal-style, her hair streaming like a banner by his side. Marion's competence fails; her armored cross-dressing is rapidly punished; she is "returned" to her domestic secondary role, as Longstride becomes Robin Hood. The audience never again sees outside the context of romance and heteronormative gender roles, for the film ends in a romanticized domestic greenwood idyll. The visual tone and language of the film shift massively in the final scene: grey colors, muck, and grit disappear into a luminescent and vibrantly lush greenwood. As Robin leads a group of men to the outlaw encampment, audiences are shown a pack of feral forest children being domesticated under Marion's caring hands. The film ends as Robin and Marion smile at each other and embrace; the final shot pulls back as Robin picks Marion up, elevating her head far above his own.

In 2018, Eve Hewson played Marian in Otto Bathurst's *Robin Hood*, featuring Taron Egerton as Robin Hood and Jamie Foxx as Yahya/John. The 2018 Marian is a woman of her time: a political organizer in the vein of Women's March activists, good at her job, intelligent. She enjoys sequential monogamous romantic relationships with first Robin and then Will Scarlet. Despite the film's attempts to objectify her (her first on screen appearance is as a masked horse thief displaying remarkable cleavage) and Robin's best efforts to reduce her impact to love interest (he pines after her and vomits when he realizes she has accepted his "death" and found love elsewhere), she maintains her autonomy, resisting her romantic partners' attempts to tell her what to think and how to act. This Marian is carefully kept as a supporting character. She is menaced with sexual violence, but she responds fiercely and refuses the authority of the mercenaries who casually threaten rape; her work as an organizer and activist is inherently supportive, and she encourages Robin to maintain his double identity as the guerrilla outlaw "The Hood" and junior representative in the Sheriff's strange parliament. Hewson's Marian disrupts the pattern by refusing to play the game, but she doesn't dispute the game's existence— much like the early ballads recognize the problems of corrupt officials but utterly fail to consider that the entire system is at fault. The Hewson performance has potential, but the potential fades as the narrative rushes to an explosive climax, setting the stage for a sequel that will likely never be made.[21]

The efforts of the 2010 film to reposition Marion in a "proper" domestic sphere are inexplicable from a director like Ridley Scott, whose reputation as a filmmaker was established on the shoulders of women characters whose arcs are narratively similar to male characters. However, these choices are in line with the pattern of neomedieval cinematic treatments of Maid Marian. This neomedievalism binds onto the significant fiscal concerns driving characterization in blockbuster summer cinema. I propose that the continual efforts to remove or negate the parity that Marian consistently seeks to achieve are directly traced to neomedievalism underwritten by fiscal panic: film producers are finally acknowledging the significant financial rewards women and feminist men give to new versions of traditional stories, but producers also fear alienating a core audience of misogynistic viewers who expect, even demand, neomedieval women behave according to sexist stereotypes. Films that are simultaneously liberal and conservative like the 2018 Bathurst production satisfy neither pole, despite their potential. The films I have surveyed in this essay first establish Marian as a strong and capable woman within the context of the production's own cultural moment—but then *every* production finds some way to reduce her to the ultra-feminine cliché of damsel in distress.

Neomedievalism traffics in easily recognizable and overly simplified tropes, and neomedievalism can be found threading through the nostalgia inherent in any Robin Hood story. This neomedievalism views women as ladies and damsels (distressed or otherwise) first; women are active characters with interior lives, depth of dialog, and independent arcs second—which usually means not at all. Robin Hood's story is prioritized and retold infinitely at the expense of Marian. As Laura Mulvey noted, the "fascination of film is reinforced by pre-existing patterns of fascination already at work within the individual subject and the social foundations that have moulded him"[22]: neomedieval Robin Hood films give us what we want to see and hear, and until we decide we want to see Marian break free of Robin, she will be struck down again and again.

NOTES

1. Laura Mulvey, "Visual Pleasure and Narrative Cinema," in *Film Theory and Criticism: Introductory Readings*, eds. Leo Braudy and Marshall Cohen (New York: Oxford University Press, 1999), pp. 833–844.

2. Sherron Lux, "And the 'Reel' Maid Marian?," in *Robin Hood in Popular Culture: Violence, Transgression, and Justice*, ed. Thomas Hahn (Cambridge: D.S. Brewer, 2000), p. 152.

3. Stephen Knight, *Reading Robin Hood: Content, Form, and Reception in the Outlaw Myth* (Manchester: Manchester University Press), pp. 187–188.

4. KellyAnn Fitzpatrick, "(Re)producing (Neo)medievalism," *Studies in Medievalism* 20 (2001): 11. See also Pam Clements, "Authenticity" in *Medievalism: Key Critical Terms*, eds. Richart Utz and Elizabeth Emory (Cambridge: Boydell and Brewer, 2014), pp. 23–24.

5. Lorraine K. Stock and Candace Gregory-Abbott, "The 'Other' Women of Sherwood: The Construction of Difference and Gender in Cinematic Treatments of the Robin Hood Legend," in *Race, Class, and Gender in "Medieval" Cinema*, eds. Lynn T. Ramsey and Tison Pugh (New York: Palgrave Macmillan, 2003), p. 199.

6. See Kevin J. Harty, *The Reel Middle Ages: American, Western and Eastern European, Middle Eastern, and Asian Films About Medieval Europe* (Jefferson, NC: McFarland, 1999). Many amateur and enthusiast web sites also provide comprehensive lists of early film productions.

7. The characters of the Robin Hood tradition occupy a peculiar status as adaptations which continually self-reference and have little connection to "original" materials. Consequently, risk is minimized because the material is exceptionally flexible. See Thomas Leitch, "Adaptations without Sources: The Adventures of Robin Hood," *Literature/Film Quarterly* 36.1 (2008): 21–30.

8. Mulvey's reading is psychoanalytic. J.R.R. Tolkien outlines the functions and limitations of "secondary belief" (audience acceptance of the narrative world's implicit laws) in the seminal essay "On Fairy-Stories." See *Tolkien on Fairy-Stories*, eds. Verlyn Flieger and Douglas A. Anderson (London: HarperCollins, 2008).

9. The matter is urgent; activist historian sites including People of Color in European Art History (www.medievalpoc.tumblr.com/) and The Public Medievalist (www.publicmedievalist.com/) provide cogent descriptions of the consequences of unquestioned bigotry.

10. Fairbanks contributed to all elements of the production, and Scott Nollen observes caustically that "Fairbanks' writing style merely was an extension of his leaping, grinning, and arm-thrusting overacting technique." See *Robin Hood: A Cinematic History of the English Outlaw and His Scottish Counterparts* (Jefferson, NC: McFarland, 1999), p. 93.

11. Nollen, p. 93.

12. The note, "translated" from medieval script to a modern cursive hand, reads: "The people suffer and perish. The women of the castle hang their heads in shame. Intrigue and death lurk in every corner. Desperately my heart cries out to you. England is doomed." The shame felt by the women of the castle is clearly connected to the woman in the montage of John's evil deeds who is whipped (as her child clutches her skirts, for even more pathos) for refusing his sexual advances, as well as Guy's sinister bargain with John to possess Marian.

13. At the trial, Marian's various crimes are listed, and she is told she is a woman who has "betrayed her own Norman people"—when asked if she is ashamed of being a traitor to her race by falling in love with a Saxon, she neatly twists their framing from the sexual to the political: "Yes, I am, bitterly, but it's a shame that I'm a Norman after seeing the things that my fellow countrymen have done to England."

14. This use of her smile resonates for modern women, who frequently endure street harassment where (usually) men demand that (usually) women smile. A woman is far more likely to experience this demand, even from other women, because women's faces are considered public property.

15. Fitzpatrick, p. 11.

16. Lux, p. 154.

17. This subplot is an apparent narrative acceleration and simplification of John's conflict with Pope Innocent III, which historically resulted in John's excommunication and the interdiction of England in 1208.

18. Lux, p. 154. The 1980s and 1990s were rich in Robin Hood materials pushing genre boundaries and the conventions of the tradition: for a discussion of Marian's roles in popular novels published at the end of the century, see Evelyn M. Perry, "Maid Marian Made Possible," *The ALUN Review* 31.1 (2003): 37–47.

19. Lux, p. 156.

20. For a fascinating and insightful analysis examining the frustration many viewers feel with the Costner film in light of Regan-era treatment of women in business settings, see Lisa Schubert, "Managing a Multicultural Work Force in Robin Hood: Prince of Thieves," *The Centennial Review* 37. 3 (1993): 571–592.

21. The Bathurst film is considered a commercial failure, reportedly unable to recoup its production costs with box office returns. Ironically, the film's most used tagline may offer a glimpse into why it failed to thrive: "The legend you know. The story you don't" is quite close to the 2010 film's tagline ("The untold story behind the legend") and also demonstrates that whatever strange and wild story is on offer, nothing significant will change in the legend. Consequently, for all of the positives the Hewson Marian presents to viewers, she is ultimately a match to Taron Egerton's flavorless Robin Hood.

22. Mulvey, p. 833.

The Women of Fritz Lang's Medieval Epic, *The Nibelungen*; or, Two Queens and a Nazi

Donald L. Hoffman

Auteur, hack, meticulous craftsman, careless drudge, Communist, Nazi, progressive, reactionary, self-destructive tyrant, helpless victim of the Hollywood bureaucracy, perhaps no figure in cinematic history has aroused such passionate and opposed reactions among critics and audiences as Fritz Lang. His career took off with great fanfare when his German films swept the world in the early 1910s and '20s, and UFA had a real possibility to beat Hollywood as the center of the world's cinematic empire. But, after his notorious flight to America, as a consequence of a fraught (and possibly fraudulent) conversation with Goebbels, his career fell into periods of highs and lows, acclaim and scorn, that culminated in the highest measure of critical success afforded an artist in 1950s America, an inquisition before the House Un-American Activities Committee. This summons resulted in no prosecution, but was followed by an extended trip to Germany (and India) for a problematic return to and revision of his most ambitious early films, including a last look at Mabuse (his archetypal, Moriarty-like villain), and his Indian epics, *The Indian Tomb* and *The Tiger of Eschnapur*.[1] Significantly, he did not return to the great successes of his German period, *Metropolis*, *M*, and *The Nibelungen*. It is easy to imagine reasons why he might not wish to return to these projects, but the only one for which he provided an answer is *The Nibelungen*. Although, not addressed, he must also have been aware of the difficulty in post-war America of finding an audience eager to see a heroic German epic.

In the first quarter of the last century, however, at least in Germany, there was an audience eager for that sort of film. The reason for this readiness has, however, been the subject of much debate. One of the first and most influential discussions of this phenomenon was Siegfried Kracauer's *From Caligari to Hitler*.[2] Kracauer's brilliant thesis, which emerged shortly after Germany's defeat in World War II, was deeply influenced by the aftermath of guilt, despair, and disillusion. In this context, he reads all German film as foreshadowing and revealing the development of a pre–Fascist investment in developing a National Socialist ideology.[3] While Kracauer made a chilling and compelling case (that also had the benefit of being sufficiently anti–German to appeal to an American readership in the post-war world), his thesis involves the major flaw of reading history backwards, seeing the Weimar Republic as primarily a prologue to the horrors of the Nazi era. More recent critics, such as Heiko Suhr,[4] have criticized this ahistorical approach, while Anton Kaes resituates Lang in a historical context, and looks backward rather than forward situating early Weimar films in the collapse of the Wilhelmine Empire and the shock of Germany's defeat in World War I. His *Shell Shock Cinema: Weimar Culture and the Wounds of War* is a powerful refutation and revision of Kracauer's thesis.[5] Rather than reading Weimar film as Fascist propaganda *avant la lettre*, Kaes makes a deeply moving and compelling case for Weimar film as deriving from the trauma of loss. It is in this period of trauma that Kaes locates the origin of the famous monsters of such brilliant Weimar films as *The Golem: How He Came Into the World* (Wegener, 1920), *The Cabinet of Dr. Caligari* (Wiene, 1920), *Nosferatu* (Murnau, 1922), and Lang's own chilling creations, the arch-villain, Dr. Mabuse—in *Dr. Mabuse, Der Spieler* (2 parts, 1922) and *Das Testament von Dr. Mabuse* (1932–1933)—and the archetypal villain-victim, *M* (1931).[6]

As if to counter the "expressionist" distortion and existential anguish of the post-traumatic cinema, Lang chooses to offer a gift to the Germans, a recreation of a Germanic heroic age. Echoing the notorious dedication of the Reichstag by Kaiser Wilhelm in 1916, Lang offered a similar dedication—*dem Deutschen Volke zu eigen*—less than a decade later, to a defeated nation, in an attempt to encourage hope for the future by recalling the glories of the past. Unlike his wife, Thea (an early fan of Mahatma Gandhi), Lang had no interest in Nazi ideology, but considerable interest in mythic narratives and technical spectacles. At the outset, he was attracted by the visual challenges of the narrative (giants and dragons and dwarves), the architectural potential of the sets (mountains, caves, forests, and oceans), and the geometrical opportunities for both massive and intimate groupings in palaces, plains, and, above all, on stairs. It involved everything that appealed to Lang at the time. And it might even help to heal.

Much of this heroic nostalgia works for *Siegfried*,[7] despite its mournful ending. The history of Siegfried is a compilation of fragments pointing only vaguely towards a nonexistent archetype. Clues to that archetype, mainly names associated with the House of Gibich, recorded in the *Leges Burgundionum*,[8] establish a setting in the fifth to the sixth centuries in a period of Burgundian migrations westward with a civic center, assumed but not proven, to be the city of Worms. Other fifth-century chronicles record the defeat of the Burgundians by the Romans led by Aetius.[9] While Attila the Hun (d. 435) was active at this time, nothing links him to the Burgundian adventures, and his actual history bears little resemblance to the story of *The Nibelungenlied*'s Etzel. Brunhild and Siegfried are more thoroughly documented, though at least a century later, but those chronicles (Gregory of Tours' *Decem libri historiarum* and the *Chronicle Attributed to Fredegar* c. 660) contribute little to the narrative of *The Nibelungenlied*, although they do document the marriage of the daughter of the Visigothic King of Spain, Brunhildis, to the Burgundian King Sigibert, King of the Franks. The quarrel between Brunhildis and Fredegunda, after the death of Siegebert in 575, may have influenced the tale of the fatal rivalry between Brunhild and Kriemhild, although with roles reversed, in what became the classic version of the narrative.

The development of the narrative from the sixth century to the twelfth involved narratives and fragments of narratives transmitted orally in versions that can be only tentatively reconstructed. Early attempts to establish a text culminate in the last of the complete medieval versions to survive, that of Hans Reid compiled between 1504 and 1516.[10] Jacob Obereit's discovery of the 13th century manuscript in 1755 sparked renewed

The famous cathedral stairs in Lang's 1924 *The Nibelungenlied*.

interest in the text, early attempts to claim it as the German Homeric epic, and inspired Goethe to give a (partial) reading to his Weimar literary circle in 1808. The 19th century was, perhaps, the great age of *The Nibelungenlied* studies yielding the influential edition of Friedrich von der Hagen, which elicited the admiration of the Brothers Grimm, who were so delighted by this authentic German epic that they could happily ignore its Dutch and Norse origins. With the classic 1826 edition by Karl Lachmann, a "final" text was established, and the narrative became irrevocably, if controversially, imbricated in any nationalist definition of German ideals or even "Germanness" itself.[11] The 19th-century cult of *The Nibelungenlied* culminated in Richard Wagner's masterpiece, *Der Ring des Nibelungen*, which far surpassed the medieval text in its susceptibility to "cultiness."

It really isn't Wagner's fault that the Nazis liked him so much. He really was not a Fascist, in fact, he was almost a Jacobin, although he did, unfortunately, share with them a virulent anti–Semitism[12] (if never close to suggesting what became known as the final solution), an enthusiastic nationalism, and a fondness for pink silk underwear.[13] The women in the family, especially Wagner's widow, Cosima, were far more responsible for organizing a concerted association between extreme nationalism and the Bayreuth Circle, a trend fanatically supported by Wagner's English daughter-in-law, Winifred, an enthusiastic Nazi. In essence, though, the Nazi fondness for Wagner seems to have been remarkably superficial, having little to do with the music, less to do with the plot, and not much to do with Brunhild (and it pretty much ignored Kriemhild). In fact, it seems to involve little more than the image of Siegfried as a gorgeous blond hunk, the model of ideal German maleness. That beautiful, blank male, however, becomes what might be called an "empty signifier," a vessel into which any ideology might be poured. So Wagner's simple-minded hero is made the vessel of an insidious agenda. Both Lang and Wagner share the unfortunate fate of being blamed for the future and supposed to incorporate a noxious ideology of which they were unaware. That there may be points of intersection is undeniable and regrettable, but the desire to honor a German heritage should not be seen as malicious in itself nor to involve a retroactive guilt.

It is not accidental that Lang should choose to film *The Nibelungenlied*. As a young filmmaker at a time when the potential for film seemed infinite, money (for a short time) seemed abundant, and the nation seemed to need comfort after the trauma of the war and the peace, Lang could not help but be attracted by the chance to create an epic film. The script written by his wife was celebratory, at least in the first half, but, if Lang was not particularly interested in the nationalist thrust of the script, he could not resist the mythological scope of the narrative and its opportunities for the grand set pieces, which he relished. And for an ambitious grandiloquent young man what could be more attractive than to compete with the *magnum opus* of the towering figure of 19th-century magnificence, Richard Wagner. He must also have relished the irony of competing with the musical icon in a soundless medium.[14]

Although Lang denied any indebtedness to Wagner, it is clear that his influence is everywhere, whether in detailed borrowings (like the dragon), determinedly anti–Wagnerian choices (like his choice to divest the saga of Wagnerian pathos and the men of Wagnerian beards),[15] or the whole-hearted embrace of a Wagnerian aesthetic. The core of that aesthetic is the notion of the *Gesamstkunstwerk*, the total artwork. For Wagner, this concept stressed the interdependence of words and music, but also encouraged a totalitarian tendency to strive for complete control over every aspect of the final product, culminating in the creation of Bayreuth, which allowed him complete control over not only the product, but also the mode of production. Lang, who never used the word *Gesamstkunstwerk*, equally wanted all aspects of production and design to contribute to a unified product. Lang did not build his own theatres or ever manage to have a Wagnerian control over all aspects of production of his films (and was often hampered, especially in Hollywood by the power of others to interfere in his films). Neither Wagner nor Lang, however, left much to chance, and both men were intensely involved in every aspect of production as far as possible.

Unlike Wagner, however, Lang did not have a demented king in love with him, and so he had to make far more compromises than Wagner. For some critics, this desire for complete control of the final product reflects a quality of psychic Nazism, conflating the desire for totality with a desire for totalitarianism.[16] It seems a bit of a stretch to go from a desire for an accurate realization of a vision to an accusation of a totalitarian ideology, but this intense desire to control the product and an impatience with variations (particularly, for Lang, in innovations proffered by actors) made both men difficult to work with. Lang, in particular, was notorious for some of his feuds; Henry Fonda, in particular, remembered his association with Lang as a difficult experience.[17] Lang's arguments with actors began as early as *Siegfried* when Paul Richter refused to be filmed naked for the scene where he bathes in the dragon's blood. (Von Harbou's husband, Rudolf Klein-Rogge, who played Etzel, agreed to act as Richter's body double.[18]) In general, Lang was tyrannical with his actors and amorous with his actresses. This tendency may have made him difficult to work with, but it does not make him a Nazi. Indeed, after his move to the United States, where his politics can be traced more easily, he was closely allied with left-wing causes and was, as a result, summoned to appear before the House Un-American Activities Committee.[19]

In 1924, however, while his politics were vague, his enthusiasm and ambition were boundless and supported by the acclaim awarded to his earlier work, particularly the breakthrough work, a masterpiece of pathos and fantasy, *Der müde Tod* (1921). This film, filled with romance, wit and invention, is also relentlessly mournful with the reunion of the lovers achieved at last, but achieved only in the world of shadows behind the wall that separates the living and the dead. Its elegiac tone reflects the Weimar trauma so beautifully analyzed by Kaes. Three years later, it seems appropriate that Lang would choose to abandon the mournfulness of his earlier film and find a subject that allowed scope for his artistic ambitions. Part I of *Die Nibelungen*, *Siegfried* allows him to do just that. But, as the atmosphere darkens with the death of Siegfried, Part II, *Kriemhilds Rache* looms, and the death spiral of the Weimar Republic haunts the film and its nihilistic conclusion. At the heart of this pair of films lie two different women, Brunhild and Kriemhild, who are a study in black and white, and even contrasting geometries of verticals, horizontals, and occasional fraught diagonals.

Although Brunhild herself does not appear until nearly half-way through *Siegfried*, her presence is established in the opening shot, a long view of her mountain-top castle poised under a huge rainbow arch that spans the horizon from edge to edge of the film's frame. It is a surprising echo of Wagner, irrelevantly recalling the conclusion of *Das Rheingold*, when Wotan and the gods cross the rainbow bridge to enter the newly constructed Valhalla. It is a surprising shot because Lang's film makes no mention of Valhalla, Wotan, or virtually any of the Wagnerian memes, so that his image is a bit of a red herring. What it does, however, is evoke enough of Wagner to prepare the viewer for a film set in a mythic world with otherworldly settings and heroic characters. It spectacularly opens the world of Brunhild; well before we meet her, we are prepared for her entrance.

Wagnerians are well-prepared for the next scene, which, ignoring all but echoes of Wotan's rainbow bridge, skips *Das Rheingold* and *Die Walküre* and lands in the peculiar world of *Siegfried*, where Paul Richter is enthusiastically forging his sword Balmung (not Wagner's Nothung), while being watched with astonishment, admiration, envy, and loathing by the malicious dwarf, Mime. Lang sticks fairly closely to Wagner's plot for a good part of the film until Siegfried's arrival in Worms, after having traveled through gorgeously filmed dense forests, and to the lair of the dragon, who guards the Niblungen hoard. Lang's Siegfried, like Lang himself, seems to have little interest in the ring (which is replaced by a significant armlet later in the film), but, after killing the dragon,[20] Lang's Siegfried still bathes in the dragon's blood, which makes him invincible, apart from the spot where a linden leaf falls on his shoulder and will leave him vulnerable to Hagen's lance. After a confrontation with Alberich, in the course of which Lang begins to diverge from Wagner, Siegfried acquires the Tarnhelm, the cap which confers the ability to become invisible or shapeshift, and the untold riches of the Nibelungen hoard.[21] Encouraged by his enormous treasure, and, of course, his Nordic profile, Siegfried feels sufficiently prepared to move on to Worms to woo Kriemhild.[22]

Arriving in Worms (leading his troop across an impressive bridge stretched between two rocky peaks), Siegfried's entrance is delayed by Hagen who warns Gunther not to admit the dragonslayer. Our first glimpse of Kriemhild finds her looking out a window spying on the hero's arrival. She seems at first to be a representative of that familiar fairy tale/romance figure, the virgin princess, guarded and pure, who falls in love at first sight. She stands straight with her arms folded, dressed in a floor-length white surcoat falling virtually without folds almost to the floor, an impression of rigid verticality reinforced by the improbably long braids that fall from her narrow golden crown. The almost geometrical white and gold is interrupted by an elaborately patterned belt around her waist. Despite her almost columnar pose, she is placed off center (far to the left of the frame) and made diminutive by the dark curtains that occupy the left quarter of the frame and the much larger dark, patterned curtain that occupies almost all the right half of the frame. In this study in black and white, the fragile maiden seems almost threatened by the dark spaces that surround her. She might seem almost an icon of vulnerability, if not for the implacability implied in those determinedly crossed arms, and the light in her eyes that might be supposed to be desire, but also seems to hint at passionate willfulness. She may be vulnerable, but she is not malleable.[23]

She is troubled, however. When her mother, Queen Ute, arrives, she shares her dream of a white dove attacked by two giant black birds. The sequence, designed by Walter Ruttman, brought an abstract expressionist style of animation and an experimental caché to Lang's film, adding very contemporary art to the *Jugendstil* classics he drew on for much of the film. The threatening seems to foreshadow the white dove Siegfried attacked by the birds of prey, Hagen and Brunhild, whose black robes and winged helmets link them with the ravens.

After entering Gunther's hall of rectilinear shapes with highly patterned carpets and wall hangings, Siegfried asks his permission to marry Kriemhild, but is cut off by Hagen, who, in contrast to Siegfried, Kriemhild, and most of the Burgundians, is dressed in black, chain mail topped by an excessively large black helmet topped by giant upright bird's wings. He demands that, in exchange for Kriemhild's hand, Siegfried must help Gunther win for his bride, the fierce Brunhild, the wild woman dwelling atop the fire-encircled mountain.[24] His request provokes our first view of the mountain maiden in action. She appears to be hunting, or perhaps on the lookout for strangers; she is as opposed to meeting strange men as Kriemhild is welcoming. From her first appearance, her dress and gesture set her in opposition to the Burgundians who will soon arrive with dire consequences for her autonomy. She is dressed in black, which instantly links her with Hagen, an association made even closer by the fact that she too wears a helmet topped with giant bird's wings, but, while Hagen's wings are phallically upright, Brunhild's are spread wide. In contrast to the effect of Kriemhild as a white column, Brunhild darts about, anxiously, if aggressively, on guard, curiously bent as she crouches and lurks behind rocks; she seems to be a bird of prey, but an anxious and vulnerable one.

Her posture seems to be seeking the horizontal as opposed to the relentless verticality of Kriemhild. Thus, while Kriemhild would, at first, appear to be appropriately timid old-fashioned wife material and Brunhild the aggressive Wild Woman, their affect suggests something different, the strong-willed tenacity of the

Hanna Ralph as Brunhild in Fritz Lang's 1924 film *The Nibelungen*.

one, and the vulnerability of the other. Things are what they seem, but not necessarily what they seem to be at first sight. These contrasts of black and white, vertical and horizontal continue to structure Lang's presentation of the two queens throughout the film.

When a battle ensues between Hagen and Siegfried over precedence (Siegfried believes that wooing Brunhild for Gunther would put him in a position of vassalage), general combat ensues. Lang shoots this scene from overhead to create a hierarchical vertical space with the heroes fighting near the throne in the upper third of the frame while the vassals descend downward. Through a door on the left, Kriemhild descends and enters the throne room, in a stately horizontal procession that interrupts the verticality of the space; she demurely but powerfully takes charge. When she offers a welcoming drink to Siegfried, the two-shot stresses the extraordinary blondness of the two and evokes a destined love more profoundly than the drink which may or may not contain the magical properties possessed by Wagner's potion.

When later Brunhild arrives in Worms, a series of virtuoso scenes trace her progress from her descent from the ship to her walk across a bridge supported on the shoulders of submerged and armored vassals, to her entry on horse through the city gates, and her arrival at the magnificent staircase of the Cathedral of Worms. Lang loved to create monumental edifices, but he is at his most spectacular here and in *Metropolis*. From the vast portal of the cathedral in the upper quarter of the frame, the immense staircase descends in four ranks that, by the end, stretch beyond the frame, creating a vast playing area that the wedding procession is barely able to fill.[25] At the bottom of the stairs, the descending Gunther meets the approaching Brunhild in a reunion that arouses her suspicions as the relentlessly geometric palace must intimidate the mountain girl who, used to rocky cliffs, must be disoriented by all these stiff horizontals.

While Gunther and Siegfried seal their oath, Brunhild's suspicions grow. Her concerns increase when the event becomes a double wedding, and the king gives his sister in marriage to the vassal, Siegfried. Later, when she and Gunther fight on their wedding night and she lays him flat, she realizes that this wimp was not the hero who defeated her three times back on the mountain. To allay her suspicions, Gunther once more calls on Siegfried to fight her in his place. Disoriented, defeated, and desperate, she is even more set on vengeance when she discovers Kriemhild wearing the armlet Siegfried had taken from her after their mountain encounter. Fraught as Brunhild's wedding night may have been, Siegfried and Gunther are more successful, when they look into each other's eyes, swearing oaths and drinking. They seem at least as enamored as Siegfried and Kriemhild when they drank the welcome/love potion and seal the oath with an embrace that seems arguably more passionate than any embrace exchanged by their spouses.

Brunhild, accepting her role as Gunther's wife, determines to exercise her rights as his queen and demands that Gunther send his sister and her vassal-husband away from the court and back to Xanten. Then Kriemhild goes to church and chooses to wear and flaunt the armlet that is the evidence of Siegfied's treachery. Brunhild, dressed in black, with a pattern of triangle shapes that suggest daggers, summons her servants and announces that she too will go to the cathedral and assert her position dressed in the regalia of the Queen of Burgundy. Her newfound self-possession is underlined by the fact that, as she announces this decision, she is still dressed in black, but now fully erect and facing the camera with her eyes blazing.

Lang cuts immediately to the cathedral. Its imposing portal, as before, occupies the top quarter or so of the frame with the giant staircase descending to fill the rest of the frame and more. This time, however, the cathedral and its steps are empty, except for two barely visible guards on either side of the door. The vast emptiness of the space is slightly disturbing with a sense of dread like an immense Max Reinhardt set (which it is) waiting for the action to begin.

And then it does. A tiny figure in white robes begins to enter from the lower left-hand corner of the frame. Barely a speck at first, she slowly begins to mount the stairs with only her white robe identifying her as Kriemdhild. As she progresses on a diagonal from lower left to upper right, the camera shifts to a surprising shot: Brunhild in black, halfway up the staircase on the left side, her black-robed figure seen from an angle that makes her seem twice as large as Kriemhild. As she spots Kriemhild, she interrupts her diagonal ascent to make a horizontal progress on the first landing of the stairs and succeeds in separating Kriemhild, a lone figure near the top, from her vassals, grouped on the stairs below the landing. Brunhild runs up the brief diagonal remaining to place herself in front of Brunhild and claims precedence: "Stay, Kriemhild, the wife of a vassal may not prcede the Queen of Burgundy" (*Siegfried* 1:34:37). Challenged, Brunhild charges that Siegfried is, indeed, Gunther's vassal and has proven it by rendering services, both acknowledged and alleged. Retorting, "Make way for the Queen, vassal woman," Brunhild prepares to enter the cathedral, but is again cut off and confronted by Kriemhild, who flashes her armlet. The conflict is no less bitter for being silent. Venom drips through the intertitles. And all is revealed; what Brunhild suspected, Kriemhild confirms. After a brief moment at mass, leaving little doubt about what she prayed for, Brunhild rushes directly and vertically down the steps with Kriemhild in hot pursuit. Running past the courtyard, through the gates and onto the bridge she crossed to marry Gunther, she is caught by Hagen, and greets him with a simple command: "Kill Siegfried."

Siegfried, unaware of what has happened, but clearly aware that something has, runs from the courtyard where he has been practicing archery, to meet his wife, just now reaching the bottom of the stairs, and embraces her. The "enemy alliance" is formed in response as Gunther, Hagen, and Brunhild rally to destroy Siegfried and avenge Brunhild. In a wonderful shot, as Hagen and Brunhild try to convince Gunther to abandon his oath of brotherhood, Brunhild reminds Gunther of how Siegfried has betrayed them both, beginning with his use of the Tarnhelm to transform himself into Gunther. As she speaks, she moves behind him for a moment, as if, in a revised version of the original transformation, she has invaded Gunther (as had Siegfried earlier) and imbued him with her spirit of implacable hatred.

With this oath, the inevitable tragic fate unfolds in a series of betrayals that Lang films with appropriate logic and occasional brilliant invention. The list of betrayals accumulates as Hagen announces a hunt. Kriemhild, sensing danger, encourages Siegfried to reveal his vulnerable spot and ironically, claiming Hagen as her protector, reveals the secret to him. While her treachery may be accidental, Hagen is fully conscious of the betrayal he commits. As the hunt commences, Hagen and Gunther with varying degrees of hypocrisy, lull Siegfried into thinking they are on a festive celebration. Kriemhild, however, has the third of her prophetic dreams.[26]

Hagen murders Siegfried and the troops bear the body back to Worms. The mournful procession wends its way through forests that recall Siegfried's youthful journey to Worms. As the news reaches Worms, Brunhild laughs with manic frenzy, horrified to have her wish fulfilled, while also relieved that her desire for vengeance has been satisfied.

The news also appalls Kriemhild, who finally understands the degree to which she has contributed to her husband's death. Not having learned her lesson, she calls on her brothers to avenge Siegfried's death and kill Hagen. The brothers refuse to renege on their duty to protect each other. The loyalty of brother to brother trumps loyalty to a "manufactured" brother. Kriemhild, abandoned and betrayed, swears to pursue Hagen to the end of world. How she, a woman alone, can do so is at this point uncertain.

Lang concludes the film with several intense, melodramatic scenes, but ends with a poignant and resonant one in the cathedral (after both queens have had bravura arias of grief before Siegfried's body). In the final moments of the film, Kriemhild enters center frame to view the bier. At Siegfried's feet, she finds a huddled Brunhild. Kriemhild walks to her and bends towards her, either to console her or confirm her death. After announcing that "the Queen of Burgundy is dead," she moves to Siegfried's body coming to a stop at the head of the bier and slowly sinks down. The film ends with the body of Siegfried flanked by the black and the white queen, both now humbled by grief, as the proud Kriemhild joins Brunhild in mourning, like her helpless and huddled. But still alive.

In an age when the New Woman was a recent discovery, the two queens may seem to be a new version of that elusive image. They both know themselves (or, at least, their passions) and are not shrinking and submissive. To be sure, they are not role models, but they do give evidence of a woman's ability to master and manipulate the rules to bend men to their will, and, by and large, they do not so in the old-fashioned way, by using their bodies (except, perhaps, in their images as mediated by men, as when Alberich praises Kriemhild, or when Gunther falls in love with what he has heard about Brunhild). Rather they master the court system of oaths and use the patriarchal law to control and ultimately destroy their men. That they themselves are ultimately consumed testifies to the depth of their resolve and their resolute determination. The drive toward self-destruction at the heart of their project identifies a flaw in their entire design, and perhaps undermines their apparent autonomy. They may have power, but they are nevertheless defective. This critique, not of a woman's ability to dominate, but of her ability to rule, may disqualify them from participating in the world of the New Woman, but, of course, as products of literary history, they are not new, but exceedingly old women. Despite being part of an exciting new medium, they are creatures of an old worldview and demonstrate, despite the power to control and manipulate, that they are not creatures of reason, but of passion.[27]

The supposed hero of the film, Siegfried, remains less a character than an icon, a vision of Nordic blonditude, smiling, reckless, the whitest of men on the whitest of horses, shirtless[28] and shiny, trotting towards his fate, the trap set by women, and executed by Hagen, their tool and their demonic master. In contrast to Kriemhild, Siegfried really is innocent. Caught between a woman and a brother, he chooses the brother, whose innocence is manipulated by others. Kriemhild, on the other hand, uses her own "innocence" to conceal (perhaps from herself as well) a more devious agenda that she is not (or may not be) aware of until it is too late.

Both the awareness and the too-lateness are the subject of the second part of Lang's *Nibelungen*: *Kriemhilds Rache* (*Kriemhild's Revenge*). If *Siegfried* compels a contrast between the two queens, *Rache* demands a comparison between two husbands. If her first husband, Siegfried, is an icon of classic Nordic male beauty, her second, who woos her (by proxy) in almost the first scene of *Rache*, is dramatically unlike him. The film opens with Kriemhild, at Siegfried's bier, acting almost as a priestess at his altar, and reminding us of what she has lost and the intensity of her grief. This staging of grief and fidelity is followed by Rüdiger arriving with the marriage proposal from Etzel (aka Attila the Hun). And then we see him. No one could be less like the blond Siegfried than the dark Etzel. His portrait is an encyclopedia of anti–Siegfried tropes. Instead of riding freely and quasi-naked through a forest, he is encased in a frame, as if surrounded by a twisted mandorla, a self-proclaimed deity, constricted by his own power; he is an icon of Oriental splendor more a carved idol than a living man. He radiates malice, as his elaborate robes of many folds rise to support a death's head. Etzel's countenance is designed to repel. Flesh barely covers his skeletal, triangular cranium, almost glowingly bald finished with a topknot sprouting off center. His eyes glitter with dark malice beneath heavy lids, and his smile is a rictus of threat.[29] As Brunhild and Kriemhild are the black and white queens (with also some contrasting verticality and horizontality), Lang introduces in *Kriemhilds Rache* a retrospective contrast of black and white husbands. It is hard to imagine the widow of the radiant Siegfried choosing to marry the dark and malevolent Etzel.

Her choice of Etzel has, of course, no element of sexual attraction. Indeed, she has not even seen him yet. She is more attracted by what she hears than by what she sees. Still possessed by her vow to avenge Siegfried, she tries to trap Rüdiger (or Etzel) into promising to kill Hagen, who the camera cuts to in closeup as Kriemhild completes her abbreviated narrative of Segfried's death, concluding with the ominous proclamation that "his assassin lives." Rüdiger does not quite fall into Kriemhild's trap but does assure her that if she were ever insulted in Etzel's court, she would undoubtedly be avenged. That is enough for Kriemhild who begins plotting her vengeance, while Hagen, anticipating trouble, returns to the hiding place of the Nibelungen Horde, and sinks it in the Rhine,[30] to ensure that Kriemhild will be powerless in her new homeland without the Horde to buy allegiances and mercenaries. When Kriemhild hears what Hagen has done, she straightaway gives her word to Rüdiger, and the deal is sealed. Cut to a last shot of the treasure "drowning" in the Rhine.

With that shot, Lang's *Nibelungen* truly ends. The geometry and black and white contrast that structured *Siegfried* are gone. Kriemhild is now always in black, and, no longer grieving for Siegfried, she becomes his avenger with the single-minded goal—to kill Hagen. To accomplish this, she marries the distant Hun, and allies herself with the dark tyrant, and sacrifices all of herself that appealed to Siegfried, so that in avenging his death, she betrays his life. When there is a recollection of the blond hero, it only serves to underline how far she has fallen. After the last visual image from *Siegfried*, *Rache* becomes a very different film from the first part of Lang's *Nibelungen*. As brilliantly explicated by Tom Gunning, the two films trace a trajectory of the fall of myth into history.[31] Gone, or at least considerably diminished, in *Rache* is much of the sheer delight in invention and camera tricks that enlivened *Siegfried*, none of the forest freedom of the first film, and none of the romance (however fated). Unlike the previous contrast of black and white, *Rache*, like its characters, is dressed in shades of black and gray (except for a few of the Burgundians, mainly Kriemhild's brothers, who, as if "trailing shades of glory," dress in ironic white to enter Etzel's court). With the inevitability of all tragedies, the fate of Kriemhild and the Burgundians unfolds once she agrees to marry Etzel (who, by the way, is the only innocent party, and who, unknowingly, also seals his own fate with his acceptance of Kriemhild's bargain). With the descent into history, the romance and adventure that garlanded Siegfried are gone, and all that remains is Kriemhild's

relentless, grim pursuit of Hagen and the annihilation of the Burgundians. It a proclamation of total war that revisits, rather than heals, the traumas of the First World War
and (almost) anticipates the Second.

The drumbeats of destruction begin relentlessly with Kriemhild's departure from
Worms. She stops to take as her only dowry a handful of earth stained with Siegfried's
blood. Queen Ute makes one last attempt to heal the family, but Kriemhild refuses to
embrace her brothers in farewell. That she refuses to embrace Gunther is not too surprising, but she also adamantly refuses to embrace Gernot and Giselher, her two younger
brothers, who are not only innocent, but also love their sister. Young, innocent, loving
and exuberantly blond, they are the closest thing to Siegfried remaining in that fallen
world. Blind to that resemblance, Kriemhild cannot see that her lust for revenge has
killed the image of Siegfried in her heart. Thus, on the symbolic level, to avenge Siegfried
she must kill his image and replace him with the dark and dwarfish Etzel.

In her the journey east, Kriemhild arrives in a world that, filled with Orientalist
fantasies, is as far from Burgundy as possible. It is a barbaric ribald place, but, apart from
the swirling barbarity, there is also a welcome more sincere, for example, than Brunhild's
welcome in Burgundy. The Huns seem to approve of their new queen, anticipating her
arrival by lurking in trees to espy her progress and be the first to get to bring the news
to the king. As she nears, the clustering Huns, drop from the tree like ripe fruit, and
hurry to Etzel. There is a touch of the barbaric in their arboreal spying, but it seems
almost pastoral compared to the men in arms in neat, yet threatening, rows, who line up
to greet Brunhild's entry into Worms. Kriemhild is neither impressed nor repelled by
this barbaric display but proceeds directly to the throne to meet her new husband and
ask him to affirm the oath Rüdiger had sworn by proxy.

The episodes of Lang's Canto III seem almost a departure from expectations. Etzel
is mocked for being uxorious and abandoning his assault on Rome; Kriemhild meanwhile
is suffering the pangs of childbirth. Motherhood may seem a total departure from her
dedication to vengeance, but actually secures her marriage to the Scourge of God and
grimly abets her plan. Despite all the layers of grotesque makeup, the repellent Hun, at
the sight of his child, breaks into a smile of such joy and love, that he becomes almost
endearing. This virtual master of the world, almost giddy with love and joy, asks his wife
what reward he can possibly give her in return for the incredible gift she has given him.
Kriemhild, the new mother, asks only one thing: "invite my brothers to visit." With this
request, the values of the West and the East collide. The East becomes the locus of loyalty
and love (until infected by Kriemhild), while the West becomes the dwelling of darkness,
where a woman can bear a child to be sacrificed to her vengeance and the whole idea of
family becomes an accursed mockery. Etzel fathered a child out of love, while Kriemhild
bore a child only to lure her brothers to their death. She has come a long way from her
"innocent" love of Siegfried.

Canto 4 of Lang's film seems to take another swerve away from the vengeance trajectory, but that swerve merely prepares a more horrendous tragic turn. The minstrels
open the canto, creating, in effect, a frame around the intercalated narrative of Giselher
and his new bride, Rüdiger's daughter. The wedding of a poignantly blond and happy
couple recalls the happier days of another couple, Siegfried and Kriemhild. But it only
draws the happy couple and the noble Rüdiger deeper into the clash of loyalties that
Kriemhild manipulates for her single-minded plans.

Lang's most spectacular images in the film cluster around the scenes of the Nibelung approach to Etzel's with racing horses and roiling troops to the spectacular final descent of Kriemhild to address the Huns in their underground dwellings that recall the misery of Alberich's forest home in *Siegfried*. Dressed in black and white of almost Byzantine splendor, she slowly descends the steep staircase to greet the Burgundians. The splendor of the robes, the height and slope of the descent, and her hieratic grandeur echo the great staircase confrontation on the steps of Worms Cathedral, but the white Kriemhild is now in Brunhild's place, dressed in black and vengeful. The contrast could hardly be more dramatic. And, note, too, that instead of the "innocent" wife ascending to be interrupted by the black queen, the vengeful Kriemhild is descending alone and powerful, and relentless.[32] Although perhaps far too literal a metaphor, a contrast of the two scenes suggests that, while Kriemhild's ascent was interrupted, her descent is inevitable.

As the camera cuts between Kriemhild offering shields full of gold to the killer of Hagen and shots of the baby in the cradle, Etzel is, unknowingly, caught between his wife and his child. Having bribed the Huns, Kriemhild tries to compel her husband, provoking the surprising, but long-delayed, response: "Don't you ever think about anything else but Siegfried?" As he moves toward compliance, he recalls a contract that would have been immediately recognizable to any German of the past thousand years or so: Hagen is a guest. Kriemhild temporizes a bit, sneaking in a proviso that he will take action if Hagen offends in Etzel's court itself. He agrees and she makes him swear—on her child's life.

There is a great Hunnish celebration, exhibiting the same sort of barbaric joy that greeted Kriemhilld at her wedding. But, as hostilities break out between the Burgundians and the Huns, Hagen's accidental arrow kills the baby. Kriemhild madly rebukes the heartbroken Etzel, holding the dead baby before him, with the words: "The Work of YOUR GUEST." Even as an intertitle, the words drip with horror and anger, but Kriemhid's response is mixed. She is not totally immune to some sorrow as a mother, but she is clearly at least as mad with joy as she is with horror, for now Etzel cannot refuse to join in her revenge against Hagen. As she gazes on her dead baby, her face reflects not the sorrow of the mother, but the joy of Siegfried's widow at moving significantly closer to achieving her vengeance. The sacrifice of her child, like the ultimate sacrifice of her family, is a small price for her to pay.

As the slaughter begins, Kriemhild views it from a position that again brings to mind how far she has come since Worms. In place of the great architectural spaces and staircases of her lost kingdom, she stands before a low uneven arch at the top of a staircase of barely a few steps. Her spaces are diminished, as her goal constricts to a single desire. When Giselher

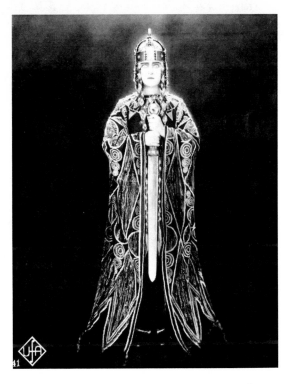

Magarete Schön as Kriemhild in Fritz Lang's 1924 film *The Nibelungen*.

arrives to negotiate a peace and save the few Huns and Burgundians who remain, she is relentless in her demand that he kill Siegfried's assassin. Rüdiger in turn appeals to Etzel, who demands that he fulfill the oath he has sworn and join the battle against Hagen. When Rüdiger points out that that would lead to the death of his child, Etzel, in a morbid and mournful moment, opens his cloak to reveal the body of his own dead child. Rüdiger then points out that Etzel does not understand the depth of German loyalty and fidelity. This instance of hyperbolic nationalism, with its disturbing Nazi resonance, is unique in the film and seems almost intrusive; it does, however, reinforce the code that structured Kriemhild's obsession, and helps to explain why the Burgundians are so adamant about protecting Hagen, who was, after all, guilty of precisely the crime of which Kriemhild accuses him.

In the tragic encounter between Giselher and Rüdiger, Rüdiger kills Giselher. This trope of conflicting loyalties in which a hero must make a choice between two equally disastrous options is formulaic in Germanic epics, a trope that, even after a millennium, remains moving in Lang's cinematic version. There is more carnage to come, however, as Hagen approaches Kriemhild with, for her, the happy news that virtually her entire family has been destroyed. The gates to Etzel's fortress start to close as the last surviving Burgundian crawls inside to burn the palace down.[33] Etzel, in a passion of loyalty to his wife and despair for his child, joins with Kriemhild in the final confrontation with Hagen. In an almost operatic, if silent, duet, Kriemhild affirms that her heart was never more filled with love.[34] While they join in a grotesque *Liebestod*, Gunther abandons his sister for the last time and, loyal to Hagen, plans to die with him. As Hagen approaches Kriemhild in anticipation of the final duel, Kriemhild says she has nothing to lose since she has already died with Siegfried and demands that he tell her what he has done with the Nibelungen treasure. When he refuses to tell her, she kills him[35] and is, in turn, killed by Hildebrand who stabs her from behind.[36] Dying, she removes the Burgundian earth stained with Siegfried's blood, clasps it to her bosom and joins it to her own. It is indeed a kind of *Liebestod*, but only if utter devastation seems an adequate substitute for ecstasy.

Lang's film is a glorious anthology of advanced (for 1924) cinematic techniques, a glorious evocation of a medieval world that draws on recollections of ancient art, romantic art, *fin de siècle* art, expressionist art, and even (thanks to Walter Ruttman) early abstract art. It is a beautiful art film, as well as a spectacle, a melodrama, a throwback and a leap forward, and an altogether remarkable film. But how does it earn its dedication to the "German people"? *Siegfried*, up to a point, works as a point of pride, a remembrance of mythic glory, and as something of an antidote to the disastrous finale of World War I, but the conclusion is less than comforting with the hero's death and his widow's cry for vengeance. It doesn't in the end relieve the trauma of that war, so much as echo it. And, then, comes *Kriemhilds Rache*, a devastatingly nihilistic film, which may be full of tragic resolution, but not an ounce of consolation.

To reconcile this opposition, I am tempted to recall a remark Lang made late in his life, years after his divorce from von Harbou (after having virtually never mentioned her name since his departure from Germany in 1933) that a marriage between a Nazi and a Communist was bound to fail.[37] To suggest that the essential differences between *Siegfried* and *Kriemhilds Rache* reflect an ideological split between the (Communist) husband and the (Nazi) wife would be critically suspect and biographically impossible to prove, I will resort to excusing the following remarks as allegorical (a mode much-favored by Lang, after all). *Siegfried* with its pure Teutonic hero and its mountain heroine (which anticipates the later mountain films [*Bergfilme*] which often featured Leni Riefenstahl). The image of Brunhild as a free spirit ranging the hills on her own and free from men reflects an ideology that would suit Thea von Harbou with her roots in the "blood and soil" nationalism, as well as her own modernist ideals in the age of the New Woman. Despite the tragic ending, the images of Siegfried and Brunhild remain positive, totally positive for Siegfried, and, while Brunhild may become vindictive, she remains a kind of Romantic figure, nevertheless, tragically betrayed and tragically avenged. There may be a consolation for the *Volk* in this film despite the grim ending, but there is a lingering aura of myth and romanticism that could permit some sense of pride to still reflect their glory on the German people. With the descent from myth into history in the second half of *The Nibelungen,* a far more cynical and unromantic tone takes over as Kriemhild replaces Brunhild as heroine. With the fall into history and, indeed, the end of history, at least for the Nibelungen, the world lacks myth leaving only an overbearing sense of dread inspired by the inevitability of annihilation. Kriemhild is powerful, calculating, and relentless, but she is not admirable or even, as it turns out, loving. Although her quest for vengeance is, she claims, rooted in her love for Siegfried, that love is pretty much cancelled (even though she may not acknowledge it) by the time she abandons him for Etzel, who is merely a means to an end, who takes Siegfried's place and eventually seems to erase him from Kriemhild's memory. Thus, while the two queens, like matter and anti-matter, destroy each other by meeting each other, Lang the communist who creates the decaying western world of Kriemhild poses the cynical antithesis to his wife's decadent nationalist theses. By the end, it becomes visible that, in this clash of ideologies, no heroic synthesis is possible and, like that marriage of the Communist and the Nazi, the ideological marriage of the two queens ends in a shattered Wasteland.

Here is no whiskey bar, as Brecht observed a few years later. Thea von Harbou was, by all accounts, a good woman.[38] She was active, even a pioneer, in women's issues (although she had a nationalist admiration for the role of the Mother, more as an ideal than as an actual role, at least for her), and she was devoted to the ideals of Mahatma Gandhi, which she shared with her patriotic Indian husband, whom she married after her divorce from Lang, and who encouraged her fierce support of Indian independence. Painfully wrong on some issues (almost a poster child for the downside of nationalism), she seems on the whole to have been a kind and caring woman, who claimed, "I don't think there is anyone who can claim that I hurt or insulted them because of their race."[39] Nevertheless, she was interned by the British in Staumühle Prison Camp from July 10 through October 10, 1945, several months longer than her colleague in German film history, Leni Riefenstahl.

Her husband had a career of ups and downs, but one that was consistently fairly successful, until his retirement, forced upon him largely by encroaching blindness. His last years, nearly forgotten in and by Hollywood and all but totally blind, were lived in near seclusion supported by some of the women who adored him (like Lotte Eisner, Lilly Latte), and sustained by his not infrequent visits to the local prostitutes, who loved his custom and put up with his customs. But in one last upward arc, Jean-Luc Godard arranged a final success by casting him in *Le Mépris* where he played the character he had taken a lifetime to perfect, himself. In that film, Lang descends an immense outdoor staircase in Capri that slopes steeply from a high roof to a garden overlooking a terrace on the edge of the Mediterranean. As he descends this grand staircase, more majestic that any staircase he created for his descending queens, he recalls his life charmingly (and carefully) relating all his favorite triumphs and grievances, defining himself as the Ultimate Survivor, the Master who is "still here" after all the black and white queens, Nazis and Communists, and Thea von Harbou.

NOTES

1. The Indian epics seem to have been a complex challenge. On the one hand, they gave the mature director with a generous budget (although not nearly generous enough—it never was for Lang) a chance to revisit a spectacular failure of his youth in the hope of turning it into a glamorous spectacle to compete with the best of the Age of the Hollywood epics (that ended with an unfortunate thud with *Cleopatra*). Unfortunately, costs, locations, and other troubles plagued the remake of which no satisfactory version exists to this day, although fragments and reconstructions give some hint of what it might have been. But there is also a hint of another agenda, and it seems almost too poignant to see a subtext motivated in part by a suppressed longing to revisit his wife Thea who was an integral part of his early career and successes, and whom he divorced not long before he left Germany in a clearly mutual decision. It would seem ironic too, although Lang never indulged in inconvenient ironies, that after her divorce from Lang, Thea took up with a young Indian nearly half her age. Once Thea left Fritz's life, she seems to have equally left his mind, but with the return to the early films, she must not have been on his mind, even for a mind as easily closed to inconvenient truths as Lang's.

2. Siegfried Kracauer, *From Caligari to Hitler: A Psychological History of the German Film*. 1947. Rev. and Expanded, ed. and Intro., Leonardo Quaresima (Princeton: Princeton University Press, 2004).

3. In Lang's case, such an argument is tempting since nearly all his films before he emigrated to America in 1933 were based on scripts or treatments by his wife Thea von Harbou, who became devoted to the Führer (and to her Indian lover).

4. Heiko Suhr, *Fritz Lang's "Nibelungen"-Rezeption mittelalterlicher Vergangenheit im Film* (Munich: GRIN Verlag, 2008).

5. Anton Kaes, *Shell Shock Cinema: Weimar Culture and the Wounds of War* (Princeton: Princeton University Press, 2009).

6. One great fan of *M* was cultivated cinema critic, Joseph Goebbels, who thought the film was "fantastic." What particularly impressed Goebbels, however, was its rejection of "humanitarian soppiness" and its arguments in favor of the death penalty. Goebbels, in this reaction, seems to reveal a certain insensitivity to nuance and the problem that M's judges are possibly even more reprehensible than M himself. The episode is discussed in Patrick McGilligan, *Fritz Lang: The Nature of the Beast* (Minneapolis: University of Minnesota Press, 1997), loc 3662 (Kindle edition).

7. Part II, *Kriemhilds Rache*, is, as we shall see, a totally different sort of film.

8. This background of the legend is summarized from the admirably concise discussion of sources in Appendix 1 ("History and Legend") in *The Nibelungenlied: The Lay of the Nibelungs*, trans. with intro. and notes by Cyril Edwards Oxford World Classics (Oxford: Oxford University Press, 2010), pp. 215–217 and Appendix II ("The Nordic Sources and the Problem of Genesis"), pp. 218–222.

9. Edwards refers to the Gallic Chronicle of 452, Prosper's *Epitoma Chronicon* (435–455).

10. See Edwards review of the texts, pp. xix–xxii.

11. It is perhaps necessary to stress that "nationalist" and "Nazi" are not synonyms. At the same time, there always seems to be a dark side to any strictly nationalist agenda.

12. Wagner's anti-Semitism has been much has been much discussed. A review of the topic can be found in Barry Millinton's *The Sorcerer of Bayreuth*, chap. 19 "Grit in the Oyster: The Role of Anti-Semitism in Wagner's Life and Work" (Oxford: Oxford University Press, 2012). Although it smacks of the smarmy "some of my best friends are" defense, Wagner had many Jewish admirers and friends. Most curious is the mutual admiration between Wagner and Hermann Levi, who conducted the premiere of *Parzifal* at Bayreuth in1882, although the composer chose to conduct the work from the Transformation Scene in Act III to the conclusion. Some have perceived this choice as Wagner's dissatisfaction with allowing a Jewish conductor to take charge of his most Christian opera. It is more likely, however, to have been the expression of the master's desire to participate in the first performance of his final opera. In any case, Levi continued conducting *Parsifal* at Bayreuth for another twelve years. (See the list of conductors at Bayreuth on *Wagnernet*, accessed 11 March 2017.)

13. A particular Nazi fondness for pink silk underwear has not been documented, but it would nicely complement the uniform.

14. Music was added to the film in a score by Gottfred Hupertz, which can best be described as "Wagner Lite."

15. These examples are cited in Lotte H. Eisner, *Fritz Lang* (1976; rpt. Boston: Da Capo Press, 1986), p. 73. Eisner also points out that Lang's *dramatis personae* do not resemble the hefty heroines and heroes of Wagnerian opera. Since the Wagnerian vocal production that was thought to require a degree of bulk is hardly a requisite for a silent film, this argument is a bit off the mark.

16. This notion is central to David H. Levin's *Richard Wagner, Fritz Lang and the Nibelungen: The Dramaturgy of Disavowal* (Princeton: Princeton University Press, 1998).

17. See, for example, Milligan, loc. 3604, for one account.

18. Referenced in "Paul Richter," *Wikipedia,* accessed 10 March 2017.

19. While not censured, he was shaken by the experience, which may be one reason for his return to Germany (of which he spoke, if at all, only with contempt during his earlier years in America) to revisit some of his youthful successes.

20. Critics are divided about whether Lang's dragon is a successful technical and dramatic achievement or a comically archaic failed experiment. I must confess I am quite fond of the beast. Two cheers for the dragon.

21. The hoard inspires one of Lang's unprecedented inventions. A great portion of the hoard is contained in a gigantic salver heaped with jewels supported by a circle of dwarfish caryatids. When Alberich is finally defeated, he turns to stone along with all his slaves and cohorts. The calcification of the bearers is a surprising event and filmed with a creepy sort of realism as each of the dwarves begins to realize what is happening and is frozen in stone in a last consciousness of horror.

22. Lang's forest bird sends Siegfried to Kriemhild, not to Brunhild. With this reorientation, Siegfried's betrayal of Kriemhild leads more tightly to the vengeance theme that will dominate Part II of Lang's *Nibelungen.*

23. Despite the apparent simplicity of Kriemhild's costume, the patterning of the belt and the curtains (to say nothing of the furniture in the room, which is revealed when the camera moves to a wide shot of Queen Ute entering the room to comfort her), seem to suggest Gustav Klimt in black and white. The influence of the riot of patterns and the rich conflicting geometricals in costumes, sets, and ceilings reflect the influence of the Viennese master, although without his gorgeous colors, and his signature swaths of pure gold. Lang himself acknowledged that Klimt "might have influenced the excessive stylization of *Die Nibelungen.*" (McGilligan, loc. 622). Kriemhild's style was also influenced by Wilhelm von Kaulbach and Franz von Stück, while Siegfried's style was based on Hans Thoma, and the forest landscapes by Caspar David Friedrich which are evocative of Böcklin (McGilligan, loc. 2210); on Böcklin, see also Eisner, *Fritz Lang,* p. 74.

24. Lang retains the fire, but eliminates any mention of its origin which, thus, allows him to skip over the complexities of Wagner's Wotan-centric plot.

25. Lang conceived this scene under the influence of the great Viennese director, Max Reinhardt. See Tom Gunning, *The Films of Fritz Lang: Allegories of Vision and Modernity* (London: British Film Institute, 2000), p. 59. As he points out, the stairs "not only create a powerful graphic image, but also stress shifting power relations and hierarchies."

26. Apart from the innovative falcon dream, she also dreams of a boar before Siegfried leaves on the hunt, and, as he is about to be killed, she dreams of the blossoming tree, which earlier sheltered the lovers as they pledged their love, and Siegfried revealed his vulnerable spot. As the blossoming tree appears to Kriemhild, the tree transforms into a skull made of twigs.

27. While not quite as dangerous to others, dueling, passionate queens remain popular, as evidence by the current hits on TV (*Feud,* which recounts the rivalry of Bette Davis and Joan Crawford), and Broadway (*War Paint* which celebrates the rivalry of Elizabeth Arden and Helena Rubenstein).

28. A minor point, perhaps, but, although Siegfried is, in fact, shirtless, his costume is far more concealing than the small to minuscule briefs or bikinis that cover (or not) the loins of contemporary beefcakes. He wears a surprisingly large animal skin (presumably an animal that he killed and skinned himself) that covers him from well above the waist to below the knees. Lang is striving, perhaps, towards Charles Darwin's stunning vision recorded in *The Voyage of the Beagle,* "A naked man on a horse is a very fine spectacle; I had no idea how well the two animals suited each other: as the Peons were galloping about they reminded me of the Elgin marbles." (November 15) It is typical of the nineteenth century to veil homoerotic attraction with a classical allusion.

29. There is historical precedent for Lang's revolting Etzel. Here is how the Huns are described by Ammianus Marcellinus: "They are quite abnormally savage. ... They have squat bodies, strong limbs, and are so prodigiously ugly and bent that they might be two-legged animals. ... They are ill-fitted to fight on foot, and remain glued to their horses, hardy but ugly beasts." See Michael Scott, *Ancient Worlds: A Global History of Antiquity* (New York: Basic Books, 2016, loc. 6147.

30. The Nibelungen treasure of the Rhine unavoidably recalls Wagner's Rhinemaidens guarding the sunken treasure. Lang's revision of Wagner (via *The Nibelungenlied*) cannot help but evoke all kinds of revisions and allusions that, unfortunately, are almost all entirely irrelevant, although Lang may not have been able entirely to forget Wagner's Schwarz Alberich, Hagen's dark dwarf father. The allusions already point to Kriemhild moving to the dark side.

31. In *The Films of Fritz Lang,* "The Decay of Myth," pp. 34–51.

32. In her glittering malice, she is something of a blend of a vindictive Byzantine Empress and the Wicked Queen in Disney's *Snow White.* More to the point, in this scene and in her later confrontation with Etzel, she seems clearly derived, visually and dramatically, from Richard Strauss' *Salome.* Her dress recalls the hieratic patterns of Gustav Klimt and echoes of the Wilhelmine era, and her relentless demand that the

oath be fulfilled to the letter recalls Salome's demands of Herod that he fulfill his oath and giver her the head of Jokanaan. (Hofmannstahl's libretto is essentially a translation of Oscar Wilde's play.)

33. The spectacular conflagration that incinerates the Hunnish fortress is impressive, and only one of the many such scenes that Lang labored over. He loved fires and explosions, and was equally meticulous in choreographing his one on one combats as well. The opportunity for this kind of bravura episode may have been one of Lang's considerations when he chose to revisit *The Indian Tomb* and *The Tiger of Eschnapur* at the end of his career.

34. How seriously are we meant to take von Harbou's Wagnerian Romanticism? If Kriemhild is being true in this exuberant response, it would mean that Etzel, in avenging Siegfried, replaces Siegfried in Kriemhild's heart, which would also mean, as suggested earlier, that Kriemhild's *Rache* is as much an attempt to annihilate Siegfried as it is to memorialize him.

35. This one-on-one male-female armed combat is unique in Germanic epic. Von Harbou may here infuse Kriemhild with some of the warrior valor of Wagner's Brunild, but, while Brunhild bears the heroes to Valhalla, she does not actually kill any of them.

36. What von Harbou giveth, von Harbou taketh away. If her duel with Hagen elevates the woman to heroic status, allowing her to be killed by a stab in the back would seem to seriously diminish her status as hero. Somewhat ominously, von Harbou may have anticipated the Nazi theory of the Weimar treachery (the stab in the back) that led to Germany's humiliation in World War I. Whatever Nazi sympathies she may have come to hold, that Nazi theory was not developed until ten years after the film was released.

37. Tom Gunning reports that "when I spoke to Lang while still an undergraduate I asked him a rather unguarded question about the role of love in his films. He responded, 'Love! Tell me, if a man is a communist and his wife is a Nazi, what happened to love?'" (p. 204).

38. There are many reports of von Harbou's many kindnesses to Jews and others throughout the war (and no reports of any traces of anti–Semitism, although one could hardly exist in Nazi Germany without being complicit with anti–Semitism). McGilligan's eulogy in the latter pages almost canonizes von Harbou, but does provide a great deal of evidence of her virtues. (See loc. 7546–7578.)

39. McGilligan, loc. 7561.

Through a Woman's Eyes

Liv Ullmann's Kristin Lavransdatter

Joseph M. Sullivan

It has been a century since the great Norwegian realist writer Sigrid Undset published *Kransen*, or *The Bridal Wreath*, the first installment of her three-part novel *Kristin Lavransdatter* (1920–1922), perhaps the most well-known work of historical fiction set in the Middle Ages ever written.[1] Together with a second medieval novel, *Olav Audunsøn: The Master of Hestviken* (1925–1927), *Kristin Lavransdatter* was largely responsible for earning Undset the 1928 Nobel Prize for Literature. In the many decades since, *Kristin* has continued, especially in Norway, to attract a dedicated readership and a good deal of critical attention, with the subject of this essay, the 1995 Liv Ullmann film *Kristin Lavransdatter*, a dramatization of *The Bridal Wreath*, representing just a single, albeit very important, witness to that lively reception.[2] In the following pages, this essay will attempt to show how the film's production was especially influenced by the fact that it was directed by a woman who had already established her reputation in front of the camera as a major bankable international star. The essay will also identify some of the more prominent themes regarding the emotional life of women, including female erotic desire and motherly love, that Ullmann picks up from Undset's novel and develops.

Apart from Sigrid Undset's sensitive portrayal of characters, it is *Kristin Lavransdatter*'s detailed depiction of medieval Norway in the first half of the 14th century that has been, since the novel appeared, the focus of both popular and scholarly interest. Indeed, as we approach the hundredth anniversary of *The Bridal Wreath*'s publication, the question of the accuracy of Undset's portrayal of medieval culture—the prime locus of scholarly debate since the novel's debut—shows little sign of abating. While Undset's detractors have maintained, for instance, that her depiction of the importance of Christian practice in medieval Norway is overstated and that the rich interior, emotional lives of especially her female characters have little grounding in medieval historical and literary documents, her supporters in the debate find exactly the opposite.[3] At least for the moment, those supporters seem to be represent the weight and direction of scholarly opinion. And, indeed, as one reads especially *Kristin*'s descriptions of medieval material culture, it is easy to appreciate how truly fine a scholar of the Middle Ages Undset was, a writer who drew adroitly on both the mass of 19th- and early 20th-century scholarship on medieval Norway as well as on primary historical and literary texts.[4]

Although the novel's careful depiction of medieval life certainly has been responsible for much of its enduring appeal, it is nevertheless important to recognize that the historical was for Undset secondary to, and primarily a backdrop for, the portrayal of basic, unchanging human experience. Indeed, for the author, her characters' experiences of love, loss, and betrayal are meant to be timeless. As Undset wrote at the end of her 1915 retelling of Sir Thomas Malory's Arthuriad, *Fortællinger om Kong Artur*, customs, modes of thought, and religious practices change, "But the human heart does not change at all across time."[5] While the experience of the heart may thus be timeless, what makes the portrayal of emotional life in *Kristin Lavransdatter* unique is its gendered perspective. Or as Liv Ullman, born 1938, explains, "Undset writes about women through a woman's eyes. And she writes about men through a woman's eyes."[6]

Behind Ullmann's own retelling of *The Bridal Wreath*, which preserves Undset's concentration on women's interior lives, lies a lifelong engagement with the material. Although we might credit Ullmann's performance in Ingmar Bergman's 1966 Swedish masterpiece *Persona* as having launched an international career that would, in subsequent decades, establish Ullmann as Norway's "most profiled woman's name in the world,"[7] it was her interaction with Undset's novel that was, perhaps, the most formative artistic experience for the young Ullmann, who, after falling in love with the novel at 14, went on, as a 21-year-old in 1959, to star in a major stage dramatization of that novel. As Ullmann has remarked, she felt "when I myself played Kristin Lavransdatter" that the role was as if created for her.[8]

The road, however, to Ullmann directing *Kristin* and, indeed, for the Scandinavian film industry even to get the adaptation of the novel in production, would be a long one. Although there was, at one point, talk of filming the novel with Ullmann playing the younger and Ingrid Bergman the older Kristin, Undset unfortunately had sold the film rights in 1947 to Hollywood, where David O. Selznick hoped to produce a *Kristin* starring his wife, Jennifer Jones.[9] While that production never materialized, the rights nevertheless were to remain in Hollywood for decades. Finally, a Swede, Ingmar Ejve, bought those rights in 1991 and approached the Norwegian state film company, Norsk Film AS, with a proposal for a joint Norwegian-Swedish production.[10] Soon after selecting a director, namely, the Swede Lars Mollin, and entering the script-writing phase, Mollin and the producers decided mutually that Mollin should step down. As executive producer—and head of Norsk Film at the time—the Dane Esben Høilund Carlsen, explained, "we agreed it should be directed by a Norwegian and by a woman,"[11] thus reflecting their belief that the novel was of special significance to women and that the film too, while certainly of potential interest also to men, clearly would be a women's film.

When the producers approached Ullmann with what she later called "the greatest offer I've received in my whole life," she had just come off her critically acclaimed directorial debut of the Danish film *Sofie* (1992), which like *Kristin* centers around a strong female protagonist.[12] Thus as an individual who had portrayed Kristin Lavransdatter as a young actress, who was both a woman and a Norwegian, and who had proven herself as a director, Ullmann seemed an ideal choice. But, while she would create what is arguably one of the most artistically crafted medieval movies ever filmed, the project would prove an exceptionally bumpy journey for Ullmann, with budget difficulties during filming and then bitter skirmishes between her and the producers in the post-production phase. Interestingly, for this "woman's" movie, many of those misunderstandings appear to have been rooted in Ullmann's gender and the unwillingness, or inability, of her male producers to work effectively with a woman.

On the set itself, things could not have gone better among Ullmann, her crew, and her actors, and Ullmann was to characterize their cooperation as "the most tremendous experience" of her life.[13] Indeed, so pleased were her cast members with their experience under Ullmann, whom they viewed as a true actor's director, that right before *Kristin*'s premiere in August 1995, nearly all of them had agreed to participate in a sequel even though they knew it would be with a different director.[14] Additionally, her harmonious work with world-famous head cinematographer Sven Nykvist—about whom she has commented, "Nykvist and I speak the same [visual] language"[15]—would not only successfully capture the singular beauty of the Norwegian landscape, its lowlands and its highlands in all seasons, but also spectacularly imbue the movie in its signature interior, domestic scenes with a richness of luminescent blues, reds, greens, and golds and a use of light and darkness that is perhaps most reminiscent of the works of the 15th-century Netherlandish master Jan van Eyck.[16]

In contrast to the harmony on set, however, Ullmann's interaction with her male producers and the officials at Norsk Film, also male, represented, as she reportedly stated, "the worst episode in my life."[17] During production, friction revolved around the budget. Planned from the beginning as the most expensive Scandinavian picture ever and with an original budget of approximately $11.5 million, the cost of the film would balloon progressively during shooting to over $15 million.[18] Furthermore, the resultant "war that raged through the entire production" was fought openly and often indecorously in the Norwegian press between Ullmann and lead producer, Esben Høilund Carlsen, with the cost overruns eventually resulting in Esben Carlsen's resignation as head of Norsk Film.[19] Asserting her lack of responsibility in the budget woes, Ullmann stated about her male associates' reluctance to work with her that "I was never involved in a decision and was never presented a budget. I was not allowed to be in meetings."[20]

In the post-production phase as well, rancor characterized Ullmann's relationship with her producers, with disagreement centering around Ullmann's unwillingness to re-edit her film to a shorter length. Although the producers had envisioned the film from the outset of the project to be about three hours[21]—and at right over three hours that is exactly the length that Ullmann achieved—*Kristin*'s German distributors, Cine-International, demanded that the film be edited down to under two and a half hours for the American and international markets. Ullmann, however, refused, remarking, for instance, "I wouldn't cut it down one minute…. Because I know for Sigrid this [refusing to shorten the movie] is OK."[22] After she learned, however, that the head Swedish producer, Göran Lindström, had begun "in absolute secrecy" to shorten the film himself,[23] and after she threatened that, if his version were sold abroad, the producers would have to market the film "without the director's [i.e., Ullmann's] name,"[24] she eventually and "with reluctance" agreed to create a shortened version.[25] By the time, however, that Ullmann had finished her new version of two hours and 21 minutes in March 1996—a full six months after the August 1995 Norwegian premiere—*Kristin* had missed its window of opportunity for successful international sales, failing to find a U.S. distributor and soon becoming a film marketed internationally for mostly women's film festivals.[26]

The effect of the protracted feuding with Ullmann's male producers over the film's editing and the resulting failure for *Kristin Lavransdatter* to achieve international theater distribution seem largely responsible for the fact that Ullmann's film is, today, both hard to obtain as well as relatively unknown outside Scandinavia, except among Scandinavian Studies scholars. In Norway, however, *Kristin* was, as Ullmann has accurately observed, "the greatest success Norway ever had in film."[27] Indeed, in a country where in the mid–1990s only three percent of box office receipts were for Norwegian films, *Kristin* had attracted to the cinema almost 14 percent of all Norwegians by November of 1995.[28] Such numbers, usually only seen for American films, were surpassed in 1995 Norway only by Disney's animated blockbuster *The Lion King*. So successful was *Kristin*, in fact, that the so-called "Kristin-Fever" postponed the Norwegian release of the Tom Hanks vehicle *Apollo 13* for a full month, the first time in recent Norwegian cinema history that an American movie had to wait until a domestic film had finished an extended run.[29] While Norwegian critics were certainly less excited than audiences about the film—typically commenting, as the *Dagbladet* reviewer did, that the movie moves a bit too slowly and "is too long"—reviews in the leading newspapers were, if not glowing, generally good.[30]

In retrospect, it is unsurprising that Ullmann's *Kristin* was so successful in Norway and that it became a true national event. Not only had Undset's novel long been a beloved part of the national patrimony, but the early 1990s also had witnessed a great blossoming of new interest for the novel and its author, with, for example, performances of new stage and ballet adaptations of *Kristin Lavransdatter*, the publication of new editions of Undset's works, and the appearance of a critically acclaimed and popular documentary film about the writer, namely, Maria Fuglevaag Warsinski's 1993 *Sigrid Undset—Et kvinneliv* (*Sigrid Undset: A Woman's Life*).[31] Moreover, daily and weekly reports in the press during filming about this "Norwegian film of the century" announcing, for example, that "Ullmann and Nykvist are names that guarantee that an attempt is being made at a level whose equal we've seldom seen in the country," stoked intense anticipation among the public, with, for example, throngs of Norwegians visiting the shooting locations.[32]

The popular welcome that *Kristin* achieved upon release, however, had certainly less to do with pre-release publicity than with Ullmann's success in fulfilling the expectations of her audience members, about whom she remarked, they "all have their opinion about *Kristin Lavransdatter* and how it should be."[33] Ullmann satisfied those expectations by, first, meticulously recreating on film the detail and fidelity to medieval reality that so characterize Undset's novel. Thus Ullmann filmed in more than 60 locations across Norway, including inside numerous surviving medieval buildings, and built from the ground up both a true-to-the-period version of Kristin's rambling family estate, Jørundgaard, as well as the medieval Norwegian stave church of Kristin's village.[34] But even more important to Ullmann's ability to meet audience expectations was certainly her careful, year-long preparation of a script that, as she accurately observed, is "partly new" but nevertheless "lies close to Sigrid Undset's spirit."[35] Indeed, Ullmann's story succeeds in preserving the basic and timeless emotional experiences that are a priority in Undset's novelistic agenda, while at the same time introducing numerous changes that both highlight those experiences already present in Undset as well as create new ones. The remainder of this essay will discuss some of the more important items that Ullmann keeps, that she intensifies, and that she innovates, with a focus on items that relate especially to women's emotional lives, particularly motherly love and female erotic desire, in a film that was to enjoy "first and foremost an unbelievably large female audience."[36]

Ullmann's film and Undset's *Bridal Wreath* tell the story of the young noblewoman Kristin from her early childhood to the time of her marriage. Kristin's parents, Ragnfrid and her beloved father, Lavrans, have already lost three boys and, therefore, their first surviving child, Kristin, holds a special place in their hearts. Although Ragnfrid and

Elisabeth Matheson (center) as the title character in the 1995 film *Kristin Lavransdatter*.

Lavrans have arranged for Kristin to become engaged to a young nobleman whom they have chosen, Simon Darre, Kristen falls in love with the dashing but irresponsible older knight Erlend while she is spending a year at a convent in Oslo in advance of her wedding to Simon. Going against the wishes of her family and betraying the mores of her society and her faith, Kristin repeatedly seeks out the company of Erlend and, after their love is discovered, refuses to give him up. It is only when Lavrans recognizes that Kristin will not change her mind that he finally consents to allow her to marry Erlend.

From the very start of her film, Ullmann not only picks up on the power of female desire that is central to Undset's novel, but her script works also to intensify its importance. Significantly, Ullmann intervenes in Undset's storyline by making Kristin's marriage ceremony—which had been *The Bridal Wreath*'s last event—the first sequence of her film. Although this shift functioned for foreign audiences, unfamiliar with how the story ends, as a spoiler by removing "suspense" from a film that needed, in the opinion of a Canadian reviewer, all the excitement "it can muster,"[37] Ullmann's move nevertheless has the effect of highlighting that Kristin ultimately will realize her wishes and that her desire will override all other considerations. For example, to satisfy that desire, she will transgress the proscriptions of her Christian faith against sex outside of marriage.[38] Thus, Kristin will enjoy sex on numerous occasions with Erlend while still engaged to another man, Simon. Perhaps more significantly, in choosing Erlend, Kristin sins against the connections that tie her to her family. Indeed, in refusing to renounce Erlend, Kristin violates her most important kinship bond, that to her father, Lavrans Bjørgulfsøn. Despite having been admonished by her father—"You must forget the man you love"—and even after Lavrans informs Erlend that he *never* will give Kristin to him, Kristin stubbornly announces to her father that, if she cannot marry Erlend, "then I'll pray God to take me away."[39] In a film whose trailer opens by announcing that this is "a story about father and daughter,"[40] Kristin's refusal to bend to her father's wishes would seem particularly significant, especially when we acknowledge that Lavrans is not only the most positively drawn, but also the most reasonably acting, major character both in the original novel as well as in Ullmann's film.[41]

Further, for Ullmann, who chose to feature a conspicuously large number of outdoor shots of mountainous Norway's majestic and often foreboding natural environs, her Kristin was cognizant of sinning not just against father, family, and church. As Ullmann explains, Kristin also feared "it might be the evil forces of nature" itself that would punish her for pursuing, at any cost, the satisfaction of her romantic desire.[42]

Ullmann further explores the nature of female erotic desire and suggests that a woman's consent is part of nourishing that desire in her interpretation of the first time that Erlend and Kristin have sex. That romantic encounter occurs when the recently acquainted couple seeks shelter from a storm in a barn and gives way to passion. Unlike in the novel, however, where Kristin is not fully willing and becomes primarily passive— "She sank back into the hay with open arms and let Erlend do as he liked" (145)—Ullmann's film makes Kristin a more willing participant and the depiction of the love-making less forced.[43] For instance, whereas in the book Kristin tries to push Erlend away from her when it becomes apparent that he wishes to have sex, Ullmann's Kristin demonstrates no such resistance. Further, following the lovemaking, Ullmann has her Erlend sensitively kiss the hymenal blood that had flowed onto Kristin's leg, immediately after which Kristin passionately kisses Erlend in return. This exchange suggests not only Erlend's respect for Kristin, and her recognition of that respect, but also it casts a distinctly more loving, gentle atmosphere of shared emotion over what had been in the book a very ambiguous episode at best. Indeed, that Kristin in Undset's original did *not* feel that the sex had proceeded according to her will is suggested by her feelings afterwards. Thus, Undset's Kristen believes of the sex that "Erlend had done this to her," and she now has the uncomfortable feeling that "she had become his possession" (146). By comparison, Kristin in the film demonstrates no such animosity to the act that has taken her virginity, or to the man who shared in that now more consensual act with her.

As in Kristin's relationship with Erlend, female erotic desire also holds a central, but nevertheless quite different, place in the relationship of Kristin's parents, Lavrans and Ragnfrid. That female desire had played an especially problematic role for the parents first becomes apparent, in both novel and film, when the protracted familial discord over Kristin's insistence to marry Erlend provides an occasion for Lavrans and Ragnfrid to revisit in conversation the awkward early days of their own marriage. When Lavrans, the audience has learned, married Ragnfrid, she was several years his senior, and he was not much more than a boy. Apologizing for not responding in those early days to her sexual entreaties and Ragnfrid's strong desire for sexual satisfaction, Ullmann's Lavrans explains that "I was so afraid," adding painfully that "I wanted only to live with you and not have you grasp at something in my heart [i.e., the will and ability to meet Ragnfrid's sexual needs] that I could not give." As in Undset's novel, Ullmann sends here, in her film, the message that it is not only reluctant women but also men—and even the best of men, like Lavrans—who can be bad lovers and the determining factor for a lack of passion in a romantic relationship. Further, Ragnfrid's thwarted sexual desire appears intended, both in the novel and the film, to contrast with the effects of her daughter's realized desire. More particularly, Ragnfrid achieves, despite her thwarted sexual desire, a long, successful marriage with a husband who deeply loves and respects her, whereas Kristin tears her family apart and deeply wounds all around her while in successful pursuit of satisfying her desire.[44]

While Ullmann leaves largely unchanged the novel's depiction of Kristin's parents, she alters fundamentally Undset's portrayal of Kristin's sister Ulvhild, making Ulvhild also a vehicle to explore female desire. In both film and book, Ulvhild is disabled as a young child when a log rolls upon her while she is playing. Though she survives, her injury leaves her unable to walk without crutches, and Lavrans and Ragnfrid, knowing that she will be unable to find a suitable husband, decide that she will enter the convent when she comes of age. In an important departure from the novel, however, in which Kristin is about seven years older than her much younger sibling, Ullmann—who never explicitly states the age difference—chooses actors for the adolescent Kristin and her little sister Ulvhild who visually appear to be almost the same age. In so doing, she introduces to the story a much-heightened emphasis on sisterhood, that is, the notion of closely related women of about the same age who share similar dreams, problems, and possibilities.[45]

That Ulvhild's specifically romantic possibilities are, however, quite different than Kristin's becomes apparent in a scene in which Kristin, about 15 or 16 years old, and Ulvhild are sitting opposite each other under trees near the family farm. When Kristin's best childhood friend, Arne—a family servant who is also deeply in love with the already betrothed Kristin—approaches Kristin, flirts with her, and begins to caress her feet, the camera shifts to Ulvhild. In a cinematic technique that is the film's most characteristic, the camera then twice lingers for what feels like an uncomfortably long period of time upon Ulvhild's face and allows those close-ups to speak for how she feels. The normally cheerful Ulvhild, with a flute dangling in a sexually suggestive way from her mouth, casts longing, searching eyes upon her sister and Arne. Clearly, the future that her parents have planned for Ulvhild in the convent as a bride of Christ is not the one that corresponds to the desire of her heart and contrasts in the most basic way to Kristin's future, which will be defined by her romantic and marital relationships with men.

In addition to its increased focus on sisterhood, Ullmann's script introduces also a far greater emphasis on yet another important woman-to-woman relationship, namely, female friendship, which Undset had only hinted at. And, once again, this type of relationship will also function as a platform for Ullmann to examine female desire. Such friendship unfolds during Kristin's year-long stay in the convent of Nonneseter in Oslo when she is about 17, and while she is betrothed to Simon Darre. Upon arriving at the convent, Kristin is introduced to the two girls who will become her companions, Ingebjørg and Helga. Whereas in Undset's novel, the companions' stories are barely fleshed out, with especially Helga playing little role, Ullmann both completes the companions' stories as well as makes their friendships to Kristin far more important to understanding Kristin herself. Ullmann suggests that all three girls are, at the most basic level, to be understood as friends when, in a departure from the book—in which only Ingebjørg and Kristin share a bed—the abbess assigns all three young women to a single bed in the dormitory that houses both novices and the young girls, such as Kristin, who are to spend but brief periods at the convent before marriage. In their bed, and, as if they are modern adolescent girls at a slumber party, the three toy with one another's hair and engage in pillow-talk, sharing their most intimate thoughts about, for example, marriage and men.

In Ullmann's script, the more significant of the two friends, Ingebjørg Filippusdatter, becomes a very different kind of character than she had been in the novel. Ingebjørg, in Undset's original story, had been a rather comic, superficial, and even amoral figure, whom the author describes as a "foolish," "flighty" "chatterbox" (114, 168, and 169).

Moreover, Undset, in the tradition of great realist writers, also fully exploits the possibilities offered by extended physical description to further the impression of the girl's ridiculousness. Thus about the "plump, fair-haired ... maiden," the narrator reports that "Ingebjørg was ... fat and sweated heavily" (106 and 120). In creating her fundamentally different Ingebjørg, Ullmann will remove, first, any association with silliness suggested in Ingebjørg's physical appearance by casting a rather normal-looking, attractive actor, Gisken Armand, to play the girl. More significantly, however, Ullmann avoids placing ridiculous words in Ingebjørg's mouth, and, instead, allows her repeatedly to be serious when appropriate to the situation. Such is the case, for example, when Ullmann's Ingebjørg warns Kristin, in utter earnestness, about Erlend's checkered past and, suggesting that she should forget him, reminds Kristin that "you shall marry Simon Darre."

It is, however, in the handling of Ingebjørg's sexual fate that the film makes her character integral to understanding Kristin and to appreciating the power of female erotic desire. As in the novel, the film informs its audience that, when the girls first meet, Ingebjørg is soon to wed a rich, but old and ugly, man. But whereas Undset never follows up on whether that union actually materializes, director Ullmann, by contrast, completes Ingebjørg's narrative by showing her departure from the convent with her future husband. That husband is, indeed, quite aged and extremely unattractive, but it is the look upon Ingebjørg's face that most powerfully suggests that her fate is not an ideal one. Once again, Ullmann uses a close-up and allows the camera's eye to dwell upon an actor's face, which in Ingebjørg's case is replete with sorrow, pain, and, especially, fear. Clearly, the director intends Ingebjørg's story to contrast with Kristin's. In comparison to Kristin, who asserts individual liberty in electing to pursue her desire, Ingebjørg's sexual future has been determined by the wishes of her family, which, in pairing her with a repulsive older man, has chosen to ignore the existence and worth of any romantic desire that the now terrified Ingebjørg might possess.

As with her Ingebjørg, Ullmann's more fully formed Helga also becomes in her script a true mirror character to Kristin and contributes, as had Ingebjørg, to the film's explorations of female friendship and female desire. Importantly, and unlike her girlfriends Kristin and Ingebjørg, the young novice Helga is not destined to marry at all, but rather her family has given her to the convent to become a nun. To tell the story of Helga and her friendship with Kristin, Ullmann skillfully deploys as a kind of MacGuffin the small brooch that Kristin's childhood friend Arne had given Kristin as a farewell gift. In the book, Kristin, in recognition of Helga's kindness to her, gifts the girl with a large silver clasp, an item that Kristin is only too happy to be rid of; indeed, she had been wearing that clasp on the night a man had attempted to rape her, "and she had never wanted to wear it since" (124). In Ullmann's script by contrast, the piece of jewelry Kristin presents Helga becomes an item most dear to Kristin's heart, namely, the very same simple brooch that Arne had given her. And the item will represent in the film not just the beginning of the girls' friendship, but its end. Thus, after Kristin abuses that friendship by abandoning Helga to spend several excruciatingly uncomfortable hours on a beach with Erlend's companion, the morally ambiguous knight Munan Baardsøn, while Erlend and Kristin sneak off to make love, Helga gives the brooch back to Kristin. The return of the precious gift stands for the end of the close friendship between the young women and, perhaps even more importantly, signifies the power of erotic desire, evident in Kristin's overriding drive to be with Erlend, to force individuals who give into it to betray the trust of those closest to them.

But even after the betrayal of friendship that redrawing Helga allows Ullmann to add to Undset's story, the director is still not done with her as a vehicle for discussing female desire. Combining Helga with another character from the novel, a certain Sister Cecilia (154), Ullmann has her Helga, still shaken from the humiliating experience with Kristin on the beach, suffer a public breakdown in the company of the girls of the convent. Declaring that she truly loves only herself and the devil, and pronouncing herself the worst of sinners, Helga announces her greatest fault: "I love no *man*. No man has tempted me!" Her self-condemnation focuses audience attention on the fact that Helga's cloistered existence has separated her from the chance, or even thought, of entertaining her sexual desire as a woman and that her sexual destiny—one that she did not choose for herself—has driven her to the verge of madness. Unmistakably, Ullmann intends Helga's thwarted erotic desire to contrast with Kristin's realized desire, just as earlier Ulvhild's unfulfilled desire had served as a kind of distorted mirror for the potential that her older sister, Kristin, will have to indulge her own romantic inclinations.[46]

While romantic, erotic love and the desire that underlies it certainly constitute one major focus of Ullmann's exploration of women's interior lives, another type of love, namely, maternal love, also forms a central discourse in the director's interpretation of Undset's novel. Such motherly love is, for example, at the core of Kristin and her mother Ragnfrid's story. In retelling that story on film, Ullmann was able to follow closely the events and dialogue provided by Undset, who believed adamantly that a woman's role as mother was the highest role to which she could aspire.[47] Thus in both book and film,

Elisabeth Matheson as the title character in the 1995 film *Kristin Lavransdatter*.

Kristin's relationship to her mother, at least on the surface, has never seemed a particularly close one, with the reticent Ragnfrid forever hesitant to show her affection openly, and Kristin, a true daddy's girl, favoring the company of her father. However, when the row among the family members over Kristin's insistence on not giving up Erlend leads to a particularly heated exchange between mother and daughter—an argument in which the mother even goes so far as to slap Kristin's face—Ragnfrid finally lets down her guard and lays bare the profound depth of her love. Accepting that "you [Kristin] never loved me much," Ullmann's Ragnfrid explains—and does so in the most intimate, maternal way—that she has allowed Kristin, from her infancy, to believe that Lavran's affection for the girl was greater than her own:

From the time when you were small, when Lavrans would come near, you would turn away from my breast and reach for him, laughing with milk spilling over your lips. God knows I was happy for you both—happy for Lavran's joy each time he saw you. But God knows too, as does the Virgin Mary, that I loved you no less than Lavrans did.... [N]ow I tell you [this], Kristin, as one woman to another.

That Ullmann perhaps wished to focus even more audience attention upon maternal love than the book had suggested is evident especially in her expanded portrayal of yet another mother-child relationship, namely, that between the village woman Gunhild and her troubled son, the young priest Bentein. In both novel and film, Bentein attempts to rape Kristin and is only prevented from doing so when Kristin throws rocks at his head, knocking him down, and flees the scene. Soon afterwards, Bentein commits yet a second atrocious act when he slays Kristin's childhood friend Arne after Arne had, presumably, defended Kristin's honor in the face of Bentein's slander. Whereas in Undset's original story, we hear little else about Bentein—except that he has escaped and perhaps has fled to Sweden (100)—Ullmann brings Bentein's story to completion and uses her new ending as a platform to highlight the power of motherly love. More specifically, Ullmann's Bentein does not escape punishment. Instead, Kristin becomes a witness as Bentein, sentenced to be hanged for Arne's murder, is paraded, seated backwards on a donkey, ignominiously through the crowded streets of Oslo. As boisterous onlookers jeer the condemned man, the camera focuses in on his mother, Gunnhild, who, lamenting her son, follows closely behind in his trail while a bystander pelts her with raw egg. In Gunhild's anguished, unflagging devotion to Bentein, Ullmann's message is unequivocal: Despite the fact that Gunhild knows that her son had tried to rape Kristin and that he subsequently murdered a man, the power of motherly love is such that it can compel a woman to overlook the most grievous failings in even the most flawed and morally corrupt of children.[48]

In conclusion, in crafting a film that not only captured but also expanded themes that were so central to the exploration of the emotional lives of women in Sigrid Undset's *Bridal Wreath*, director and scriptwriter Liv Ullmann showed enormous respect for, as well as great understanding of, the earlier artist's thematic intentions. Indeed, in fully developing the themes of, for instance, female erotic desire and motherly love, Ullmann faithfully followed Undset's lead in placing discourses speaking to the emotional lives of both younger women and more mature women in the very center of the dramatic action. Furthermore, that Ullmann was able to reproduce successfully in her *Kristin Lavransdatter* the reality of medieval Norway that was so much a part of Undset's novel and that she was able to bring the film project—a huge enterprise by Scandinavian standards— to its completion in spite of the often glaring lack of support she received from male studio executives and producers, testify to the directorial skill and outright persistence of Ullmann, one of the great women of modern film. Without a doubt, her *Kristin Lavransdatter*, with its signature presentation of both men's and women's experiences through the perspective of a woman's eyes, deserves to be much better known among students of the Middle Ages and recent film.[49]

NOTES

1. Sigrid Undset, *Kristin Lavransdatter: Kransen* (Oslo: Aschehoug, 1920). The novel's first part is also known in English simply as *The Wreath*.

2. References to the film are from Liv Ullmann, dir., *Kristin Lavransdatter: The Restored Director's Cut*, DVD (1995; Chicago: Home Vision Entertainment, 2004).

3. On the debate, see Claudia Burguson, "Arrested in Parody: The Performance of Erlend Nikulaussøn in *Kristin Lavransdatter*," *Scandinavian Studies* 82.3 (2010): 290–294; and especially Olav Solberg, "'Oppfostret

i historie'—Om det historiske i *Kristin Lavransdatter*," *Edda* 94.2 (1994): 99–101. For a reasoned case for considering the novel as historically realistic, see Solberg, pp. 99–101.

    4. Carl Bayerschmidt, *Sigrid Undset* (New York: Twayne, 1970), p. 89.

    5. "Men menneskenes hjerter forandres aldeles intet i alle dage." *Fortællinger om Kong Artur og ridderne av det runde bord* [*Tales of King Arthur and the Knights of the Round Table*] (Oslo: Aschehoug, 1915), p. 252. This quotation, which so concisely captures Undset's attitude toward changeable history and unchangeable human emotion, is a commonplace in Undset scholarship. All translations in this essay from Norwegian into English are my own, except as otherwise noted.

    6. Linton Weeks, "The Burning Midnight Sun of *Kristin Lavransdatter*," *Washington Post* 20 December 1995: C01.

    7. "mest profilerte kvinnenavn ute i verden." Mona Levin, "Når den ny Liv blomstrer," *Aftenposten* 24 December 1994: 22.

    8. "...da jeg selv spilte Kristin Lavransdatter." Liz Buer, *Dagbladet* 16 November 1994: 10.

    9. Lars Ditlev Hansen, "I Kristins årestue på Jar," *Aftenposten* 9 June 1994: 68, and Phyllis Ellen Funke, "From the Icy North, A Tale of Love and Rebellion," *New York Times* 7 April 1996: 2, 22.

    10. See, for example, Marlene Edmunds, "Carlsen Steps Down at Norsk," *Daily Variety* 22 December 1994: 1. The project, with Norsk Film in control, would eventually receive funding from Scandinavian (60 percent), German (20 percent), and other European (20 percent) sources.

    11. Marlene Edmonds, "Ullmann Helms Norwegian Epic Slated for '95 Debut," *Variety* 31 October 1994: 63.

    12. "det flotteste tilbudet jeg har fått i hele mitt liv." Bjørn Bratten, "Liv Ullmanns hemmelige prosjekt," *Dagbladet* 14 October 1994: 2.

    13. "den vakreste erfaring." Per A. Christiansen, "Applaus for Liv Ullmann," *Aftenposten* 13 April 1996: 12.

    14. The producers signed the well-known Norwegian female director Eva Isaksen for the second part of the *Kristin* trilogy. The project, however, never progressed past initial planning. About the affection her actors had for Ullmann, see, for example, Liv Ullmann, "Liv Ullmann: Out of Bergman's Shadow," interview by David Brooks Andrews, *Moviemaker* (January/February 1996), in *Liv Ullmann Interviews*, ed. Robert Emmet Long (Jackson: University Press of Mississippi, 2006), p. 160.

    15. Liv Ullmann, "Actress Behind the Camera: An Interview with Liv Ullmann," interview by Richard Porton, *Cinéaste* 26.2 (2001): 37.

    16. See, especially, van Eyck's *The Arnofini Wedding*, 1434, oil on oak panel, 32.4 in. × 23.6 in., National Gallery, London. Nykvist (1922–2006), winner of two Oscars, is most well known for his work on the films of fellow Swede Ingmar Bergman. Critics often have celebrated his use of light, which is frequently compared to that of the Scandinavian impressionists. See, for example, "Sven Nykvist (1922–2006)," IMDb.com, http://www.imdb.com/name/nm0005815/?ref_=nv_sr_1 (accessed 14 March 2017).

    17. "den verste episoden i mitt liv." Per A. Christiansen, "Nyfrisert 'Kristin' i New York," *Aftenposten* 12 April 1996: 34. Ullmann later denied having said this. See Christiansen, "Applaus," 12.

    18. That is, respectively, 46 million and 60 million Norwegian kroner. I have given the dollar figures above to reflect the value in 2017 dollars.

    19. "en krig som har rast gjennom hele produksjonen." Bjørn Bratten, "Sandman ut mot Ullmann: Liv får kritikk etter 'Kristin' overskridelser," *Dagbladet* 22 December 1994: 4.

    20. "Jeg har aldri vært med på en beslutning eller vært forelagt et budsjett. Jeg har ikke fått være meg på møter." Levin, "Når den ny Liv blomstrer," 22.

    21. Lars Ditlev Hansen, "Lavransdatter til 46 millioner," *Aftenposten* 5 May 1994: 56.

    22. Robert E. Lauder, "Liv Ullmann Talks About *Kristin Lavransdatter*," *Crisis Magazine: A Voice for the Faithful Catholic Laity* (1 December 1995), http://www.crisismagazine.com/1995/liv-ullmann-talks-about-kristin-lavransdatter (accessed 8 May 2017).

    23. "i all hemmelighet." Ullmann quoted in Tryve Aas Olsen, "Liv Ullmann er forbannet," *Dagbladet*, 25 October 1995, 36.

    24. "bort regissørens navn." Bjørn Bratten, "Forandrer ikke mening," *Dagbladet* 10 October 1995: 35.

    25. "med sorg." Maria Brit Espinoza, "Liv klipper med sorg—men har full kontroll," *Dagbladet* 20 December 1995: 43.

    26. See, for example, "Amongst Women: Michael Dwyer Previews a Number of Forthcoming Film Festivals Around the Country," *Irish Times* 7 November 1997: 13.

    27. Liv Ullmann, "Trolling for Authenticity," interview by Jeffrey Gantz, *Boston Phoenix*, 15 December 1997, in *Liv Ullmann Interviews*, p. 163.

    28. Marlene Edmunds, "Scandi Film Biz Blows Mostly Cold, Danes Notwithstanding," *Variety* 14–20 October 1996: 49, and Edmunds, "TV Coin Boosts Film Production," *Daily Variety* 4–10 December 1995: 44.

    29. Håkon Moslet, "Kristin-feber," *Dagbladet* 29 August 1995: 31, and Nora Sørensen, "Hanks må vike for Ullmann," *Dagbladet* 12 September 1995: 45.

    30. "filmen er for lang." Thor Ellingsen, "Film: Kristin Lavransdatter," *Dagbladet* 22 August 1995: 28. *Kristin*'s relatively few non–Scandinavian reviewers generally shared similar, albeit harsher, sentiments regard-

ing *Kristin*'s length and pace. See, for example, the largely negative review by Brendan Kelly, "*Kristin Lavransdatter* (Norwegian-German-Swedish)," *Variety* 11–17 September 1995: 111.

31. See, for instance, Trude Ringheim, "Undset-feber," *Dagbladet* 9 October 1994: 11, and, especially, Gunnar Iversen, "Clear, from a Distance: The Image of the Medieval in Recent Norwegian Films," *Scandinavica* 39.1 (2000): 15.

32. "århundrets norske film." Unsigned, "Elisabeth den tandre: Klar for rypejakt—og forberedt på filmslakt," *Dagbladet* 19 August 1995: 52; "Ullmann og Nykvist er navn som garanterer at det gjøres forsøk på et nivå som vi knapt har sett maken til her i landet." Per Haddal, "Film—Norge bør ikke klage," *Aftenposten* 23 June 1994: 16; Unsigned, "Turister vil hjem til Kristin Lavransdatter," *Aftenposten* 25 July 1994: 4.

33. "Alle har sin mening om 'Kristin Lavransdatter' og hvordan det skal være." Lars Ditlev Hansen, "'Kristin Lavransdatter' on location: Kirkebrann med stram regi," *Aftenposten* 14 July 1994: 38.

34. So realistic was Ullmann's Jørundgaard, adding brand new buildings to several reconstructions of medieval buildings that the community of Sel had previously built on the location, that the set after filming became, and remains to this day, an open-air medieval center. See the museum's website, *Jørundgard: Kristin Lavransdatters hjem*, http://www.jorundgard.no/ (accessed 24 May 2017), and also Ellen Rees, "Dreaming of the Medieval in *Kristin Lavransdatter* and *Trollsyn*," *Scandinavian Studies* 75.3 (Fall 2003): 412. Rees's study investigates the extent to which Ullmann's film and another 1990s Norwegian medieval film, *Trollsyn* (1994), use constructs of the medieval and contribute to notions of Norwegian identity.

35. "en del nytt" and "ligger nært opp til Sigrid Undsets ånd." Hansen, "I Kristins årestue," 68.

36. "først og fremst et utrolig stort kvinnepublikum." Ketil Bjørnstad, *Liv Ullmann—Livslinjer*, 2d ed. (Oslo: Aschehoug, 2005), p. 235.

37. Pat Donnelly, "*Lavransdatter* a Powerful Tale of Lust and Life," *The Gazette* [Montréal] 3 September 1995: F3.

38. The portrayal of Christian practice is the subject of Peter G. Christensen's excellent comparative analysis of the novel and film, "Liv Ullmann's Handling of Religious Themes in Her Adaptation of Sigrid Undset's *The Wreath*," *Scandinavian Canadian Studies* 19 (2010), http://scancan.net/christensen_1_19.htm (accessed 24 May 2017).

39. English language quotations from the film are from the first-rate subtitles included on Liv Ullmann, dir., *Kristin Lavransdatter: The Restored Director's Cut*, DVD. I have occasionally changed the punctuation of the subtitles and italicized words to reflect more closely the flow and emphasis of the actors' voices.

40. "Theatrical Trailer," from Liv Ullmann, dir., *Kristin Lavransdatter: The Restored Director's Cut*, DVD.

41. Undset seems to have based Lavrans on her own beloved father, the renowned archaeologist of Iron Age Europe, Ingvald Undset, who died in 1893 when the novelist was just eleven years old. See, for instance, Bayerschmidt, *Sigrid Undset*, p. 22.

42. Liv Ullmann, "Interview with Liv Ullmann, Key Largo 2001," from Liv Ullmann, dir., *Kristin Lavransdatter: The Restored Director's Cut*, DVD.

43. All English language texts and page number references from the novel are from the superb translation Sigrid Undset, *Kristin Lavransdatter I: The Wreath*, trans. Tiina Nunnally (New York: Penguin, 1997).

44. In the two remaining parts of Undset's trilogy, Erlend proves to be a poor husband, little interested in his familial responsibilities and also unfaithful to Kristin. For a synopsis of the latter two parts, see Bayerschmidt, *Sigrid Undset*, pp. 96–104. In the interest of space, I have not discussed here the film's and the novel's portrayals of two other important instances of female erotic desire and its role in forging marital-type relationships. Thus Kristen's aged friend, Fru Aashild, had been led by her desire decades earlier to go against the wishes of her family and to marry a much younger man, Bjørn. And Erlend's mistress, Eline Ormsdatter, followed her desire when she chose to transgress against her marriage to an elderly man to be with Erlend and to have illegitimate children by him. In Ullmann's film especially, Eline's unhappy marriage to the old man also echoes the marriage into which Kristin's convent friend, Ingebjørg (see below), is forced by her family to enter.

45. Ullmann concentrates audience attention upon the relationship of Kristin and Ulvhild by also choosing not to include in her script the novel's third, much younger sister, Ramborg.

46. In the interest of space, I have chosen not to discuss the one significant female friendship that both book and film share, namely, that between Kristin and the much older Fru Aashild.

47. About Undset's conservative and arguably reactionary views on motherhood, see, for example, Ebba Haslund, "Sigrid Undset—en antifeminist?" in *Sigrid Undset i dag*, ed. Pål Espolin Johnson (Oslo: Aschehoug, 1982), pp. 14–17 and 26–27.

48. In consideration of space, I have not discussed the film's and the novel's treatments of the story's other important case of motherly love, namely, that of Inga for her deceased son, Arne.

49. With its very solid attempt—and, indeed, relative success in comparison to other Middle Ages films—in reproducing particularly the material aspects of high and late medieval culture, *Kristin Lavrandatter* is an exceptionally fine film for teaching about daily life in the Middle Ages. As Ullmann, however, evidently created the film with audiences in mind that already had a good knowledge of Sigrid Undset's novel, it is easy to miss important plot details and to fail to appreciate Ullmann's artistry in modifying the original story without first reading Undset's *The Bridal Wreath*. (In fact, most critical interpretations of the film have failed to notice just

how extensive Ullmann's changes to the original truly are.) I, therefore, recommend reading the novel in the excellent translation by Nunnally, or at least selected parts of it, prior to screening. Also recommended for those wishing to teach the film alongside the book, and for their more advanced students, is a succinct interpretation of the novel that puts it also into its recent cultural context internationally, namely, Otto Reinert, "Unfashionable *Kristin Lavransdatter,*" *Scandinavian Studies* 71.1 (1999): 67–80.

Gender, Violence and Medievalism in *La Passion Béatrice*

Andrew B.R. Elliott

In the introduction to her 1986 essay on medieval and early-modern women, Mary Beth Rose argues that "medieval and renaissance women seemed vague, shadowy presences, existing on the periphery of history and in the margins of literary culture."[1] While Rose was referring to the presence of medieval women in the historical record, her comment seems equally relevant to their depiction in medieval cinema, and even more so the discussion of these cinematic depictions in academic scholarship. Even writing over 30 years later, it is hard to summon up more than a handful of examples of medieval women on screen who are able to demonstrate agency in anything more than that "vague, shadowy presence." Even less frequently encountered are films wherein the central protagonist, in this case the titular character, is a woman who operates for a significant part of the screen time outside of the shadow of male oppression. It is thus tempting to see in *La Passion Béatrice* a progressive, empowering, and refreshingly different film that dares to depict genuine female agency within an overwhelmingly patriarchal medieval world. However, even a cursory glance at the film reveals, for those familiar with it and with the vaguely historical tale on which it is loosely based, a markedly different take on female power.

Part of the problem, however, lies not in the medieval treatment of women but in our modern approaches to that period. My argument in this essay is that the traditional invisibility and oversight of medieval women is not a reflection of any specifically medieval antecedents, but rather a reflection of the ideological positions from which we view those Middle Ages. In other words, throughout Bertrand Tavernier's difficult film *La Passion Béatrice*, the problematic marginalization of medieval women is not a historical issue, but a result of the continued (and often unacknowledged) tendency to foreground male privilege in the present. This marginalization, I will suggest, relies implicitly on universalized and trans-historical ideas about entrenched and "natural" gender roles. Moreover, in order to deliver its extended meditation on goodness, evil, morality and the breakdown of the family, the film ends up reinforcing fixed, intransigent, and essentialist stereotypes about medieval women.

Despite offering what seems, on the surface, to be an empowered and enfranchised medieval world, the extended on-screen suffering of the titular Béatrice becomes an unwitting metaphor for the assumed mistreatment and invisibility of medieval women in history, and thus from a psychoanalytical perspective does not challenge, but rather reflects, the continued modern subjugation of women. As such, Tavernier's medieval women are less a reflection of medieval gender relations than they are a reflection of contemporary gender troubles (to allude to the title of Judith Butler's canonical work[2]), which are transported back to the Middle Ages as a site of contested values. In this essay, I explore Tavernier's film as precisely such a contested site, to show how an entirely constructed Middle Ages is used as a pretext (what I have elsewhere called a "paradigm"[3]) in which contemporary debates about gender and morality are played out.

The film itself begins, tellingly, not with the women of the de Cortemare estate (the invented family to which Béatrice belongs), but with the departure of the castle's lord, setting in motion a visible absence around which the plot revolves. An empty hillside frames the title credits, shot from a static camera that gazes dispassionately at the rolling hills of southwest France. Adopting the wide angles and the long takes traditionally favored by the director,[4] the landscape's stillness is underscored by the gradual appearance of a speck that arrives slowly over the horizon of the hill in the foreground. The speck slowly turns into two human figures riding on the same horse, which rides towards the camera in an excruciatingly slow advance, finally revealing that the speck is a man and a child.

Then we are treated in the first cut of the film, to a low angle long shot of the pair as they come to a halt and the boy dismounts, shortly followed by the man. The pair turn away from the camera to stare out at the scenery, and the man—the father, we assume by this point—places a protective, perhaps even at this point proprietorial, arm around the boy's shoulders. A second cut moves to a mid-range two shot with the pair on the right of the screen looking out of the frame to the left, the father's full beard and long, blond hair contrasting sharply with the bright red hair of the child, before a long pan follows their gaze, sweeping back across the empty landscape to the original establishing perspective, wherein more specks have appeared on the horizon. Slowly, inexorably, children on foot begin to fill the screen, with additional figures on horseback trudging over the hillside to reveal a troupe of brightly-colored but indistinct figures, with a corpulent priest in the center of the frame, who walks awkwardly using a cross as a makeshift walking stick.

In keeping with the slow setup of many of Tavernier's films, even as the characters move in and out of focus and out of the frame to the right, the static camera refuses to shift its gaze. Instead, the camerawork continues to favor long, static takes, recording the commentary from a distance, and typically using open frames to construct a non-judgmental pro-filmic space. Such a non-judgmental space thus creates an aesthetic distance from the events that unfold in the film that often imparts a sense of inevitability to those events. The cut switches to a low-angle shot of the still-moving troupe, an effect that creates a jumbled and occasionally blurred procession of moving figures, occasionally obscured by horses moving in front of the camera. Finally, our first individual female figure approaches the two males, before a zoom-in on the flanks of a horse gives way to a mid-shot of the priest to the right of the frame, followed by a long-shot of what can be assumed to be a family, kneeling on the left, with the priest's huge cross cutting the frame in two.

Such long, open takes often allow Tavernier suddenly to switch to a form of visual metonymy to highlight collective struggles through individual sufferers. The opening of *Béatrice* offers, for instance, a strikingly similar composition to the closing of his 1976 *Le Juge et l'assassin* (*The Judge and the Assassin*), where the long take is juxtaposed with a sudden cut to an individual child soldier bringing home news of the death toll of the Paris communes. Tavernier repeats the trope in the opening scenes of *Béatrice*, in which the camera operates as a silent witness to the passing crowd but is interrupted by a sudden cut that brings into focus the individual lives of the de Cortemare family as a symbol of greater suffering and sadness.

Thus the film's first close-up zooms in on the father (we assume) looking down to the right of the frame with the priest's black-clad hand reaching in and blessing him. A match-cut offers the son receiving a similar blessing, with the *mise-en-scène* offering a perfect mirror, a trick that Tavernier repeats with the woman accompanying them, whose pure white robes, veil and brightly-lit upturned face give us our first hint of the binary division of gender roles between the cold emotionless menfolk and the spirited and spiritual womenfolk of the Cortemare estate. An extreme close-up, finally, frames the father and mother exchanging a passionate kiss before the father leaves the frame to the left, after which the extended leave-taking sees the father and his knights ride out of the frame to the left. The boy pursues his father, calling after him, "Père! Père!"

When the boy catches up, the father blesses his son, giving him a dagger, and then takes his leave by warning him to protect his mother on the grounds that "she is so beautiful, and men are so brutal."[5] Not only do the first words of dialogue of the film confirm, for the first time, that the trio are indeed a family, but they also introduce an entire ideology of war, threat, protection, family values, and chauvinism. Beneath the command from the father to son is the bestowal of a belief not in the essential fickleness of women—which might perhaps be expected from medieval culture and medieval Christian thought in particular, at least in the popular imagination—but in the brutality of men. Though seemingly warning against the wife's infidelity, the command is framed as a condemnation of the menfolk and their presumed incapacity to resist the beauty of the mother, marking the boy's mother as more of a Virgin Mary than an Eve. However, the next scene offers a blow-by-blow reversal of the first, with the boy, François, returning to the castle, this time in search of his mother. As he runs through the castle in a series of rapid and disorienting cuts, he reverses his previous pursuit by calling out, "Mère! Mère!"—before he stumbles upon his mother naked, already in bed with her lover. Unthinkingly, François unsheathes his dagger and plunges it into the chest of the lover, chastising his mother in the process. From Virgin Mary to Eve, Tavernier's use of parallel editing implies that the two events take place at precisely the same time, so that the time it takes for the boy to catch up with his father is all it takes before the mother has already transgressed his paternal interdiction. As such, his father is right about the infidelity, but wrong about his wife's complicity and willingness, and within three lines of dialogue, the masculinity of the film's protagonist is demonstrated to be in crisis.

Thus, the dominant themes of the film are already sketched out fully within its two opening scenes, just as the ailments of certain trees can be traced back to their roots, as the voice-over has reminded us during the prologue. The ambiguous position of religion in Tavernier's film is introduced with the priest blessing the men leaving for violent glory; the ruptures underlying the seeming blissfulness of family life are exposed by the departure of the father and the instant infidelity of the mother; the inherent violence of the patriarchy is embodied by the father's absence and the vindictive cruelty of the son. Furthermore, the *mise-en-scène* says more than it means to. Up to this point, no words have been spoken by any female character, and nor are any of the women named—there is no chance of the film passing the Bechdel test here.[6]

It is in the context of a cruel, swift, and overwhelming male justice, then, that the sudden switch to the youthful, passionate, and delicate voice-over of Julie Delpy's Béatrice creates such a stark contrast. Her voice-over is deliberately confusing in the temporal planes it invokes: she speaks as the eponymous Béatrice, whom the young boy seen in the opening scene will grow up to father. The film thus starts with Béatrice's grandfather, before the story passes to her father, François; while Béatrice describes the psychological effect of Francois' mother's infidelity on the young boy, the accompanying images switch back to the long takes and distant camera shots to witness his self-imposed exile on the roof of the castle, awaiting his own father's return. Immediately afterwards, Tavernier deploys another sudden generational switch, which highlights the loneliness of all three generations by opening with Delpy's pale face in profile looking out from the castle roof.

We hear her voice before we see her, and her voice-over willingly self-identifies Béatrice not as the protagonist and titular character, but as the offspring and "possession" of her father, François. The cold, empty frames foreshadow the loneliness of the de Cortemares; the distant camera denotes the cruelty of the family. The opening of the film already suggests that the dynasty is irrevocably built on cruelty and lovelessness, wherein the patriarchy exists for protection instead of affection, power in place of love, and vengeance in place of kindness and forgiveness. Moreover, the family is normalized by the film's consistent reference to religion—as the priest in the opening section, the saints to whom Béatrice prays, the blessings and the observances all make clear, the de Cortemares are a devout family. However, already by the opening scenes, we are presented with a twisted version of medieval Christianity wherein God's mercy and grace are eschewed, replaced by a crude Manicheism reflecting a violent dichotomy between good and evil with no room for ambiguity. The dark brutality of the father's childhood is suddenly undermined by a close-up of the tender, fragile beauty of a young Béatrice looking out of the frame and into the distance, waiting for the return of her own father, François, in a visual and narrative echo of her father's own lonely vigil. Thus, even when empowered, her agency is expressed by her inactivity; instead of running the castle in the absence of masculine agency, she is first glimpsed passively waiting for the menfolk to return.

Béatrice's gradual empowerment is thus systematically reconfigured throughout the film, not as a kind of proto-feminist emancipation, but as a kind of agency operating in a purely reactive capacity. Her management of the castle and estate is only permitted in the absence of the menfolk, and the entire purpose of her assumption of the role is to raise sufficient ransom so as to guarantee their safe return. Thus, her agency is only designed to re-establish the male-domination to which the estate, and family, are "naturally" subjected. Such a willingness is represented visually, too, in Béatrice's jaunts through the countryside; in her vibrant, immaculate red dress, with golden hair flowing freely, she is depicted as a kind of nymph of the forest, recalling Emmanuelle Béart's eponymous *Manon des sources* released one year earlier. However, her liberation outside of the castle, narratively speaking, serves to hasten the return of her father and brother even though it is only made possible by their absence. Indeed, the symbolic value of her red dress as index of freedom is bathetically undermined by later scenes in which the same red dress is seen torn, dirty, and faded as she is imprisoned within the castle, only to be removed altogether as she barricades herself into her chamber after her father rapes her.

Julie Delpy as the title character in the 1987 film *Béatrice*.

The introduction of Béatrice, and of her quotidian routine in the female-dominated castle, is sharply and decisively ended with the long-awaited return of François. Structurally, the film can be divided loosely into what I will call three "acts," each of which revolves around the variously distorted male-female relationships and the equilibrium of gender roles. In the first of these acts, introduced in the brief sketch above, it is the absence of the men from the estate and the freshness of Béatrice's youth that signal the hope for the future. Bookended by shots of Béatrice looking out hopefully into the distance, her construction as a giddy teenager sees her tripping lightly around the castle, giggling with her maid and grandmother, and devoting most of her attention to picking wildflowers, catching birds, and ensuring domestic harmony and aesthetic pleasures. In this feminine world, her interactions with male characters play on a cruel binary between absent men and emasculated figures, such as the retainer who regales the castle's inhabitants with well-known stories of his pilgrimage to Jerusalem, or else the handicapped boy Jehan, whom Béatrice treats tenderly and who follows the maiden around loyally like a surrogate son.

In this section, as a proleptic nod to the imminent darkness that will accompany the return of her father, her bucolic idyll is shot through with golden sunshine and bright, primary colors, from the red of her dress to the dappled sunlight as she climbs trees to capture her birds. However, even here, her agency is continually undermined; although she is nominally in a position of power, even in her moments of absolute authority (such as when she negotiates the sale of lands to the local lawyer), her powerlessness is restored by her admission of illiteracy, which leads the lawyer literally to guide her hand as she signs the deeds of sale.

With the hints of a potential love flourishing between herself and the lawyer, even while these hints are expressed in terms of *fin amor*, Béatrice herself thus becomes symbolically part of the chattels and valuable jewels of the castle, having passed already from the father's possession to the lawyer's, in the same transaction as the father's lands are sold to the same buyer. As such, by the close of the first act, Béatrice has surrounded herself with a kind of ersatz surrogate family consisting of an absent husband, a handicapped son, and a menagerie of semi-feral birds, who long to escape the moment their cages are open. The symbolism of these wild, beautiful spirits trapped in gilded cages scarcely needs to be mentioned, and the shots of the birds are visually echoed by shots of Béatrice herself perched in branches, or in her flights through the country estates, her long sleeves flapping behind her in the breeze.

The second act is framed by a similar visual parenthesis in the brutal and destructive return of François, under cover of darkness, together with his *écorcheurs*—his marauding and pillaging retainers. Their arrival at night, amid a blanket of snow, offers a powerful visual contrast with the perpetual spring of Béatrice's first act, throwing the flower-decked "merry, merry month of May," as Lerner and Loewe's *Camelot* might describe it, into a sudden winter of violence, cruelty, and bloodshed.

The scene depicting François' return is unrelenting and seems to be a bricolage of other medieval films, particularly those coming from a European art house tradition. The *écorcheurs'* procession through local villages is a direct reversal of the finely-appareled knights of Rohmer's *Perceval le Gallois* (1978) and the Grail-seeking knights of *Excalibur* (1981). Where the latter two appear in literally shining armor, riding to provide assistance to the weak in accordance with the courtly and chivalric codes, Tavernier's bathetic knights wreak havoc, death, and destruction on all that they see around them. As they ride back from war, they create their own Terre Gaste, burning villages and pillaging food and wealth, and ultimately amassing little more than a pathetic plunder of cheap metal armor and iron tools. In one of the most disturbing scenes (in a film which is, on the whole, disturbing), the *écorcheurs* come across a woman in labor in the woods. The scene operates as a gruesome reversal of the rescue of Mia in Bergman's *The Seventh Seal* (1957). In Bergman's film, the condemned knight distracts Death long enough to save Mia, Jof, and their baby allowing them if not life, then at least hope of life. In *Béatrice*, when the troupe encounters the woman, a rapid cut reveals that she has suffocated her new-born baby in the snow amid a pool of blood, and the high-angle shot literally looks down on her as a kind of impassive judgment while she feebly pleads with the "knights" for mercy. Forced to abandon the child, the woman is roughly thrown onto a horse as a trophy and obviously intended as booty for François' men to enjoy. The parting exchange between Arnaud (Béatrice's brother) and his father makes explicit the disdain for women rampant among the troupe: on discovering that the dead child was a girl, Arnaud seeks his father's approval with his suggestion that "wenches don't have a soul."[7]

Though perhaps not quite so explicitly in this second act, the women of the castle also suffer cruel treatment on the return of their lord. Despite the tender hopefulness of Béatrice on the arrival of her father and of her brother, her father's first action is not to embrace her but to grip her wrist forcefully in a powerful foreshadowing of bodily possession and domination. A brief summary of the treatment of the women is not enough to convey the physical and verbal cruelty meted out to the female occupants of the castle from François' return onwards. Besides his coldness and impassivity, François' behavior rapidly deteriorates to include the physical abuse of family and servants, such as a brutal scene in which the same woman who was earlier "rescued" in the forest is kicked awake as François begins to rape her, only to discard her literally by throwing her aside when he suspects she is ill or dying from fever. A later scene sees François raping another female servant, only interrupting his violent actions to force his son to join in, brutally beating him when he fails to do so.

In fact, even his son and sole heir is implicitly transfigured as a female member of the household when his father systematically undermines his already fragile masculinity. Though his disdain for his son is scarcely concealed from the outset, it is not long before we explicitly witness the son's humiliation as his father recounts his ironic exploits and alleged "conquests," in which a petrified Arnaud, frozen with fear in the face of what seems to have been his first sight of open battle, soils himself. As François recounts it, he and his brave warriors were forced then to leave the fray, rushing back to rescue his son "covered in shit," only to find themselves surrounded by enemy soldiers and taken prisoner: as such, the humiliation of Arnaud also contains a subtext of boastful masculinity that explains and implicitly exculpates François' own humiliation. The "sins of the father" are thus borne by the son, so that any doubts surrounding François' reputation as a warrior and as a male patriarch are assuaged by the ritualized unmanning of Arnaud who is thus responsible by implication. This "unmanning" of Arnaud is continued in later scenes, such as when François tells Béatrice that she should have been born as his son, when Arnaud's response to his father's madness is to secure himself in the castle, while Béatrice follows her father's childhood instincts and seeks self-imposed exile and isolation on the open rooftop. François's assault on Arnaud's masculinity reaches its apogee in a haunting scene in which the father forces his son to put on a red dress (visually recalling Béatrice's dress) as a ritual humiliation and undermining of his masculinity. Once the boy is dressed as a woman—and thus visually constructed as a counterpart to his sister—François and his retainers rally together with their horses and dogs to hunt him like an animal, a scene that despite its cruelty still does not quite represent the nadir of his father's depravity.

The second act also adopts a set of binary oppositions as metaphors for the return of the father and a shift from the daylight to the nocturnal (both literally and figuratively), and from the open air to the stale, shadowy enclosure of the castle. The bright, bucolic *mise-en-scène* of the earlier act is totally undermined by the return of François in this second act, which is dominated by night-scenes, shadow, and interior scenes rather than by the exterior locations, dappled sunlight and bright primary color palette reflecting Béatrice's own adolescent metaphorical springtime. The claustrophobic tension of the castle is further underscored by the use of tapestries, curtains, and wooden partitions to divide the space of the castle into smaller, cramped spaces in which men sleep side-by-side on straw scattered around the central hall, where dogs bark relentlessly, children pilfer, underlings are beaten without reason, servants scurry out of striking distance from their lord, and the women of the castle barricade themselves into bedrooms, sleeping three to a bed with the curtains drawn around them. Similarly, after several uncharacteristic close-ups and cutaways in the first act, the pace slows down in this second act to return to Tavernier's more familiar style of unflinching long takes, wide-angles, and open frames.

Tavernier's style owes much to André Bazin's criticism, and particularly to his dismissal of the "myth of total cinema," a predominant understanding of cinema as an impassive means of capturing reality. After a series of breakthroughs in photographic technologies in the late 19th century, according to Bazin many theorists began to see the camera as a means of capturing the truth, and thus saw cinema or moving pictures "as a total and complete representation of reality."[8] Bazin's criticism, however, is that such a naïve view of the camera overlooks the artistry of cinematography as well as the limitations of the frame; as a piece of technology used to mask and frame reality rather than slavishly to record it, the camera—and by extension cinema—cannot show everything but is instead always offering a viewpoint that is partial and fragmented.

Working in the shadow of Bazin and the French New Wave directors, Tavernier's style as a director demonstrates their collective influence in the presentation of a fragmented and partial Middle Ages, which are here paraded impassively before the viewer as an inexorable and relentless descent into brutality and chaos wherein we can never see the total picture. Tapestries and arches frame, mask, and constrain the screen; forests and horses block key shots and obscure the action from our vision. In one pivotal scene, curtains divide up the womenfolk sleeping in the same room, so that a rampaging François must tear away the drapes in order to discover where the occupants of his castle have hidden themselves. These Middle Ages, like those of John Huston's *A Walk with Love and Death* (1969) or Paul Verhoeven's *Flesh + Blood* (1985), the latter of which shares dark and unflinching depictions of incestuous rape, are no sanitized version of Merrie England. Instead they welcome dirt, dirtiness, and grime, as a wide-angled camera sits back dispassionately recording a depiction of a ruthless, cruel, and uncaring world. The religious themes are closer to Robert Bresson's *Lancelot du lac* (1974) than to Ingmar Bergman's eschatology in *The Seventh Seal*. Unlike Tavernier, Bergman sees redemption even through the death of his protagonist; the salvation of his medieval people relies ultimately on the sacrifice of his knight, Antonius Block. Bresson, instead, sees a dark and dismal world suffering not the punishment of God, but his total indifference to such suffering.

In fact, Tavernier's *Béatrice* bears some striking similarities to Bresson's *Lancelot du lac*, not least in its thematic obsession with a search for grace and redemption in a brutal world. In Bresson's 12th-century Camelot, there is scarcely any room for religion; the knights spend a good deal of time castigating themselves for their impieties, transgressions and sinful nature, which led to the failure of their spiritual quest, but they still fundamentally seem to fail to grasp the spiritual nature of the quest itself. There is clearly a greater focus in *Lancelot du lac* on the ramifications of fundamentally human flaws. No *deus ex machina* is allowed to rise and effect the court's redemption, even after Lancelot's plea to God not to abandon Camelot and its occupants ("ne nous abondonnez pas [...] ne m'abandonnez pas"). However, "invoked, prayed to, supplicated, God never responds,"[9] and the film closes with the end of chivalry made manifest only by the cinematic incarnation of a court tearing itself apart over petty rivalries. The spiritual redemption, it seems, comes only from the renunciation of earthly sins, and perhaps only by the final and ultimate removal of the armor of pride, allowing for a final redemption of sin. Bresson's film thus offers a visual and thematic parallel to that of Tavernier, offering a world in which events unfold according to the whims of local lords under the uncaring eye of an indifferent God, a deity who is as little concerned for his devout female servants, such as Béatrice and the unnamed recluse (played by Albane Guilhe), as he is angered by François' various direct challenges to his authority. Tavernier's Middle Ages are thus a

Middle Ages of no time or place, where God is oblivious to the taunts of men, and refuses to intervene to protect devout innocents like Arnaud and Béatrice.

Having thus established a fundamental dualism between the dark violence of masculine authority and the innocent brightness of feminine devotion and nurturing, the film's third act is thus free to move towards its denouement and its ultimate attempt at a reconciliation of medieval femininity. Beginning with François' attempt to legitimize his rape of his own daughter by forcing her to marry him and ending with the daughter's rejection of the father's patriarchal power, the third act is delineated by total descent into madness and rejection of humanity and compassion. In doing so, Tavernier tightens the plot to focus almost entirely on the father-daughter relationship, so that "the essential drama of *La Passion Béatrice* concerns the two intensely emotional characters whose relationship descends into a terrible conflict of love and hatred, and the film's single close-ups and medium close-ups ensure that the images that echo longest after the film are human faces drawn by anguish."[10]

With the systematic undermining of Arnaud's masculinity, culminating in his becoming the prey of a gruesome "hunt" sequence, the father-daughter binary opposition functions as a metonymic device to juxtapose the male-female relationships, further underscoring the brutality of the father and the violence that inheres in the patriarchal insistence on the absolute power of the *pater familias*. As Lisa Manter suggests,

> part of what makes François's behaviour as lord and father truly horrific is its juxtaposition to Béatrice's daughterly devotion. To concentrate the viewer's attention on this father-daughter conflict, Tavernier alters the Cenci story [the "true" story on which the film is based] so that the roles played by the stepmother, the older and younger brothers, and the members of the church hierarchy are downplayed to emphasize the relationship between François and Béatrice.[11]

It is at this stage that the reductive simplicity of such a gender dualism really begins to show the ideological fault lines of the 20th, and not the 14th, century. The film's attempt to challenge unchecked masculine authority is resolved not by exploring gender as a construct, but rather by forcing the innocent Béatrice to adopt her own form of violence as a retribution against the patriarchy. As Laurence de Looze puts it, in a world where "social power is marked as masculine and masculinity is defined as symbolic possession of the phallus [, Béatrice ...] must become a 'man' during the course of the film in order finally to defeat her deranged father."[12] The problem, however, with such an attempt is that it clumsily equates agency and power purely with violence, which, as I have argued elsewhere, only serves to reinforce the specifically masculine understanding of power even further.[13]

The problem with de Looze's parallel is, however, that it flattens the nuances of the film. The idea that Tavernier was relying on a contrast between female passivity and male agency precludes the possibility that he was also trying to address an oversight in the general depiction of medieval women on screen. In reality, once we recognize the visual parallel between the young François exiled on the rooftop and the adult Béatrice adopting the same site as a refuge from her own father, it is obvious that the film is trying to explore more than a clumsy gender binary, but rather represents a rather complicated meditation on the place of gender and agency during a period of grotesque sexual assault and violence. The fact that Arnaud is unable to enact the military exploits demanded of him (and thus the romantic tales of feats of arms undermined by François' description of a cowardly Arnaud) and that Béatrice is also prevented from fulfilling the marriage demanded by courtly love shows that Tavernier is rebelling against the strictures of medieval gender. Instead, the meaning of the film's depiction of gender and agency is embedded in a fundamental queerness, dependent on a complex maelstrom of entangled issues. By concentrating only on a polarity of male/female agency, as de Looze argues, Tavernier has simplified the fluidity of gender constructs into a spectrum of which we glimpse only the two outermost extremities.

Such a simplification is perhaps partly explained not by the issue of gender in the Middle Ages, but by its legacy in our cultural memory of the period. In this respect, what is particularly telling is the complex relationship between the story retold in the film and its claim to be based on an actual "true" story. As stark, shocking, and dysfunctional as the de Cortemare family may be, the essential outlines of the film's plot are taken from a purportedly true version of events carried out by the Cenci family in Italy in the late 16th century. As Manter summarizes it:

> In brief, the story, recorded in legal documents, chronicles, and popular legend, concerns the patricide of Francesco Cenci, a Roman nobleman, who had a record of violence and sexual license. After years of abuse, his wife Lucrezia, eldest son Giacomo, and daughter Beatrice (both from a previous marriage) arrange to have him killed. Their conspiracy came to light, and Pope Clement VIII sentenced them to public execution in 1599. The youngest son, Bernard, was spared but forced to watch his family executed.[14]

The story, replete with its shock and gore, was thus sufficiently sensational as to invite later artists and writers to depict its central themes.[15]

The tale of the Cenci family has been revisited numerous times in literature, poetry, theatre, opera and the visual arts, and became something of a Victorian phenomenon with a sculpture by Harriet Goodhue Hosmer in 1857, a photographic series by Julia Margaret Cameron in 1866, and perhaps most famously a 17th-century painting of Beatrice by Guido Reni (now thought to be painted by his assistant, Elisabetta Sirani ca. 1662). Reni's painting in turn appeared in Herman Melville's 1852 novel, *Pierre*, and Nathaniel Hawthorne's *Marble Faun* (1860), though it is unclear if Tavernier would have known of her depictions there. It is, however, likely to have been the most well-known versions, *The Cenci: A Tragedy in Five Acts* by Percy Bysshe Shelley (1820), the short story "Les Cenci" by Stendhal (1837), and *Les Cenci*, Antonin Artaud's adaptation of the Shelley play in 1935, that seemingly most influenced Tavernier's version, as well as a film version made by Riccardo Freda in 1956, entitled *Beatrice Cenci*, which was later re-released under the more salacious (and alarming) title of *Castle of the Banned Lovers*. Though the latter film is somewhat brusque in its treatment of the tale, and clumsily insensitive in places, François Amy de la Bretèque argues that originally Tavernier wanted to make a homage to Freda's version, but transported the setting to the late Middle Ages, since it seemed to reflect a decline of values and the chaos of the Hundred Years War as it has been collectively remembered.[16]

In fact, the choice to shift the temporal setting is not incidental to the question of gender. Again, as Manter argues,

> by projecting this Renaissance story backward onto the Middle Ages, to a time of shifting norms and instability, the narrative of *Béatrice* can be read as supporting a history that is 'continuist and teleological' since the events of the tragedy should never have occurred in the modern period. In other words, if the brutality and sexual deviance of the [Renaissance] Cencis are transferred to the [medieval] de Cortemare family [...,] then the dramatic action is fittingly barbaric rather than perverse.[17]

Similarly, in his discussion of the film's aesthetic style, Stephen Hay argues that the *mise-en-scène* of the film is typical of Tavernier's historical filmmaking with its "wide framing and camera movements, designed to emphasise its characters' searchings and wanderings."[18] Unlike Tavernier's earlier historical works *Que la fête commence* (1975, a.k.a. *Let Joy Reign Supreme*) or *Le Juge et l'Assassin*, which are set in the Regency and post–Commune periods respectively, as the director's only medieval film *Béatrice* relies on a more mythical sense of disorientation which deliberately works against the demands of realism. Such effects include a greater reliance on dissolves and fades, rather than on direct cuts, slow-motion or other anti-realistic images using jump-cuts and dissolves, which, as Hay observes, "clearly strengthen the film's important dream-aspect, but do not represent an essential change in approach."[19]

Consequently, even from the directorial style of the film, it is clear that the film's focus on Béatrice as a complex, rounded and pitiful character, together with its temporal shift from the Renaissance to the Middle Ages, means that the film is not only about gender and the corruption of male power, but it is also about a specifically *medieval* version of that corruption and brutality. By deliberately shifting an early modern tale to a late medieval setting, Tavernier is playing on a specific understanding of the Middle Ages as a period of brutal, unchecked, male violence—and of medieval women as the victims of that violence. The only way for the director to emphasize the extent of that violence, however, is to insist on the passivity and meekness of a saintly, innocent, and pure Béatrice. In this way, the shift to an earlier period reveals less about history or the Middle Ages, and more about *our perceptions* of those Middle Ages, and the historical capital of modern audiences in understanding what that period means to us in the 20th and 21st centuries.

Because of this paradigmatic borrowing, in which the Middle Ages becomes a useful repository for modern fears and anxieties, Tavernier's medieval world becomes a bricolage, a world constructed from fragments of other medieval representations of those worlds. Speaking psychoanalytically, that bricolage of familiar medieval paradigms thus becomes a screen on which contemporary (to the 1980s) gender issues are projected. Instead of retelling the story of one dysfunctional family, Tavernier constructs Béatrice as the paragon of filial devotion and feminine passivity in a brutal and violent male world that is the progenitor of our own, modern world. As such, just as the root poisons the branch, as the film's prologue warns us, so too do our medieval predecessors' attitudes toward gender poison and contaminate our own modern attitudes. In this respect, the film is more of an example of a neomedievalist fantasy (which is rooted in the present) than of a medievalist attempt to depict the Middle Ages and the conditions of women within the period.

Thus, as suggested in the introduction to this essay, the gender debates of *La Passion Béatrice* are not about medieval women, but their descendants in France in the late 1980s. Scripted by Tavernier's wife, Colo O'Hagan Tavernier, and starring their son, Nils Tavernier, as Arnaud, the focus on a family is perhaps understandable. However, the relevance to the present of the depiction of a corrupted family is less so, unless understood as a reflection of a broader "crisis of masculinity" which Phil Powrie argues characterized French cinema in the 1980s.[20] Within this apparent "crisis," traditional gender roles began to find themselves challenged by the new faces of French cinema such as Tavernier, Jean-Jacques Beineix, Bertrand Blier, and Josiane Balasko.

In the new generation of 1980s and 1990s films, the bastions of square-jawed masculinity began to take on new roles that overtly called into question the immutability of masculinity. The rugged masculinity of Gérard Depardieu, for instance, found itself lampooned in the comedy crime drama *Tenue de soirée* (a.k.a. *Ménage/Evening Dress*, Bertrand Blier, 1986) with his depiction of Bob, a bisexual, cross-dressing, petty criminal who seduces both members of a married couple. A year later, the same year in which *La Passion Béatrice* was released, Depardieu would further undermine his rugged, tough star persona in his portrayal of the titular hunchback in *Jean de Florette* (1987), a role that once again worked against his earlier action-based roles. Perhaps most significantly for my purposes here, one of Depardieu's most enduring roles remains his depiction of Martin Guerre in Daniel Vigne's *Le retour de Martin Guerre* (1982, a.k.a. *The Return of Martin Guerre*) a deeply flawed character whose masculinity is overtly challenged in a memorable, and disturbing, charivari, in which his manhood is publicly challenged by a carnivalized and symbolic castration.[21]

Set against such a backdrop, *La Passion Béatrice*'s construction of medieval femininity is forced to rely on its irreconcilable polarity between father and daughter only by entrenching their gender roles according to simplified ideas of purity versus barbarity, innocence versus *Weltschmerz*, and sanctity versus corruption. The juxtaposition of a destructive, hegemonic male violence and the redemptive, healing innocence of femininity are, of course, painted too crudely and do injustice to both, especially in the periodic return throughout the film of a mirror image in which Béatrice kneels before a crudely carved Madonna, a trope that clumsily compares the corruption of Béatrice's innocence with the statue's purity and sanctity. However, in the context of broader challenges to patriarchal and hegemonic masculinity of the 1980s, the kind of masculinity most prevalent in hard-body Hollywood action films like *Rambo* or *The Terminator*,[22] the depiction of medieval male power as inherently flawed has repercussions in the ways in which we view ourselves.

It is in this final, psychoanalytical, reading of the film that the underpinning attitudes towards gender, and the degree to which they are anchored in present—and not past—concerns, begin to emerge. In his article on the film, de Looze rightly reads *La Passion Béatrice* as a psychoanalytical allegory throughout, basing his reading on the "Freudian/Lacanian observation that sexuality is not innate but acquired."[23] Reading beyond the specific issue of sexuality, and adopting an entirely presentist perspective, that same psychoanalytical reading perhaps explains why, despite offering an interesting and potentially provocative female figure amid a paucity of empowered medieval women on screen, Tavernier's film falls back on a rather clumsy gender essentialism.

Given the film's focus on brutality and primitivism and given the shift of setting from the Renaissance to the Middle Ages, it is reasonable to conclude that the film sees the medieval world as a form of childhood. Indeed, already from the pre-title sequence, the epigraph of the film makes such a reading explicit in its claim of the Middle Ages that "their universe is at the same time vast and fierce, haunted by the powers from up above, a universe where the Sacred brushes daily with the Barbaric[…]. These are savage children. They are what we still are at night, in our dreams. They are our unconscious."[24]

As such, the reading of the medieval world not as a historical world in its own right but only as a dream of our infancy recalls Umberto Eco's argument that the period is often used to diagnose our own trauma and pathologies. The constant return to the Middle Ages is, in this reading, the result of an eternal search for our roots. "Looking at the Middle Ages," writes Eco, "means looking at our infancy, in the same way that a doctor, to understand our present state of health, asks us about our childhood, or in the same way that the psychoanalyst, to understand our present neuroses, makes a careful investigation of the primal scene. Our quest for the Middle Ages is a quest for our roots."[25]

In this context, the voice-over heard in the opening scenes begins to adopt a new meaning. As the young François chases his father off to war, the voice-over comments that "there are some stories that are like certain trees, of which it is necessary to know the roots in order to better grasp the sickly twisting of the branches, the rush of blood in the foliage, the poison in the sap."[26] In this psychoanalytical context, from the perspective of contemporary gender studies, the subtext is perhaps even more disconcerting, since it embeds within a timeless narrative a gendered binary of purity and innocence, rather than acknowledging the inherent violence of the patriarchy.

In fact, by continuing the logic of the tripartite structure suggested above, it becomes possible to read in Tavernier's film a way of seeing medieval women not as individual agents capable of self-determination and autonomy, but as either meek, passive playthings of a medieval patriarchy or else as pale imitations of male agency. In both cases, the psychoanalytical explanation proposed in the prologue indirectly inculpates the female characters as somehow responsible for the unnatural and brutal actions of the menfolk. Thus, the neomedieval—rather than medieval—reading of the Cenci case as retold by Tavernier's film makes for a problematic reading of the relationship between gender, violence, and empowered female agency on screen. In part, I suggest, this problematic psychoanalytical reading is due to the tripartite structure of the film which separates the key plot points into the absence of male agency and the passivity of the female characters.

To explain in more depth, the division of the film into the three acts that I have proposed above separates the action into the comings and goings of François and the emergence into adulthood of Béatrice. Combining these three sections with the psychoanalytical reading of the prologue thus implicitly apportions blame for the breakdown of the family unit to a dysfunctional family unit caused not only by the violence of the father but also by the failure of the son to demonstrate sufficient male agency; these two themes dominate the first and third sections respectively, characterized by François' attack on his mother's lover and by Arnaud's failure to replicate such male violence against women in particular. The dysfunctionality of the family is not only highlighted in the second act by the inability of the daughter to accept her place as meek, docile and fundamentally passive, but also by her inability to act as an independent, female agent of history because of the sexual assault and violence of the father.

Again, two key elements of the film demonstrate the ways in which the prevention of female agency is depicted through often violent subjugation. The first, Béatrice's acceptance of the marriage proposal, offers a degree of conformity to audience expectations of the medieval according to which the daughter becomes part of the chattels of the family estate to be "sold off" to the highest bidder, but it is undermined by the return of the father, who prevents her from enacting that traditional role of a meek and dutiful daughter. However, the distressing reversal of the father's prevention of the marriage is made manifest through his cruel treatment of her, leading to his violent rape, which offers an inverted and disturbing parallel to the marriage: if Béatrice is his "property," then his incestuous rape is the consummation of the owner's rights, as witnessed by his attempt to legitimize the rape when he asks the priest to marry them.

A further level of misogyny emerges through the psychoanalytical reading of these three acts, since their ordering implies a level of responsibility and teleology. Most particularly, the violence and lack of empathy of François are ascribed to his loneliness and abandonment as a child, proposing a logic which traces the root cause of such a lonely and isolated childhood to his mother's infidelity during his father's absence. In turn his father's absence, following the same logic in which the "poison in the sap can be traced back to the roots," leads to the demonstration of a violent and brutal masculinity in François, whose excesses are corrected in the sensitive Arnaud, who thus becomes aligned with the female members of the estate who are rendered ineffectual (François' mother), invisible (François' wife), or inadequate at the daily management of the estate (Béatrice herself, as well as Arnaud).

Further, the absence of the men is enacted as a thematic repetition of the opening sequence of the film in which the men leave for battle. Significantly, although the film shows his departure, we are never shown François' father's return to the castle, and nor is any real concrete information supplied about his fate. Thus, the only return we see is that of François himself, coldly returning with his band of *écorcheurs* to take the place of the "good" father; having unsuccessfully deployed violence on the battlefield, they thus resort to male-agency-as-violence on their return. The simplicity of the equation is thus brutal; the medieval world of the film is one which equates male agency as performed through violent acts, and its obverse—femininity—is demonstrated through the failure to enact violence (in the case of Arnaud, who is both feminized by his forced cross-dressing and finds his agency undermined in a scene where he breastfeeds from a wet nurse in his helplessness and desperation).

The logic of this equation of agency with violence is thus signaled in the third act by the return of the father and the restoration of patriarchal power. Indeed, the brutality of this logic is visually reinforced by the chilling scene in which Arnaud becomes the quarry in a vicious and disturbing human hunt. As mentioned earlier, during this scene Arnaud is forced to wear a red dress which visually evokes Béatrice, and which visually demonstrates the final emasculation of Arnaud in a procession from verbal abuse (when François recounts the embarrassing cowardice of Arnaud on the battlefield) to sexual abuse (when François attempts to coerce Arnaud into raping the servant girl, and suggests a male substitute when the latter indicates his reluctance) to physical abuse in his chasing and, it is implied, desire to kill his son as prey.

By coding Arnaud as feminine within the brutal male world, the logic follows that he is as guilty as the women of the estate of being unable to maintain a family and its estate and is thus "deserving" of punishment in the same way as the women, in this distorted logic which equates agency with violence and the gendered absence of power. The scenes of Arnaud stumbling over rocks in his frantic attempt to escape the hunt offer a bathetic repetition of Béatrice's agility in leaping through the fields and hills in the second act of the film. The cinematography also points backwards to the opening scene witnessing the departure of François' own father. Moving from a focus on the landscape from a static camera, the horsemen come into focus moving from left to right across the screen, with shots in which a horse's flanks block the screen in a direct repetition of the same shots as discussed in the opening of this essay.

In contrast to the opening scene, the static camera is also juxtaposed with a series of tracking shots, swift and clumsy pans that follow Arnaud in his desperate flight, with rapid cutting between shots, all of which recall Béatrice's playful excursions earlier in the film as she climbed trees gaily, capturing birds in her own, gentle hunt. The cinematography thus combines both François (static camera) and Béatrice (moving and fast-paced editing) to suggest, cumulatively, that Arnaud is more daughter than father. The hunt sequence thus undermines the last tenet of kindness and tenderness by the ironic repetition of the film's very few moments of happiness and tenderness, replaced by brutality, loss of control and a total lack of empathy and compassion. The fact that, during the hunt, Béatrice is picked out by the camera as riding at the tail end of the trail of horses only serves to demonstrate the polarity of the gendered logic of male agency and male violence. The punishment of women—including Arnaud—here becomes a trope representing the cycle of violence that can only be escaped by violence, namely the killing of the father.

The problem with the depiction of male agency as violence, of course, is that the film's surface logic seems to suggest that such tropes are a staple trope of the Middle Ages, endemic to a culture of masculinity, brutality and patriarchy. As mentioned above, the premise of the film's source material (the tale of the Cencis in Renaissance Italy) places the culpability firmly on the family and not on the father. Whatever the sins of the father, the horror and fascination of the tale seem to have been caused by the "unnatural" and ungodly acts of the daughter in her patricide. Certainly, the gruesome punishments of the family, including the hanging of Beatrice herself, suggest that for Renaissance Italy it was the unthinkable killing of the patriarch which was the real sin. The absence of direct censure in Tavernier's version of Béatrice, accordingly, might seem to be a more modern and sympathetic retelling of the story.

In terms of its representation of gender, *La Passion Béatrice* is thus more of a neomedievalist fantasy reflective of attitudes towards women at the end of the 1980s than a medievalist text aiming to understand the realities of medieval women. Despite its attempt to offer a more sensitive and nuanced portrayal of medieval life, *La Passion Béatrice* nevertheless relies on a fundamental gender essentialism. When coupled with the problematic implications of the above psychoanalytical reading, such gender binaries mean that the film's insistence on the feminine saintliness of Béatrice as a typology of medieval femininity only works if medieval men are understood as uniquely, overwhelmingly, and unfailingly masculine. As Amy S. Kaufman argues, "behind such works of medievalism lurks the odor of nostalgic fantasy, a longing for the opposite side of the disempowered feminine equation: a muscular medievalism," a medievalism which reflects a "need for the suffering and exploitation of women in order to validate [and in the case of Tavernier, to critique] its vision of masculinity."[27] The somewhat disappointing conclusion, then, of Tavernier's examination of female suffering is that, by trying to buck the trend in the representation of medieval women as passive and ineffectual, Tavernier makes recourse to a prevalent neomedievalist fantasy of female suffering and exploitation which ultimately undoes some of the nuance of gender. By constructing medieval women according to overly simplistic, preconceived categories, *La Passion Béatrice* unwittingly reproduces some of the essentialist gender paradigms it otherwise seeks to leave behind.

NOTES

1. *Women in the Middle Ages and the Renaissance Literary and Historical Perspectives* (New York: Syracuse University Press, 1986), p. xiii.

2. Judith Butler, *Gender Trouble: Feminism and the Subversion of Identity* (Routledge, 2011).

3. Andrew B.R. Elliott, *Remaking the Middle Ages: The Methods of Cinema and History in Portraying the Medieval World* (Jefferson, NC: McFarland, 2011), pp. 46–48.

4. Stephen Hay, *Bertrand Tavernier: The Film-Maker of Lyon* (London: I.B.Tauris, 2000), p. 129.

5. "Elle est si belle, et les hommes si brutaux." Translation my own.

6. The Bechdel Test is a cultural meme used to outline the extent to which women are consistently

marginalized in contemporary cinema by outlining the frequency with which they are unnamed and offered no agency except insofar as their actions relate to male characters. Beginning life as a joke in the popular comic strip *Dykes to Watch Out For* penned by cartoonist Alison Bechdel in 1985, the episode describes how the main character will only go to see a film if there are (1) at least two women in it (2) who talk to each other (3) about something besides a man. Despite the humorous connotations, the test has gained greater currency in recent scholarship owing to the assertion that despite being incredibly simple, a staggering number of mainstream films consistently fail the test. For more, see Christa van Raalte, "No Small-talk in Paradise: Why *Elysium* Fails the Bechdel Test, and Why We Should Care," in *Media, Margins and Popular Culture*, ed. Einar Thorsen, Heather Savigny, Daniel Jackson and Jenny Alexander (London: Palgrave Macmillan, 2015), chap. 1.

7. "Les garces n'ont pas une ame." Translation taken from film subtitles.

8. André Bazin, "The Myth of Total Cinema," in *Technology and Culture: The Film Reader*, ed. Andrew Utterson (London: Routledge, 2005), pp. 33–36.

9. Estève, quoted in Joseph Cunneen, *Robert Bresson: A Spiritual Style in Film* (London: Continuum, 2003), p. 154.

10. Hay, p. 126.

11. Lisa Manter, "The Law of the Daughter: Queer Family Politics in Bertrand Tavernier's *La Passion Béatrice*," in *Queer Movie Medievalisms*, ed. Kathleen Coyne Kelly and Tison Pugh (Farnham, Surrey: Ashgate, 2009), p. 30.

12. Laurence de Looze, "Modern Approaches and the 'Real' Middle Ages: Bertrand Tavernier's *La Passion Béatrice*," in *Studies in Medievalism*, V, ed. Leslie J. Workman (Woodbridge, Suffolk: Boydell & Brewer, 1994), p. 186.

13. For a full explanation of this argument, see Andrew B.R. Elliott, "Unmasking Marian: Representing Violence, Gender and Agency in Medieval Films," in *Gender, Agency and Violence: European Perspectives from the Early Modern Period to the Modern Day*, ed. Ulrike Zitzlsperger (Cambridge: Cambridge Scholars Publishing, 2013), pp. 173–187.

14. Manter, p. 21.

15. Manter, p. 21, note 5.

16. François Amy de la Bretèque, *Le Moyen Âge au cinéma: Panorama historique et artistique* (Paris: Armand Colin, 2015), p. 181.

17. Manter, p. 22.

18. Hay, p. 129.

19. Hay, p. 129.

20. Phil Powrie, *French Cinema in the 1980s: Nostalgia and the Crisis of Masculinity* (Oxford: Clarendon Press, 1997), esp. pp. 171–182.

21. William F. Woods, *The Medieval Filmscape: Reflections of Fear and Desire in a Cinematic Mirror* (Jefferson, NC: McFarland, 2014), pp. 138–140.

22. See, for instance, Joan Mellen, *Big Bad Wolves: Masculinity in the American Film* (New York: Pantheon Books, 1977), chap. 6; Steve Neale, "Prologue: Masculinity as Spectacle: Reflections on Men and Mainstream Cinema," in *Screening the Male: Exploring Masculinities in the Hollywood Cinema*, ed. Steve Cohan and Ina Rae Hark (London: Routledge, 1993), pp. 9–20; Yvonne Tasker, *Spectacular Bodies Gender, Genre and the Action Cinema* (London: Routledge, 1993), esp. pp. 230–244.

23. de Looze, p. 186.

24. Translation from Hay, p. 124.

25. Umberto Eco, "Dreaming of the Middle Ages," in *Travels in Hyperreality*, trans. William Weaver (London: Picador, 1987), p. 65.

26. Translation taken from Manter, p. 19.

27. Amy S. Kaufman, "Muscular Medievalism," *This Year's Work in Medievalism* 31 (2016): 56–66; citations come from p. 58 and p. 61.

Lady Godiva on Film

Icon of Faith, Icon of Feminism or Erotic Simulacrum

Sandra Gorgievski

Medieval Legend and Iconography

The story of the 11th-century historical figure, Lady Godiva of Coventry, has grown into a legend that turns the private plight of a pious medieval woman into a powerful erotic myth which still fascinates the collective Western imagination today, especially in English-speaking countries. Beyond the overt transgression of Godiva's naked ride through the streets of Coventry, Greek or other pagan female deities riding a horse possibly coalesced into cult images well before the 11th century and thus contributed to the flourishing of the legend during the Middle Ages. In the 19th century, a substantial body of paintings and a number of civic processions in Coventry revived the myth in a particularly vivid way as part of the medieval revival in Victorian England, only to have the legend wane in its popularity in the 20th century. Compared to the extraordinary presence of other medieval women (either historical figures like Joan of Arc or legendary ones like Guinevere, Isolde or Morgan le Fay) in film and on television, neither medium has been particularly attracted to the story Godiva and her (in)famous ride. Except for a few feminist avatars more or less taken straight from Tennyson's poem, on-screen images of Godiva in romantic comedies, or even in soft-core pornographic films, have erased the ambiguous aspects of what was once a legend richly informed by both primitive fertility rituals and by religious traditions as recorded in medieval chronicles. As iconography is more than a simple historical document, a "*momentum*" which reveals individual as well as collective memory in all its social and cultural dimensions,[1] these films will be discussed in relation to the evolving iconography of Godiva in the Western world.

Lady Godiva was the wife of Leofric, Earl of Mercia, who played an important political role in England before the Norman Conquest. Chronicles mention her as a particularly pious and charitable woman who gave precious donations to the Church—hence her Old English name *God-gifu* ("good gift") later adapted into Latin as "Godiva." Indeed, both Leofric and his wife were generous benefactors and founded the Benedictine monastery of Coventry (1043), where they were to be buried. Roger of Wendover recounts the 1057 events which gave birth to the legend in his 1235 chronicle *Flores Historiarum*.[2] Godiva allegedly begged her husband not to impose an excessive new tax on the people of Coventry. She was so adamant in her requests that he challenged her to ride naked across the city market swarming with people in return for his abatement of the tax. The chronicle specifically mentions that she unraveled her tresses to veil her naked body before venturing on the ride, accompanied by two knights. The city was thus spared further taxation, though for clearly extraordinary conditions. And significantly the 13th-century chronicle, written by a monk at St. Albans Abbey, merely mentions the fact that Godiva rode exposing her bare legs, thus toning down the erotic potential of such an image better to emphasize her decision to ride unclothed in the service of higher, religious ideal. Interest in the specific religious aspects of her story faded after the medieval period, but Godiva's ride would continue to attract interest, doubtless because of its ability to advance any number of agendas in keeping with its original mythical associations that pre-date the Middle Ages.

Often presented as a determined woman opposing unjust male domination, Godiva is also associated with the chthonic power of the horse especially as the horse is related to stories involving the underworld. And as other medieval chronicles emphasize, the ride on horseback in the legend is symbolically important. Ranulf Higden, a 14th-century Benedictine monk of St. Werburgh's Monastery in Chester, focuses on a particularly relevant detail in his retelling of the Godiva story (1364),[3] in which the tax is specifically on horses. And Higden further juxtaposes the exemplary tale of the pious countess riding naked in broad daylight with a tale in which a richly-clad prostitute—a personification of Venus, the goddess of love—riding a mule nightly torments a newly married young man.[4] The secondary tale reveals the intrinsically ambivalent figure that Lady Godiva presents and associates her with the lusty, luxuriant appeal of the Roman Goddess enthralling men's senses. Godiva's horse may then symbolize impetuous, animal desire, while her unraveled hair adds to the voluptuous, brash image of erotic vitality.[5]

Indeed, Godiva's legend can be a conflation of various mythical trends. Anglo-Saxon and Germanic traditions have kept a more macabre and nocuous significance of the horse from Greek mythology.[6] For example, the psychopomp deity Hecate, who also provides protection and guarantees prosperity, is accompanied by two mares; the chthonic god of the underworld Hades rides in a chariot drawn by four black horses. Perhaps more significant to the development of Godiva's legend is the Celtic Epona, a goddess of fertility and protection, who rides a horse and who, as is often the case with hippomorphic divinities, is also associated with the passing of time, death, and the journey into the other world. Cult images of Epona (in multiple mediums) show a female figure riding side-saddle or astride or standing in an imperial position surrounded by horses. She always wears a long dress hiding her feet or subtly revealing her legs under her pleated cloth. These details suggest a possible connection with Godiva, as Epona contributed to the development of mythical images of equine goddesses in Romano-Celtic areas during the Middle Ages.[7] Furthermore, hippomorphic goddesses in Indo-European myth and folklore also entail rituals of horse-sacrifice, which contain an erotic dimension. A king (figuratively) lives with a mare in order to fertilize and renew his reign; the mare is then sacrificed, thus ensuring a fruitful reign for the monarch.[8]

But medieval monks could hardly be expected to dwell on the ambivalent figure of the countess exposing her naked body to the gaze of all the inhabitants, and still emphasize the Christian aspects of Godiva's story. They, therefore, reduced any powerful mythical imagery in that story to mere details (her bright white legs for Wendover, her nightly counterpart for Higden) that at worst suggest possible seduction of any bystanders through sight. Apart from a 14th-century glass window formerly set in Trinity Church in Coventry—and now reduced to fragments[9]—there is no surviving portrayal of Godiva in medieval iconography, perhaps because she was not associated with a male hero (like Isolde or Guinevere), or because she could not be appropriately represented in Christian devotional and cultic art. What's more, details about the reception of the relevant chronicle texts during the Middle Ages remain unclear.[10]

In the 17th and 18th centuries, the legend changed significantly as it was retold in a new literary genre, popular English songs and ballads, which erased the religious contents to the profit of the erotic one. As public nudity was still prohibited, the inhabitants of Coventry supposedly hid in their homes to save the Countess from shame, and the new character of a transgressive tailor, "Peeping Tom," emerged, only to be punished for his voyeurism by being struck blind. A taboo linked to the secret celebration of rites of fertility lies beneath the surface morals of these songs and ballads, so that the voyeur plays the sacrificial role of the scapegoat who works for the community's welfare and fertility.[11] The introduction of this detail into Godiva's tale suggests that erotic, frightening images of femininity are relegated to the unconscious and to the dark aspect of blindness. From the blinding of Oedipus and Venus's blindfolding Cupid's eyes, to Artemis's metamorphosis of Actaeon into a stag for having peeped at her naked body, this taboo leads to a process of disavowal and denial and is transformed into a story of salvation.

In the 19th century, Godiva's fame grew in England in popular culture,[12] while a rich iconography of the legend flourished, in which painters toned down her piety and humility in favor of more contemporary concerns. Lord Alfred Tennyson, in his 1840 poem "Lady Godiva," glorified the chaste victim and liberating, self-sacrificing heroine, thereby combining a widespread taste in England for the medieval with his own socialist as well as feminist interests. Godiva revolts against Leofric's grim, tyrannical exploitation of the people to give voice to distraught mothers whose children will starve if they must pay the tax. She courageously rides alone without any escort, but she imposes a condition on the people of Coventry who must shut their windows and remain inside their homes. The Romantic imagination replaced the witnesses of her humiliation with staring gargoyles, gabbles, chinks, holes and gaping rampart murdresses. The voyeur is punished even before he actually sees Godiva. Female determination and sacrifice turn the ride into a triumphant event, at the sound of the "twelve great shocks of sound" at noon. The 1857 edition of Tennyson's poem was illustrated by the Pre-Raphaelites John Everett Millais, Dante Gabriel Rossetti and William Holman Hunt, where Godiva is decently clothed to emphasize her chastity.[13]

Indeed, Godiva soon became a favorite subject for 19th-century painters, whether they specialized in female nudes (John Collier, Edwin Landseer, Marshall Claxton, Jules Joseph Lefèbvre) or in medievalism (William Holeman Hunt, Edmund Blair Leighton),[14] where the horse is an important presence in the nude paintings which portray the ride through the streets. Pre-Raphaelite painters preferred to depict Godiva at the moment when she makes her decision alone in a room, in scenes of domestic introspection tinged with Victorian modesty. She appears as a liberating heroine in keeping with the medieval legend, but as a result deprived of a whole range of larger associations because of the absent horse.

The famous civic processions at the Coventry Festival further reduced Godiva to an icon of popular entertainment and enthusiasm. A local figure, she became a commercial attraction between 1678 and 1854, a victim of the voyeurism of the crowd for hours.

Although the women on parade were always covered with cream-colored gowns, the procession led to a controversy about its decency in 1854 and was resumed thereafter less frequently.[15] Cheap erotic postcards of beauty contests in the 1860s involved more and more suggestive costumes, from a short gown to a mere body suit.[16] Wavering between solemn procession and pantomime, charity feast and folklore fair, one can see her parade on a white horse down the streets swarming with people, accompanied by a nun (*British Pathé Gazette*, 1920–1929); side by side with Cleopatra, a guillotine and an Arab prince (*British Pathé Gazette*, 1936); or with Elizabeth I, suffragettes asking for their rights and a delegation of nuns, while a man in the crowd is wearing a handkerchief on his eyes for fun (*British Pathé Gazette*, 1951).[17] And such scenes of popular entertainment were replaced at the beginning of the 20th century by films about the famed Coventry Countess.

Godiva in the Silent Film Era: Exhibitionism and Voyeurism

The legend first appears in silent films that highlight its melodramatic aspects. Lines from Tennyson's poem are used as titles in such films, thereby emphasizing the pathos of the narrative being shown. In a faithful adaptation of Tennyson's poem, the opening sequence of the 1911 American *Lady Godiva*, directed by J. Stuart Blackton, shows the countess (Julia Swayne Gordon)[18] surrounded by the people of Coventry. Her exaggerated melodramatic gestures—kneeling and pleading in front of Leofric, spreading her arms in horror at the announcement of the condition he sets not to tax the people—clearly associate her with the archetypal heroines of virtue rewarded in silent pictures. A close shot on a dark wooden door gradually opening reveals a starving, rebellious mob kneeling down to arouse Godiva's pity. It is followed by a series of overly emotional shots of women in rags and tatters, weeping when the herald publicly announces the Godiva's husband's demand in the marketplace, and in counter shots during Godiva's ride itself. The cheap sentimentalism of these sequences best illustrates Tennyson's lines: "all the mothers brought their children, clamoring, 'If we pay, we starve!'" The sequence depicting the ride through the town shows the door opening again on Godiva's figure on a white horse, clothed in a black cloak which she abruptly and theatrically shakes off. The camera switches to a static frontal shot of the countess, accompanied by a servant, riding towards the camera with her body completely hidden by her hair. The 17th-century character of the voyeur is fully developed into a morally degraded character—an ugly drunkard in black (in contrast to Godiva's white steed), sardonically smiling and cutting through the wooden shutters with a symbolically phallic knife. He is filmed from the back, peeping through the chink of the wood, thus preventing the spectator from seeing Godiva. Immediately struck blind, he writhes back in an exaggerated way. Godiva on her horse then appears on the screen with her back facing the camera, fully exposing her radiant white back, buttocks and legs to the spectator's voyeurism, in a strikingly erotic image. The last sequence stages the popular triumph following the suppression of the tax; the door melodramatically opens again on Leofric applauded by the people, followed by Godiva blessing them all.

The overt sentimentalism of images is counterbalanced by the final daring shot of Godiva's naked body in a scene that is strongly reminiscent of erotic postcards from the early 20th century. The legend might be seen as narrative pretext, but the association with the horse is meaningful. In a 1910 Anglo-Danish film *Afgrunden* (*The Abyss*),[19] the liberating, erotic power of the horse is underlined when a lady suddenly abandons her conventional husband to follow a gypsy she has just seen dancing in a circus. She elopes with him riding on his horse, and then delights in taking part in circus acts in which she tantalizes her lover by wearing straight, black satin gowns and by performing sensuous, lascivious dances, until she is finally punished for her lust and jealousy by being taken away by the police.

The 1921 *Lady Godiva* by German director Hubert Moest also emphasizes the melodramatic by introducing the story of two star-crossed lovers: the unscrupulous schemer who has become Earl of Mercia succeeds in marrying the mayor of Coventry's daughter Godiva, in spite of her betrothal to another man with whom she is in love. When Godiva and her still unidentified lover are discovered in each other's arms, the Earl threatens to destroy Coventry if his adulterous wife refuses to reveal her lover's identity. During her ride, the inhabitants of Coventry duly look away from the countess, but the husband plays the part of the voyeur. The lover comes to rescue Godiva from humiliation, hiding her body with his own cloak. The Earl is thwarted, but the countess's infidelity is only redeemed by her death.[20] When the film was released in the United States in May 1922, significantly it was advertised as "great in eye-appeal, wondrous beauty, stupendous crows, massive sets, and a story of a wonderful sacrifice."[21] In the title role, the film features Moest's own wife Hedda Vernon, who was also featured in his film *Das Frauenhaus von Brescia* (*The Women House of Brescia*, 1920). This highly controversial film set in 14th-century Europe was rejected by the British Board of Film Classification because it depicted the melodramatic fate of female prisoners of war who prostituted themselves to save other women. The film relied on the same mixture of sacrifice, voyeurism, and exhibitionism as his adaptation of the Godiva legend.

The 1928 British film *The Lady Godiva* written by George Banfield dramatically stages the sufferings of the people of Coventry, as well as those of Godiva. It is framed by sequences showing two contemporary tourists in Coventry who travel back in time to the 11th century, only to discover the harsh realities of medieval life: after a shot of the Lady Godiva statue at the Coventry Museum, the film cuts to a sequence straight from Chaplin's *Kid*: a bed-ridden mother and her child are starving in a barely-furnished bedroom while the aged father is robbed of his purse by tax collectors. Beyond the obvious nod to the medieval legend and Leofric's excessive taxation, such scenes of poverty and deprivation may reflect the concerns of the female audiences at the time, as British women's pictures were not necessarily limited in their themes to romance.[22]

The film reworks the pseudo-historical details of the legend by featuring soldiers wearing stereotypical Anglo-Saxon costumes and Viking helmets. Low-angle shots underline the authoritative, dominating position of Leofric, whereas a helpless Godiva (Gladys Jennings) and her people are shown beaten down in high-angle shots. In a series of pathetic, melodramatic portraits, close-ups reveal the suffering faces of the people of Coventry. Yielding to their entreaties, Godiva begs her husband in humble attitudes of piety. While she is listening to the condition imposed by her husband, the camera gives access to her interior tumult in a further close-up. Her determination is then underlined as a title resolutely announces her decision: "I will do it." In the same streets of Coventry where the two tourists wander in the film's opening sequence, the voyeur is depicted as a wicked dwarf-like character rubbing his hands together in glee at the prospect of transgressing the herald's order which also appears in the titles: "No eye shall look." A strip-tease-like sequence subtly depicts Godiva's long hair hiding her back while her dress slowly falls to her feet, and a curtain theatrically falls to hide the view from the townspeople. When the horse is brought in in the dark, Godiva's silhouette appears in half-light; a counter shot reveals the Peeping Tom hiding behind a window and cutting a hole through the shutters, followed by a close-up on his eyes staring through the chink. A high angle shot reveals the countess' body half hidden by her falling hair, followed by shots of grotesque, wide-eyed gargoyles, then of the horse's legs and Godiva's white legs, just as in the medieval texts. Such self-conscious devices underline the mixture of exhibitionism and voyeurism in the legend. The voyeur is struck blind while the countess is looking at the sky as if in meditation. The count apologizes and makes amends, even kneeling in front of his wife while she is gazing up into the distance. The idealized image of the heroine eventually dissolves to a final shot on the two tourists in 1928, showing the emotional impact of the legend and her fame on them.

Gladys Jennings, who is featured as Godiva, also appeared as a melodramatic character embodying courageous love and daring elopement in *The Prey of the Dragon* (directed by F. Martin Thorton, 1921) and in the Scottish highland period drama based on Sir Walter Scott's poem *Young Lochinvar* (directed by Will P. Kellino, 1923): in 15th-century Scotland, Lochinvar falls in love with Helen (Jennings), rescues her when she is in distress and elopes with her, despite the fact that they are both betrothed to another partner.[23] Jennings later seemed to be typecast in the late 1920s. In *Piccadilly* (directed by E.A. Dupont, 1929), she is identified as an example of "old-fashioned Victorian femininity," and a "conventional, passive, long-suffering and long-haired" fiancée in contrast to another type of more modern young women who demonstrate intelligence, confidence, courage, self-sufficiency, and who would rather wear short skirts and cropped hair to highlight their erotic and slightly androgynous appearance.[24]

Early silent films, although they can depict an active woman, usually provide images of erotic contemplation. Such moments of visual pleasure have been described by feminist critics as freezing the narrative to display stereotyped images of women: "in a world ordered by sexual imbalance, pleasure in looking has been split between active/male and passive/female."[25] The powerfully erotic close-ups of Godiva's legs in the silent film era paved the way for the now conventional shots of women's legs in the films of such sex-symbols as Marlene Dietrich and Marilyn Monroe.

A Cold War Feminist Heroine?

The Hays Code enforced in the 1930s may explain an absence of American Godiva films, although Ernst Lubitsch's irreverent *Design for Living* (1933) contains significant allusions to her legend. The artist George Curtis (Cary Grant) is identified by Gilda Farrell (Miriam Hopkins) as the painter who depicted Lady Godiva on a bicycle: "A bicycle seat is a little hard on Lady Godiva's historical background." This reference is one of the numerous sexual innuendoes which created censorship difficulties for the director, although the film was approved for release by the Hays Office before its restrictions would be more strictly enforced the following year.

Censorship can also be seen as a productive process in which the censored elements of the legend do not totally disappear, especially after the Second World War. The 1955

American film *Lady Godiva of Coventry*, directed by Arthur Lubin, is a swashbuckler that mingles medievalism, adventure and romance, in the wake of Sir Walter Scott's novels adapted to the screen by Richard Thorpe for the Metro Goldwyn Mayer in the 1950s.[26] The Middle Ages provide an exotic location in time and space while the plot reworks cold-war issues using the opposition between the Saxons and the Normans to advance its political agenda. In one poster for the film, Godiva is seen riding naked on her horse in a lascivious pose, looking straight into the viewer's eye. Another design shows the Hollywood kiss which guarantees romance. The levying of the tax is introduced to show Godiva's generosity and altruism, but not to justify her sacrifice. She becomes the voice of the weeping mothers and energetically asks for her husband's mercy. She is also on equal terms with her husband in the Saxon resistance, in an overtly feminist discourse. A victim of her political success, she is accused of adultery by her husband's Norman enemies and condemned to be punished with the humiliating ride followed by a public stoning. Although King Edward the Confessor disapproves, Godiva challenges the Normans to demonstrate her Saxon loyalty. The ride is supposed not only to individually restore Godiva's honor, but also to reaffirm social conventions such as marital fidelity and submission to the king.

The titles conventionally open on a pseudo-manuscript (as is often the case in period films at the time) showing an image of Lady Godiva's ride, followed by a narrative that provides a political context for the legend in terms of the opposition of the Saxons to their Norman overlords. But our expectations are unmet, as we must wait until the very last, climactic sequence of the film to watch Godiva's famous ride. Throughout the film, Godiva is characterized as a strong, self-assertive woman, a far more feminist heroine than Tennyson's Victorian lady. Gender issues are clearly tackled as she is the only female character in the film with any agency. She generally feels at ease with men, whether with aristocrats once she marries Leofric, or with the rabble as she can speak just like them, but her femininity is often repressed. As the sheriff of Lincolnshire's sister, she comes into contact with prisoners who become her steadfast friends when she secretly brings them food and drink. She daringly stands against her husband when he mistreats a woman or delivers misogynous discourses, but she offers to help him flee when, on the king's unjust orders, he must marry a stiff, mean and futile Norman girl who stands in contrast to her. Respect, honesty, straightforwardness, determination, rashness, tactical intelligence, and enthusiasm earn her public recognition and a solid reputation among the Saxon barons. She is endowed with masculine physical qualities—she is strong (she can lift a heavy wooden table), warrior-like (at least for the 1950s standards), irascible, and possessed of a loud voice which can be heard above the clamor of soldiers. She doesn't hesitate to flee into the forest and hide with renegades from the Normans. She strongly influences her husband's strategies and blackmails him (refusing to share their bedroom) until he yields to her worthy schemes. Far from being reduced to a repressed, male-like supportive figure or a virago, she can also cajole and enthrall the Earl. Lubin thus prepares the spectator for her final act of courage and rebellion, rather than sacrifice, against Norman injustice.

Irish-born actress Maureen O'Hara was no random choice to impersonate Godiva. A popular actress in the 1950s, she regularly starred in adventure films in multiple genres and had already become a icon of female adventurism. Film posters encapsulate the ideals of romance and freedom that she embodied at the time in mass culture, whether she languorously kisses a pirate or an Oriental, seduces a cowboy, or lasciviously appears as a saloon dancer.[27] O'Hara was a sexually provocative figure during the 1950s in America, wearing tight, suggestive dresses with deeply plunging necklines, in intensely deep shades of dark blue, green velvet, violet and black. In *Lady Godiva*, her body lines are well displayed under her red plaited hair or pony tail. In spite of her sex appeal, she is protected by her uncouth Saxon friends who almost on cue intrude anytime the count tries to embrace her.

The exhibitionism of the final three-minute-long parade comes as a reward for the voyeurism of the spectator, when she finds herself exposed naked on her horse. The ghastly silence of the empty streets contrasts with the former joyful, noisy scenes in the swarming marketplace. The deserted streets appear in medium shot while the sinister sound of the horse's shoes resounds on the pavement. Godiva enters the frame slowly riding towards the fixed camera accompanied by a nun. The shot cuts to a close shot on

Maureen O'Hara as the title character in the 1955 film *Lady Godiva of Coventry*.

O'Hara's upper body showing her unraveled, immeasurably long hair, which partly hides her body. The camera then tracks along her slow ride down the narrow, oppressive streets and under arches. Her shadow is projected onto the houses' high walls and closed shutters, filmed in low-angle shots that seem to crush her. Godiva's straight profile and hieratic pose contrast with her sensuous white legs exposed by her side-saddle position, referencing the medieval tradition while also presenting her as the object of spectacle. Outdoor tracking shots alternate with indoor shots of a family hiding behind shutters, of the king kneeling in prayer, of wicked Normans plotting, and of Peeping Tom drinking in a tavern. The blinding of the voyeur takes place off frame and seems to be directed at the spectator when a torch is suddenly brandished towards the camera. Godiva fully appears through the small frame of the tavern's half-open window. The procession then disappears into the distance outside the town, heads towards a convent whose heavy wooden doors close on Godiva's weary face. The image is disquieting as it fades out on the two black silhouettes of nuns filmed from the back.

The next shot transforms the former humiliation into triumph, as a radiant, self-assured Godiva appears at court. Her courage has apparently inspired her husband who heroically protects the king from a Norman trap and saves the country from chaos. The film ends like a stereotypical romance, when Godiva pretends to faint in her husband's arms in order to elope with him and enjoy a benighted marital life. The happy ending is underlined by the joyful soundtrack and the blissful smiles of the Saxon soldiers. A complex character in a patriarchal movie, Godiva appears as dutiful wife, feminist activist and sex symbol, precisely what the "American way of life" was ready to imagine in the 1950s.

A Testimony to the Sexual Revolution: Godiva as Pretext or Simulacrum?

After the 1970s challenged traditional sexual, familial and societal patterns, only a few films focusing on Godiva were released. Most of them reduce the rich and complex erotic potential of Godiva's ride to some empty nod, a mere object of male desire devoid of mythical connections in films that are no longer even period pieces. The greater diffusion of images of female sexuality in the late 20th century may account for the limited number of film adaptations of a Godiva story that relies solely on sexual transgression. In a postmodern era which tends to blur the difference between reality and a constructed representation of reality, or simulacrum—according to Jean Baudrillard's concept of "hyperrealism" that substitutes signs of the real for the real itself and the impossibility of staging an illusion[28]—Godiva's phantasm of a female naked body in modern processions would perhaps appear as something more real than actual reality.

The X-rated 1969 German film *Lady Godiva Rides*, directed by Stephen C. Apostolof, uses the legend as vague pretext to stage a series of lascivious, pornographic scenes. When Leofric finds his wife Lady Godiva in bed with her lover, they have to flee to the United States, and Godiva ends up in a brothel. When her lover wants to save her, he is challenged to a duel by the owner of the brothel. In his discussion of the seduction of images, Baudrillard sees in porn films some "disenchanted simulation," something "more real than the real, and the height of simulation."[29]

A more humorous nod to the voyeurism and exhibitionism of the legend appears

Kim Novak as Lady Godiva in the 1969 film *The Great Bank Robbery*.

in the 1969 American film *The Great Bank Robbery* directed by Hy Averback. Kim Novak stars as a crook surrounded by male friends who pose as leaders of a church in Friendly, Texas, in the 1880s, while they carefully plan a bank robbery. Novak's character reworks the iconic Lady Godiva riding on a white horse as a thoughtful trap to distract a guard's attention while her accomplices enter the bank unseen.[30] The voyeurism of the scene is highlighted by alternating low-angle shots of the bank guard watching down in disbelief from beneath the window blinds with high-angle shots of Novak displaying her voluptuous charms, wearing a sheer body suit with some flowers in the deserted, hot, dusty yard below. The stifling atmosphere is erotically suggestive, but, when the voyeur calls his colleagues to watch with him, she mysteriously vanishes off the frame. After a series of teasing parades distracting the guards, the bank robbery is pulled off.

In the long-running irreverent series on British television featuring Benny Hill, Lady Godiva is parodied on the day of her ride in a buffoon-like sequence, but the comic surprisingly refrains from his usual grotesque shots of scantily-clad women. Godiva's body is shown and remains carefully hidden under a large cloak.[31] Playing the role of Godiva's groom as well as that of Peeping Tom, Benny Hill emphasizes his familiar position as voyeur obsessed with female bodies in close-up shots of his goggled eyes staring at the camera.

Two British films starring Godiva were released more recently. A 2008 British film *Lady Godiva* directed by 20-year-old director Vicky Jewson reworks the legendary ride in present-day England. In a romance made for a targeted audience of teenagers, the two protagonists emancipate themselves from smothering mothers and escape from painful memories of a dead brother and absent fathers. The film opens as a period piece in rural England as young Godiva (Phoebe Thomas) is undressing, having a cleansing river bath to prepare for her ride, while two knights are engaged in combat. She rides astride naked (only covered with her long, curly red hair) into the ramparts of a castle (Carcassone, Southern France). People duly avert their eyes from her, except for a young Peeping Tom who is merely scolded for his outrage and never mentioned to the Earl of Mercia (James Wilby). A private meeting in the castle shows a caricatured scene with a submissive Godiva facing her husband's wrath and humiliation as he threatens her with a knife and is unexpectedly rewarded with the exclusive contemplation of his wife's naked body. The sentimental prologue underlies fantasies of male-dominating gaze, somewhat limited by the ingenuous, teenage-like body of the actress.

The film then fast forwards to contemporary Oxford where altruist art teacher Jemima (Phoebe Thomas) needs to raise funds to re-open the charity art factory her late brother had created. Too proud to get financial support from her rich lover Michael (Matthew Chambers), she complies with his silly, childish bet that she can embody Godiva's audacious ride through Oxford's streets to garner financial support from the local gentry. In this conventional romantic idyll, nods to the legend seem to be limited to Michael's obsession with horses, money and female nudes: a talented horse trainer and womanizer, he dubs himself "the Lady Godiva Man" (borrowing a pompous title from his best-selling autobiography), calls his favorite white horse "Lady Godiva," enjoys glamorous sex-filled lifestyle, but improbably discovers true love with awkward, innocent and modest Jemima. The film's seems to be an attempt to remake the highly-successful *Notting Hill* (directed by Roger Mitchell, 1999), though its stars lack the genuine eccentricity of Hugh Grant and Julia Roberts.

The modern Godiva/Jemima simply delights in artistic representations of horses—whether in drawings, sculptures and paintings, and a large reproduction of George Stubbs' "Whistlejacket" (1762) hangs in her class and appears on the cover of her favorite book. Whistlejacket is painted without a rider in a jumping position, half-way equestrian figure and half savage. Its blond, long, undisciplined tail and unkempt mane suggest an impulsive, nervous temperament closer to that of Romantic paintings than to the celebration of royal power and authority horses are often associated with.[32] The horse's pathos-filled eyes express the uncontrollable, savage spirit that the film strives to associate with the apparently reserved, timid art teacher, who ultimately dares to defy powerful men in order to assert her passion for art. John Collier's famous painting "Lady Godiva" (1898) briefly appears on Jemima's computer, as if to bridge the gap between past and present. Collier's paintings often associated female temptation with the wilderness of exotic animals.[33] In his painting, Godiva's white body is sketched on the horse's red and gold caparison and a richly decorated saddle. Her humble position, recoiling with bended head as if in prayer, contrasts with the horse's majestic uplifted head. The streets are imbued with a pale, surreal halo which captures the viewer's imagination.

Nothing of the sort takes place in Jemima's gently audacious, cabaret-like strip-tease through the streets of Coventry—a naive act of bravado which is supposed to signal her coming of age as a mature young woman, by being ready to strip naked in front of a friendly crowd including her newly reconciled mother, and her future mother- and sister-in-law. This complex set of supportive female characters finally supplants the otherwise cheap sentimentalism of the film and counters the patriarchal burden of absent fathers and brothers. The "excessive visibility" of the mothers and of female-to-female relationships[34] at first limits the coming of age story of the two protagonists, but eventually becomes part of the film's final reconciliation.

The two dream-like sequences in slow-motion of the two lovers riding, kissing or making love in a stable to the sound of singing angels clearly meet the conventions of romantic comedy. Apart from the opening period sequence which reminds the viewer of the medieval legend, the overwhelming number of incidental references to Lady Godiva reduces the film's links to the legend to the merely anecdotal. The final ride through overcrowded Oxford streets filmed through the frame of a TV show resembles a Coventry fair exhibition in which the actress appears wearing a flesh-colored thong and tights. As compensation for this teasing sequence, men regularly appear half-naked in the film, as if to minimize any sense of voyeurism directed at women. The pattern of visual pleasure in looking, identified by feminist criticism as active/male and passive/female, is reversed. After feeling humiliated, Michael joins the crowd of spectators and makes amends, eventually applauding his lover's act of courage, contrary to the rigid behavior of monolithic, misogynous Leofric in the medieval prologue. Beyond the character's efforts to stand against adversity and the conventional satire of the greedy local investors, there is hardly any sense of social protest in the nude exhibition of Godiva.

In the 2007 British *Lady Godiva: Back in the Saddle* directed by Baz Taylor, the viewer's expectations are humorously deceived. During the title sequence, a Bayeux tapestry-like cartoon recounting the legend in a distorted, bawdy way parodies the cinematic pattern of the medieval-like prologue, following the irreverent cartoons from *Monty Python and the Holy Grail* (1975). Godiva appears in her bra and panties surrounded by cabaret-like dancers, and an Arabian Prince even intrudes, foreshadowing the ludicrous events that occur later in the film. The viewer is then plunged into contemporary Coventry as an anonymous voice over reminds the spectator of Godiva's legend in sculpture and painting. Coventry is threatened by greedy American and local investors who have corrupted the local mayor into selling them the park in which Lady Godiva actually rode, in order to turn it into a dream casino. The rampant threat of progress and dehumanization is denounced by a local history teacher (James Fleet) as he gets fired from college after one of his pupils spits on Collier's painting of Godiva during a college-sponsored visit to the Herbert Art Gallery. As the socially awkward teacher piteously claims, there are "no more causes" to be fought for. Yet the comedy shows the ridiculously portrayed mayor's involvement with the greasy local Mafioso and sinister Native Americans from Wisconsin, as well as with sexy dancers and ambitious secretaries. A parade featuring Lady Godiva's ride is even organized, preceded by a beauty contest won by the seductive fiancée of the caricatured, cruel mafia chef. The ride is staged as part of the local fair to gain support from the population and to appeal to the foreign investors with a pageant that includes Indian tepees on chariots, soldiers in Union Blue uniforms, and the naked Godiva partly hidden with her long blond hair and wrapped in white silk. Top-model-like Godiva (Faye Tozer) is reduced to a gorgeous, exotic figure along side American Indians, Arabian backdrops, and faux medieval pageantry.

But all these disparate scenes are simply distractions. The genuine Lady Godiva figure in the film is someone who doesn't need to flaunt her body to save her town. The mayor's ex-wife Catherine (Caroline Harker) gets involved, and against all odds, derails the plan to build the casino. A simple, strong-headed, supportive and generous woman, she allies herself with the history teacher to disrupt the parade and convince the people of Coventry that they still need a park in which to walk their dogs and to roam about peacefully. Her scurrilous ex-husband, the mayor, plays the part of Leofric as he is finally influenced by his ex-wife's steadfast moral values, chivalrously helps the other Godiva dismount from her horse (she was badly wounded by an arrow), covers her with his coat and elopes with her, while the tepees are set afire and the farcical procession is dispersed. A romance develops between Catherine and the good-natured history teacher, who eventually finds a job appearing in period piece TV shows. The city's savior and heroine is rewarded by the people of Coventry with a flower bed bearing her name in the park. The modern-day civic battles seem at best silly, and the nods to Godiva's myth (Collier's painting in the museum and in the mayor's office, the Coventry statue, the parade) turn out to be parodies of historical icons. An unpretentious and self-deprecating comedy, the film owes much to the British genre of the romantic comedy in the wake of *Four Weddings and a Funeral* (directed by Mike Newel, 1994)[35] with its series of witty coincidental meetings, unexpected romances, mild derision, and happy endings. The references to the medieval tale of Lady Godiva both celebrate and deflate the legend, while playing with the spectator's expectations, before rewarding them with a dose of mock-heroism.

Conclusion

Godiva's avatars in the cinema fulfill or play with their audiences' shifting "horizons of expectations" according to time period and country of production. This phenomenon, as described by Hans Robert Jauss, is based on

> overt and covert signals, familiar characteristics, or implicit allusions. It awakens memories of that which was already read, brings the reader to a specific emotional attitude, and with its beginning arouses expectations for the "middle and end," which can then be maintained intact or altered, reoriented, or even fulfilled ironically in the course of the reading according to specific rules of the genre or type of text.[36]

The patterns of cinematic references to the legend of Lady Godiva involve the audience's expectations of a film's genre (melodrama, swashbuckler or romantic comedy), the version of the legend an audience is familiar with—medieval texts, British painting, Victorian poetry, or popular culture—and the opposition between poetic and practical language, imagination and the day-today reality of the audience. The underlying mythical basis of the legend tends to be overlooked by the collective historical unconscious, starting with the medieval monks who adapted the hippomorphic deity to Christian themes of sacrifice, then by the Victorian painters who portrayed the liberation of unconscious impulses, and by the variegated images and costumes of medieval women in films throughout the 20th and 21st century. In period films, the 11th century is more or less accurately portrayed as an imaginary background on which to project fantasies of female stars embodying modern mythologies—from the ambivalent liberated, housewife of America in the 1950s to the more liberated women in later British romantic comedies. Actresses *disguise themselves as*, rather than impersonate, Lady Godiva, but they still revive on the screen the ambivalent pattern of voyeurism and exhibitionism of the medieval legend in collective aesthetic experiences of mass-entertainment where the spectator is less passive than expected.

FILMS CITED

1911   USA *Lady Godiva*, dir. J. Stuart Blackton
1921   Germany, *Lady Godiva*, dir. Hubert Moest.
1928   UK *The Lady Godiva*, dir. George Banfield.
1955   USA, *Lady Godiva of Coventry*, dir. Arthur Lubin.
1969   West Germany, *Lady Godiva Rides*, dir. Stephen C. Apostolof.
1969   USA, *The Great Bank Robbery*, dir. Hy Averback.
2007   UK, *Lady Godiva: Back in the Saddle*, dir. Baz Taylor.
2008   UK, *Lady Godiva*, dir. Vicky Jewson.

NOTES

1. Jean-Claude Schmitt, *Le corps des images. Essais sur la culture visuelle au Moyen Âge* (Paris: Gallimard, 2002), p. 55.

2. *Rogeri de Wendover Chronica, sive Flores Historiarum (1235)*, ed. H.O. Coxe (London: English Historical Society, 1841) I, pp. 496–498.

3. *Polychronicon Ranulphi Higden with the English Translations of John Trevisa and of an Unknown Writer of the Fifteenth Century*, ed. C. Babington and J.R. Lumby (London: Longman, 1865–1886).

4. André Crépin, "Lady Godiva, le mari, le voyeur et l'artiste," *Bulletin des Anglicistes Médiévistes* 19 (1981): 255–266.

5. Sandra Gorgievski, "Lady Godiva," in *Dictionnaire des mythes féminins*, ed. Pierre Brunel (Paris: Éditions du Rocher, 2002), p. 831 [830–836].

6. Gilbert Durand, *Les structures anthropologiques de l'imaginaire* (Paris: Dunod, 1969–1992), pp. 78–79.

7. Sandra Gorgievski, "Lady Godiva: mythe et réalité d'une maîtresse femme," in *Voix de femmes au Moyen Âge*, ed. Leo Carruthers (Paris: AMAES, 2011), pp. 245–246, 262 [243–266].

8. Miriam Robbins Dexter, "The hippomorphic goddess and her offspring," *Journal of Indo-European Studies* 8, 3–4 (1990): 293–294 [285–308].

9. "The Legend of Lady Godiva," in *A History of Warwick*, Volume 8: *The City of Coventry and Borough of Warwick*, ed. W.B. Stephens (London: Oxford University Press, 1969): 1 [242–247].

10. The reception of the two medieval Latin texts is difficult to assess, and the translation into vernacular English was hazardous: Ranulf Higden was translated in 1387 by John Trevisa and published in 1482 by Caxton; the two thirteenth- and fourteenth-century manuscripts of Roger of Wendover were translated only in 1841 by Coxe.

11. René Girard, *Le bouc émissaire* (Paris: Grasset, 1982).

12. For a comprehensive historical study, see Daniel Donoghue, *Lady Godiva, A Literary History of the Legend* (Oxford: Blackwell, 2003).

13. Alfred Tennyson, *Collected Poems* (London: Moxon, 1857).

14. Gorgievski, "Lady Godiva: mythe et réalité d'une maîtresse femme," pp. 248–254.

15. Ronald Aquilla Clarke and Patrick A.E. Day, *Lady Godiva, Images of A Legend in Art and Society* (Coventry: Leisure Services Arts and Museums Division, 1982).

16. Albert Smith and David Fry, *Godiva's Heritage, Coventry Industry* (Berkswell: Simanda Press, 1997), pp. 4–28.

17. https://www.youtube.com/watch?v=CvZVfUtmHr8 [consulted 11 March 2017].

18. The actress also appeared as the highly desirable Countess Olivia in the film adaptation of Shakespeare's *Twelfth Night* (Eugene Mullin, 1910).

19. https://www.youtube.com/watch?v=9qrG-luCW0k [consulted 11 March 2017].

20. Kevin J. Harty, *The Reel Middle Ages: American, Western and Eastern European, Middle Eastern, and Asian Films About Medieval Europe* (Jefferson, NC: McFarland, 1999), p. 294.

21. *South Bend News-Times* 15 November 1922: 17. https://newspapers.library.in.gov/cgi-bin/indiana?a=d&d=SBNT19221115.1.17 [consulted 20 March 2017].

22. Nathalie Morris, "Pictures, romance and luxury: women and British cinema in the 1910s and the 1920s" in *British Women's Cinema*, ed. Melanie Bell and Melanie Williams (New York: Routledge, 2010), p. 20 [19–33].

23. Harty, p. 564.

24. Laura Mulvey, "Love in two British films of the late silent period: *Hindle Wakes* (Maurice Elvey,

1927) and *Piccadilly* (E.A. Dupont, 1929)," in *Europe and Love in Cinema*, ed. Luisa Passerini, Jo Labayani, and Karen Diehl (Bristol: Intellect, 2012), p. 95 [87–100].

25. Laura Mulvey, "Visual Pleasure and Narrative Cinema" in *Film Theory and Criticism: Introductory Readings*, ed. Leo Braudy and Marshall Cohen (New York: Oxford University Press, 1999), p. 837 [833–44].

26. Richard Thorpe's adaptations of Sir Walter Scott's novels *Ivanhoe* (1952) and *Quentin Durward* (1955) were followed by *Knights of the Round Table* (1954), adapting Sir Thomas Malory's *Le Morte DArthur*.

27. Maureen O'Hara features in *Sinbad the Sailor* (Leslie Hale, 1947), *Flame of Araby* (Charles Lamont, 1951), *Bagdad* (Charles Lamont, 1949), *Rio Grande* (John Ford, 1950), *The Redhead of Wyoming* (Lee Sholem, 1953), and *War Arrow* (George Sherman, 1953).

28. "Of the same order as the impossibility of rediscovering an absolute level of the real, is the impossibility of staging an illusion. Illusion is no longer possible, because the real is no longer possible. It is the whole political problem of the parody, of hypersimulation or offensive simulation, which is posed here. For example: it would be interesting to see whether the repressive apparatus would not react more violently to a simulated hold-up than to a real one? For a real hold-up only upsets the order of things, the right of property, whereas a simulated hold up interferes with the very principle of reality. Transgression and violence are less serious, for they only contest the distribution of the real. Simulation is infinitely more dangerous since it always suggests, over and above its object, that law and order themselves might really be nothing more than a simulation." Jean Baudrillard, *Jean Baudrillard, Selected Writings*, ed. Mark Poster, trans. Jacques Mourain (Palo Alto: Stanford University Press, 1988–2001), p. 180.

29. Baudrillard, p. 157.

30. https://www.youtube.com/watch?v=jSEQULgF66c [consulted 11 March 2017].

31. https://www.youtube.com/watch?v=V-LGgOuzhgc [consulted 11 March 2017].

32. Rachel Barnes and Simon Barnes, *The Horse. A Celebration of Horses in Art* (London: Quercus, 2011).

33. Collier's "Circé" lies in an odalisque position close to a tiger embedded in a dark forest; "Lilith" stands in an exotic forest with a boa entwined around her sensuous, naked body. A melancholy "Water Nymph" contemplates her image in the dark water where her body is mirrored; "Eve" runs away into a deep wood, as if trying to escape from some off frame voyeur or serpent.

34. Judith Mayne, *The Woman at the Keyhole: Feminism and Women's Cinema* (Bloomington: Indiana University Press, 1990), p. 26.

35. James Feet (here as history teacher) is featured as Tom in *Four Weddings and a Funeral*.

36. Hans Robert Jauss, *Toward an Aesthetic of Reception,* trans. Timothy Bahti (Minneapolis: University of Minnesota Press, 1982), p. 23.

Hidden in Plain Sight

Heloise in Clive Donner's Stealing Heaven

KRISTIN L. BURR

The story of Heloise and Abelard brings together two exceptional minds, reckless love, overwhelming physical passion, tragedy, and lives that stayed intertwined even after the pair took religious vows; it is small wonder that the couple holds enduring appeal. Besides editions of their letters, biographies and scholarly studies, Heloise and Abelard have inspired creative works in German, French and English, including Marion Meade's *Stealing Heaven: The Love Story of Heloise and Abelard*.[1] The sole feature film recounting the pair's tale, however, is Clive Donner's 1988 *Stealing Heaven*, based on Meade's novel.[2] Critical response to the couple's cinematographic representation was generally unenthusiastic. Reviewers praised Mikael Salomon's cinematography, the period detail, and the attractive stars (Kim Thomson and Derek de Lint), but offered overall assessments ranging from "interesting in a morbid way" and "over-pretty, comic" to "surprisingly effective."[3] Medievalists, too, find fault with the film. Andrew Larsen remarks on the film's historical errors—including that construction of Notre-Dame de Paris did not begin until after Abelard and Heloise's liaison and that Heloise actively instigates the affair.[4] Emily Sutherland and Tony Gibbons take similar issue with Meade's novel, citing it as an historical novel "which, although very readable, has serious inaccuracies."[5]

Since neither Meade nor Donner sought an entirely faithful reconstruction of the lives of their subjects, I will leave aside these valid historical questions and consider instead the ways in which the film transforms the image of Heloise and her relationship with Abelard.[6] Given that Meade states that the Middle Ages "was a lousy time in which to be a woman,"[7] it is not surprising that the novel focuses on the limits placed on medieval women. The film removes this focus, both in the ways in which it modifies characters—particularly women, but also Abelard—and in which it details the challenges that Heloise does (or does not) face. One might think that Donner's Heloise would reach new levels of independence and radiance. Paradoxically, the opposite holds true. The screen version of Heloise is intellectually brilliant, passionate, and committed to her beloved, just as she is in the book. Yet her relationship to Abelard overshadows everything else, and Heloise becomes less complex.[8] She remains an extraordinary heroine, but her star dims, concealed behind the love and desire that are all to her.

In part, this transformation occurs because the film concentrates on the first half of the novel. By the midpoint of Meade's work, the castrated Abelard has suggested that he and Heloise enter religion. The rest of the novel recounts their story as they navigate their new lives, with a heavy emphasis on Heloise. Chris Bryant's screenplay, on the other hand, devotes little time to these events. Abelard's castration takes place nearly an hour and a half into the two-hour movie. Within 15 minutes, we see Abelard's physical and emotional suffering, Heloise's cursing of her uncle, Abelard's decision to become a monk, and Heloise's acceptance of Abelard's wish that she, too, take vows. The film's final 15 minutes cover the rest of the couple's lives, particularly Heloise's work at the Paraclete.

This condensation of the novel in the screenplay is not atypical, nor does the emphasis on Heloise and Abelard as a couple necessarily reduce Heloise's agency. Indeed, her strength of character seems superior to Abelard's because she is so clearly exceptional. The film takes pains to underscore Heloise's intellectual prowess, often in scenes that are either missing or heavily modified from the book.[9] In the novel, when the adolescent Heloise is summoned to Paris by Fulbert, for instance, she travels from the convent at Argenteuil to Paris with a butcher. In the film, Heloise is accompanied on her journey by the Bishop of Paris.[10] During Heloise's ride in the bishop's litter, the two engage in a spirited theological discussion. Upon reaching Paris, the bishop praises Heloise's wit and education. Fulbert is especially pleased with Heloise's performance when the bishop invites himself to dinner. From the beginning, Heloise's sharp mind distinguishes her, making her more comfortable in the world of the intellectual conversations of high-ranking church officials than among the women of Argenteuil.[11]

While the film insists upon Heloise's superiority, Meade's depiction of the community at Argenteuil reveals the constraints placed on medieval women. Before departing from Argenteuil, Heloise attends prime. Meade fits a wealth of information into the short scene: some of the nuns are absent, still abed after drinking and gossiping after matins; the nuns at the service skip over sections of the office to finish more quickly; and the two sides of the choir are on different verses. In addition, Lady Alais, the abbess, is no role model. She offers perfunctory blessings unless guests are present, dresses extravagantly, and tends toward laziness.[12] Much later, Heloise discovers that Lady Alais is intimately involved with Astrane, a lame novice left at the convent as a child. The convent is more worldly than religious. Instead of condemning the women, however, Meade underscores the lack of opportunities afforded to them. Watching the nuns' half-hearted attempts to finish prime, Heloise recognizes the root of the problem: "Most of these women wouldn't be here if the choice had been theirs. Obviously."[13] Lady Alais is no exception. She looks more like a duchess or countess—which she might have been "if her father had not had three daughters to marry and a son who spent money on tournaments and fashionable cloaks."[14] These women have no religious calling; social circumstances have dictated their fate.[15]

Not all women embrace their destiny readily. Heloise's faithful friend Ceci, whom she first meets when both are children at Argenteuil, stubbornly tries to choose her own path rather than accepting the religious life that her family seeks to impose upon her. Soon after Heloise leaves for Paris, Ceci flees Argenteuil, making the long journey to Fulbert's house, where she is eventually sent back to the convent. Years later, Ceci runs away again, this time with a passing jongleur. This disappearance, too, is temporary; she finally returns, abandoned and pregnant.[16] The episodes point both to the potential for women to resist choices made for them and to their lack of real power to do so.

Meade's portrayal of marriage also calls attention to the lack of options available to women. When Abelard sends a pregnant Heloise to his family's home at Le Pallet, Heloise discovers a small fortified castle inhabited by Abelard's sister Denise, her husband, her sister-in-law, and a passel of children. Neither of the women is in a happy marriage. Denise wed William at 13, against her wishes, disappointed not to have had a wealthy husband. Abelard's brother Dagobert, Alienor's husband, lives at the duke's palace and visits his wife infrequently—just often enough to keep her pregnant. Alienor points out that the 18-year-old Heloise is old to become a first-time mother. These women's lives, too, are chosen for them.

Women of lower social classes fare worse. Meade uncovers Fulbert's hypocrisy through the character of Agnes. Both the canon's housekeeper and his lover, Agnes is frequently pregnant. Meade implies that Fulbert is responsible for at least some of those pregnancies and that he may be the father of Agnes's daughter Petronilla, who also serves in the house. The latter shocks Heloise with her vulgarity and openness about sex, and she eventually dies in childbirth. Throughout her novel, Meade underscores the difficult predicament of women—whether in the secular or sacred world.

Heloise is exceptional, yet she shares the same options as the other women. In both the novel and the film, no one seems to know quite what to make of her extraordinary mind. Fulbert voices the choices available to his 14-year-old niece: she can become a bride of Christ or of man. Fulbert's preference in Meade's book is clear. He deems it a pity that Heloise has no desire to take the veil.[17] Nonetheless, he does not insist, nor does he make a consistent effort to find her a husband. He drops the subject in the novel in the space of two pages. He takes greater pains in the movie, organizing a forest luncheon to introduce Heloise to a prospective spouse—an afternoon that Heloise endures with difficulty, appalled after the potential groom tosses a dead deer at her feet and offers to teach her to hunt. In the face of Heloise's opposition to the marriage, Fulbert cedes to her wishes, although he continues to discuss possible matches. He acknowledges that Heloise is exceptional, noting that her accomplishments surpass even those of most adult men,[18] yet much of the challenge is born of Heloise's image of herself. She does not wish to take religious vows because she lacks the vocation—which has not prevented many of the other women at Argenteuil from becoming nuns—nor does she view marriage as desirable. Rejecting both the religious life and marriage, Heloise has no socially acceptable path.

The film minimizes Meade's critique of the limitations placed on women by eliminating or modifying secondary female characters. Ceci, faithful to Heloise even in the face of extreme hardship, is missing entirely. Likewise, Astrane, who plays a pivotal role in Argenteuil's fate, is written out of the film. The abbess at Argenteuil, too, plays a smaller part. The film's abbess is more maternal and more spiritually inclined than Lady Alais; when a feisty Heloise asks impertinent questions of the prioress, it is the abbess who indulgently takes Heloise's side. Agnes is simply Fulbert's housekeeper, and Petronilla becomes downright spiteful. She spies on Heloise and Abelard during an assignation in the stables and then whispers about it to her lover, one of Abelard's students, making the affair public and playing a role in the couple's eventual downfall. She uses the information to her advantage, asking Heloise for a dress in return for her "friendship." She looks out only for herself.

Male characters in the film, on the other hand, emerge mainly unchanged from their depictions in the novel. Two men who disappear in the film—Bernard of Clairvaux and Peter the Venerable—are from the novel's unadapted second half.[19] Suger, who also plays a key role in the novel's second half, has his role modified slightly so that he is one of the film's villains. He appears early, and neither the students nor the Parisians bear him much love. He recognizes that Abelard's lectures are far more popular than anyone else's, but he is critical of the disrepute Abelard brings by challenging God's word and by his inappropriate behavior. His relationship with Abelard is similarly conflicted in Meade's novel. The main male characters from the first half of the book, Fulbert and Jourdain, play much the same parts in both novel and film.[20]

Bryant's screenplay further removes the spotlight from Heloise by transforming her relationship with Abelard's family, thereby minimizing the challenges that she faces. In the film, when she arrives in Le Pallet to await Astrolabe's birth, Heloise finds a warm welcome. Abelard's sister, here named Jeanne, tells the new arrival: "You must have changed my brother. It's you he loves now, not logic." Jeanne raises Astrolabe after Heloise and Abelard depart, but the family is reunited once Astrolabe is a young man: an elderly Abelard gazes down at the well-established Paraclete and greets Heloise with praise ("Noble indeed. Worthy even of you"). Behind him, Jourdain remarks on the odd first name of his new squire before stepping aside to reveal Astrolabe. Mother and son embrace, with keyboards swelling in the background.

Meade, though, focuses on the distance separating Heloise from Abelard's relatives. Denise and Alienor accept their place as mothers and wives without question. Heloise is different. She shocks Denise by saying that she does not want a wedding, and Denise criticizes the name that Heloise gives to her son as "stupid."[21] She is so unsupportive that, when Heloise returns to see her son—whom she never wished to leave—she discovers that Astrolabe is now called Peter (after his father) and that he considers Denise his mother. Denise has destroyed all of Heloise's letters to Astrolabe and convinces the boy that Heloise will steal him from his home. She further tells Astrolabe that his mother is a whore.[22] The novel offers no happy family reunion.

Heloise's past with Abelard leads to particular suffering in her relationship with Suger. Vacillating between admiration and envy, the abbot of Saint-Denis offers some protection to Abelard. The same does not hold true for Heloise and, consequently, the women around her. Visiting Argenteuil, Suger has inside information going back years, asking about a nun who committed suicide yet is buried in the cemetery, several others who were pregnant, and Ceci's unreported disappearance.[23] Given Lady Alais's lack of leadership and the nuns' questionable level of spiritual devotion, Suger's reproaches are valid. Nonetheless, he seems to be more intent on punishing Heloise than on reform. To the abbess's defense of Heloise as Abelard's wife, he responds harshly: "Leman first, wife second. Bore a brat out of wedlock. Once a whore, always a whore."[24] He minces no words in denouncing Heloise's role as prioress and disagrees with her decisions. Undeterred by Suger's hostility, Heloise asks for news of Abelard. Suger grudgingly offers minimal information followed by blame: "Sister Heloise, if it were not for you, Peter Abelard would be a whole man today."[25] She can do nothing to redeem herself in his eyes.

The scene of the convent's closing is memorable in Donner's film. The expelled nuns trudge through mud as thunder cracks. Heloise's few prized possessions are soaked in the pouring rain.[26] One nun stumbles and falls as she holds the convent's large crucifix. Donner follows the nuns' strenuous journey with scenes of Abelard at the Paraclete. There is a knock on the door as a student quietly sings "Sealed with a Kiss," calling to mind Abelard's relationship with Heloise.[27] An exhausted and sick Heloise falls into Abelard's arms. Her enduring love for Abelard becomes clear from the moment she begins to recuperate from her illness, and Abelard is equally open in his affection. The two begin their conversation with a flirtatious exchange. "So, my lord," says Heloise, "I am in your bed again." Abelard responds, "I'm glad you are." Heloise explains to Abelard that, not knowing where else to go, she came to the Paraclete. Abelard does not hesitate to help: "You're home. Home. I'm giving this place to you." The two exchange tender looks, and Heloise assents: "Then it will be our home together." Their profound love remains, and the attraction has not dimmed. When Abelard calls her "my love," Heloise reveals, "You still make love to me in my heart." Without negating the perils faced by the nuns between Argenteuil and the Paraclete, the film places the emphasis squarely on the love that unites Heloise and Abelard.

The challenges during Heloise's voyage from Argenteuil to the Paraclete in the film pale in comparison to those in Meade's novel. Suger will stop at nothing to close Argenteuil, although it takes him five years to succeed in doing so. Besides relying on the information provided by Astrane, he produces a forged charter stating that the convent belongs to Saint-Denis. The nuns have 30 days to find other convents or ask to be released from their vows. Heloise faces repeated rejection when she seeks places for herself and Ceci: "Always there was some excuse—no room, or her application was being carefully reviewed and so forth. Heloise marveled at the power of Abbot Suger."[28] His reach extends to his influence over the king, who rejects the convent's appeal. Once the convent is officially the abbey's property, no one rushes to claim it, testifying to Suger's true motives.[29]

Ceci and a puppy are Heloise's only companions in exile in the novel. In the nearly two years they travel before settling at the Paraclete, the pair suffers many tribulations: they beg for alms in Paris, visit Jourdain and the now senile Fulbert, journey to Brittany in a blizzard, have most of their possessions and their horse stolen, lose the puppy to wolves, and spend nights in filthy huts. It is a year after Argenteuil's closure before the two reach Saint-Gildas, and Abbot Abelard asks them to go when he realizes that Heloise still tempts him. After the visit to Le Pallet and her repudiation by Astrolabe, Heloise falls extremely ill. During Heloise's long recovery, Ceci sends word to Abelard but receives no reply. At last, he arrives, and it is at this point that he offers her the Paraclete, explaining: "You were dearest to me when we lived in the world, and now you are dearest to me in Christ."[30] There are no loving glances, no reminders of their past joy, no implication that the Paraclete will be "their" home. In fact, Heloise and Ceci find a frosty welcome when they arrive with Abelard in Quincey, the village nearest to the Paraclete. The villagers have unpleasant memories of Abelard's students, bear no love for Abelard, and are unhappy that brigands have stored loot at the Paraclete. It takes Heloise many months to begin to win their trust. Moreover, the Paraclete has barely been developed. Abelard sees the property through the lens of his memories, recalling his thousands of students. Ceci is less impressed when she realizes that the new convent consists of a chapel and two "graceless rectangular structures, which looked like empty boxes," asking, "Is this all?"[31] Abelard's gift has its disadvantages.

The Paraclete owes its eventual success to Heloise's determination. We see her hard at work in the film, but the extent to which she is willing to do anything necessary receives greater attention in the novel. Meade devotes nearly a quarter of her work to Heloise's years as abbess, where she truly shines. Despite resistance, Heloise does not hesitate to learn to plow, to do other manual labor, to insist upon the convent's water rights and other needs, and to welcome increasing numbers of nuns.[32] She displays a talent for leadership and becomes the convent's fierce defender. She boldly approaches Pope Innocent for a charter—which he grants along with the protection of the Apostolic See—requests that Abelard write a new Rule for women, and files lawsuits against monks whom she feels are trying to take advantage of the Paraclete. She also displays courage in facing down Suger when she travels to court to accept the king's offer of tax advantages. After reminding Louis of their long-ago meeting, Heloise turns the conversation to the convent's extraordinary growth. Suger, standing behind the king, quickly reminds him that he has granted the convent exemption from the duty on goods bought in the kingdom. Heloise voices her gratitude, yet asks for an exemption on goods they sell, as well.[33] The king immediately agrees, and Suger must acquiesce. Heloise emerges victorious, having turned her expulsion from Argenteuil into her greatest accomplishment.

While the Paraclete may be a testament to God's glory, the inspiration for Heloise's work is not divine. Abelard turns to God as a result of his castration; the violent act inspires the opposite reaction in Heloise. Her nagging doubts about the Church—visible in the hypocrisy she sees at Argenteuil, her lack of religious vocation, her feelings about relics, and the conflicting statements she recognizes in the writings of the Church Fathers, the liturgy, and canon law[34]—beget a spiritual crisis. She characterizes God as cruel, finding it unjust that Abelard alone was punished for their physical intimacy.[35] Furthermore, she does not forgive God for Abelard's suffering, telling Jourdain: "I serve God, but I accuse him, as ever."[36] Nor does she expect much for herself, convinced that she will not die from a grave illness because God wishes to torture her.[37] Her faith is in her beloved, and she agrees to become a nun because it allows her the possibility on occasion of seeing Abelard. Consenting to Abelard's request, Heloise conflates human love and religious faith: "I will do it. But it's you who has been crucified. You are my lord, and I will love no other." Her heart and soul, she declares to God as she takes her religious vows, belong to Abelard, and in this conviction, she never wavers.[38] Responding to Jourdain's praise after the Paraclete is flourishing, Heloise forthrightly announces: "I built this house for Abelard. Nothing was done for God."[39] Her steadfast love for Abelard motivates all of her actions.

Although the film devotes little time to the religious life of Heloise and Abelard after their affair, it succeeds in capturing Heloise's attitude. In this regard, relics are crucial. In both the novel and the film, Fulbert does a booming business in selling relics.[40] It is in the invention of a different "relic," however, that the film evokes Heloise's spiritual misgivings. Adopting the book's structure, the film opens with a scene in which an elderly nun is on her deathbed; the rest of the story is told as a flashback. The film heightens the suspense by setting the opening scene during a storm.[41] The dying woman pushes away a crucifix, whispering a request to a nearby nun. The nun goes to the chapel to retrieve a small crucifix, bringing it in with a clap of thunder. The aged nun removes an object from a hole in the base, holds the mysterious item to her heart, and hurls the crucifix across the room, breaking it. With a whispered "I understand," the scene ends, and we are taken into the past, where young women sit asking questions of the prioress. In just a few minutes, the film has established that the woman (whom we take to be Heloise) is not motivated by her devotion to God as she lays dying.[42]

The item that the nun wants to hold as she departs from this world, we learn, is an everyday object that becomes a relic. During their passionate affair, the couple takes a walk in the woods. Heloise catches a dove's feather, proclaiming it her own holy relic and the day a holy day. The film's final minutes return to the opening scene. Once more, the dying nun clasps the item from the crucifix's base in her hands. This time, we see that it is the feather. In the background, the dialogue from the scene in the woods plays. Doves fly across the sky, and Abelard's voice is the last sound that Heloise hears: "My love. I'm here. I'm waiting." Abelard and love are at the heart of Heloise's veneration.

The feather becomes a visual reminder of Heloise's rejection of God. After Jourdain informs Heloise of Abelard's castration, Sister Cecilia exhorts the upset woman to accept God's will. Heloise categorically refuses: "The will of God? There is no God." When Sister Cecilia crosses herself, Heloise does not back down: "Pray until your knees are raw. No one will hear but the spiders!" She voices similar sentiments when she comes to Paris to care for Abelard. Whereas Abelard views his mutilation as God's just vengeance for his lust, Heloise cannot accept the violent act as divine punishment, declaring: "I spit on God and all his saints. When I heard of this thing, God died." Her repudiation of God takes tangible form when she takes religious vows. Before the ceremony, she takes a small crucifix—the one that appears in the film's opening and closing moments—and places the dove's feather in a hole in the base. As she enters religious orders, she kisses the crucifix's base rather than the crucified Christ, justifying her action to those present: "I am unworthy. Therefore, I cannot kiss my Lord." She replaces religious faith with human love.

Heloise's renunciation of God comes across as an act of defiance and anger. While she is bitter in the novel, as well, she never fully denies God. Instead of rebellion, her decision to place Abelard rather than God at the center of her life has the effect of accentuating her devotion. She is faithful despite repeated doubts about Abelard's feelings. She expresses her belief that Abelard never loved her and that he sees her solely as the instrument of his salvation to Jourdan and Ceci, respectively; she accuses Abelard, too, of lust rather than love.[43] By describing Heloise's unerring love, Meade places the focus on her heroine. Even in scenes centering on Abelard's troubles, we see them through the lens of Heloise's concern and compassion.

This dedication continues throughout her entire life. Just as Heloise hears Abelard tell her that he is waiting for her as she dies in the film, so does she see him at the moment of her death in the novel, feeling herself pulled through blackness to a green meadow with a stone wall: "Someone was sitting on the wall, and when he saw her, he grinned and stretched wide his arms. She rushed forward."[44] Love has inspired her. In Donner's film, love inspires Abelard, as well; he may struggle with justifying his desire for Heloise and his religious faith and see his castration as divine—and merited—punishment, yet aside from angrily telling her to leave when she comes to nurse him after he is castrated, he never falters in his kindness. He takes care of her, offering her the Paraclete as a home, working alongside her to build a chapel for the nuns (even giving her posies as they labor), asking to consecrate the finished chapel so that that they will see each other again, and reuniting Heloise with Astrolabe. His affection for Heloise remains constant even if he cannot act on his desire. The elderly Abelard tells Abbess Heloise: "You are still the girl in the meadow chasing the feather. Strange, isn't it, the one you love never seems to grow old." After expressing his wish to be buried at the Paraclete, he continues, "And perhaps in God's time, you will share my bed." The two press their lips to their clasped hands and gaze into each other's eyes. This is their final scene together, and in the film's last moments, we return to Heloise on her deathbed, hearing Abelard's voice. A title then appears on the screen noting that lovers still leave flowers on the pair's shared grave in Paris's Père Lachaise cemetery. Until the very end of the film, we see Heloise and Abelard as a pair, with the emphasis on their mutual love.

This is hardly the Abelard of Meade's novel, where the celebrated philosopher's

Kim Thompson as Heloise in Clive Donner's 1988 film *Stealing Heaven*.

shortcomings place the focus more squarely on Heloise's constancy and patience. The softening of Abelard's character begins from the moment Heloise meets him in the film. Shortly after her arrival in Paris, Heloise is horrified to see a child trampled by a horse ridden by one of Suger's men. A tall man moves the limp body to the side and picks up the coins tossed onto the boy. Berated by Heloise, he protests that he does not want the money to be stolen and then sends his students in search of the child's parents. In the meantime, he places coins on the child's eyes and mouth, where touching them would be sacrilege. Dabbing at Heloise's tears, he takes her home—finally realizing who she is because the bishop has spoken about her. Heloise does not know who has helped her until she is told that it was Abelard. The scene accomplishes several things: it establishes that Abelard and Heloise are well-matched; it vilifies Suger; and it creates an image of Abelard as thoughtful and kind, justifying Heloise's feelings.

Heloise is quickly smitten with Abelard in the novel, as well, but the circumstances are quite different. Before seeing Abelard, she has heard much about him thanks to her friendship with Jourdain—and the young man has spoken of Heloise to Abelard, too. Although Heloise has no desire to wed, she dreams about a lover. Days later, Heloise stops at the baker's, where she sees a tall man asking one question after another about the bread and its ingredients, oblivious to the impatience of the baker and the other customers. Intrigued by the man's looks and voice, Heloise is also impressed by his wit, on display when he defends himself to an angry customer, telling her: "it took Our Blessed Savior three days to rise from the tomb and he was the Son of God. The least you can allot me is three minutes to purchase a loaf of bread."[45] By the time Heloise leaves the bakery, she announces to the surprised Ceci: "That man is mine."[46] Meade highlights the role of destiny—Abelard is the lover in Heloise's dreams—and the speed with which Heloise realizes that Abelard is meant for her. Absent, however, is the image of a tender-hearted Abelard that we see in Donner's film.[47]

The film further softens Abelard's image when he comes to lodge with Fulbert and during his seduction of Heloise. Donner's Abelard does not initiate the discussion of moving into Fulbert's home. He has already proven his devotion to his studies by rejecting the prostitute his students have hired to seduce him—another scene missing in the novel—and it is the bishop who promises to find him respectable lodging.[48] Only then does Abelard select Fulbert's residence. This Abelard has assured his students that God has given him the gift of teaching in return for his celibacy and that taking a woman would be like spitting in the face of God: "He would take away his gifts and damn me for all eternity. And He would be right." He finds himself tempted by carnal thoughts once he begins working with Heloise, yet he experiences these feelings despite himself.

Abelard finally submits to his destiny, but not without a struggle. He tells Heloise to leave his room as she leans over his shoulder and blots a drop of ink as he writes, and then opens the window to rub snow on his face. Following a debate between the pair over whether temptation comes from God or the devil, the scene shifts to a topless Heloise wafting the smoke from a love potion given to her at Argenteuil over her face and torso. The film then cuts to Christmas Eve mass at Notre-Dame, where the smoke from the censer recalls the smoke from the charm. Abelard and Heloise look at each other, their eyes meeting. The camera moves once more to Heloise in her room, rubbing the charm's smoke across her breasts and then down toward her genitals. Finally, it returns to the cathedral, where a smiling Fulbert, eyes closed, is oblivious to all that is happening around him. Assured by Abelard that it is practically the law to offer a kiss when asked on Christmas Eve, Heloise laughingly satisfies Jourdain's request with a small peck. Later, sitting before the fire, Heloise asks Abelard: "Do you not owe me something, my lord?" Abelard reminds her that Jesus was betrayed by a kiss, to which Heloise responds that the kiss—and by extension, their love—was preordained. The two soon go to Abelard's room, where they give in to their passion. The next morning, Abelard leaves while Heloise is still in bed, riding into the woods to a wayside crucifix and crossing himself. When Heloise asks him where he has been, he replies, "Trying to make peace with my God." Heloise does not share his worries: "I've tried very hard to feel I've sinned all through mass. All I can feel is happy!" Abelard tells her that their making love must never happen again and leaves. Even as he succumbs to temptation, Abelard resists, and the film emphasizes his doubts and regrets.

The themes of temptation and desire subtend the entire film: the initial scene of Abelard teaching finds him seeking to define temptation, and Abelard and his students sing bawdy songs. Heloise demonstrates a special interest in erotic material. The first time that she sneaks into Abelard's room to look at his books, she discovers a translation of a risqué Catullus poem. The film hints at Heloise's role as temptress from our introduction to the young heroine, who is asking provocative questions about reproduction and male genitalia. A poster for the film highlights the carnal nature of the couple's love. Heloise, shoulders bare, leans against a shirtless Abelard, whose lips rest on his lover's head. Heloise has her hand on Abelard's chest in an intimate gesture. The pair is set against a blue and pink backdrop reminiscent of clouds and a sunset. In the upper left, the text reads: "One of history's greatest erotic romances. Unforgettable love. Unforgivable sin." While Abelard and Heloise equally experience desire and the love scenes have them both nude, Heloise in particular is associated with sexual curiosity.

Abelard's concern for Heloise, as well as her role in perpetuating the affair, are evident until the two are discovered *in flagrante delicto*. Having heard talk about his relationship with Heloise, Abelard fears for her reputation. He announces to Fulbert that he will lodge elsewhere.[49] Heloise suffers profoundly from his departure, leading Jourdain to arrange for the two to meet at his room. As they sleep unclothed after making love, Fulbert and his men burst in. Back at the canon's residence, Fulbert and Heloise argue passionately. A furious Fulbert accidentally cuts his hand, promising: "By God, this isn't the only blood that will flow!" Heloise's pursuit of Abelard and lack of care for her reputation have led to tragedy. While Abelard is not blameless, the film depicts him as conflicted, worried both for himself and for Heloise.

The novel mutes Heloise's responsibility. Abelard is the source of the request to lodge with Fulbert, sending Canon Martin with the message. Both Fulbert and his friend find the query unusual; as Fulbert probes, Martin replies that Abelard "says that his household problems are hindering his studies. He *says* that his servant robs him blind and the expense of maintaining his own lodgings is more than he can afford. That's what he *says*."[50] The repetition of "says," along with Meade's use of italics, suggests that the men find Abelard's reasons suspect.[51] Abelard displays much greater agency in the novel, and the scene hints at his ulterior motives. Jourdain seizes on Abelard's upcoming arrival to tell Heloise unequivocally: "Fulbert mustn't. He must not."[52] He further relates to Heloise that Abelard has compared himself to a hungry wolf and Heloise to a tender lamb. This Abelard displays little fear of what God will think.

Abelard orchestrates Heloise's seduction with equal care. After a post-mass feast at Fulbert's, Abelard offers his cup to Heloise, encouraging her to drink. When she asks if he would make her drunk, she wonders if she imagines him whispering, "I would, lady."[53] Moments later, he tells her that she owes him a kiss. Heloise hesitates, afraid that her uncle will awaken, but Abelard persists, surprising her when he puts his tongue into her mouth. Over the next few days, nothing seems to have changed between them, until on New Year's he stuns her by saying that he dreamed that they were lying together. Before long, the dream becomes reality, although not without trepidation on Heloise's part. When Abelard lays her on the bed and touches her breast, and she asks him to return to kissing her and eventually pushes him away, worried: "It's a fearful sin."[54] Abelard, intent on undressing Heloise, reassures her: "If we intend no sin, it can't be one. That is my belief."[55] After hesitating once more, Heloise surrenders to Abelard's wishes, swept up in her love and desire for him. Meade's Abelard is calculating, concerned with satisfying his lust rather than with the potential for sin; Heloise is the one who expresses doubts.

Abelard's arrogance and egotism come into full display after his castration.[56] Heloise thinks only of Abelard: she falls ill upon hearing the news and is determined to return to Paris to care for her husband, angry at God for unjustly punishing Abelard. Abelard, too, thinks only of himself: he rants about eunuchs as abominations to God and fears what others will say: "How can I show my face in public? So that everyone can point at me, every tongue deride me, a monstrous spectacle to everyone I meet?"[57] He focuses on his suffering and shame.

While Abelard's self-absorption during his recovery is excusable, his attitude is harder to justify when he decides that both he and Heloise should take religious vows. The identity crisis that Abelard undergoes—"I *was* a philosopher. Now it is my desire to become a monk"[58]—has important consequences for the woman who loves him. Characteristically, Abelard underscores what the decision means for him, grateful that God has freed him from temptation and worldly distraction. Heloise realizes that his wish for her to become a nun has little to do with her best interests: "To keep from losing her, he was willing to bury her."[59] Moreover, Abelard does not take vows until he has watched Heloise utter hers.[60] Abelard can no longer continue his physical affair with Heloise, but he wishes to ensure that no one else takes his place—in her heart or in her bed. Donner's Abelard is more spiritually driven. He wishes to become a monk to make amends to God, and he takes his vows first, with a teary Heloise in the back of the chapel. Afterwards, Abelard explains to Heloise that he wishes her to join a religious community for her own safety. There is no suggestion that he wants to prevent Heloise from loving another man.

For most of the second half of the novel, Abelard proves to be blind to Heloise's difficulties. On the heels of Heloise's horrible winter journey, Abelard sees only her accomplishments, lauding her for being able to manage everything by herself: "God, what a marvelous woman you are!"[61] Although Heloise has taken every opportunity to ask people about Abelard, he has no idea that she has found no community after Argenteuil's closure and heaps scorn on the women who chose to be released from their vows. He later bristles when he hears of many visitors—including men—to the Paraclete as Heloise builds the community, resists Heloise's desire to travel occasionally (despite the fact that her reasons for doing so are in the Paraclete's interests), and includes in his Rule for women the requirement that the abbess be cloistered. Heloise does not always respect Abelard's wishes, but his repeated attempts to keep her isolated from other men point both to the stereotypical belief that women cannot master their lascivious nature and to his selfish hope to prevent Heloise from loving anyone else since he cannot have her.[62] Consciously or not, Abelard tries to control her.

Meade's portrayal of the philosopher turned monk is rarely flattering. Although Heloise and Abelard are physically separated for much of the novel, Abelard maintains a strong presence thanks to the updates that Heloise hears from Jourdain and, eventually, Astrolabe. Abelard deeply wounds Heloise with his letter of consolation to his friend, filled with what Heloise views as distortions and omissions about their affair and an emphasis on Abelard's suffering. Given Abelard's lack of consideration for Heloise, it is little surprise that the general consensus is that he brings many of his troubles upon himself. He faces one challenge after another after he takes his vows: Suger both helps and hurts him, the monks of Saint-Gildas dislike him, the inhabitants of the village nearest to the Paraclete display animosity toward him, and, most importantly, Bernard of Clairvaux is determined to have Abelard and his work condemned as heretical. Abelard's troubles predate his affair with Heloise; shortly after Heloise speaks to Abelard for the first time, Jourdain tells his friend that Abelard has enemies, attributing them to the philosopher's rebellious tendencies. Informing Heloise that Suger has sent Abelard to the isolated Breton abbey of Saint-Gildas, Jourdain notes that Abelard's most dangerous enemy is Abelard himself.[63] The pride that has always been one of Abelard's flaws eventually leads to his condemnation. During the assembly at Sens, Bernard of Clairvaux denounces Abelard's arrogance. In front of King Louis, Queen Eleanor, and the bishops, abbots, counts and monks gathered to hear the men present their cases, Bernard acknowledges that Abelard is a stronger speaker but proclaims that Abelard's words condemn him, listing his heresies. To everyone's surprise, Abelard remains quiet, refusing to be judged and promising to appeal to Rome before leaving the cathedral. In the letter that Astrolabe hands to Heloise, she finds Abelard's profession of faith, written before Bernard's speech. The letter could have saved Abelard—the Pope upholds the judgment of heresy—but rather than make it public, he leaves it for Heloise's eyes. He will not back down.

Poster for Clive Donner's 1988 film *Stealing Heaven* (collection of Kristin L. Burr).

The film takes a more ambiguous approach to Abelard's hubris, focusing on his mastery in teaching. Donner almost always shoots Abelard teaching from below, making him seem larger than life; or from above, where the students, Church officials, and few women watching testify to Abelard's popularity. By surrounding Abelard with his students yet separating him enough that he remains the focal point, Donner creates a visual representation of Abelard's appeal and talent. Suger's criticisms may be a reaction to Abelard's arrogance, yet the film implies that he is jealous of Abelard's intellectual superiority and ability to draw crowds. The bishop notes that Suger's lectures are only half full, and his main concern once Abelard's affair with Heloise is discovered is that Paris risks losing France's greatest teacher. Abelard may be pretentious, but that flaw is never rendered explicitly.

While Meade's Abelard is frequently portrayed harshly, he grows kinder toward Heloise as he ages. She is astonished to learn from her son that Abelard often speaks of Heloise, praising her as the most admirable woman he has ever known, thereby encouraging Astrolabe to be more kindly disposed toward Heloise than he was when she visited him at Le Pallet. Moreover, Astrolabe tells his mother that Abelard's *Sic et non* is Heloise's book: she gave Abelard the idea, and he based the work on her research.[64] Abelard displays greater generosity to Heloise after he is condemned at Sens, apologizing for the pain that he has caused her. The two entwine their hands, and for the first time in years, Abelard affectionately calls Heloise "Ladylove."[65] By now, Abelard is showing signs of serious illness. Treating Heloise with kindness and later reconciled with Bernard of Clairvaux, Abelard dies in peace. The news of his passing affects Heloise deeply; she transforms her emotional pain into physical suffering by biting her fingers until they bleed, wishing for her own death.[66]

Devoted to Abelard during his life, she feels no less strongly after his death, and she is determined to carry out Abelard's wish to be buried at the Paraclete. When Brother Thibaut claims that the abbey where Abelard dies has the right to keep his body and that he has already been interred, Heloise shocks the monk by suggesting that they unbury him.[67] Fortunately, Peter the Venerable has the same thought. He arrives at the Paraclete with a wagon bearing Abelard's body, which he had disentombed during the night. He recognizes what Abelard long resisted, telling Heloise that Abelard belonged at her side: "He is the other half of you. God is keeping him for you."[68] In her grief, Heloise finds comfort. She is able to spend the 21 years between Abelard's death and her own continuing her work at the Paraclete—and still steadfast in her love. While this love is at the core of who she is and what she accomplishes, Meade does not permit Abelard to dominate the story. Instead, she uncovers the many reasons to admire Heloise. By the time Heloise dies, six daughter houses have been founded from the Paraclete, which has received papal bulls from six popes, multiple royal charters, and extensive property. The esteem shown to her by popes, kings, and Peter the Venerable, among others, is warranted.

Heloise is remarkable in Donner's film, as well. Nevertheless, what is her story in the novel becomes on screen merely a love story. By eliminating much of the material from the book's second half, moving the focus away from the constraints on women, and creating a kinder portrait of Abelard, the screenplay has the paradoxical effect of reducing Heloise's complexity. She is brilliant, fiery, and passionate—but she is also consistently defined by her relationship with Abelard. The spotlight shifts off of Heloise and onto the couple that she forms with Abelard, keeping her hidden in plain sight. The time is ripe, perhaps, for another big screen version of the lovers' tale, and this time, one in which Heloise truly shines.

NOTES

1. Marion Meade, *Stealing Heaven: The Love Story of Heloise and Abelard* (1979; rpt. New York: Open Road Media, 2014). See also Luise Rinser, *Abaelards Liebe* (Stuttgart: S. Fischer, 1991); Antoine Audouard, *Adieu, mon unique* (Paris: Editions Gallimard, 2000); Jean Teulé, *Héloïse, ouille!* (Paris: Julliard, 2015); and Sherry Jones, *The Sharp Hook of Love* (New York: Gallery Books, 2014).

2. *Stealing Heaven*, directed by Clive Donner (1988; MGM Home Entertainment, 2015), DVD. Other filmed and theatrical versions exist, but they are rare: Jacques Trébouta directed the two-part French *Héloïse et Abélard* that aired on television in 1973 (for which Régine Pernoud served as historical advisor), and artistic director John Sparks staged a January 2008 reading of *Heloise and Abelard: A New Musical* at Theatre Building Chicago.

3. The citations come respectively from Rita Kempley, "*Stealing Heaven*," *Washington Post*, 28 April 1989, http://www.washingtonpost.com/wp-srv/style/longterm/movies/videos/stealingheavenrkempley_a0c9ce. htm; Michael Wilmington, "*Stealing Heaven* Updates Heloise and Abelard," *Los Angeles Times*, 28 April 1989, http://articles.latimes.com/1989-04-28/entertainment/ca-1645_1_movie-reviews-convent-castration; and Caryn James, "Doomed Passion of Abelard and Heloise," *New York Times* 28 April 1989, http://www.nytimes. com/movie/review?res=950DE1D8143FF93BA15757C0A96F948260. The critics vary in their opinions of the quality of acting, with Kempley characterizing de Lint's Abelard as a "lunk—you have the feeling that the filmmakers couldn't get Gérard Depardieu," but James describing his performance as thoughtful and complex. Both Kempley and Wilmington note that the film feels more modern than medieval; Wilmington sees the 1960s, whereas for Kempley, Thomson and de Lint are "more like those wild and crazy hepcats in Madonna's 'Like a Prayer' video." James offers the kindest review, comparing *Stealing Heaven* to "a poor cousin to 'The Lion in Winter' crossed with 'Camelot' and highlighted with steamy sex scenes." More recently, in her review, Traxy Thornfield finds the production value less than impressive, but the story draws her interest: "… it's technically a mediocre film, and the script and cinematography isn't [sic] the most inspiring ever, and this is quite possibly a low-budget TV movie, but OMG the romance totally works." Traxy Thornfield, "Film Review: *Stealing Heaven* (1988), directed by Clive Donner," *The Squeee* (blog), April 29, 2013, http://www.thesqueee. co.uk/stealing-heaven-1988/

4. Andrew E. Larsen, "*Stealing Heaven*: The Great Medieval Love Story on Film," *An Historian Goes to the Movies: Exploring History on Screen* (blog). Nov. 10, 2014, https://aelarsen.wordpress.com/2014/11/10/ stealing-heaven-the-great-medieval-love-story-on-film/ Larsen still deems the film "a far better medieval romance than many other films." He does not address the novel, which he had not read.

5. Inaccuracies include Heloise's journey to Paris with the butcher and her travels with Ceci after being expelled from Argenteuil. Emily Sutherland and Tony Gibbons, "Historical Fiction and History: Members of the Same Family," *TEXT* 13.2 (2009), http://www.textjournal.com.au/oct09/sutherland_gibbons.htm

6. Meade intended to write a biography of Heloise, but insufficient material led to a historical novel instead, which she qualifies as a "blessing in disguise." Meade, p. 3. In the film, Nick Bicât's keyboard-heavy score reminds viewers that they are not in the Middle Ages.

7. Meade, p. 1. While there are reasons to dispute this generalization, doing so is not my objective here.

8. Abelard, too, is more unidimensional. Glorianna Locklear sees Donner as replacing the historical Abelard's intellectual power with sexual charisma and little else and argues that Donner imposes twentieth-century thought on twelfth-century concerns. Glorianna Locklear, "Delicious Poison: Heloise and Abelard Out of Time," *Popular Culture Review* 4.1 (January 1993): 45 [39–47].

9. Larsen considers the film to be mainly Heloise's story, finding her more interesting than Abelard. He praises Kim Thomson's portrayal of Heloise as a relatively strong-willed woman who is Abelard's intellectual equal. Larsen supposes that the novel, like the film, focuses exclusively on the love affair.

10. Heloise is named for the first time when the abbess introduces her to the bishop.

11. The same qualities are evident in other scenes in the film that are absent in the novel, as when Heloise and Abelard return from an outing and Abelard tells a suspicious Fulbert that they were studying Augustine's *Confessions*. Heloise saves the moment by answering Fulbert's questions about the work, which she has read earlier.

12. Meade, pp. 23, 26.

13. Meade, p. 17. Heloise herself began attending prime as a young child from defiance rather than faith. She wished to be there not to worship, but because she was neither required nor permitted to get up for the service—which piqued her interest and made her beg the nuns to take her along.

14. Meade, p. 25.

15. Financial concerns are essential in convents' decisions of which women to accept. After months of walking following Suger's closure of the house at Argenteuil, Ceci's feet are so swollen that she and Heloise stop for three weeks at the ironically-named Our Lady of Hope, where the abbess explains that she can welcome them permanently only if they have dowers or other money to give to the convent. Meade, p. 306.

16. Meade, pp. 266–268.

17. Meade, p. 35.

18. Meade, p. 35.

19. Also missing is Fulbert's uncouth brother Philip, who helps him with the castration; presumably, his character disappears to simplify the story.

20. Changes to these characters are minor. Meade hints that Fulbert secretly loves Heloise but does not act on (or perhaps even recognize) his feelings. In the film, Heloise meets Jourdain in Paris, but the novel depicts their meeting during a visit to Fulbert's brother's domain. He has ties to both Heloise and Abelard in Meade's work, and his role as go-between makes more sense.

21. Meade, p. 166. Besides her sentiments about marriage in general, Heloise resists Abelard's offer to wed her because she wants to protect Abelard: she argues that marriage would disgrace him and that family life is incompatible with philosophy. She finally agrees but is outraged when Fulbert reveals the secret marriage.

22. Meade, pp. 318–321.

23. Suger's initial visit comes before Ceci returns. It later becomes clear that Astrane is Suger's source, using the information to hurt Alais, with whom she has fallen out. In exchange, Suger untruthfully promises Astrane the position of prioress at another convent.

24. Meade, p. 261.

25. Meade, p. 264.

26. These include the small crucifix that we see in the film's opening and closing scenes.

27. The song is heard at key points: first the night after Abelard has met Heloise, and then again when news begins to spread about their affair.

28. Meade, p. 288.

29. Meade, p. 289.

30. Meade, p. 325.

31. Meade, p. 327.

32. These nuns include two of Abelard's nieces and Astrane, forgiven for her betrayal.

33. Meade, p. 387.

34. Meade, p. 114.

35. Meade, p. 211.

36. Meade, p. 295.

37. Meade, p. 322.

38. Meade, p. 229. When Suger allows the nuns at Argenteuil to return to the secular life, Heloise refuses because her vows are to Abelard. Meade, *Stealing Heaven*, p. 286.

39. Meade, p. 401.

40. Meade's discussions of relics create an image of Fulbert as motivated by financial reward rather than spiritual commitment. He devotes more of his time to his profitable dealings in relics than to his obligations as canon. Others note his priorities: Abelard argues that Fulbert loves relics, Heloise, and, especially, money. Jourdain disagrees, placing Heloise at the top of the list. In Donner's film, viewers see Fulbert working on reliquaries, and, when Heloise asks her uncle how he can sell relics that are supposed to be in Venice, he flippantly replies that they miraculously reproduce themselves.

41. In contrast, the weather is balmy as the novel begins. Moreover, Meade's initial scene, titled simply "May 16, 1163," recounts a series of memories in the dying abbess's mind, juxtaposed with the few sounds and sensations that the woman notices as she grows close to leaving the physical world.

42. Locklear notes that the scene sets up Donner's premise that human love is all and that it creates dramatic suspense, making the viewer want to know what the hidden object is and why it is important. Locklear, p. 43.

43. See Meade, pp. 275, 364, 376. While Jourdain and Ceci seek to reassure her, Heloise's uncertainty remains.

44. Meade, p. 440.

45. Meade, p. 70.

46. Meade, p. 71.

47. To be sure, Abelard is kind to Heloise. When Jourdain introduces the two after one of Abelard's lectures, Abelard sees that Heloise is hurt and arranges for a horse to take her home—but he does not display the benevolence that he does with the trampled child.

48. The scene's placement underscores the negative image of Suger, who offers this criticism and calls Abelard a fornicator in the film immediately after Abelard resists the temptation of a prostitute his students have paid to seduce Abelard as a bet.

49. In the novel, Abelard moves out of Fulbert's residence because Fulbert has heard rumors and wants to protect Heloise's name. Abelard announces the decision to Heloise jointly with Fulbert, yet the idea is not his.

50. Meade, pp. 83–84.

51. Martin advises Fulbert to accept Abelard as a lodger for the money. The men briefly consider the impropriety of bringing together Abelard and Heloise, but Fulbert naively supposes that Abelard has no interest in women and that Heloise is not interested in men. Meade, p. 85.

52. Meade, p. 86.

53. Meade, p. 98.

54. Meade, p. 103.

55. Meade, p. 104.

56. Meade relates the details of the castration from a medical student's perspective (a surgeon accompanied Fulbert and Philip). Donner's film portrays the castration less graphically, interspersing scenes with Heloise dreaming fitfully in the convent where she stays for her safety and images of Fulbert summoning men, entering Abelard's room, and binding him as he struggles. We hear Abelard's scream as the scene changes to the morning mist at Argenteuil. There, Heloise tucks her dove's feather "relic" into her bodice.

57. Meade, p. 215.

58. Meade, p. 222.

59. Meade, p. 226.

60. Meade underscores the new life that awaits Heloise by interweaving the young woman's memories of her past in Paris with her religious ceremony.

61. Meade, p. 311.

62. Abelard's fears are unfounded. Not once is Heloise tempted to break her vows to Abelard.

63. Meade, p. 297.

64. Astrolabe and Heloise finally make their peace over discussions of logic, with Heloise offering help to her son. Meade, p. 382.

65. Meade, pp. 419–420.

66. Meade, p. 431.

67. Meade, p. 431.

68. Meade, p. 436.

Catty Queen Consort, Lioness in Winter and Loyal Queen Mother

Images of Eleanor of Aquitaine in Film

Fiona Tolhurst

Eleanor of Aquitaine's appearances on the big screen are not numerous, but they are varied—both in how much power Eleanor has, and how positively or negatively she is portrayed. These varied appearances are colored by two markedly conflicting images of Eleanor, both grounded in mythmaking: the Black Legend, which presents her in strongly negative terms, and the Golden Myth, which presents her in strongly positive ones.[1] With its point of origin in the medieval period, the Black Legend denigrates Eleanor by claiming that she prioritized her love life over political interests, parented poorly, sought divorce from Louis VII and selected Henry II as her second husband, rebelled against Henry, usurped male authority by dressing as a man, slept with numerous lovers, was guilty of incest, and murdered Henry's mistress Rosamund Clifford. The Golden Myth—a product of 20th-century scholarship inspired by Second-Wave Feminism—repackaged Eleanor as a female hero by exaggerating her achievements and scope of influence and by perpetuating the myth of her exceptionality.

As is true of cinema medievalia in general, viewers do not learn much about the Middle Ages from films in which Queen Eleanor appears. However, viewers can learn about how filmmakers have used a complex medieval woman to explore and define women's roles in the 1950s, 1960s, and later. Six live-action films present an Eleanor of Aquitaine who can be powerless or powerful, evil or good, and disrespected or honored depending on which elements of the Black Legend and Golden Myth each film draws upon, and the attitudes toward women prevalent at the time that film was made.[2]

Eleanor as Catty Queen Consort in Becket

The film adaptation of Jean Anouilh's 1959 play *Becket ou l'honneur de Dieu* [*Becket, or the Honor of God*], which Paramount released in 1964, would have been very different if the resurgence of feminism in the United States that began in the early 1960s had influenced its script. However, Peter Glenville's Eleanor can be neither a major character nor an object of her husband's affection, for screenwriter Edward Anhalt did not alter the play's focus: King Henry's love of Thomas Becket, love which remains unrequited because Becket is incapable of love until—after Henry makes him Archbishop of Canterbury— he becomes willing to act on (and eventually die for) the love of God's honor. The homosocial tension between Henry and Becket never manifests itself as homosexual behavior, yet the intensity of Henry's love for his closest friend makes Eleanor irrelevant to her husband's emotional life.[3] It also makes her the target of many a scathing rebuke from the king, and (because the film's director justifies Henry's scorn for Eleanor) a character that film critics have scorned in like manner.[4] But Eleanor, played by Pamela Brown, eventually gains some depth as a character because she expresses frustration with her powerlessness and resists Henry's verbal abuse of her.

Eleanor's first interaction with Henry in *Becket* establishes their marital dynamic: she makes catty comments out of jealousy, and he rejects her as boring and disloyal; nevertheless, the queen tries to defend both her wifely rights and the value of their life together. Because the screenplay contains no mention of the Aquitaine, the source of Eleanor's political power, she remains limited to the roles of wife and mother. The director makes this limitation visible by consistently presenting Eleanor as "literally hemmed in—by elaborate gowns and wimples."[5] After the queen cattily notes that the new Archbishop of Canterbury is too busy "fitting sandals on beggars" to visit Henry, she—apparently out of jealousy that Henry is more interested in Becket than he is in her—complains about how Becket undercut her position as wife when he "lured [Henry] away from the duties [he] owe[s] to [her]" by taking him to whorehouses. Although the whoring episodes show viewers that Henry led Becket astray, Eleanor's loyalty to her husband causes her to assume that Becket is the instigator of these illicit sexual encounters. Yet Henry uses her assumption that her rival for Henry's love is to blame as an opportunity to demean her by suggesting that their sex life is a duty from which he is now happily freed. Having failed to assert her expectation that Henry will again share a bed with her, Eleanor attempts to defend the value of family life. However, when Eleanor expresses her hope that, once Henry realizes that Becket has "used" him, he "might appreciate the joys of family life again," Henry brands her as boring and catty because of her "everlasting back-biting." Even the queen's platitude "One performs according to one's gifts" earns her a condescending "Yes" from her husband, consistent with his dismissal of her as producing a truly mediocre tapestry—thereby mocking the women's work to which she is relegated.

Henry's verbal abuse of Eleanor continues even in the presence of their children. Although Eleanor's actions offer no corroboration of this charge, Henry accuses his wife of undermining him by planning to wield power when he is dead. In this film, the Black Legend is invoked through Henry's harsh words but not validated through anything the queen does. Henry's labeling their children as his wife's "loyal vermin" presents her to viewers as disloyal, and—because the directorial point of view coincides with the king's— viewers are likely to accept his assessment.

In her second appearance in *Becket*, Eleanor expresses loyalty to her husband by gloating over Thomas Becket's impending destruction in court, yet Henry makes what viewers might perceive as the move of a traditional husband in the 1950s and 1960s: he puts his wife firmly in her place and silences her through his verbal aggression. As soon as Eleanor asks why she should not gloat "at seeing [Henry's] enemy perish," Henry gives her a tongue-lashing that denies her the wifely right to take pleasure in her husband's political triumph, brands her as catty and selfish, and dismisses her as inherently worthless. The director reinforces Henry's harsh assessment by making Eleanor's focus on her "puny little person" evident in the extravagant headdress that accentuates her crown, an expression of self-importance that contrasts with the king's bare head but full assertion of kingly power.

In response to this verbal aggression, Eleanor attempts to assert the value of both their family and her primary commodity as a woman, her virginity, but the king's harsh words dismiss and silence her. The queen's defensive remark that she has given Henry both children and "[her] youth" earns her further verbal abuse. Henry dismisses his queen's gift of her body by branding that body "an empty desert" in which he has suffered emotional isolation. When Henry concludes this speech by praising Becket as "red-blooded, generous, and full of strength," his implication is that Eleanor is cold, selfish, and weak. Although Eleanor's earlier protest suggests that she believes she *has* been a wife to Henry, his degrading language silences her. She stands by, neither speaking nor behaving in any way that undermines Henry, as he puts her in her place once again. The king tells the bishop and nobleman who come to speak with him that he is "surrounded by fools"—inviting both these men and the film's viewers to conclude that Eleanor is the greatest fool of all.

When Henry clutches at his heart as he bemoans losing Becket, he risks effeminacy; nevertheless, he seems clever and powerful as he uses patriarchal power to undermine and dismiss Eleanor. Henry undermines her through his contempt for and demonization of her, such as when Becket's mention of Henry's son and heir gives the king another opportunity to brand his wife as disloyal as well as imply that she is an idiot like her son, and sly rather than clever: "He's an idiot. Sly like his mother." Henry's plea, "Thomas, don't you ever marry," continues to demonize her by suggesting that marriage has ruined his life. The king's first insult to young Henry reveals that he considers his wife to be dis-

Pamela Brown as Eleanor of Aquitaine in the 1964 film *Becket*.

loyal and his son moronic: "You look to me, sir, not your mother. Sit, you witless baboon." The boy's blank stare and silence reinforce his father's assessment of him. Consequently, Henry's subsequent dismissal of his son with a kick to the backside seems justified—a gesture that undermines the queen's status by mocking the heir she has produced. Henry then exercises his patriarchal privilege first by scornfully inviting Eleanor to spew all of her bile "once and for all in one great whine" and then by demeaning her (along with his mother Empress Matilda) in the presence of many noblemen with the comment "I retch with boredom at the sight of you."

Despite Henry's verbal abuse, Eleanor manages to criticize him, to protest her situation, and to express frustration with her powerlessness in the male-dominated world of *Becket*. In response to Henry's complaint that he was suckled by a peasant girl rather than his mother, Eleanor criticizes his unkingly behavior: "That, no doubt, is why it is so difficult to see the king beneath your crown." This insult reveals a witty side to her character that prevents viewers from completely dismissing her as a fool. Furthermore, despite her husband's invitation to whine, Eleanor does not; rather, she protests the disrespect she has suffered as the wife of an adulterer—even positioning herself above Henry through her pity for him. The first part of Eleanor's speech in this scene is an attempt to assert her right to a modicum of respect from Henry as his wife and queen consort. The second part of her speech, however, expresses her frustration with her lack of power in Henry's world. She does so by threatening to "complain" to all the powerful males she can think of: "[her] father, ... [her] uncle the emperor, ... all the kings of Europe," and God himself.

Although Eleanor resists patriarchal power, Henry can do exactly as he pleases, and what pleases him is to disrespect his wife. In the world of *Becket*, Henry can laugh at his wife's threat to call upon God, for Henry is sure that He will not come to Eleanor's aid. Because the film's screenplay gives Eleanor no access to political power, either through the Aquitaine or through influencing her husband's decisions, this queen consort remains a powerless punching bag for Henry. As a result, all Eleanor can do is protest before being bullied into silence.

The Lioness in Winter

Anthony Harvey's *The Lion in Winter* was released in 1968, just as its American viewers were receiving conflicting messages about gender roles. From Second-wave Feminism, a movement inspired in part by Betty Friedan's *The Feminine Mystique* (1963), Americans knew that many women were no longer satisfied with just being housewives: they wanted access to jobs other than the traditional women's jobs of secretary, teacher, and nurse as well as to choose when, or if, to have a family.[6] From mainstream culture, Americans also knew that many of their neighbors saw the women's movement as a threat to the American way of life. Katharine Hepburn, the daughter of a suffragette mother who fought for women's right to vote and a physician father who was a leader in the field of sexual hygiene, brought to the role of Eleanor of Aquitaine a feminist energy, and Hepburn's feminist persona makes more palatable to viewers a complex screenplay that includes key aspects of the Golden Myth, several nods to feminist perspectives on sex and marriage, and a focus on behavior and characteristics attributed to Eleanor because of the continuing cultural power of the Black Legend.

James Goldman's screenplay connects its Eleanor of Aquitaine with three aspects of the Golden Myth: she presides over courts of love; she is a cultured woman of southern France who educates her son Richard; and she is a proto-feminist of sorts. Eleanor herself articulates the Golden Myth's claim that she presided over courts of love when she speaks to her son Richard of her former desire for both poetry and the poets who wrote it. In this same conversation, the queen also asserts her cultural sophistication by reminding him that she taught him all the skills of a cultured man. Eleanor's claim that she both presided over courts of love and dressed as an Amazon while on Crusade mark her as the walking embodiment of Amy Kelly's version of the Golden Myth.[7] Furthermore, when Eleanor speaks of her escapade as an Amazon, she does so to Henry—her husband and king whose patriarchal power she resists—as a feminist assertion of the free expression of female sexuality. The queen's account of this adventure gains feminist traction through Hepburn's clipped and assertive manner of speech. First, she asserts that she "made poor Louis" take her on the Second Crusade, and then she punctuates the audaciousness of her participation in a male martial activity sponsored by the Church with "How's that for blasphemy?" She then revels in how she and her female entourage used their inappropriately sexualized costumes to overwhelm both King Louis and the troops: "I dressed my maids as Amazons and rode bare-breasted halfway to Damascus. Louis had a seizure, and I damn near died of windburn, but the troops were dazzled." This speech certainly packages Hepburn's Eleanor as a medieval proto-feminist.

The lioness in winter's comments about motherhood also make her sound like a 12th-century proto-feminist. To Richard, Eleanor explains that the best time of her life was early in her marriage, when she had Henry all to herself: "There was no Thomas Becket then, or Rosamund … no rivals, only me." When the queen says sardonically, "Had I been sterile, darling, I'd be happier today," she becomes a feminist spokeswoman who does not find motherhood fulfilling. As she acknowledges the medieval requirement that a queen produce at least one male heir, Eleanor's sardonic tone and frank expression of both a desire for political power and an understanding of sexual politics mark her as a modern incarnation of Henry's queen: "good, good, Louis. If I had managed sons for him instead of all those little girls, I'd still be stuck with being Queen of France, and we should not have known each other. Such, my angels, is the role of sex in history."

Despite Goldman's including some nods to 1960s feminism in his screenplay, *The Lion in Winter* reflects traditional American values by defining Eleanor's identity through her roles of wife and prisoner. Her husband's characterization of her as being "like a democratic drawbridge" and her retort—"At my age, there's not much traffic anymore"—situate her, as a woman, as a sexual commodity. In addition, the queen demonstrates an emotional need to remain Henry's wife that is so strong that she will do anything to retain that role. When Henry claims that he will annul Eleanor and replace her with "A new wife," Eleanor warns him, "Don't leave me, Henry. I'm at rock bottom. I'll do anything to keep you." She then demonstrates her capacity to "do anything" when she claims to have slept with—and even loved—Henry's father. In the midst of making this claim, she threatens, "I'll kill you if you leave me." Although being a queen consort who defines herself as a wife limits the queen's range of possible actions, her being Henry's prisoner reduces her to plotting against him. She admits to Richard, "I scheme a lot, I know. I plot and plan. That's how a queen in prison spends her time." Henry's power over Eleanor is so complete that she admits to him that she can accept remaining his prisoner as long as she can see Henry "now and then" at "Christmas courts and state occasions"; of these opportunities to function as his wife she declares, "It's enough." However, despite her acceptance of her roles as wife and prisoner, Eleanor is a character marked by the many crimes that the Black Legend has attached to her name.

Because her status as lioness in winter is predominantly a function of the Black Legend, Eleanor cares about love, sex, and domestic life more than about the politics of who gets the throne. When arguing with Henry about which son will become king, she admits, "I care because you care so much." This admission makes clear that neither the succession plan nor the political welfare of England is her concern. Eleanor's obsession with lost love, Henry's sex life, and her own position in a love triangle with Henry and his mistress Alais becomes evident when Eleanor insists on watching Henry and Alais kiss. She insists because she watches them "every night" and "conjure[s]" this scene before going to sleep. The queen's focus on domestic life remains palpable when she insists that Richard marry Alais in exchange for her giving up the Aquitaine. When Henry admits that he loves Alais, Eleanor says, "Thank God. You frightened me. I was afraid this wouldn't hurt." This desire for revenge is the product of Eleanor's unrelenting focus on domestic life. According to *The Lion in Winter*, Eleanor's focus on Henry makes her the bad parent created by the Black Legend.

Because *The Lion in Winter* is primarily a family drama, one of Eleanor of Aquitaine's defining characteristics is that she is a bad parent—a woman who has warped her sons' characters and judges or ignores them rather than expresses affection for them. As a result, her sons hate her and condemn her as a bad mother. Viewers will immediately perceive Eleanor as a bad parent when she greets her sons at Chinon, for she judges John and Richard rather than expresses maternal love and says nothing at all to Geoffrey. Although this initial interaction with her sons suggests that she is a bad mother, her sons tell her so, such as when John asserts, "You can't hurt me, you bag of bile." Although Eleanor tries to deny her responsibility for John's character flaws when she says to Henry, "Don't share John with me. He's your accomplishment," Henry reminds her that this son who "steal[s] and whore[s] and whip[s] his servants" is "the man [they] made him." In Harvey's film, Eleanor's influence on Geoffrey's bad character is even more evident than her influence on John's. When Eleanor criticizes Geoffrey's desire to see his parents "go picnicking on one another" by declaring, "You have a gift for hating," her son replies, "You're the expert; you should know." According to Henry, Geoffrey is inhuman, "wheels and gears" rather than "flesh," and Geoffrey blames his mother for making him this way and consequently hates her. When Eleanor encourages Geoffrey to be Richard's chancellor, Geoffrey expresses his hatred for her by telling her to go "rot."

Because Richard is the son to whom Eleanor is closest, his behavior and assessment of her condemn her most strongly. Eleanor reminds her son of their close, perhaps too close, relationship when she idealizes it: "The sun was warmer then, and we were every day together." Her husband confirms viewers' impression that the mother-son bond is almost Freudian in terms of its closeness when he says accusingly, "You threw me out of your bed for Richard." Goldman's screenplay suggests that Richard's defects of character, as a soldier and a man, are primarily his mother's fault. Henry criticizes both the pleasure his son takes in killing and his homosexuality, blaming these defects of character on Eleanor. Henry's comment that Eleanor visited Richard "anywhere he was killing people" implies that she encouraged this bloodlust. In addition, when Henry learns from King Philip of France that Philip had sex with Richard as well as that Richard loves Philip still, Henry claims that Eleanor will be "pleased" when she learns that her son is homosexual.

Furthermore, after Richard informs his father that Eleanor "knows" about the sexual encounter with Philip and even knowingly caused it to happen by sending Richard to Philip, Henry blames his wife for what he sees as his son's sexual deviance by declaring to Richard, "How completely hers you are." The screenplay shows that Richard is completely hers, both in his self-identification as "a sometime poet" who has apparently been shaped by her teaching him poetry, languages, and what is beautiful and in his contempt for Henry's mistress Alais to whom Richard refers as "the family whore." Because Richard knows his mother better than his brothers do, his assessment of her as a parent condemns her even more effectively than Henry's: "You love nothing. You're incomplete. The human parts of you are missing. You're as dead as you are deadly." Even more damning is Eleanor's admission that she knowingly and out of laziness gave Richard the opportunity to rape the future king of France: "I was tired. I was busy. They were friends." Eleanor's lack of affection for her children is evident in a comment to Henry, "I don't much like our children," and an admission to Geoffrey: "There are times I think we loved none of our children." Although *The Lion in Winter* portrays Henry as a bad father, the screenplay focuses primarily on Eleanor's parental sins.

Harvey's lioness in winter is a walking embodiment of the worst aspects of the Black Legend; the film likens her to demonic beings as well as connects her with rumors of adultery and incest. Medieval charges of demonic ancestry enable Goldman to liken her to two evil creatures: Medusa and the dragon. In the film's opening scene, Henry refers to Eleanor as "the new Medusa" and then "the gorgon." He then updates her embodiment of the image of womanly evil by referring to her as "the great bitch." Just before he kisses Alais in front of Eleanor, Henry brands his wife "the dragon in the doorway." The screenplay does not go as far as to say that Eleanor had an affair with her uncle Raymond of Antioch, but it does condemn her as a serial adulterer. Henry's comment "Let's have a tally of the bedspreads you've spread out on" works with his characterization of his wife as a "democratic drawbridge" to connect her to rumors of affairs with many men. However, Eleanor admits to what sounds like adultery with Henry when she was still married to Louis: "He[nry] came down from the North to Paris with a mind like Aristotle's … and a form like mortal sin. We shattered the Commandments on the spot." This shattering of commandments could include both coveting thy neighbor's wife and adultery. In addition, Goldman's screenplay blackens Eleanor's name by making her the one to seek an annulment in order to marry her new lover, Henry. The queen also admits that she had a number of other lovers when she explains to Richard that men were one of her "many appetites" when she was younger: "I wanted poetry and power and the young men who create them both. I even wanted Henry, too, in those days." However, one of the lioness in winter's sexual relationships links her with incest as it was defined during the Middle Ages: intercourse with either a blood relative or a godparent, godchild, or in-law.[8] Eleanor not only admits to having had sex with her father-in-law but also presents herself as reveling in the beauty of his body. Her description of Geoffrey the Fair's rough arms with their scars provides proof of the affair while her assertion "I loved your father's body. He was beautiful" makes her an unrepentant medieval perpetrator of incest.

The Lion in Winter also associates its Eleanor of Aquitaine with the rumor from the medieval Black Legend that she cruelly murdered Henry's mistress Rosamund Clifford. Although Harvey's Eleanor denies killing Rosamund, her gloating over her rival's death and sardonic comment that "I never liked her much" make the queen seem capable of committing the murder. More importantly, when Eleanor asserts that she would never have allowed this mistress (like Alais does now) to usurp the position of queen consort by "heading Henry's table," viewers may well wonder whether the rumor is true. The queen's declaration, "That's *my* chair," not only makes clear that she will not tolerate losing her position as queen consort but also makes Alais's conclusion—"And so you had her poisoned"—seem reasonable to viewers.

In addition, *The Lion in Winter* elaborates upon the murderous aspect of the Black Legend by making Eleanor cruel enough to facilitate the murder of Henry's future son, to enable her sons to kill Henry, and to encourage Henry in turn to kill their sons. After taunting Henry with the fact that, given his age, he has little time to beget a son on Alais, Eleanor states unequivocally that she is ready to have Richard kill any future child. When Henry asserts that Eleanor would not "let [Richard] do a thing like that," she declares that she would encourage him: "Let him? I'd push him through the nursery door." Refuting Henry's claim, "You're not that cruel," she reveals that she is: "Don't fret. We'll wait until you're dead to do it."

Later, in the cellar scene, the queen first gives her sons the daggers needed either to escape or to kill their father, and then encourages her husband to kill their sons. Furthermore, Richard asserts that, because Eleanor's behavior taught him to be an assassin, killing his father would simply fulfill his mother's murderous desire. When Eleanor tries to distance herself from this association with murder, Richard accuses her: "Where do you think I learned this from? Who do you think I studied under?" If Richard is an "unnatural animal" for planning to assassinate Henry, then the roots of that inhuman behavior are the many "battles" she fought with her king and lord and her murderous intentions. In contrast to Henry who cannot bring himself to execute Richard, Eleanor encourages her husband to kill all three of their sons: "This was treason, wasn't it? You gave them life. You take it." This Eleanor of Aquitaine is, for the most part, a walking embodiment of the Black Legend.

The Lioness in Winter Spoofed

The script of the 1984 comedy *The Zany Adventures of Robin Hood* spoofs *The Lion in Winter* by invoking two key aspects of both James Goldman's original stage play and Anthony Harvey's adaptation of the play for the screen: the family drama that is the plot's focus, and the clever and sexually inappropriate Eleanor at the heart of that family drama. Ray Austin's lioness in winter is competent in political matters, but she embodies several aspects of the Black Legend: she is a bad parent whose failure to love John as a child has made him an evil adult; she is lustful in her desires and potentially a source of corruption for Robin and Lady Marian; and she is a woman who disguises herself in a way that violates normative female roles.

Before viewers see Austin's Eleanor of Aquitaine, they have a definite image of her as a bad parent. In the opening scene in which Roddy McDowall's Prince John complains on a therapist's couch about his childhood, Eleanor receives just as much blame as her deceased husband Henry for John's emotional instability and cruelty. Perhaps spoofing *The Lion in Winter*'s inclusion of Freudian ideas of both psychosocial development (Richard's homosexuality as a result of his overly close relationship with his mother) and family dynamics (the sons' desire to kill their father) in its tale of a medieval royal family, *Zany Adventures* labels John "neurotic" in its opening credits in order to prepare for

John's Freudian tirade. The prince blames his problems on his father and mother, but, because King Henry is dead, viewers have only Queen Eleanor to look to for evidence of negative influence on the younger generation—and she provides it.

Austin's Eleanor is lustful, and therefore a potentially corrupting influence on both Robin Hood and Lady Marian. Janet Suzman's physical appearance and behavior make her Eleanor a lustful older woman. Suzman's straight gray hair contrasts with Morgan Fairchild's golden mane, and her heavy use of eyeliner (even when in bed) gives her a sexy and yet somewhat sinister appearance. This makeup works with Suzman's sardonic tone to suggest that she might be doing a sendup of the sexy and sardonic Katharine Hepburn. The behavior of Suzman's Eleanor is lustful, for she greets Robin Hood invitingly when he enters her bedroom through the window. Even his unintentional pulling of her bed toward him, after she anchors his rope to the bed, presents Eleanor as moving closer to Robin while she is still dressed in a negligée. After Robin departs to find Marian, Eleanor expresses regret that she cannot have this "cute" younger man to herself. Clearly, this older woman would readily sleep with the film's hero if she could, so she is a potential threat to his relationship with Marian. However, when interacting with Marian, Eleanor becomes the voice of sexual experience rather than desire—encouraging a virgin who worries about becoming an old maid to satisfy her desires rather than jump in the moat every day to cool the heat of her passions. Then, after Marian declares her intention of keeping her promise to King Richard by remaining a virgin until she marries, Eleanor suggests that Marian encourage the attentions of Sir Guy de Gisbourne in order that Eleanor's plan of obtaining the tax money Guy and John raise for Richard's ransom can come to fruition. Luckily, Marian resists both Eleanor's corrupting influence and Robin's desire to consummate their relationship as soon as they are engaged—in part by continuing to use the moat as an aid to self-control. Because these characters function in a light-hearted comedy, the hero and heroine easily resist Eleanor's potentially bad influence.

Although the script of *Zany Adventures* does not clarify for viewers why Eleanor twice disguises herself as a nun and thereby violates normative female roles by appropriating the moral authority of a holy woman, Eleanor's disguise provides an amusing clash between her lustful nature and holy appearance. It is possible that screenwriter Robert Kaufman was familiar either with the fact that Eleanor attempted to escape Henry's clutches after the 1173 rebellion by dressing in men's clothing, or with the legend that Eleanor dressed herself and her female entourage as Amazons, so he decided to spoof one or both of these appropriations of male authority. Eleanor's first errand in the nun's habit is with Marian to seek Robin Hood's help in securing Richard's ransom. Her second errand with its usurped air of moral authority is to offer Robin the solution to the problem of the lack of available tax money: seek the Jewish moneylender named Jehoudi. Eleanor's drinking heavily in bed before donning her disguise for the second time emphasizes the clash between her role as loyal queen mother and reputation as lustful wife of King Henry.

Nevertheless, Austin's Eleanor engages viewers because, in a film full of inept comic characters, she is both politically astute and pragmatic in her solutions to problems. When Marian informs her of John and Guy's plan to retain the tax money they collect from the Saxon peasants, Eleanor works with Marian to seek the aid of Robin and his merry men. When she learns that there is too little money in England to pay the ransom, she sends Robin to negotiate with Jehoudi. Therefore, the queen mother orchestrates Richard's release. She is also pragmatic when Robin needs to get Jehoudi's aid as well as the peasants' support: she tells Robin to make whatever promises are necessary to achieve

Richard's freedom. Her final action in the film signals that she will continue to guide King Richard now that he is back in England. After Richard tries to call back the brother he has just exiled because he does not want to cope with the competing demands of the peasants unleashed by Robin's promises, Eleanor accompanies her son as he returns to the throne room—where she occupies the throne next to his. Clearly, this Eleanor will continue to make sure that England survives, despite the foolishness of her sons.

The Lioness in Winter Hallmarked

The fact that Hallmark Entertainment chose to remake the 1968 *Lion in Winter* shows that the original film remains the best-known appearance of Eleanor of Aquitaine on the big screen. *The Lion in Winter*'s ongoing impact on the image of Eleanor in the popular imagination is evident in the online *Encyclopædia Britannica*'s entry on her, which includes a montage of images derived from the 1968 film.[9] Nevertheless, this remake is as problematic as the original film because both James Goldman's play and the 1968 film based on it have "focused perhaps undue attention" on the issue of "the impact that [Eleanor's] maternal feelings might have had on the destinies of her inheritance and lordship."[10] Both play and film have a plotline that links the queen to the Black Legend through a focus on her failure to love and parent her sons appropriately, as well as through her exploits as Amazon, adulteress, and murderer. To watch the 2003 remake of *The Lion in Winter* is an unsettling experience because the script is nearly identical to the one used in the original film, yet the remake's emotional impact on viewers is quite different. Andrei Konchalovsky's characters speak the original lines in the same order as Harvey's characters. However, two factors change the meaning of these lines: the transformation of Eleanor into a sadder, gentler figure whom a Hallmark audience will like and the addition of an initial scene. Unfortunately, this opening scene falsely sets high feminist expectations, but the film fails to meet those expectations due to the Hallmarking of both Eleanor and her family system.

Konchalovsky's film begins with a scene absent from the original *Lion in Winter* that prepares for the family drama of 1183 by establishing the main characters' traits. In this additional scene, the civil war of 1173 has just ended. The on-screen narrative declares, "Henry's ambitious sons, Richard and Geoffrey, hungry for power, have risen up against him, spurred on by their iron-willed mother, Eleanor of Aquitaine." One of Henry's men informs him that he has won the field and that "victory is complete." At that moment, Eleanor enters riding a white horse and in armor—including a helmet with chainmail flaps that disguises her gender by covering her hair; in response to her arrival, Henry says, "There she is." This entrance creates a new dynamic for the Golden Myth by presenting the queen as a powerful leader of troops, and it positions viewers to expect further feminist behavior from Eleanor, such as her appropriating male roles, throughout the rest of the film. When Richard declares that he has 50 men to bring to battle, Eleanor speaks as the military leader of the rebellion, for she tells her son firmly that this battle is lost. When Richard continues to yell that he could win, she slaps his face and informs him "now we retreat," as she makes plans for her sons to go to Paris while she goes to Poitiers and declares (pointing at Henry), "He won't always win!" This opening scene establishes the queen as her husband's enemy and as a woman whose idea of motherhood is the toughest embodiment of tough love.

Nevertheless, the end of this opening scene signals that the rest of the 2003 film will present Eleanor not as an empowered female but as a tragic heroine. She arrives at Salisbury Castle a prisoner dressed completely in black, as if she were in mourning. Although her commanding gaze at the troops assembled before her causes them to remove their helmets and kneel to her, neither this gaze nor her physical resistance to entering the sparsely furnished bedroom that she will inhabit after the guard slams the door in her face changes the fact that Eleanor, as Henry's prisoner, will suffer because he has the power to do with her as he likes.

The 2003 production of *The Lion in Winter* lacks much of the power of the original because it Hallmarks Eleanor's sons and husband by softening their edges. John Light's Geoffrey is still the plotter he was in the 1968 film, but he lacks John Castle's brooding intensity and chilling emotionlessness. The obesity of Rafe Spall's John makes him physically softer around the edges than Nigel Terry's John, and both his waddling walk and his infantile behavior make him a pathetic figure. Spall's John spits a pit out of his mouth while his father philosophizes to Philip about politics and becomes the butt of many a joke. In contrast, Terry's John is a character viewers must take seriously when he reminds Henry that he wants the kingdom but cannot have it until "daddy" is dead and buried. In this production, even Richard has his softer side, for Anthony Howard tears up when his father claims that history will report how King Henry disowned his sons. Patrick Stewart's Henry is a softened version of Peter O'Toole's. One reason is that Stewart lacks O'Toole's physical stature, but another is that he makes Henry gentler and more loving than does O'Toole.

In this film's opening scene, Stewart's Henry is unwilling to kill his wife and sons despite young John's harsh reaction to his mother and brothers' attempt to take the kingdom: "We must chase and kill them.... They deserve to die ten times over." Later, Henry gently caresses Alais's face and holds her hand before kissing her lovingly under the mistletoe he has brought, despite informing her, "I'll use you as I like." In addition, Stewart's Henry exudes genuine love for his wife, both when he excitedly awaits Eleanor's arrival on the parapet alone—not with Alais—and when he banters with Eleanor more playfully than aggressively. Alais's behavior encourages viewers to interpret Henry as still being in love with Eleanor, for Alais is nervous because she fears that Eleanor will manage to reestablish her connection with Henry.

Resembling this gentler, more loving Henry, Glenn Close's Eleanor is a tragic heroine who speaks the same lines as Katharine Hepburn yet softens them through gestures and tears. Close plays the tragic heroine to great effect when—instead of scratching her forearm to prove her sincerity to Richard, as Hepburn does—she cuts open the palm of her hand, a gesture that draws from her son a kiss on that wound. The queen is again a tragic heroine when Henry offers her freedom in exchange for the Aquitaine. Close's Eleanor tears up immediately, then speaks her lines about riding "bare-breasted halfway to Damascus" softly—not with the feminist sarcasm and self-satisfaction of Hepburn's Eleanor. The 2003 lioness in winter is much more fragile than her 1968 counterpart, but her fragility makes her likable and contradicts her feminist image in the opening scene. In contrast to Hepburn's Eleanor, who is so verbally adept that viewers assume that most if not all of her words are lies, this Eleanor genuinely and passionately loves Henry.

In keeping with her role as tragic heroine, Close's Eleanor reveals her love for Henry more intensely and more often than Hepburn's version of the character. This Eleanor shows her emotional pain at losing Henry's love when declaring, "I could peel you like a pear, and God himself would call it justice!"—shaking with the intensity of her emotions. The queen has affection in her voice both when she says to Henry, "That's my woolly sheepdog," and when she confesses, "You are still a marvel of a man." When Close's Eleanor banters with Henry, there is often affection in her eyes. Even in the middle of an argument with Henry during which the king aggressively throws a pillow at her and knocks over a chair, Eleanor expresses her love for her husband by pressing her cheek against his hand as she asks, "How, from where we started, did we ever reach this Christmas?" Her love for Henry is likewise evident when, just after he informs her that he plans to annul their marriage, she must turn her face away from him to hide her tears. When Close's Eleanor agrees with Henry that the most terrible lie is the one she saved up for now, that she still loves him, the line sounds tragic rather than sardonic. Close's Eleanor must again turn away from Henry after they reminisce about their passionate first meeting in order to hide the love that puts her at a strategic disadvantage.

When Hepburn's Eleanor confesses that she wants to die because she has lost Henry and can never have him back, her tenderness clashes with viewers' predominant impression of her as sardonic, vengeful, and untruthful. However, when Close's Eleanor makes the identical confession, it rings true because it is consistent with Close's tragic and sentimental portrayal of the queen throughout the film. When Konchalovsky chooses to end Henry and Eleanor's final verbal battle by having their faces touch and their bodies lean against each other, viewers are left with the final impression that the king and queen love each other and will always do so. These gestures are the final confirmation of how this director has Hallmarked Eleanor. Konchalovsky has made Eleanor readable rather than inscrutable, emotionally expressive rather than restrained, and weaker because she is so weepy.

Eleanor as Disrespected and Demoted Queen Mother

Because Ridley Scott's 2010 *Robin Hood* begins with the death of King Richard I, the queen mother lacks her usual motive for ransoming her captive son. The grimness of this film's medieval England, however, requires that the thoroughly absolutist, dishonorable, and (as it turns out) foolish King John have voices of reason to override his decisions, including that of Eleanor of Aquitaine. Eileen Atkins plays an entirely good and wise Eleanor who indirectly saves her son from deposition, yet the film's screenplay situates the queen mother in a man's world in which her sons disrespect her and demote her to a position of powerlessness. Eleanor's potential power disappears the moment at which she crowns John; as a result, she can only temporarily restrain John's tyranny from the sidelines—despite her loyalty to both England and her son.

In Scott's *Robin Hood*, Eleanor of Aquitaine is a queen mother who receives more respect from Richard's subjects than from her sons: Richard disrespects her in her absence, while John disrespects her to her face and scornfully dismisses her. Richard's subjects treat Eleanor with the deference appropriate to her position. When Eleanor leads the royal party that walks toward the dock where the bearer of her dead son's crown will arrive, the cry "Part for the Queen!" causes the crowd to immediately make way for Eleanor. Nevertheless, her first mention in this film disrespects her authority while portraying her as an obstacle to effective rule. King Richard is the first character to refer to his mother, but he does so in a resentful tone. Richard remarks to Sir Robert Loxley, "I have a mother that won't die, and a brother who wishes me dead. First thing I'm going to do is lock them up." This comment encourages viewers to assume that the queen mother is an annoyance to the king as well as an obstacle to the effective exercise of his royal power, an obstacle he wishes to eliminate as soon as he returns to England. This context makes her tyrannical son's rude and aggressive treatment of his mother seem acceptable—even appropriate.

As the king, John's first private words to his mother reinforce Richard's words to Loxley by disrespecting the authority of the queen mother and portraying her as interfering with *his* exercise of royal power. John's retort to Eleanor's advice regarding taxation is "Spare me your farmyard memories. You have none, and I don't understand them." This snide remark suggests that the queen mother is a liar, making up nonsense, and John does not even grant his mother the dignity of looking at her as he insults her. He talks over her while offering a knowing look to another man, his chancellor, William Marshal.

Early on in *Robin Hood*, it is clear that Eleanor of Aquitaine possesses symbolic rather than political power. Eleanor's gown and matching mantle of blue and gold brocade indicate her royal status, but her full wimple, which covers not only her hair but also her ears and neck, presents her to viewers as a widow and mother mourning her son—not as a woman wielding political power. Eleanor wears a jeweled circlet on top of her wimple, but the fact that both John's wife Isabella and Marshal's wife wear similar circlets provides viewers with visual confirmation that Eleanor is no longer Queen of England. Nevertheless, the queen mother—as Richard's chief mourner—exercises considerable symbolic power. Eleanor's physical position in relation to the other characters gives her prominence: she stands in front of both John and Isabella, who stand to her left, and Marshal and his wife, who stand to her right. Eleanor then presides over the ceremony of receiving and conferring the crown. First, she silences the heralds who play joyful music for what might have been Richard's homecoming. Then, Robin Longstride, impersonating Richard's friend Loxley, kneels before her and offers the crown. The crown's cover, a cloth decorated with Richard's coat of arms (three gold lions on a red ground), marks it as the Lionheart's—perhaps to foreshadow that John will not measure up to his brother's standard of conduct. Eleanor slowly lifts the cloth and maintains her dignity despite having to handle the object that signifies that her beloved son is dead. Her quivering lip reveals her love for her son. The queen mother—performing the function of the Archbishop of Canterbury—then takes up the crown, commands John to kneel, places the crown on her younger son's head, and declares to the assembled crowd, "Long life, my son. Rise now. A king is dead. Long live the king." As she announces Richard's death, the pain of Eleanor's loss is evident both in her quavering voice and in her closing her eyes to prevent tears from falling. Nevertheless, she maintains her composure as she kneels to the new king—a gesture that all those present emulate. The coronation is the high point of Eleanor of Aquitaine's power in this film.

However, from the moment the queen mother transfers the crown from her dead to her living son, the difference between a woman's symbolic power and a king's absolute authority becomes evident. King John is the one who tells all to rise after he receives the crown, and, within seconds, he begins to exercise his monarchical rights by withholding the ring that he begins to give to Robin-as-Loxley for delivering the news of Richard's death, doing so on the basis that Walter Loxley (Robert Loxley's father) owes taxes to the king. John taps this ring on the crown while asserting that this is "[his] crown," a signal

Eileen Atkins as Eleanor of Aquitaine in the 2010 film *Robin Hood*.

that John is already exercising his absolute power and will continue to do so. Eleanor remains silent as her son John dismisses Robin-as-Loxley, for she can do nothing to alter his behavior. This scene sets the tone for the mother-son interaction to come.

Both the wisdom Eleanor offers to John during their discussion of taxation and her implied criticism of his character receive such harsh dismissal from her son that viewers must realize a key fact: she is powerless to influence the new king as an advisor. After John mocks his mother's homespun wisdom regarding taxation policy—"Milking a dry udder gets you nothing but kicked off the milking stool"—and condescendingly invites Marshal to join him in disrespecting his mother, Eleanor's behavior reveals her lack of either political power or influence on her son. When Godfrey (the henchman John trusts but who is really the French king's agent) rejects Marshal's advice that John use loans to finance his government, Eleanor can only look on with concern. She can say nothing, for she has been put in her place. When it becomes clear that John is ready to use "mounted men" who will force "merchants and landowners to fill [John's] coffers or their coffins," Eleanor refuses John's invitation to support this policy. She even expresses implied criticism of John: "Richard commanded loyalty not by threats, but by example." In response, John again disrespects and dismisses her, laying most of the blame for the crown's money problems at her feet, while the queen mother remains wide-eyed and quivering but silent (not unlike her counterpart in *Becket*). Because King John has dishonored both his brother's memory and the Third Crusade, Eleanor slaps John across the face. However, this slap is the final gesture of a frustrated, and likely disgusted, queen mother who only temporarily and symbolically threatens John's power, for John mocks her again as soon as she leaves the room. Although the three thrones on the dais provide places for both John's mother and his wife, Eleanor never obtains the dignity that would have come with sitting on one. Instead, John claims, "I broke her skin more than she did mine," and then replaces his chancellor Marshal with Godfrey. John's words make clear that his mother's opinions will not alter his actions in the least.

Out of loyalty to her son and the realm, Eleanor of Aquitaine uses the wisdom that comes with age to save John from deposition, yet the manner in which she must save him reveals her lack of power. When Marshal praises the queen mother as "much wiser than [her] owl," she labels this wisdom as a function of age—asserting that she has "lived longer" than her owl. Her loyalty to her son is evident in her willingness to "point him to his duty" as king, despite the awkwardness of having "to scold him like a child." Her sighing and looking away from Marshal as she commits to this task underscore this awkwardness. Because her son no longer respects her, Eleanor must work behind the scenes: she goes to John's queen, Isabella, to convince her to inform her husband of Godfrey's collusion with King Philip of France. When she presents herself to the Queen of England, she does so humbly in a plain dress and cap—without gown or crown. These clothes signal Eleanor's acceptance of her loss of even symbolic power. When Isabella asks why Eleanor cannot reveal to John the actual source of the information regarding the conspiracy, Eleanor's reply reveals that she can no longer attempt to advise her son: "A mother he mistrusts bearing the word of a man in dishonor? No." Eleanor makes clear that, because John has rejected both his mother and his former chancellor, only Isabella's words can influence John: "If you wish to be queen, *you* must save John. And England." Although Eleanor is wise to exploit both her daughter-in-law's desire for power and her son's love of his wife to restrain John's tyranny, the queen mother achieves only a temporary improvement in her son's behavior that she must engineer offstage, without her son knowing she is helping him to retain the throne.

Eleanor's final appearance in Scott's *Robin Hood* reinforces viewers' understanding that this admirably honest and loyal Eleanor cannot combat the evil actions of her son because she functions in a man's world. The queen mother's powerlessness becomes obvious when John swears "on [his] mother's life" to write the charter that viewers know as the Magna Carta, but then refuses to honor it when he is in the presence of the northern barons to whom he made that vow. When John asserts his absolute power by burning the charter, Eleanor must observe with silent concern, which is all she can do in a film that centers around Russell Crowe "beefily inhabiting" the role of Robin Longstride and that celebrates the hero for inventing the concept of the Magna Carta and defending England from the French.[11]

Eleanor as Loyal and Powerful Queen Mother

Of all of Eleanor of Aquitaine's screen incarnations, Martita Hunt's Eleanor in Disney's *The Story of Robin Hood and His Merrie Men* is both the most powerful and the most positive one to date—interestingly Hunt also played the role of Eleanor's mother-in-law, the Empress Matilda, in *Becket*. Hunt's portrayal of Eleanor is surprising given that the Disney film was released in 1952, during a period many viewers associate with conservatism in the form of what Michael R. Evans terms "the reimposition of traditional gender roles"; nevertheless, there were progressive forces at work too: the doubling in a decade by the end of the 1950s of the proportion of women earning salaries for working outside the home and "a changing attitude towards the role of powerful women."[12] Lorraine K. Stock has interpreted the queen mother's "prominence" in this film within a more specific cultural context, "the iconic role of Eleanor Roosevelt in America during World War II."[13] Hunt's Eleanor certainly looks like the first lady with whom she shares a name. Evans notes that Eleanor Roosevelt's active role in both American politics throughout the 1950s and the development of the United Nations could have made her a model for the strong, positive Eleanor in this film, even if a specific link between the modern and medieval Eleanors is difficult to prove.[14] Nevertheless, there is another possible explanation of why Hunt's Eleanor is so powerful and yet such a positive female figure: the emergence in the 1950s of the Golden Myth that produced a feminist reassessment of Eleanor of Aquitaine.

Whatever combination of cultural factors influenced screenwriter Lawrence Watkin and director Ken Annakin, they created an Eleanor who plays a traditional but pivotal and entirely positive female role: that of ideal and heroic loyal mother. Of course, her positive role suits the Disney formula of creating a strong contrast between good and evil characters. Hunt portrays Queen Eleanor as a stately and important woman admirably loyal to her son King Richard I, perceptive in detecting wrongdoing, and heroically brave when combating villains.

The Disney film signals the queen mother's political importance through both the manner in which she enters the plot and her initial actions. This Eleanor commands viewers' immediate attention and respect because she is stately: a tall, broad-shouldered woman with an aquiline nose, Hunt walks slowly and regally. The queen's political importance is evident in her magnificent robes and crown, a crown that gains prominence because her son King Richard does not wear one. As Richard gives instructions to his brother and soon-to-be regent John, Richard underscores Eleanor's importance by telling John to ensure the wellbeing of both the kingdom and their mother. Eleanor's initial actions are consistent with her high status. Her first action is to assert her independence by responding to Richard's reminder to John that he must care for their mother while Richard is on Crusade with "A lady with two sons like you can look after herself." Although Eleanor reinscribes traditional gender roles by asserting her competence based on the sons she has borne, she successfully resists Richard's infantilization of her. Demonstrating her full control over her own household, the queen mother's first public action is to accept Maid Marian as its newest member—without any input from her sons. The fact that Queen Eleanor is the head of a household separate from Richard's reinforces viewers' perception of her high status and strong character: she is a powerful and independent woman.

Because Watkin's screenplay omits even a mention of Richard I's wife Berengaria, Eleanor is the only royal woman in the film, and she exercises her authority without hesitation. The queen displays her authority both when she encourages Marian to live up to her "sweet and gentle" name, and when she pledges to keep the young woman safe during her father's absence while on Crusade with the king; therefore, Eleanor—not

Richard—has Marian as a ward. Later, the queen again displays her commitment to protecting Marian by refusing to give her permission to go to Robin. Eleanor is clear that she has Marian "in trust from [her] father"; as a result, although John is willing to let Marian risk being hit by real arrows because she has already been hit by Cupid's, Eleanor forbids her charge from setting foot outside the castle walls. The final action of Queen Eleanor in her first scene in this Robin Hood film likewise marks her as powerful. Because the king is departing for the Third Crusade, Eleanor offers him her blessing in the form of a kiss on the forehead. This kiss validates the nobility of his cause while showing that Eleanor is the only person with the status necessary to match the Archbishop of Canterbury's ecclesiastical blessing with a secular one. At this moment, she functions as if she—not John—will be regent.

The queen mother's next two on-screen appearances in *Robin Hood and His Merrie Men* give her opportunities to exercise power as if she were regent as well as to show that, as a supporter of King Richard, she protects people from John. In the Nottingham fair scene, it is Eleanor—rather than Prince John—who presides over the shooting contest. Her doing so in a crown makes her further seem more like a regent than her crownless son. While John and the Sheriff of Nottingham lurk on the edges of the dais, Eleanor and Maid Marian are front and center. The queen mother reinforces her status as a defender of the good when she responds to Robin's excellent shot with visible admiration. Eleanor then performs the function that King Richard would have, had he been present: she gives the prize of the gold arrow to Robin's father Hugh Fitzooth, who has split Robin's arrow. Eleanor's graciousness to both father and son marks her as an ally of Richard and Robin, not of John. The next time viewers see Queen Eleanor she is traveling to London in style, carried on a litter and again wearing sumptuous clothes and a crown. When Robin advises his father to seek Eleanor's protection because he has publicly criticized the sheriff, and then one of the sheriff's men murders Hugh, viewers learn that the queen mother could have prevented Hugh's death. These two scenes reinforce the image of Eleanor as possessing both good moral judgment and political power.

Because the earlier scenes have already established her status as Richard's most powerful ally, the queen mother can perform her main function: loyally protecting Richard's interests, despite John's machinations, and working with the Archbishop of Canterbury to raise the 100,000 mark ransom required to get Richard out of Austria. Consequently, Eleanor as a good "regent" counters John's actions as evil regent. Eleanor's initial assumption is that John can be relied upon to help raise the last quarter of the ransom because John and Richard are "blood brothers," but when the archbishop informs her that John has refused to contribute anything to the cause, she declares, "John shall not hold back money in the face of the king's need." When she next sees John, the queen mother makes clear to her son that she intends to use her power to help Richard. First, she reminds John that he could have listened to her messengers regarding the ransom. Then, when John pleads poverty, she reminds the prince that he has been collecting new taxes. Clearly, she is politically savvy and sees through her younger son's lies. In the Nottingham Square scene, Eleanor publicly works with the Archbishop of Canterbury to collect the remaining ransom money. The fact that Eleanor is seated at the center of the dais, while John sits on her left and the archbishop on her right, signals that the queen is in charge of raising the funds and that the archbishop—like her—is a good character. After Robin and his men force the Sheriff of Nottingham to donate much more than he intended by filling an enormous coffer with his valuables, Queen Eleanor says that "the sheriff's heart is bigger than we knew," but she says so knowingly. Her sardonic tone makes clear that John and the sheriff are disloyal to Richard.

In her final appearance in Disney's 1952 Robin Hood film, Eleanor of Aquitaine displays heroic bravery in the face of danger and continues to be a champion of good. When the Sheriff's men try to steal the ransom that she and the archbishop are taking to Austria, Eleanor bravely commands, "Hold, and put down that chest!" Speaking like a loyal regent, she then adds, "I am Eleanor Queen of England, you traitorous dogs." In this moment, she is kingly rather than womanly. She neither hides when Robin and his men come to the rescue nor hesitates to brand the would-be thieves "cut-throat knaves"—even though she doesn't have Robin's information that these men are the Sheriff's, and not his. After Queen Eleanor hears the confession of one of the Sheriff's men, she continues to be a champion of the good embodied by Robin. She praises him saying, "God bless you for the deed you have done." Continuing to fulfill what she calls her "duty to this girl," she grants Robin permission to seek Marian. The queen then sets off with the archbishop to deliver the ransom that will free the king.

Eleanor's final deed in this film is achieved when she is offstage, yet it provides compelling evidence of her being a true "good guy" in the Disney tradition and a powerful and pivotal female figure. The queen arranges for Maid Marian to marry the Earl of Loxley, whom she knows (but Marian does not) is the recently elevated Robin. Robin's assertion that he "cannot question the dictates of the queen mother" provides a final reminder to viewers that this Eleanor of Aquitaine is powerful and uses her power to aid the right—whether that aid take the form of freeing the rightful king from captivity or ensuring that the young woman she has sworn to protect achieves a marriage that both suits her station and fulfills her heart's desire. This action makes Eleanor a pivotal figure in the film's plot who makes possible Richard's return to England and the marriage of the hero and heroine.

Conclusion

Despite its production during the resurgence of the feminist movement that began in the early 1960s, *Becket* presents a powerless and totally disrespected Eleanor because its homosocial plot necessitates the demonization of women. In contrast, *The Lion in Winter* presents a complicated Eleanor who embodies many elements of the Black Legend yet remains appealing to viewers for two reasons: she is a romantic figure who reflects the Golden Myth's claims that Eleanor was exceptional and presided over courts of love, and she speaks like a modern feminist thanks to Hepburn's portrayal. The 2003 remake of *The Lion in Winter* sets high feminist expectations with its opening scene, but it fails to meet those expectations because of the Hallmarking of both Eleanor and her family system. *The Zany Adventures of Robin Hood* offers a comic version of the queen, one who is competent in her management of political matters yet receives with Henry the blame for making John immoral and embodies the adulterous aspect of the Black Legend. The 2010 *Robin Hood* presents an entirely good Eleanor, but it positions her in a man's world in which her sons disrespect her and the screenplay demotes her to powerlessness. Surprisingly, it is the 1952 *Robin Hood and His Merrie Men* that offers viewers the most powerful and positive image of Eleanor of Aquitaine, likely in response to both cultural attitudes at work in 1950s America and the Golden Myth.

NOTES

1. For an overview of Eleanor's life, see Elizabeth A.R. Brown, "Eleanor of Aquitaine Reconsidered: The Woman and Her Seasons," in *Eleanor of Aquitaine Lord and Lady*, ed. Bonnie Wheeler and John Carmi Parsons (New York: Palgrave Macmillan, 2003). For a medieval basis of the Black Legend, see Richard of Devizes, *Cronicon Richardi Divisensis de Tempore Regis Richardi Primi* [*The Chronicle of Richard of Devizes of the Time of King Richard the First*], ed. and trans. John T. Appleby, Nelson's Medieval Texts (London: Thomas Nelson, 1963), pp. 25–26. For the origins of the Golden Myth, see Amy Kelly, *Eleanor of Aquitaine and the Four Kings* (Cambridge: Harvard University Press, 1950) and Régine Pernoud, *Aliénor d'Aquitaine* (Paris: Albin Michel, 1965) and *Eleanor of Aquitaine*, trans. P. Wiles (New York: Coward-McCann, 1968). On the development of the Black Legend and Golden Myth, see Michael R. Evans, *Inventing Eleanor: The Medieval and Post-Medieval Image of Eleanor of Aquitaine* (London: Bloomsbury, 2014), pp. 19–67, 91–104; and Ralph V. Turner, *Eleanor of Aquitaine: Queen of France, Queen of England* (New Haven: Yale University Press, 2009), pp. 299–313.

2. Richard Burton, Peter O'Toole, *Becket*, directed by Peter Glenville, Paramount, 1964; Peter O'Toole, Katharine Hepburn, *The Lion in Winter*, directed by Anthony Harvey, Avco Embassy, 1968; George Segal, Morgan Fairchild, Roddy McDowall, Janet Suzman, *The Zany Adventures of Robin Hood*, dir. Ray Austin, Charles Fries Productions, 1984; Glenn Close, Patrick Stewart, *The Lion in Winter*, directed by Andrei Konchalovsky, Showtime/Hallmark Entertainment, 2003; Russell Crowe, Cate Blanchett, *Robin Hood*, directed by Ridley Scott, Universal, 2010; Richard Todd, Joan Rice, *The Story of Robin Hood and His Merrie Men*, directed by Ken Annakin, RKO Radio-Disney British Productions, 1952.

3. Laurie A. Finke and Martin B. Shichtman discuss the deeply homosocial, nearly homoerotic Henry-Becket relationship in *Becket*, in *Cinematic Illuminations: The Middle Ages on Film* (Baltimore: Johns Hopkins University Press, 2010), p. 97.

4. For instance, when Kevin J. Harty praises Glenville's *Becket* as "excellent in every way," he notes one exception: "its reduction of Eleanor of Aquitaine into a simpering fool," *The Reel Middle Ages: American, Western and Eastern European, Middle Eastern and Asian Films About Medieval Europe* (Jefferson, NC: McFarland & Company, 1999), p. 35. Yet *Becket*'s Eleanor, played by Pamela Brown, is more than a "simpering fool."

5. Finke and Shichtman, pp. 98–99.

6. Betty Friedan, *The Feminine Mystique* (New York: W.W. Norton, 1963).

7. Kelly, pp. 100–101, 163, 165–67; 35, 38–39, 41, 47–48, 50, 56, 72, 169, 234, and 257.

8. Elizabeth Archibald, *Incest and the Medieval Imagination* (2001; rpt. Oxford: Oxford University Press, 2003), pp. xiv–xv, 5–6, 11, and 27.

9. Régine Pernoud, "Eleanor of Aquitaine, Queen Consort of France and England," *Encyclopædia Britannica*, https://britannica.com/biography/Eleanor-of-Aquitaine accessed 16 May 2017.

10. John Carmi Parsons and Bonnie Wheeler, "Prologue Lady and Lord: Eleanor of Aquitaine," in *Eleanor of Aquitaine Lord and Lady*, p. xx [xiii–xxix].

11. Peter Bradshaw, review of *Robin Hood*, *The Guardian* 13 May 2010, https://www.theguardian.com/film/2010/may/13/robin-hood-review-russell-crowe

12. Evans, p. 106.

13. Lorraine K. Stock, "Now Starring in the Third Crusade: Depictions of Richard I and Saladin in Films and Television Series," in *Hollywood in the Holy Land: Essays on Film Depictions of the Crusades and Christian-Muslim Clashes*, ed. Nickolas Haydock and E. L. Risden (Jefferson, NC: McFarland & Company, 2009), p. 108.

14. Evans, p. 106.

The Lady *Is* for Burning

The Cinematic Joan of Arc and Her Screen Avatars

Kevin J. Harty

Cinema medievalia may have had its beginning with the story of Joan of Arc. In 1895, Alfred Clark was directed to broaden the Edison Manufacturing Company's approach to film production and distribution. To do so, Clark turned away from popular theatrical amusements to historical scenes based on well-known works of art as the inspiration for a series of kinetoscopes representing "larger-than-life, semi mythical moments. These films, which were taken outdoors, involved elaborate historical costumes." Among those films was *Joan of Arc*, "which showed the French heroine being burned at the stake."[1] While the Joan film in the series no longer survives, it marked the beginning of a rich tradition of cinematic responses to the life and legend of the Maid of Orléans.

The historical facts about the life of the person who is now St. Joan of Arc are well documented thanks to the detailed records that survive first from her original trial in 1431, which condemned her to death and led to her execution at the stake in Rouen on 30 May, and then from her second trial in 1456, which nullified the 1431 verdict and rehabilitated her reputation.[2] Given then what is known—and, in some cases, what is falsely thought to be known—about Joan's actual life and her multiple afterlives, filmmakers have had an ongoing fascination with Joan of Arc for more than a century, and the corpus of that cinematic fascination can be divided into three general categories: films which depict in whole or part the life of Joan, films in which characters play Joan on stage or screen, and films in which characters channel Joan as an avatar to advance a number of agendas.

Being Joan

Two short late 19th-century Brothers Lumiére films directed by Georges Hatot survive: the 1898 film *L'Execution de Jeanne d'arc*, and a kind of travelogue shot in 1899, *Domrémy*, which featured a walkabout in Joan's home village. The first full attempt to tell the story of Joan's life on film is Georges Méliès's 1900 film *Jeanne d'arc*.[3] The film runs more than 200 meters and presents 12 scenes (*tableaux*) from Joan's life in front of painted backdrops. Joan was played by Jeanne Calvière, the "première danseuse à cet moment au Tríanon–Lyrique de Paris," who was supported by an elaborately costumed cast of almost 500, including Méliès himself and his wife both playing multiple roles. The film culminates in an apotheosis, in which the smoke of the pyre in Rouen gives way to reveal a bank of clouds, in the center of which sit God and the saints awaiting the arrival of the new martyr. This final tableau is part of the film's three-fold emphasis on Joan as a national hero, as a maid of the people, and, finally, as a potential saint of the Catholic Church.[4] And this final scene in Méliès's film reflects an on-going debate about how to view Joan: was she a daughter and a saint of a Catholic Church that had earlier burned her at the stake for heresy; was she a secular hero and the mother of a nation; or was she some kind of fraud or hysteric?

Other Joan films would soon follow. In 1901, the Italian director Mario Caserini made *La béatification de Jeanne d'arc*, with his wife, Maria Gasperini, in the title role. A second Italian film based on Friedrich Schiller's 1801 play, *Die Jungfrau von Orleans*, was released in 1908, *Vita di Giovanna d'arco*, also directed by Caserini and written by Guido Gozzano, with Tina Malli and Aldo Maricci—but little information survives about these two films.[5]

Fuller records do survive for other silent Joan films. In 1909, coincidental with Joan's beatification ceremony, Pathé Frères released Albert Capellani's *Jeanne d'arc*, which tells a familiar story of Joan from her simple beginnings in Domrémy to her death at the stake in Rouen. But Capellani's cinematic techniques would prove revolutionary for their time. Gone initially are Méliès simple *tableaux* as Capellani skillfully balances location and studio shots. Here Joan (Léontine Massert) is clearly a military leader, and a sequence of long shots halfway through the film presents Joan's soldiers attempting to scale the famous tower at Orléans, Joan's wounding, and her quick recovery to rally her troops under a banner displaying the French *fleur-de-lis*. Such scenes do contrast with the tableaux used later in the film to show Joan's capture at Compiègne.[6]

In his film, Capellani also nods to contemporary politics. While the director's sympathies clearly lie with the republican view that Joan is a national heroine, Capellani does not totally ignore the competing Catholic royalist view that sees her as a potential saint. In 1904, France and England had signed an *entente cordiale* to check German aggression in Europe or Northern Africa, and the 1905 law formalizing the separation between church and state in France only widened the divide between those holding royalist and republican views of Joan's place in the French national consciousness. In Capellani's film, Joan's enemies are never identified as English troops, and, in the final scene depicting her burning, the director gives pride of place on the canopied judges' dais to the French bishops rather than to English soldiers.

In 1913, Nino Oxilia cast the opera diva Maria Jacobini in the title role of his *Giovanna d'Arco*. The film carefully balanced two conflicting views of Joan at the time. Anatole's France's massive two-volume *Vie de Jeanne d'Arc* (1908) had contained a less-than-flattering account of Joan that tried, in part, to explain her remarkable life as the result of a series of ongoing neuroses, but such a psychological dismissal of the Maid of Orléans was soon countered by two vehement responses taking a decidedly different view of the Maid, Andrew Lang's *The Maid of France* (1908) and Gabriel Hanotaux's *Jeanne d'Arc* (1910). While Oxilia's film covers familiar enough ground in retelling the story of Joan from her days as a simple peasant at home to her death at the stake, it also contains several additions unique to the director's view of his title character. Joan is always in the film accompanied by a companion named Bertrand, though the specifics of their relationship are never detailed. In her final captivity, Joan is almost murdered by the frustrated Earl of Stafford, and then almost tricked by her confessor, Loyseleur. Joan subsequently forgives the priest, and her confessor is shown in his final appearance in the film groveling in the dust begging for her pardon. To make his final verdict on Joan perfectly clear, and to thereby counter Anatole France's view of Joan, Oxilia ends the film with an intertitle reading "A saint has passed to her rest." When the film was released in 1914 in the United States, a brief note in *Moving Picture World* called it "a great production" and contemporary reviews of the film praised the overall production in general and Jacobini's performance in particular.[7]

The cinematic Joan would be part of a call to arms for the United States to come to the aid of France during the First World War in Cecil B. DeMille's 1917 spectacle, *Joan the Woman*, whose screenplay by Jeanie Macpherson borrows heavily from Schiller's 1801 stage play, while omitting Schiller's ending, in which Joan escapes the English and the Inquisition. Joan twice appears in the film silhouetted against a *fleur-de-lis* that slowly turns into a cross, and in the film's prologue, an English soldier in the trenches in France, Eric Trent (Wallace Reid), discovers a fragment of a sword he imagines to be Joan's. Armed with that sword, Trent believes that he is spiritually and historically connected to Joan as he volunteers to go on a suicide mission against the Germans, France's new invaders. The film's scenario soon establishes that Trent is really a modern-day reincarnation of a 15th-century English soldier of the same name who was rescued by, and subsequently fell in love with, Joan, whom he unwittingly betrayed into the hands of her executioners. In a moment of true pathos, Joan admits that, were things different, she would return his affections. Seeing her burn at the stake, Trent feels his life is over, and, in the film's epilogue, the modern-day Trent does indeed die on his suicide mission.

DeMille's reading of the life of Joan is both personal and political. The initial intertitles establish that the film is "founded on the life of Joan of Arc, the Girl Patriot, Who Fought with Men, Was Loved by Men and Killed by Men—Yet Withal Retained the Heart of a Woman." His Joan (played by the opera singer Geraldine Farrar) has then a possible suffragist context, an interesting response to the life of a woman who was seen by her accusers as a political, religious, and sexual heretic. Sumiko Highasi expands upon the film's several political agendas:

> DeMille's epic was in fact part of public discourse enlisting support for an embattled France symbolized by Joan of Arc.... Patriotic appeals associated with the Maid of Orleans were useful in overcoming American prejudice against Parisian avant-garde movements that contravened sacrosanct notions of genteel culture. An ad, for example, addressed the reader as follows: "Would Joan of Arc Be Burned Today? ... Is the World Freed of the Arch-Enemies of Truth—Ignorance and Superstition?"[8]

In one of the film's more original and jarring touches, and a scene that stirred protests against the film in Catholic circles, Joan appears before a court of Ku Klux Klan–like white-hooded accusers who torment her at Bishop Couchon's behest.[9] The Klan had reorganized itself in 1915 in what would turn out to be a tide of rising nativism that swept across the country and that the film industry viewed with some alarm. DeMille's *Joan* then becomes, among other things, part of a discussion of the Klan across three films by two directors. D.W. Griffith's 1915 film, *The Birth of a Nation*, was accused of contributing to the rise of the Klan and to the growing tide of racism across the country. In 1916, Griffith responded to criticism that he was a racist sympathetic to the Klan with a second film *Intolerance*. DeMille's *Joan* would further advance a negative view of the Klan by linking them to Joan's judges—and, as Albert Capellani's 1908 film had shown, how a director portrays Joan's judges can speak volumes about the contemporary politics that underlie a Jehanne film.[10]

Joan's judges would become the focus of the next—and arguably the greatest—film portrayal of Joan, Maria Falconetti's in Carl Theodore Dreyer's *La Passion de Jeanne d'Arc* (1927–1928). The film treats only the events of Joan's trial. The screenplay was the result of a collaboration between Dreyer and Joseph Delteil, who had published a well-received biography of Joan in 1925,[11] though the film's original cut was modified so as not to offend the Catholic Church, whose spokesmen balked at what they saw as its negative portrayal of the ecclesiastical authorities and their actions at the trial.

Records from the trial detail Joan's 29 interrogations by the church tribunal under the direction of the Bishop of Beauvais, Pierre Cauchon. Dreyer's film condenses them into one long tribunal on the last day of Joan's life. In rapid succession, we see Cauchon convening the court, Joan's movement back and forth from her cell to the court, and her final journey to the public square where she dies at the stake. Dreyer's use of closeups was revolutionary in his day, and "convinced many viewers that cinema could be intellectually respectable."[12] Dreyer's aim was to mirror the historical records of the trial in Rouen to document Joan's passion as mirroring that of Christ—early in the film Joan appears wearing what appears to be a crown of thorns—and Dreyer is unflinching in his desire to portray Joan's suffering and the hypocrisy of the ecclesiastical authorities who condemned her—hence calls in some Catholic quarters for the film to be censored before its release:

> The records give a shattering impression of the ways in which the trial was a conspiracy of judges against the solitary Jeanne, bravely defending herself against men who displayed a devilish cunning to trap her in their net. This conspiracy could be conveyed on the screen only through the huge closeups that exposed, with merciless realism, the callous cynicism of the judges hidden behind hypocritical compassion—on the other hand there had to be equally huge closeups of Jeanne, whose pure features would reveal that she alone found strength in her faith in God.[13]

Despite its innovative techniques and the intensity of its portrayal of Joan, Dreyer's film would prove a commercial failure when a now all-but-forgotten Jehanne film would prove a success in the same year that Dreyer's failed. *La merveilleuse vie de Jeanne d'Arc*, starring the 17-year-old Simone Genevois as Joan and directed by Marco De Gastyne, tells a fuller story of Joan's life with an emphasis on her military exploits. As the first intertitle, quoting the 19th-century historian Jules Michelet, reminds the audience: "Let us always remember that our fatherland was born from the heart of a woman, from her love and her tears, from the blood she spilled for us."[14] The film begins with scenes from Joan's childhood, introducing her closest companion, Rémy Loiseau, whom Joan will decide against marrying—she will instead be the bride of France. Loiseau will follow Joan into battle and die at Compiègne.

Joan soon enough rallies a motley crew of Frenchmen to her cause further establishing her place in the history of France:

> And soon in, in the heart of the country, another army arises made up of all those who are able to leave their family, their house and their mistress to serve a cause which they sensed was miraculous and which was no other than the birth of France.... In a few days, Joan turned these rough looters and debauched rovers into disciplined soldiers, giving them a sense of national identity and restoring them to the faith.[15]

The film characterizes Joan's trial and execution as simply a continuation of her battles against the English on behalf of France. Acknowledged a saint in the film's last intertitle,

Joan is more importantly portrayed as the mother of the nation—she dies for France. Not surprisingly, in making his film, De Gastyne had the full backing of the French government. Using the proverbial cast of thousands that included members of the French military, the director eschewed Dreyer's signature use of closeups. The coronation was filmed inside the recently restored Cathedral at Reims; the trial scenes, in the Abbey at Mont St.-Michel; and a screening was even contemplated—but eventually canceled—for inside the Cathedral of Notre Dame in Paris. The name of Joan's childhood companion, Loiseau, appears later in the film on gravestones marking those who have fallen for France in her wars throughout history. The film's original script even called for the actors to use French uniforms from the First World War, further emphasizing the director's view of Joan as a national heroine rather than a saint of the church.

Cinematic disagreements about whether Joan was a secular or religious icon pale in comparison to the controversy surrounding the next Jehanne film that was released, *Das Mädchen Johanna*, directed in 1935 by Gustav Ucicky. The film bore a Nazi stamp of approval, and perhaps the fingerprints of Reichsminister for Propaganda Joseph Goebbels. The hero of the film is not Joan, but King Charles, who is portrayed as a wily leader willing to make any sacrifice—including Joan's life—for the good of the nation. Whereas the historical Charles sought to remedy his nation's humiliations at the hand of the English in the Hundred Years War, the film's Charles stands ready to remedy Germany's humiliation by France after World War I.[16]

Such jaundiced presentations of history and legend lead to further misreadings of familiar scenes and characters. The film strips Joan's life of almost all its religious associations. The barons of France are reduced to a drunken mob calling for Joan's execution as a witch—thus mitigating Charles's decision to sacrifice Joan. The film is filled with crowd scenes—reflecting Nazi reliance on mass rallies to encourage their supporters. Joan pleads with Charles to free Lorraine, her homeland long subjected to foreign domination—as it was once again in 1935, according to Nazi propaganda, thanks to the Treaty of Versailles. The film was further assured of Nazi orthodoxy because everyone associated with the film in front of and behind the camera had well-established National Socialist pedigrees. And the levels of less-than-subtle propaganda continue to rise in the film, all with the intent of glorifying a self-sacrificing leader whose only concern is the good of the nation.

Not unexpectedly, the German critical reaction to the film was overwhelmingly positive, but so too inexplicably, for the most part, was the American, British, and French. Joan's ashes are claimed in the film's last scene by a group of dirndl-clad young women with braided blonde hair, but such a German appropriation of France's national symbol is at least inappropriate if not something approaching the obscene, and a clear example of medievalism gone terribly awry. Upon learning of Joan's death, the film's Charles opines: "This death will return to the people a faith in their divine mission and it is under this sign that the people will be able to vanquish the enemy"—the same response that Goebbels would deliver upon learning of Adolf Hitler's death ten years later.[17]

While Jehanne films had previously waded into the debate about whether Joan was more properly framed as a secular or a religious symbol—the mother of a nation, or a saint of the Church—the Nazi film represents an unparalleled use of Joan to advance a decidedly more troubling agenda whose consequences would lead to global conflict and genocide on an unimaginable level. A notably blander political agenda informs Victor Fleming's 1948 film *Joan of Arc*, with Ingrid Bergman in the title role. Bergman had planned to star in a film about Joan a decade earlier but the approaching war made it impossible to produce a film in which English soldiers and their allies burn a French national heroine at the stake.[18] RKO promoted the Fleming film heavily in an attempt to cash in on the post-war popularity of historical and religious. As early as 1943, *Variety* had called upon Hollywood to make fewer war films and turn instead, especially in light of the success of *The Song of Bernadette*, to religious films as a form of popular entertainment.[19] And the success of Olivier's 1944 film *Henry V* suggested film audiences were also hungry for historical dramas. Fleming's *Joan of Arc*, with a screenplay by Maxwell Anderson and Andrew Solt from Anderson's stage play *Joan of Lorraine*, combined then the religious with the historical, and the film is further notable for its lavish use of Technicolor. Anderson's play featured a play within a play, which the film abandoned, relying instead on the transcripts of Joan's

Angela Salloker as Joan in the 1935 Nazi-sponsored film *Das Mädchen Johanna*.

actual trial for the scenes of her interrogation. Critical reaction to the film was decidedly mixed, with the most positive reviews coming from the religious press. The sets and costumes were singled out for praise, while the acting was generally considered one-dimensional.[20]

Both the original stage play and the film recognize the emerging Cold War. In both, Joan confronts Charles, criticizing him for suing for peace rather than continuing to fight until his enemies are vanquished. In the play, the scene keeps shifting back and forth from the medieval to the present to highlight the play within the play and thereby dilutes the message about the dangers that the free world still faces after the end of the Second World War. But, in the film, the message is much more straightforward: "Your enemies need a little peace, my king, but not you. Let them go to their island, and they can have a good and lasting peace. No, we have only to go forward, and their last great stronghold is ours."[21] The end of the Second World War has not brought any lasting security. America's enemies, and the enemies of her allies, stand ready to strike at any moment and destroy the free world.

Bergman would return to the screen as Joan in a lesser known 1954 film *Giovanni d'Arco* based on Paul Claudel and Arthur Honnegger's 1939 oratorio *Jeanne d'arc au bûcher*. The film's agenda is apolitical. Roberto Rossellini, the director, was interested in creating what he called "pure cinema," a film that would simply be a meditation on the life of Joan as she awaits entrance into heaven. Bergman remains stationary throughout the film chained to the stake while she speaks with her confessor, and their dialogue gives way in flashbacks to scenes in Joan's earlier life. Critics were divided in their reactions to the film. To some it was a banal failure in comparison to what Dreyer had accomplished. To others, the film offered clear and keen insights into the spiritual dimensions of the life of someone who remains perhaps the most enigmatic of medieval woman.[22]

Joan would appear in two additional films in the 1950s, but her story would in both cases be subsumed into a cinematic anthology. The French film *Destinées*, released in the United States in 1954, consists of three linked episodes, each with a different director, about women and war, one loosely based on the story of Lysistrata, one about an American woman who travels to Italy after the Second World War to claim her husband's body from his Italian mistress, and a third entitled "Jeanne," directed by Jean Delannoy with Michèle Morgan in the title role. Delannoy had originally wanted to direct a feature length film in the late 1940s, but his project was coopted by Fleming's film. Instead, Delannoy, perhaps in a bit of directorial pique, decided to make a short film about an apocryphal event associated with Joan that did not appear in Fleming's film: Joan's briefly restoring to life an infant who has died so that it can be baptized and go to heaven. But the alleged miracle is the center piece of a muddled tale about Joan that sees her restoration of the child to life as proof of the later charge that she is a sorceress, and, therefore, worthy of her death at the stake in Rouen. Joan consciously abandons her saints—thereby forfeiting her own saintly status. And Joan's role as warrior is further downplayed—as it was in the Rossellini film—suggesting that female heroism and personal sacrifice were in the 1950s no longer box office draws nor cultural role models to be imitated.[23]

Joan's story would be further muddled on the screen in Irwin Allen's 1957 film *The Story of Mankind*, in which the Spirit of Man (Ronald Coleman) and the Devil (Vincent Price) stage a debate before God in an extra-terrestrial courtroom whether about mankind should be allowed to destroy itself with the hydrogen bomb. The film is comprised of 56 scenes, running from two to five minutes—though the one featuring Joan is an exception and runs ten minutes. The scenes begin with cavemen and continue to the Second World War. The cast is a Hollywood who's who—and the net effect is at best comic if not crazed: Hedy Lamarr (woefully miscast as Joan), Groucho Marx (Peter Minuit ultimately playing Groucho Marx), Harpo Marx (Sir Isaac Newton), Peter Lorre (Nero), Virginia Mayo (Cleopatra), Agnes Morehead (Elizabeth I), Charles Coburn (Hippocrates), John Carradine (Pharaoh Khufu), Dennis Hopper (Napoleon), Edward Everett Horton (Sir Walter Raleigh), Marie Wilson (Marie Antoinette), and Reginald Gardiner (Shakespeare), among others. Critics were not amused, and the director did not help his film's critical reception, or box office success, when he told *Newsweek* that "history is still something like hearing a joke for the second time. The punch line has gone out of it. So we have added a gimmick."[24]

The film's approach to history is decidedly sexist. While the stories of the great men of history balance the evil with the good, almost all the women in the film are (in)famous for their misdeeds, and wicked men are made so by the minor women characters who surround them. Elizabeth I and Joan stand out as exceptions to this sexist bias. Elizabeth is granted a reprieve because her story is told by an admiring Shakespeare. Joan's story, on the other hand, is told by the Devil who sees her as a victim of the evil judges who condemned her. Lamarr's Joan becomes a minor player in the story of *man*kind (emphasis mine)—more specifically, she is simply one of the many unfortunate victims of the Inquisition. She is not a saint of the church; she is not the mother of a nation; she is simply another casualty in history's long catalogue of the misdeeds of men for whom, the Devil says, it is "natural" to kill women.[25]

Another 1950s Joan would at least present, with mixed success, a departure from earlier characterizations of the Maid of Orléans. *Saint Joan*, Otto Preminger's 1957 film, starred Jean Seberg as Joan and Richard Widmark as the Dauphin, with a screenplay by Graham Greene, loosely based in turn on Shaw's play. Seberg's flippant Joan is self-willed and has the somewhat annoying habit of referring to the Dauphin as "Charlie." In the film's opening scene, Charles is visited by Joan's ghost after her second trial has rehabilitated her. The film then flashes back to selectively-chosen familiar scenes from Joan's life.

In Fleming's film, Charles betrays Joan out of jealousy when she receives more adulation than he at the coronation. Widmark's Charles is more impetuous than thin-skinned. He simply dismisses Joan who at her trial talks more than she suffers. The film comes full circle finally back to Charles's bedside when the spirits of Bishop Cauchon, the Earl of Warwick, and the English soldier who had made Joan a cross to hold at the stake appear beside Joan. Cauchon and Warwick have been condemned to hell, as has the English soldier who is given a one-day reprieve each year as repayment for his kind deed.

Both a commercial and a critical failure, Preminger contented himself with referring to *Saint Joan* as his "most distinguished flop."[26] Seberg was cast for the role of Joan after a much-publicized national search for the perfect actress to play the title role, but in vacillating between the childlike and the childish throughout the film, she is clearly ill-prepared to assay Shaw's Joan, and Preminger seems to have misread Shaw's play, despite his assertion that he was "strictly adhering to the Shaw dialogue."[27] In Preminger's view, Joan is right, and everyone else in the film is wrong. Shaw presented a much more complex case for Joan's story—her accusers have their day. Under Preminger's direction, a play running nearly three and a half hours is reduced to a film of less than two hours, and the Shavian debates about Joan's role in both the rise of French nationalism and of Protestantism have all but been ignored and ended up on the cutting room floor.[28]

Films about Joan of Arc are not only reactions to the times in which they are made, but they can also be reactions to previous films about the Maid of Orléans. Robert Bresson's 1962 film *Le procès de Jeanne d'Arc* counters the Hollywood commercialization of Joan in by Fleming and Preminger, while also nodding in the direction of Dreyer's 1927–1928 silent masterpiece. Like Dreyer, Bresson limits his film to Joan's trial, and his emphasis is on her faith in God no matter what happens. The director, himself ardently Catholic, would in 1974 present his meditative response to the failure of Arthur's knights to find the Holy Grail in his *Lancelot du lac*. In the Jehanne film, Bresson forces us to remain at a distance from Joan—he does not imitate Dreyer's use of close ups. Indeed his approach borders on the voyeuristic as he gives us camera shots though doorways and peepholes. Dreyer played up the pathos of Joan's death at the stake—as her body is consumed by the flames, riots break out among the crowds that have gathered to watch the spectacle in Rouen. In Bresson's final scene, Joan's body is gone. Instead, the chains that bound her hang empty from the stake, now a symbol of hope. As Bresson himself explained: "Joan's will extended to accepting God's grace even if it meant the end of her earthly life and the beginning of a purely spiritual one. All of the machinations of the court have merely fulfilled the promise of her faith."[29] Bresson is more than happy to take sides in the debate over the status of Joan and of her legacy. For him, Joan is clearly a saint of the Church.[30]

Joan achieves grace in the film—but, in Bresson's view, grace is not a gift; it is a goal for the Christian to achieve in both the medieval and the modern worlds.

Politics more than religion have colored Joan's cultural presence especially in France for almost the last 50 years thanks to the adoption of Joan as a standard bearer for the far-right wing policies of Jean-Marie Le Pen's National Front. With its emphasis on France for the French and its anti-immigration platform, the historical Joan's attempts to drive foreigners from French soil make her a medieval fellow traveler in the eyes of Le Pen and his followers. Such a misuse of Joan might, one would expect, lead to a cinematic response in one way or another, though Jacques Rivette's two-part 1993 film *Jeanne la pucelle*, with Sandrine Bonnaire as Joan, displays little interest in politics—the director simply wanted to make a film in which Bonnaire could star.[31] Each part of the film, *Les batailles* and *Les prisons*, runs almost three hours. Yet despite the film's length, there is a sparseness to the way in which it tells Joan's story. Sets and costumes are minimal; references to precise dates and times provide short cuts to advance the film's narrative; witnesses appear at strategic points in each film to fill in any gaps in the narrative and to explain, where necessary, any political or religious complications at play in the film's scenario. Harlan Kennedy's more than slightly irreverent review of the film captures Rivette's somewhat casual, off-the-cuff approach to Joan's story:

> Heroic Joan and human Joan get equal weight. Now she strides out to battle, features steeled with fearlessness; now she blubs over an arrow wound or screams at the news of her imminent barbecue. Now we the audience clamber up wanton castles, dodging arrows and spears. Now we loll in a castle listening to characters discuss bills or meal menus, or learning how to spit-roast a hare (first catch it, then kill it, then pass it to someone else for skinning and skewering).[32]

Missing from Rivette's film are large battle scenes and any kind of greater agenda—again the director seems simply to have been interested in making a very, very long film starring Bonnaire.

Luc Besson's 1999 film *The Messenger: The Story of Joan of Arc* with Milla Jovovich as Joan offers yet another approach to Joan. Besson's Joan witnesses the murder and then rape of her sister by the English, and such atrocities and the ever-present violence that is part of her childhood lead to Joan's initial visions. Several years later, on the basis of her visions, Charles gives her an army. Her initial successes secure Charles's coronation, but the now king soon sees her as threatening both his new position and the balance in his treasury. Charles essentially sells Joan out, and her trial judges are at first hesitant to condemn her, themselves partially convinced of the credibility of her visions. Cauchon and her English captors argue about whether Joan is a heretic who should be burned, but, when Joan recants and denies her visions so that she might take confession, Cauchon with some relief announces that she can no longer be burned as a witch. Back in her cell, Joan is visited by an unnamed cloaked visitor—the personification of her conscience—who further questions whether Joan's visions were indeed ever from God. Meanwhile, Joan's frustrated English captors devise a way to have her declared a witch who must be burned, and a somewhat still skeptical Cauchon surrenders Joan to her fate, as she is burned at the stake in the marketplace of Rouen. While a postscript to the film confirms that Joan is today indeed a saint, Besson seems less interested in Joan in terms of either side of the usual debate about whether she is a saint or the mother of a nation. Rather, his film attempts a psychological study of Joan that sees her at times as a hysteric traumatized by a lifetime surrounded by war. As such, the director offers up a decidedly postmodern reading of Joan, who, like anyone else, will inevitably return from war suffering from PTSD.[33]

While both Dreyer and Bresson limited their cinematic examinations of Joan to her trial, Bruno Dumont's 2017 film *Jeannette* is a rock opera focusing solely on Joan's childhood. As source for his film, Dumont turned to Charles Péguy's monumental late 19th-century mystery play, *The Mystery of the Charity of Joan of Arc*.[34] In Dumont's film, Joan is at first a precocious eight-year shepherdess (Lise Leplat Prudhomme), who worries about how war with England is depriving the children of France of food, and then a mature teenager (Jeanne Voisin) gradually convinced of the validity of her mission to save France, if she can only get her parent's permission to leave home—bathos rather than pathos at times informs Dumont's postmodern approach to Joan. To say that his approach is idiosyncratic would be an understatement. Key to the film's portrait of the young Joan is its use of music and dance, drawn from multiple genres. Both the younger and the older Joans effortlessly switch from speech to song to dance—they twirl, do cartwheels, stomp, and headbang. And the results are jarring. As Glenn Kenny points out, in a reversal of what we might expect, the film does not drag the medieval into the modern world, rather it "throws the modern back at the medieval, making no distinction between religious ecstasy and that experienced in certain contemporary contexts of music and ritual."[35]

Sam Wells' 1999 experimental film *Wired Angel* offers another postmodern reading of Joan, here played by Caroline Ruttle. The black and white film is set in a bleak modern industrial landscape infused with medieval iconography. Joan is seated in her cell, as voiceovers remind her of the interrogation she has undergone and the fate that awaits her. In a throwback to Méliès's 1900 silent film, Wells does not so much present a traditional narrative as much as a series of aural and visual tableaux with a Catholic mass as his film's centerpiece—indeed his Joan is silent throughout, and there is no traditional dialogue in the film, just the voiceovers, often distorted, in both English and French, and a score that is a mix of styles from the medieval to the modern, all to suggest that Joan's story is one for the ages, not simply that of a medieval saint.

The historical Joan makes perhaps unexpected minor appearances in a number of other films, usually to fill out some narrative thread of their plot. The 1933 *Mystery of the Wax Museum* and its 1953 remake, *House of Wax,* are B-movie horror-mysteries in which people are murdered and dipped in wax to create lifelike sculptures. In both films, one of those sculptures is of Joan of Arc. On a lighter note, in the 1989 sci-fi comedy *Bill & Ted's Excellent Adventure*, the eponymous slacker heroes travel back in history in a telephone-booth-shaped time machine to assemble a group of figures so they can complete their history assignment and graduate from high school. Among those they whisk away from the past to present-day California is "Miss of Arc," whom they find in prayer on the eve of the battle to recapture Orléans from the English.

Playing Joan

While this essay is concerned with Joan's appearances on screen, she continues to have an equally rich and complicated—though alas never fully studied—life on the stage. Plays by major dramatists such as Schiller, Shaw, Brecht (three times), Anouilh, Anderson, and Feiffer, as well as by any number of others, have attempted to dramatize different facets of Joan's life and to use that life to advance a number of agendas. Stage actors too have found in Joan an unparalleled role that challenges them in ways few other roles for women do. George Bernard Shaw once stated that it "is quite likely that sixty years hence, every great English and American actress will have a shot at 'St. Joan,' just as every great actor will have a shot at 'Hamlet.'"[36] And the list of actors who have played his Joan is impressive as is that of those who have played other Joans.[37]

In several films, the central character establishes her gravitas by assaying the role of Joan on the stage. In a variation on the combined plots of two classic films *Stage Door* (1937) and *All About Eve* (1950), an aspiring understudy assumes the role of Joan of Arc when a more established star cannot or will not perform. In the 1938 film *Dramatic School*, it is Louise Rainer who, with the aid of Lana Turner, lands the leading role, originally intended for Paulette Goddard, in a new play about Joan of Arc. In the 1948 film *The Miracle of the Bells*, an aging Polish actor's anti–American sentiments get her fired by studio chief Lee J. Cobb—who delivers a bravura pro–American, anti–Eastern Europe speech when he fires her. Cobb then hires a young unknown actress played by Valli to play Joan. In a wonderfully over-the-top melodramatic touch, Valli's Joan succumbs to tuberculosis as she is playing the dying Joan at the stake. The cinematic convention is reversed in the 1931 film *Cock of the Air*, in which a stage actress of questionable morals cedes the role of Joan of Arc to her understudy only to return to the stage to reclaim the role once the understudy garners positive notices.

Taking on the role of Joan can also signal that an actress has turned her life around. Henry Koster's 1942 at times silly romantic comedy, *Between Us Girls*, casts Diana Barrymore as a successful young actress fresh from a stage triumph playing the aged Queen Victoria. She is next set to take the lead in the stage version of Somerset Maugham's short story "Rain," but, once she find true love, she abandons her earlier carefree lifestyle and any interest in the more steamy role of Sadie Thompson and takes to the stage instead as Joan because, as she says, "being in love gives a girl that Joan of Arc look!"

In yet another variation on having someone play Joan to validate herself, Gleb Panfilov's 1970 Russian film *Nachalo,* or *The Debut*, has a loyal Communist party member leave her job on a collective factory assembly line after she has an unhappy love affair to play the lead in a local amateur production of Shaw's play. The play's successful run completed, she returns to the factory floor having recovered from her personal pain and better prepared to do her part to improve the economy of Mother Russia.

Both versions of *The Little Drummer Girl*—the 1984 film and the 2018 television mini-series—open with the central character playing Shaw's Joan so convincingly that she is recruited to be a terrorist. And in Godard's 1962 film *Vivre sa vie*, the distraught central character finds solace in watching a screening of Dreyer's *Passion*. More disturbingly, the 2000 direct-to-video film *Live Virgin* pits two rival Jerry Springer–like talk show hosts against each other in a ratings war. For a half-million-dollar fee, the one hires the 16-year-old daughter of the other to appear on his show to lose her virginity on air before an international audience. When she arrives on the set for the live telecast, the daughter is dressed as Joan of Arc because "Joan was the most famous virgin of all times."

Channeling Joan

Film characters have regularly channeled Joan of Arc to advance any number of plot lines and agendas. Perhaps the earliest cinematic Jehanne avatar is the title character

Valli as Joan in a stage production in the 1948 film *The Miracle of the Bells*.

in the 1911 film *The Mexican Joan of Arc*. The film's connection to Joan is solely titular. The plot involves the widow Talamantes whose two sons and husband are summarily executed by a corrupt judge in the employ of Mexico's president. Vowing revenge, the woman, normally deprived of any agency in a culture ripe with machismo, succeeds in exacting retribution on both the judge and the president. Like Joan, she is a woman on a mission to right the wrongs her fellow citizens suffer at the hands of their oppressors.

DeMille's 1917 film *Joan the Woman* purposefully joins the national discussion of what America's role in the First World War should be. Any number of other films channel Joan also to urge a more whole-hearted American response to the Great War, and this use of Jehanne avatars in turn plays upon the archetype of Joan as warrior maiden.

In late September 1915, the French launched an attack on the Germans at Artois with the British doing the same at nearby Loos in what was to be the major Allied offensive on the Western Front that year. The Allies had the initial advantage at Loos, yet the French and the British were eventually routed. British casualties alone at Loos were a staggering 61,000, more than three times those of the Germans. In face of this disaster, the popular press in both France and England serialized the memoirs of a 17-year-old hero, Émilienne Moreau, who not only survived the occupation and bombardment of her home town, but who also valiantly aided the French in their attempts to drive the German occupiers out of Loos and the surrounding areas. Moreau's story soon found its way to the screen in Australia in George Willoughby's 1916 *The Joan of Arc of Loos*. To the account found in the memoirs, Willoughby's film adds a love interest for Moreau and an appearance on the battlefield by an armor-clad figure who is identified in the film's credits simply as "the angel," but whose presence is clearly meant to suggest that the real Joan of Arc has sanctioned Moreau's exploits as a latter-day recreation of her own. The angel is a woman in full medieval battle armor brandishing a sword, *the* image of Joan of Arc used throughout World War I for purposes of stirring up pro–Allied sentiment.[38]

During World War I, Australian filmmakers seemed rather taken with christening women heroes as latter day Joans of Arc. On October 12, 1915, a British nurse, Edith Cavell, was executed in Belgium by a German firing squad for allegedly assisting Allied prisoners of war to escape. News of her execution shocked the world, and Cavell instantly became a flash point for anti–German propaganda among the Allies. Within months of her death, three Australian films competed to tell her story, one with the telling subtitle *Nurse Cavell, England's Joan of Arc*.[39]

But real historical figures such as Moreau and Cavell were not the only women linked to Joan of Arc by filmmakers. Even fictional young children could be inspired by Joan of Arc to do their part to help the Allied cause as William Bertram's 1917 film *The Little Patriot* makes clear. One day, young Marie Yarbell goes to school where her teacher reads her class the story of Joan of Arc. Marie is inspired by the story to undertake various patriotic and preparedness activities, including organizing her male playmates into a kind of home watch, which foils an attempt by German spies to destroy an American armaments factory.

Earnest orphans too could do their part to root out German spies, especially if they were young girls much cleverer than the men with whom they fell in love. In 1918, George Loane Tucker cast the noted comedienne Mabel Normand against type as the title character in *Joan of Plattsburg*. An orphan named Joan (Normand) passes the time reading about Joan of Arc and soon becomes convinced that she is the reincarnation of her namesake. In a dream sequence in the film, Normand even imagines she is the armor-clad Joan of Arc. The orphanage, which it turns out is run by German spies, is located in upstate New York in Plattsburg near a major military training camp. Like Joan of Arc, Normand's Joan hears voices, though the voices she hears are those of German spies plotting against the government to steal the secret plans for a new wireless device that will turn the tide of the war in the Allies' favor. When Joan realizes what the Germans are up to, she reports them to the commander of the camp, with whom she is in love, and who, with Joan's help, captures the spies and secures the secrecy of the wireless project.

The story of Joan of Arc inspired yet another young screen hero to aid in the defeat of the Germans in World War I. In Joseph De Grasse's 1918 film for Universal, *The Wild Cat of Paris*, Collette, a prostitute and Apache dancer, leads her fellow dancers to the defense of France after she sees a painting of Joan. Collette's dance troupe repels the Germans when they reach the outskirts of Paris. Eventually, Collette even abandons her wild past to become a nurse at the front where she meets, saves the life of, and eventually marries the American artist whose painting of Joan was her original inspiration.[40]

The Second World War would see a similar use of Jehanne avatars in film, though somewhat unexpectedly in a more than zany 1942 musical comedy *Joan of Ozark*, starring Judy Canova as "a hillbilly Mata Hari" who accidentally shoots down a pigeon carrying messages between Nazi spies working in America. As Robin Blaetz points out, the film both recalls the story of Joan as woman warrior and makes fun of it.[41] And Canova's Joan is more passive than her World War I cinematic counterparts, as is Michèle Morgan in the title role of another 1942 film *Joan of Paris*. Here the Jehanne avatar is a waitress in a coffee bar in occupied Paris who comes to the aid of a downed RAF pilots led by the Free French's Paul Henreid. In the film, men are saved because women, Morgan's Joan and an elderly British agent, are expendable. With Paris in the hands of the Nazis and the war seemingly going badly for the Allies, Morgan's nightly prayer to her namesake patron saint is for a new dress.[42]

In contrast, Ulrike Ottinger's 1989 feminist adventure fantasy, *Johanna D'arc of Mongolia*, channels Joan to empower women. The film's plot is fairly straightforward. Seven European women from various backgrounds, all passengers on the Trans-Siberian/Trans-Mongolian Railway, are taken hostage by the Mongolian Princess Ulan Iga, who forces them to spend the summer with her band of women warriors on the steppes of her remote country. What follows is anything but violent conflict. Rather, the women find a cultural affinity with their captors, who soon become more like hospitable hosts. The princess soon bonds with Giovanna, a French ethnologist who conveniently speaks Mongolian, as the film attempts to reconcile modernity with cultural authenticity. Equally active is the title character in the 2005 Hungarian film opera *Johanna*, a nurse who works to save patients in a mental institution that is more properly a house of horrors.

With perhaps uncharacteristic directness, Umberto Eco once explained the continued postmedieval fascination with all things medieval in this way: "It seems that people like the Middle Ages."[43] It seems, too, that people like Joan of Arc, and no one approach has informed cinematic depictions of Joan. Brian Stock has noted that an interest in the

Inés Sastre as Giovanna (left) and Xu Re Huar as Princess Ulan Iga in the 1989 film *Johanna D'arc of Mongolia*.

Middle Ages can mask religious archaism and political reaction in any postmedieval period.[44] The same can be said for the continued interest in Joan. Fifteenth-century France found her both sinner and saint. She was viewed at best with respectful curiosity for the next three centuries. A return to an interest in Joan in the 19th century evidenced a conflict between views of Joan as a saintly daughter of the Church and as the mother of a nation.[45] Filmmakers have in turn wrestled with Joan the simple peasant girl, Joan the wily politician, Joan the androgyne, Joan the woman, Joan the doubting sinner, Joan the standard bearer of a nation, and Joan the self-assured saint. In doing so, filmmakers have mirrored the continuing revisionism that complicates the story of an ignorant, simple 15th-century peasant girl who managed in less than two years to change the course of European history—of someone whom Mark Twain would call "by far the most extraordinary person the human race has ever produced."[46]

NOTES

1. Charles Musser, *Before the Nickelodeon, Edwin S. Porter and the Edison Manufacturing Company* (Berkeley: University of California Press, 1991), p. 56. Of the films Clark made in 1895 for this series of kinetoscopes, only *The Execution of Mary, Queen of Scots* survives. On the cinematic lives of Joan of Arc, see Robin Blaetz, *Visions of the Maid: Joan of Arc in American Film and Culture* (Charlottesville: University of Virginia Press, 2001); Kevin J. Harty, "Jeanne au cinéma," in *Fresh Verdicts of Joan of Arc*, ed. Bonnie Wheeler and Charles T. Wood (New York: Garland, 1996), pp. 237–264; Kevin J. Harty, *The Reel Middle Ages: American, Western and Eastern European, Middle Eastern and Asian Films About Medieval Europe* (Jefferson, NC: McFarland & Company, 1999); and Nadia Margolis, *Joan of Arc in History, Literature, and Film: A Select, Annotated Bibliography* (New York: Garland, 1990).

2. See Pierre Duparc, ed., *Procès en Nullité de la Condamnation de Jeanne d'Arc*, 5 vols. (Paris: Librairie C. Klincksieck, 1977–1988); Daniel Hobbins, trans. *The Trial of Joan of Arc* (Cambridge: Harvard University Press, 2005); Régine Pernoud and Marie-Véronique Clin, *Joan of Arc*, revised and trans. Jeremy duQuesnay Adams (New York: St. Martin's Press, 1998); Régine Pernoud, *The Retrial of Joan of Arc*, trans. J.M. Cohen (New York: Harcourt, Brace and Company, 1955); and W.S. Scott, *The Trial of Joan of Arc* (Westport, CT: Associated Booksellers, 1956).

3. See Jacques Malthête, "La *Jeanne d'Arc* de Georges Méliès," *1895. Mille huit cent quatre-vingt-quinze* 36 (2002), posted on line 17 January 2007, accessed 17 February 2017. URL: http://1895.revues.org/140 ; DOI: 10.4000/1895.140. The film can be viewed on line at https://search.aol.com/aol/video?q=lumiere+brothers+jeanne+d%27arc+film&s_it=video-ans&sfVid=true&videoId=361FB5CE3777EA22AC58361FB5CE3777EA22AC58&s_chn=prt_watch-test-g&v_t=comsearch-b.

4. Joan was not beatified until 1909, and canonized until 1920. The fullest description of the Méliès film can be found in *The Warwick Film Catalogue* (London: Warwick Trading Company, 1901), pp. 69–72. Slightly different details about the film can be found in two other catalogues of early films, *The "Walturdaw" Catalogue of Animated Pictures* (London: Walturdaw, 1904), pp. 16–17; and *The Complete Catalogue of Genuine and Original "Star" Films (Moving Pictures) Manufactured by Geo. Méliès of Paris*. (New York: Georges Méliès, 1905–1906), p. 20.

5. For what scarce information survives about many early Joan films, see Blaetz, Harty, "Jeanne au cinema" and *The Reel Middle Ages*, and Margolis, as well as Maria Adriana Prolo, *Storia del cinema muto italiano* (Milan: Poligono, 1951). Also useful for its survey of Joan's cinematic career is [*Jeanne d'arc à l'écran*] *Études cinématographique* 18–19 (1962). The two Brothers Lumière films have at various times been available for viewing on television in programs tracing early cinema history, on the internet, or at film and Jehanne archives.

6. See Richard Abel, *The Ciné Goes to Town* (Berkeley: University of California Press, 1994), p. 268. Contemporary reviews of the film were mixed. See Harty, "Jeanne au cinema," p. 260, n. 6.

7. *Moving Picture World* 7 March 1914: 1215. For contemporary reviews of the film, see Harty, "Jeanne au cinema," p. 260, n. 9.

8. Sumiko Higashi, *Cecil B. DeMille and American Culture: The Silent Era* (Berkeley: University of California Press, 1994), p. 140

9. See Higashi, pp. 137–139. Higashi details in full the multiple agendas behind the film in the fifth chapter of his book, pp. 117–141.

10. Further underscoring the role *Joan the Woman* would play in rallying support for American involvement in the First World War, two very different versions of the film were released, one for European audiences—streamlined to emphasize Joan's mythic role in the history of France—and one for American audiences, longer and more diffuse with an overly romantic—in several senses of the term—view of Joan. See Blaetz, pp. 47–64.

11. Carl Theodor Dreyer, *Four Screenplays* (Bloomington: Indiana University Press, 1970), pp. 25–76.

12. David Bordwell, *Filmguide to* La Passion de Jeanne d'arc (Bloomington: Indiana University Press, 1973), pp. 60–61.

13. Quoted by Ib Monty in *The International Dictionary of Films and Filmmakers*, ed. Nicholas Thomas, 2nd ed. (Chicago: St James Press, 1990), vol. 1, p. 691.

14. Blaetz, p. 89. The film was lost to the archives until 1966 when the Cinémathèque Française screened a restored version with a new score, which was eventually shown on French television and then released on VHS and DVD. Reviews of the screening of the restored version and its later television broadcast can be found in *Variety* 1 October 1986: 36; *Télérama* 2348 (11 January 1995): 102; and *Le monde radio-télévision* 15–16 (January 1995): 7. The files of the British Film Institute in London contain a typescript ("The Glorious Life of Joan of Arc") in English by Ros Schwartz of the scenario for the 1986 restoration. I quote from that typescript here.

15. Schwartz, p. 6.

16. See Blaetz, pp. 88–89, and her earlier dissertation, "Strategies of Containment: Joan of Arc in Film" (Ph.D. diss., New York University, 1989), p. 48.

17. For a complete discussion of the film and of its more than myopic critical reception outside of Germany when it was released, see Kevin J. Harty, "The Nazis, Joan of Arc, and Medievalism Gone Awry: Gustav Ucicky's 1935 Film *Das Mädchen Johanna*," in *Rationality and the Liberal Spirit, A Festschrift Honoring Ira Lee Morgan* (Shreveport: A Centenary [College of Louisiana] Publication, 1997), pp. 122–133.

18. See James Damico, "Ingrid Bergman from Lorraine to Stromboli: Analyzing the Public's Perception of a Film Star," *Journal of Popular Film* 4 (1975): 3–19; and Adrienne L. McLean, "The Cinderella Princess and the Instrument of Evil: Surveying the Limits of Female Transgression in Two Postwar Hollywood Scandals," *Cinema Journal* 34 (Spring 1995): 36–56.

19. "Next Cycle to Be Religious, with Interest in War Yarns Receding," *Variety* 24 March 1943: 1.

20. See Harty, *The Reel Middle Ages*, p. 271.

21. Compare Maxwell Anderson, *Joan of Lorraine* (Washington, DC: Anderson House, 1946), pp. 92, 98, 101–102; and Maxwell Anderson and Andrew Solt, *Joan of Arc* (New York: W. Sloane Associates, 1948), p. 96.

22. See the debate about the film's merits between Michel Estève and Claude Beylie in *Etudes cinématographiques* 18–19 (Fall 1962): 65–78.

23. For a more detailed discussion of the film, see Blaetz, *Visions of the Maid*, pp. 149–152.

24. *Newsweek* 6 May 1957. For a list of other reviews of the film, see Blaetz, *Visions of the Maid*, p. 224.

25. For further discussion of the film, see Blaetz, *Visions of the* Maid, pp. 154–156.

26. Harry and Michael Medved, *The Hollywood Hall of Shame* (New York: Perigee Books, 1984), p. 224. For a list of reviews, see Harty, *The Reel Middle Ages*, p. 462.

27. Gerald Pratley, *The Cinema of Otto Preminger* (New York: Castle Books, 1971), pp. 119–120. Shaw himself had earlier written a screenplay for a film version of his *Saint Joan*, about which Preminger seems to have been unaware. See Bernard F. Dukore, ed., *The Collected Screenplays of Bernard Shaw* (London: George Prior Publishers, 1980), pp. 49–59, 179–221.

28. See Ellen C. Kennedy's review "Saint Joan," *Films in Review* 8 (June-July 1957): 281.

29. See Gaylyn Studlac, "The Trial of Joan of Arc," in *Magill's Survey of Cienma*, ed. Frank N. Magill, Foreign Language Films, vol. 7, TAL-Z (Englewood Cliffs, NJ: Prentice-Hall, 1985), p. 3166.

30. Bresson has commented extensively on the religious motivation behind his Jehanne film. See Robert Bresson, *Bresson on Bresson, Interviews 1943–1983*, ed. Mylène Bresson, trans. Anna Moschovakis (New York: New York Review Books, 2016), pp. 85–122.

31. Sandrine Bonnaire, *Le roman d'in tournage: Jeanne le pucelle* (Paris: Lattes, 1994), p. 11.

32. Harlan Kennedy, "Sam & Jim's Excellent Adventure and Other Side Trips at the 44th Berlin Filmfestspiele," *Film Comment* 30 (May-June 1994): 72–73.

33. For more extensive postmodern readings of Besson's *The Messenger*, see Nickolas Haydock, "Shooting the Messenger: Luc Besson at War with Joan of Arc," *Exemplaria* 19.2 (Summer 2007): 243–269; and Susan Hayward and Phil Powrie, *The Films of Luc Besson: Master of Spectacle* (Manchester: Manchester University Press, 2009).

34. Charles Péguy, *The Mystery of the Charity of Joan of Arc*, trans, Julian Green (New York: Pantheon Books, 1950). Péguy spent nearly fifteen years writing this work.

35. Glenn Kenny, "A Patron Saint of Headbangers," *New York Times* 13 April 2018: C8.

36. Edward Betts, "'Too Busy to Bother About It!'—Shaw Unperturbed by Immortality," *The Era* 10 January 1934: 1.

37. For a selection of responses that actors have had to playing Shaw's Joan, see Holly Hill's *Playing Joan, Actresses on the Challenge of Shaw's* Saint Joan (New York: Theatre Communications Group, 1987). Of course, women have also played Hamlet on the stage—Sarah Bernhardt played both Joan and Hamlet—and many Shakespearean male roles have recently been played by women, notably Glenda Jackson's Lear in London in 2016 and in New York in 2019.

38. For a fuller discussion of *The Joan of Arc of Loos*, see Kevin J. Harty, "Warrior not Warmonger:

Screen Joans during World War I," in *Magistra Docitissima, Essays in Honor of Bonnie Wheeler*, ed. Dorsey Armstrong, Ann W. Astell, and Howell Chickering (Kalamazoo, MI: Medieval Institute Publications, 2013), pp. 132–134.

39. See Harty, "Warrior not Warmonger," pp. 134–135.

40. See Harty, "Warrior not Warmonger," pp. 135–138; and Blaetz, *Visions of the Maid*, pp. 48–49, 65–69, and 73.

41. Blaetz, *Visions of the Maid*, pp. 113–116.

42. For a fuller discussion of *Joan of Paris*, see Blaetz, *Visions of the Maid*, pp. 106–113. Morgan would later appear as Joan herself in the Jehanne episode in *Destinées*. Henreid's role in the film recalls the one he played earlier in another World War II film released in 1942, and *Joan of Paris* does at times seem a bit like *Casablanca* light. In the 2002 film, *The Uncertainty Principle*, at least the main character prays to Joan of Arc for relief from her abusive husband, and not for anything so stereotypically gendered and mundane as a new dress.

43. Umberto Ecco, *Travels in Hyperreality*, trans. William Weaver (New York: Harcourt, 1983), p. 61.

44. Brian Stock, *Listening to the Text* (Baltimore: Johns Hopkins University Press, 1990), p. 73.

45. A recent excellent study by Gail Orgelfinger discusses Joan's reception from the early fifteenth to the early nineteenth centuries. See *Joan of Arc in the English Imagination, 1429–1829* (University Park: Pennsylvania State University Press, 2019).

46. Mark Twain, *Personal Recollections of Joan of Arc* (1896; rpt. Mineola, NY: Dover Publications, 2002), p. 329.

About the Contributors

Kristin L. **Burr** is a professor of French at Saint Joseph's University in Philadelphia and coeditor of *Shaping Identity in Medieval French Literature: The Other Within* (2019). Her research focuses on gender roles in 13th-century Old French literature. She has published on topics ranging from medieval French verse romance to the fabliau. In her current research, she examines the role of love tokens and relics in Old French narrative.

Andrew B.R. **Elliott**, a senior lecturer in media and cultural studies at the University of Lincoln, is the author of *Remaking the Middle Ages* (on medieval film) and editor of *The Return of the Epic Film* and *Playing with the Past* (on the 21st-century epic and historically-themed video games, respectively). He has published on a number of topics relating to historical film, television and video games, from the classical world to the Middle Ages. His latest book is *Medievalism, Politics and Mass Media: Appropriating the Middle Ages in the Twenty-First Century*.

Sandra **Gorgievski** is an associate professor of English at the University of Toulon, France. Her interests include medieval studies and the reception of the medieval imagination today, especially in popular culture. After working on the Arthurian myth (*Le mythe d'Arthur, de l'imaginaire médiéval à la culture de masse*) and on images of angels (*Face to Face with Angels. Images in Medieval Art and in Film*), she is researching the representation of the crusades in medieval illuminated manuscripts and in film. She has coedited a book on medievalism in film and theater (*Le Moyen Age mis en scène: perspectives contemporaines*).

Joan Tasker **Grimbert** is a professor emerita of French and medieval studies at the Catholic University of America. A specialist on Chrétien de Troyes and the Tristan legend, she has published extensively on Arthurian literature and film and has authored, edited, or coedited six books. In previous film essays, she has analyzed Rohmer's *Perceval le Gallois*, Truffaut's *La Femme d'à côté*, Delannoy and Cocteau's *L'Éternel retour*, Gunnlaugsson's *I skugga hrafnsins*, Bresson's *Lancelot du lac*, and the potion scene in four Tristan films. Her most recent essay complements her contribution here by focusing on the film Tristan.

Kevin J. **Harty** is a professor of English at La Salle University, where he served for 20 years as the assistant chair and chair of the department, as director of the university's general education core, and as special assistant to the provost. He has published widely in the areas of medieval studies and medievalism. His previous books include *The Reel Middle Ages*; *King Arthur on Film*; *Cinema Arthuriana*; *The Vikings on Film*; and *The Holy Grail on Film: Essays on the Cinematic Quest*, all from McFarland.

Donald L. **Hoffman** is professor emeritus at Northeastern Illinois University in Chicago. He has published essays on Arthurian and medieval literature from Chrétien and Thomas Malory to Samuel Selvon and Ishmael Reed, along with several articles on film. He is coeditor with Elizabeth Sklar of *King Arthur in Popular Culture*.

Valerie B. **Johnson** is an assistant professor of English at the University of Montevallo. Her research addresses eco-political symbolism in Middle English literature, ecocriticism, medievalism and neomedievalism, and Robin Hood studies.

Amy S. **Kaufman** is a former professor of Medieval Studies turned freelance writer who has published a number of essays on the Arthurian legend and on medievalism in contemporary culture. Her new book, *The Devil's Historians: How Modern Extremists Abuse the Medieval Past* (cowritten with Paul Sturtevant), will be published in 2020 by the University of Toronto Press. She is currently working on a political memoir about the decline of academia and the rise of Donald Trump, as well as a novel set in 12th-century Córdoba.

Joseph M. **Sullivan**, an associate professor of German at the University of Oklahoma, has published extensively on medieval courtly literature and the modern popular reception of the Middle Ages. His focus is the tradition of King Arthur in Europe north of the romance countries. He recently published an edition with facing-page English translation of the anonymous 13th-century Arthurian romance *Wigamur*, and he is preparing a critical edition of Leiden Manuscript B of Wirnt of Gravenberg's ca. 1215 *Wigalois*, also with an English translation.

Fiona **Tolhurst**, an associate professor of English and the chair of Language and Literature at Florida Gulf Coast University, is the author of two books: *Geoffrey of Monmouth and the Feminist Origins of the Arthurian Legend* and *Geoffrey of Monmouth and the Translation of Kingship*. She has contributed entries on Eleanor of Aquitaine and Empress Matilda to *The Encyclopedia of Medieval Literature in Britain* and an essay about female figures in the extant works of Geoffrey Monmouth to the forthcoming voluem *A Companion to Geoffrey of Monmouth*.

Usha **Vishnuvajjala** is a postdoctoral fellow in the Department of English at Temple University. Her research focuses on gender in medieval literature and medievalism, and she is currently completing a monograph, *Feminist Medievalisms*, under contract with Arc Humanities Press/Amsterdam University Press, and coediting a volume on medieval women's friendships with Karma Lochrie.

Index